LADYFOOD

A Collection of Recipes Enjoyed
by Ladies & Gentlemen

Printed and bound by
Specialty Publications
Taylor Publishing Company
Dallas, Texas

FOREWORD

Ladyfood is a collection of recipes featuring that special type of food most often served for brunches, lunches, teas and even dinner parties. *Ladyfood* is usually elegant, preferably simple and yes, meant for ladies and gentlemen, too. The cookbook title came from a gentleman who said his favorite dinners as a child were on the days his mother entertained. "Then," he said, "dinner was left-over, *ladyfood*."

The Dallas Alumnae Chapter of Gamma Phi Beta International Sorority has compiled *Ladyfood* with the cooperation and support of many Gamma Phi Betas internationally. These members submitted numerous excellent recipes, and after testing and careful selection, it was still necessary to consolidate some similar or identical recipes. We hope this is understandable to those individuals.

Our gratitude goes to every Gamma Phi Beta who contributed to this book with special appreciation to all members of the cookbook committee who have worked in many capacities in preparing this cookbook.

All proceeds from this cookbook will go to support Gamma Phi Beta philanthropies and scholarships.

Explanation: The name of the Gamma Phi Beta who presented each recipe is followed by the name of the college or university she attended. The city and state indicates the Alumnae chapter and/or the city where she now resides.

ACKNOWLEDGEMENTS

CO-CHAIRMEN
Sandra Graham Cude
Sara Hess McElhaney

DISTRIBUTION CHAIRMAN
Pat O'Connell Mullins

TESTING CHAIRMAN
Fran Kirk Cranfill

CONVENTION CHAIRMAN
Jane Dick Ladewig

COLLEGIATE CHAPTER PROMOTION
Carolyn Coe Cole

NATIONAL OFFICER PROMOTION
Sue Herzog Johnson

CELEBRITY RECIPE CHAIRMAN
Virginia Forsythe Vint

ALUMNAE CHAPTER PROMOTION
Beth McCallon Wheeler

TASTING LUNCHEON CHAIRMAN
Irene Braden Loosley
LUNCHEON CO-CHAIRMEN
Dorothy Chase Jones
Betty Mae Conner Jones

RETAIL STORE PROMOTION
Pat Taylor Clapp

DALLAS TELEPHONE COORDINATOR
Gayle Howard Young

PUBLICITY CHAIRMEN
Helen Jane Bellke Wambolt
Vicki Veach

TREASURER
Latane Jordan Graham

ASST. TREASURER
Harriet Lishen Baldwin

ILLUSTRATOR (Division pages)
Marjorie McLouth Thomson

CONSULTANT
Marilyn Krebs Culwell

PROOFREADING CHAIRMAN
Sylvia Hardy Trewin

PROOFREADERS
Marilyn Cooke Sullivan
Betty Irion Bookout

DALLAS ALUMNAE PRESIDENT
Kay Reynolds Bennett

TYPISTS
Nan Blake
Joan Lonnborg De La Garza

Terry Gallagher
Sue Herzog Johnson
Pat O'Connell Mullins
Sylvia Hardy Trewin

SPECIAL RESOURCES CHAIRMAN
Harriet Lishen Baldwin

RECIPE TESTERS

Harriett Lishen Baldwin
Barbara Fort Beasley
Kay Reynolds Bennett
Cindy Blanton
Betty Irion Bookout
Holly Hawkins Bowler
Margaret Miller Browne
Patricia Taylor Clapp
Carolyn Coe Cole
Frances Kirk Cranfill, Chairman
Lewise Bailey Crockett
Candy Ayars Crowther
Sandra Graham Cude
Marilyn Krebs Culwell
Victoria Shurtz Downing
Mollie Ellis Ellis
Jackie Williams Farley
Jean Patton Fortune
Sharon McFarland Groves
Jacqueline Percival Hall
Janis Walker Hallmark
Linda Edwards Haney

Ann Sokol Heath
Gayle Marye Gurst
Molly Garrison Ingram
Pat Krebs Irvin
Bettye Mae Conner Jones
Dorothy Chase Jones
Carolyn Vestal Kelly
Margaret McGill Kunkel
Jane Dick Ladewig
Karen Schott Lawson
Irene Braden Loosley
Karen Luddeke
Charlotte Briggs Marlo
Lynn Baxter Maguire
Kathryn Critchfield McCarville
Cissie McKee McDaniel
Sara Hess McElhaney
Ann Punyan Miranda
Virginia Dodds Mistrot
Cheryl Bozeman Mitchell
Dorothy Jackson Myers
Cheryl Stoner Myhra

Margaret Eglin Nicholson
Suzanne Osburn
Judy Tonning Price
Sue Ward Ragsdale
Ann Taylor Ricker
Rhonda Reed Russell
Marilou Deaner Sargent
Dianne Hafford Schayot
Pamela Ann Smale
Linda Speckmann
Marilyn Cooke Sullivan
Martha Terrill Terrill
Sylvia Hardy Trewin
Claire Howard Upham
Nancy Luft Vermeer
Beth McCallon Wheeler
Marcia Orning Williams
Julie Winans
Anne Yeager
Gayle Howard Young

1980 COMMITTEES

CHAIRMAN
Harriet Lishen Baldwin

DISTRIBUTION CHAIRMAN
Jeanne Flowers Smith

RETAIL STORE PROMOTION
Pat Taylor Clapp
Harriet Lishen Baldwin
Kay Reynolds Bennett
Fran Kirk Cranfill
Sandra Graham Cude
Latane Jordan Graham
Irene Braden Loosley
Sara Hess McElhaney
Sylvia Hardy Trewin
Virginia Forsythe Vint

TREASURER
Linda Edwards Haney

SECRETARY
Barbara Ivy Ashby

PROOFREADING CHAIRMEN
Sandra Graham Cude
Sylvia Hardy Trewin

DALLAS ALUMNAE PRESIDENT
Fran Kirk Cranfill

OUT-OF-TOWN PROMOTION
Jane Dick Ladewig

PUBLICITY
Melinda Murphy Smith
Terry Bohling Davis
Kathryn Craven Melady

COOKBOOK COORDINATOR
Nan Mulvaney

TABLE OF CONTENTS

APPETIZERS 7

BEVERAGES 29

BREADS 37

ENTREES 57

Beef
Cheese
Eggs
Chicken
Seafood
Lamb
Pork

SALADS 121

Dressings
Sauces
Soups

VEGETABLES 171

SWEETS 193

Cake
Cookies
Desserts
Pies

Appetizers

ANGOSTURA DIP

1 cup mayonnaise
1 teaspoon curry powder
1 teaspoon prepared mustard
½ teaspoon onion salt
1 teaspoon Angostura bitters
½ teaspoon paprika

Mix well and serve with any raw vegetable — especially good with carrots, celery, radishes, green onions, cauliflower and cucumbers.

Claire Casaday Wagner, University of Arizona
Lubbock, Texas

ARTICHOKE BITES

1 box Melba rounds
1 can artichoke hearts, cut into quarters
¾ cup mayonnaise
Parmesan cheese

Spread Melba rounds on cookie sheet; place artichoke quarter on each round. Mix mayonnaise and Parmesan cheese to taste; drop this mixture from teaspoon onto each stacked round. Run under the broiler until hot and bubbly. Keeps well on an electric heating tray.

Edith Cameron McMillen, Memphis State
Starkville, Mississippi

ARTICHOKE PATE

1 6-ounce jar marinated artichoke hearts
8 ounces cream cheese
½ teaspoon Worcestershire sauce
1 teaspoon onion juice
½ teaspoon oregano
2 tablespoons Parmesan cheese

Soften cheese at room temperature. Drain artichoke hearts. Cut cheese into chunks, drop into food processor. Add artichokes and remaining ingredients. Add marinade from artichokes to make proper consistency. Serve with crackers.

Audrey Bashaw, University of Washington
Riverside, California

PICKLED ARTICHOKES

2 9-ounce packages frozen artichoke hearts
4 tablespoons salad oil
2 tablespoons vinegar
½ teaspoon salt
½ teaspoon sugar
½ teaspoon oregano
½ teaspoon prepared mustard
¼ teaspoon pepper
2 bay leaves
2 cloves garlic

Cook artichoke hearts according to package directions. Drain. In a bowl, combine rest of ingredients. Stir in artichoke hearts. Cover tightly and refrigerate until thoroughly chilled, one hour or longer. Turn hearts occasionally. If frozen artichokes are not available, canned artichoke hearts may be substituted. Makes 8 to 10 servings.

Marion Kaeser Piper, University of Illinois
St. Louis, Missouri

ASPARAGUS CANAPES

2 cans asparagus spears
1 large and 1 small loaf (thin) white bread
2 5-ounce jars Blue Cheese spread
8 ounces cream cheese
1 beaten egg
1 tablespoon mayonnaise
1 ¼ cup melted butter

Cut crust from bread and roll each slice out flat. Mix together cheeses, mayonnaise, and beaten egg. Spread mixture on bread. Top each slice with one stalk of asparagus. Roll up each and cut into 3 pieces. Dip each piece in melted butter. When ready to bake, place on ungreased cookie sheet and bake at 350 degrees for 15 minutes or until brown. This can be made ahead and frozen.

Carolyn Kelly, Southern Methodist University
Dallas, Texas

AVOCADO COCKTAIL

1 part chili sauce
½ part tomato juice
Worcestershire sauce, a dash
1 tablespoon lemon juice, or to taste
Onion juice to taste
Avocados (cut in cubes)

Combine liquids and freeze to sherbert consistency. Put avocado cubes in glasses and cover with sauce or slush. Particularly nice to serve in "icers" bedded on crushed ice. Serve with corn chips.

Connie Spanier, Oregon State University
San Francisco, California

BOLOGNA STACKS

1 12-ounce package of sliced bologna
1 8-ounce package cream cheese
1 teaspoon cream style horseradish
Dash Worchestershire sauce

Mix softened cream cheese with horseradish and Worchestershire. Spread on slices of bologna. Stack four or five topping with a plain slice. Chill. Cut in about half-inch squares and insert a cocktail pick or toothpick.

Pauline Sawyer Umland, Boston University
Peninsula, California

BEEF ROLL-UPS

1 package dried beef
1 3-ounce package cream cheese, softened
⅛ teaspoon garlic salt
½ teaspoon horseradish
Dash of Worcestershire
1 teaspoon grated blue cheese
Olives
Sweet pickles
Dill pickles

Add garlic salt, horseradish, Worcestershire and blue cheese to softened cream cheese. Mix and spread on 2 slices of beef. Roll around small dill or sweet pickles or olives.

Sue Ragsdale, Southern Methodist University
Dallas, Texas

BRAUNSCHWEIGER DIP

1 pound braunschweiger
1 cup sour cream
½ package Good Seasons Blue Cheese Salad Dressing Mix

Allow braunschweiger to sit out at room temperature to soften. Smash it with a spoon or fork. Add other two ingredients and mix together with a hand mixer. Serve with potato chips, crackers, rye bread rounds, or raw vegetables.

Linda Schreiner, University of Nebraska
Omaha, Nebraska

BEER CHEESE

3 rolls Kraft nippy cheese, room
   temperature
1 ¼-ounce Roquefort cheese,
   room temperature
2 tablespoons butter, room
   temperature
1 medium onion, minced
2 cloves garlic, minced
1 teaspoon Worcestershire sauce
1 teaspoon Tabasco sauce
¾ cup beer, heated and cooled
Round rye bread, unsliced

Cream butter with cheeses. Add onion, garlic and sauces. Add beer slowly to consistency of dip. Scoop out middle of round bread and tear into bite sized pieces. Pour cheese mixture into middle of bread and dip bread pieces with cheese. Can make ahead and refrigerate. A winner with the men. Great for casual parties and picnics.

Karen Burton Dekoker, University of Michigan
Birmingham, Michigan

CHEESE BALL

1 8-ounce package cream cheese,
   softened
½ pound Roquefort cheese
2 glasses Old English cheese
1 tablespoon Worcestershire
   sauce
½ teaspoon Tabasco sauce
1 lemon, juice and grated rind
1 clove garlic, pressed or cut fine
2 tablespoons grated onion

Mix ingredients thoroughly with a pastry blender. Roll into ball. If desired, roll in chopped parsley and/or nuts. For milder flavor use only ¼ pound Roquefort cheese.

Mary Jane Brown Monnig, Washington University
St. Louis, Missouri

CHEESE BALL

1 pound Wisconsin mild cheese,
   grated
1 large (8 ounce) cream cheese
2 tablespoons finely grated onion
1 clove garlic, minced
½ cup finely chopped peanuts or
   pecans
2 tablespoons finely chopped
   minced parsley

Mix first four ingredients and place in refrigerator until chilled enough to form ball. Roll ball in chopped nuts and minced parsley. Serve with assorted crackers.

Latane Jordan Graham, Memphis State University
Dallas, Texas

CARLA'S CHEESE BALL

2 8-ounce packages cream cheese
1 8½-ounce can crushed
   pineapple, including juice
½ chopped green pepper
2 teaspoons chopped onion
1 teaspoon salt
2 cups chopped pecans
Crackers

Mix all ingredients in an electric mixer. Form into ball. Top with chopped pecans and serve with favorite crackers.

Pat O'Connell Mullins, St. Louis University
Dallas, Texas

PECAN CHEESE BALL

1 8-ounce package cream cheese
1 2-ounce package Roquefort
cheese
1 8-ounce jar processed cheddar
cheese
1 tablespoon grated onion
1½ tablespoons Worcestershire
sauce
½ cup chopped pecans
2 tablespoons chopped parsley

Allow all cheese to come to room temperature. Blend well, add onion and Worchestershire sauce. Line bowl with plastic wrap and pour in the cheese mixture. Cover. Place in refrigerator until firm. One hour before serving, remove cheese ball and roll in chopped pecans and chopped parsley. Serve with thin wheat crackers.

Carolyn Stephonson, California State-Long Beach
Bal Harbor, California

CHEESE BONBONS

¾ cup margarine
1½ cup sharp cheese
¼ cup grated Parmesan cheese
1½ cup flour
1 teaspoon salt
1 teaspoon paprika or red pepper
Small pecan halves

Cream shortening until light and fluffy. Add shredded sharp cheese and parmesan cheese. Sift dry ingredients and add to creamed mixture. Form dough into small balls, about one inch in diameter. Put on baking sheet one inch apart. Press pecan half on each. Bake at 350 degrees for 15 minutes or until lightly brown. Yield about seven dozen.

Frances Kirk Cranfill, University of Tulsa and
Washington University
Dallas, Texas

Shirley Davis Tompkins, Iowa State University
Fort Worth, Texas

CONVENTION CHEESETTES

2 sticks margarine, softened
2 cups flour
½ teaspoon salt
8 ounces sharp cheese, grated
½ teaspoon Tabasco
Dash of Worcestershire sauce to
taste
2 cups Rice Krispies or 1 cup
finely chopped pecans

Mix well first six ingredients. Add Rice Krispies or chopped pecans and mix in carefully. Roll in balls size of small marbles. Flatten with a fork. Should dough become too soft to roll, place in refrigerator a few minutes. Bake at 350 degrees for 15-20 minutes. Makes about 80 large or 150 bite size pieces. May be kept in ice box a long time. Flavor is improved if heated slightly before serving.

Elaine Campbell Simpson, University of Iowa
Washington D.C.

Beatrice Brown Freeman, Iowa State University
Aiken, South Carolina

Frances Kirk Cranfill, University of Tulsa and
Washington University
Dallas, Texas

CHEESE PUFFS

2 sticks margarine
2 cups shredded cheese
1 egg white, slightly beaten
¼ teaspoon garlic salt
1 tablespoon milk
1 loaf unsliced bread

Combine *all ingredients at room temperature* except bread in a mixer. Beat until smooth. Take crusts off bread. Cut in 1 inch cubes. Spread five sides of cubes. Put un-spread side on greased cookie sheet. FREEZE. Store in plastic bag. Place un-spread side on greased cookie sheet to bake. Bake at 375 degrees for 10-15 minutes.

Diana Winterhalter, Michigan State University
Columbus, Ohio.

CHEESE SPREAD

1 8-ounce package cream cheese
2 small jars pimiento cheese
1 small jar Old English cheese
3 tablespoons mayonnaise
1 tablespoon Worcestershire
½-1 teaspoon Accent
3 cloves garlic

Soften cheeses to room temperature. Mix cream cheese with Old English cheese, then mix in pimiento cheese, 1 jar at a time. Add mayonnaise, Worcestershire, Accent and minced garlic. Can serve in dish or chill and shape into cheese ball.

Jacki Falkenroth, University of Nevada-Reno
Chicago, Illinois

PARMESAN GARLIC CHEESE SPREAD

1 cup grated Parmesan cheese
2 3-ounce packages cream cheese, softened
½ cup butter or margarine, softened
⅓ cup milk
⅛ to ¼ teaspoon garlic powder (to suit own taste)

Beat all ingredients except garlic powder until creamy. Add garlic powder to taste and mix well. Pack into a two cup crock or non-metal container; cover tightly. Refrigerate at least 24 hours, no longer than 2 weeks. Remove from refrigerator one hour before serving. Serve with crackers or toasted French bread.

Mary Gillham Solomon, University of Missouri
Warrensburg, Missouri

CURRIED CHICKEN DIP

1 8-ounce package cream cheese
1 pint of sour cream
¼ teaspoon lemon pepper
½ teaspoon curry powder (or more if you like)
2 tablespoons minced chives
2 tablespoons capers, drained
2 7-ounce cans deboned chicken or 1¾ cups leftover cooked and cubed chicken

Combine cheese, sour cream and seasonings (except capers). Blend until smooth. (Use blender or food processor, if available). Add the chicken and fold in capers. Chill and serve with your favorite chips. Yields about 2 cups.

Sandra Graham Cude, Memphis State University
Dallas, Texas

CHICKEN PATE

2 cans Underwood chicken spread
1 cup chopped pecans
½ cup chopped green onion
1½ tablespoons soy sauce
1 tablespoon wine vinegar
⅓ cup mayonnaise
Salt and pepper to taste
8 ounces sour cream

Mix first seven ingredients together. Press into a shallow serving dish. Top with sour cream. Chill well, at least 24 hours. Serve with crackers or rye rounds.

Jean Anderson Allard, University of Washington
Modesto, California

WALNUT CHICKEN APPETIZERS

2 whole chicken breasts, skinned
    and boned
1 teaspoon salt
⅛ teaspoon pepper
1 teaspoon soy sauce
1 tablespoon dry sherry
2 egg whites
¼ cup cornstarch
2 cups coarsely chopped walnuts
Cooking oil

Cut chicken into bite-size pieces and mix with salt, pepper, soy sauce and sherry. Beat egg whites until foamy, add cornstarch and fold in until smooth. Heat oil to 350 degrees. Dip chicken in egg white mixture and coat with walnuts. Fry 8-10 at a time until golden brown. Remove from oil and drain on paper towels. Serve hot.

Ruth Ann Morse Gray, University of Arizona
Orange County, California

GREEN CHILI BITES

1 package Francisco brand sour
    dough French rolls
¼ pound butter, softened
1 cup diced green chilies
⅛ teaspoon garlic salt
½ pound grated sharp cheddar
    cheese
½ cup mayonnaise

Split sour dough rolls, then cut each half in two again. Mix remaining ingredients and spread on pieces of bread. Broil until bubbly.

Janet Smith Sprouse, Colorado College
Coos Bay, Oregon

CRAB DIP

16 ounces softened cream cheese
¼ cup finely chopped onion
⅛ to ¼ teaspoon horseradish or
    Tabasco
1 can crab, drained (check for
    tabors)
Dash of pepper

Cream all ingredients except crab. Add crab. Bake at 325 degrees for 15-20 minutes or until it starts to bubble. Serve with ripple potato chips.

Lynn Bruning, Kansas State
Shawnee, Kansas

CRAB IMPERIAL MOUSSE

1 8-ounce package cream cheese
1 can cream of mushroom soup
1 cup mayonnaise
Dash salt
1 teaspoon Worcestershire sauce
2 tablespoons gelatin
1 onion, grated
1 cup chopped celery
1 6-ounce can crabmeat

Heat cheese, soup, mayonnaise, salt and Worcestershire sauce in double boiler until smooth. Remove from fire. Add gelatin dissolved in ⅓ cup cold water. Add 1 small onion grated, 1 cup chopped celery and 1 can crabmeat (or equivalent fresh king or dungeness crab). Put into fancy mold and chill until firm. Unmold and serve with crackers or party rye bread slices as an hors d'oeuvre. Delicious!

Jeanne Abbott, University of Missouri
Anchorage, Alaska

HOT CRAB SPREAD

½ pound crab meat (fresh, canned or frozen)
2-3 tablespoons cream
1 teaspoon minced onion
1 garlic clove, pressed
2 tablespoons lemon juice
8 ounces softened cream cheese
2-3 drops Tabasco sauce
2-4 tablespoons mayonnaise
½ teaspoon minced chives
½ teaspoon Worcestershire
⅛ teaspoon salt

Drain crab and sprinkle with the lemon juice. Mix other ingredients and add to the crab. Bake at 350 degrees until bubbly. Serve with crackers or melba toast.

Kay Reynolds Bennett, Texas Tech University
Dallas, Texas

Florence Roy White, University of Illinois
Washington, D.C.

MICHIGAN STATE CRAB AND AVOCADO DIP

1 8-ounce package of cream cheese
1 large avocado, chopped
2 teaspoons Worcestershire sauce
1 tablespoon lemon juice
¼ teaspoon salt
¼ cup sour cream
1 10-ounce can of crab meat, drained (or equivalent in two smaller cans)

Blend together avocado, Worcestershire sauce, lemon juice and salt until well mixed and smooth. Add sour cream and cream cheese, blend until smooth. Stir in crab meat and refrigerate until ready to serve. Serve with potato chips, or crackers.

Susan Henning Kirkpatrick, Michigan State University
Audubon, Pennsylvania

DIVINE CRAB PATE

2 6½-ounce cans crab meat
1½ envelopes unflavored gelatin
¼ cup water
1 can mushroom soup, heated
1 cup mayonnaise
2 8-ounce packages cream cheese
1 tablespoon Worcestershire sauce
1 tablespoon onion
2 tablespoons celery
Juice of ½ lemon
¼ teaspoon garlic powder

Dissolve gelatin in water and combine with heated soup. Add cream cheese, and beat till smooth. While cooling, place all other ingredients in blender to mince. Add to soup and gelatin cheese mixture. Turn into mold and refrigerate until firm. An oiled mold in shape of fish is recommended. Arrange on platter after removal. Place pimento stuffed olive (slice) for eye.

Judy Wilkins Schumann, Iowa State University
Greater Kansas City

Connie Spanier, Oregon State University
San Francisco, California

APPETIZER CREAM PUFFS

1 cup water
½ cup butter or margarine
1 cup flour
4 eggs
Filling:
8 ounce package of cream cheese (room temperature)
1 can chopped green chilies with juice

Heat water and butter to a boil, stir in flour. Using a wooden spoon, stir until mixture forms a ball and comes away from the side of pan. Remove from heat and add eggs, one at a time, blending well. Drop by rounded teaspoonfuls onto an ungreased cookie sheet. Bake at 350 degrees for 25-30 minutes. While still slightly warm, slit open puffs with a sharp knife. Stuff with the filling, but not more than a few hours ahead of serving time so they won't get soggy.

Ann Taylor Ricker, Oklahoma State University
Dallas, Texas

HOT CHEESE DIP FOR FONDUE

1 pound Old English cheese
½ cup evaporated milk
1 teaspoon garlic salt
1 tablespoon Worcestershire
  sauce
1 tablespoon mild yellow mustard

Slowly heat cheese, adding other ingredients. Serve in fondue pot over very low heat. Use dry French bread, cut in large cubes, with fork for dipping. Crisp fresh vegetables, such as green pepper, carrots, celery, turnips, zucchini, radishes and cauliflower, could be used.

Pat Stow Jackson, Iowa State University
Rock Rapids, Iowa

CALIFORNIA CRAB SPREAD

1 cup finely flaked crabmeat
2 tablespoons dried parsley
1 teaspoon dried minced onion
3 tablespoons mayonnaise
¼ teaspoon curry powder
1 teaspoon fresh, frozen or
  bottled lemon juice

Combine all ingredients. Let stand at least ½ hour in refrigerator before using, to blend flavors. Serve with crackers.

Barbara S. Brode, Pennsylvania State University
Pomona Valley, California

BARBEQUE CHICKEN WINGS

3 pounds wings
1 cup sugar
½ cup vinegar
1 teaspoon salt
1 tablespoon soy sauce
3 tablespoons catsup
½ cup chicken stock

Cut wings into 3 parts. Boil tips in small amount of water (enough for ½ cup stock). Dip other parts in egg and then in cornstarch and fry until golden brown. Combine remaining ingredients. Lay wings in baking dish and cover with sauce. Bake at 350 degrees for 30 minutes; turn and bake 30 minutes more.

Kay Johnson Marovich, Kansas State University
South Bay, California

CHILI-CHEESE DIP

1 8-ounce package cream cheese
1 16-ounce can chili without
  beans
1 large package tortilla strips

Cook chili and cream cheese over low heat until cheese is melted. Serve in fondue dish or chafing dish with warmed tortilla strips.

Carolyn Stephonson, California State-Long Beach
Bal-Harbor, California

COOKIE'S CRABBY CANAPE

7 ounces drained crabmeat
24 large white de-stemmed
  mushrooms
1 egg
2 tablespoons mayonnaise
1 slice lemon
1 stick butter
½ diced medium onion
½ cup bread crumbs
Dash salt

Melt butter. Clean mushrooms. Dip cap lightly in butter and place in baking pan. In bowl, mix: crabmeat, mayonnaise, lemon juice from slice, egg, salt, onion. Mix well, then add ¼ cup breadcrumbs. Put remaining ¼ cup breadcrumbs in melted butter. Fill caps generously with crabmeat mixture. Sprinkle melted butter and breadcrumbs on top. Place in 350 degree oven for 10 minutes or until golden brown. Serve hot.

Kathryn (Cookie) Hart, Lehigh University
Philadelphia North Suburban, Pennsylvania

DILL DIP

1 cup mayonnaise
1 cup sour cream
1 teaspoon horseradish
1 teaspoon dill weed
1 tablespoon dried minced onion
1 tablespoon dried parsley
½ teaspoon salt

Mix all ingredients together and store in covered container in refrigerator at least 24 hours . . . longer if possible. Serve with fresh vegetables. Excellent!

Julia Terry Templeton, Southern Methodist University
Charleston, South Carolina

Mary Sue Davison, University of Wisconsin-River Falls
Portage, Wisconsin

ITALIAN EGGPLANT APPETIZER

3 cups eggplant, peeled and cut in
  ½ inch cubes
⅓ cup chopped green pepper
1 medium onion, coarsely
  chopped
2 cloves garlic, crushed
⅓ cup olive oil
1 cup canned tomato paste
1 4-ounce can mushrooms with
  liquid
¼ cup water
2 tablespoons red wine vinegar
½ cup stuffed olives, cut in half
½ cup pitted ripe olives, cut in
  half
1½ teaspoons sugar
½ teaspoon oregano
1 teaspoon salt
⅛ teaspoon pepper

Place ingredients through olive oil into large covered sauce pan and cook for 15 minutes, stirring occasionally. Add remaining ingredients and cook covered for 30 minutes or until eggplant is tender. Chill. Serve with crackers. Makes one quart.

Judith Renje Seybt, Washington University
St. Louis, Missouri

HAM DELIGHTS

Meatballs:
2 pounds ground fresh pork
2 pounds ground ham
2 eggs
2 cups crushed graham crackers
1½ cups milk
Sauce:
1 can tomato soup
1 teaspoon dry mustard
½ cup vinegar
1 cup brown sugar

Ask your butcher to grind pork and ham together. Mix all meatball ingredients together and form into balls. Mix all sauce ingredients together, pour over meat balls and bake at 300 degrees for 2 hours, uncovered. Baste with sauce every half hour. Makes 30 meat balls. Good for a large party.

Dru Mort Toebben, University of Nebraska-Lincoln
North Platte, Nebraska

HAMBURGER-CHEESE DIP

2 pounds ground beef
½ large onion
2 green onions, including some
 tops
¼ green pepper, chopped
2 hot chili peppers, crushed
1 can tomato soup
1 can cream of mushroom soup
1 tablespoon chili powder
1 teaspoon garlic salt
1 pound Velveeta cheese

Brown meat drain off fat. Add onions, peppers and soups, add seasonings. Cook 20 minutes. Add Velveeta cheese, (cut in chunks) and stir until cheese melts. Serve hot with heavy chips such as Doritos.

Shirley VonRuden, Kansas State
Hutchinson, Kansas

HAMBURGER PIZZA DIP

½ pound ground chuck, cooked
 and drained
3 jars processed sharp cheese
¼ cup tomato sauce
1 to 2 teaspoons chili powder
¼ teaspoon onion salt

Combine all ingredients with the meat. Simmer 10 minutes. Serve with tortilla chips or fritos.

Barbara Bishop Mennell, Oklahoma State University
St. Louis, Missouri

COCKTAIL HOT DOGS

¾ cup mustard
10-ounce jar red currant jelly
cocktail frankfurters or hot dogs
 cut into bite sized pieces

Simmer mustard and jelly together. (Fondue pot works well). Add hot dogs. Serve with toothpicks when sauce thickens. Throughout party, more hot dogs can be added to remaining sauce.

Cathy Frost, Michigan State University
Birmingham, Michigan

LINCOLN LOG

1 8-ounce package cream cheese
¼ cup Swiss cheese, cubed
2-3 teaspoons horseradish
⅓ cup dried chopped beef

Cream together the cream cheese, horseradish and Swiss cheese. Roll on waxed paper to form a log. Roll onto serving plate and cover with dried beef. Refrigerate overnight for best flavor. Slice and serve with crackers.

Pat O'Connell Mullins, St. Louis University
Dallas, Texas

PIQUANT COCKTAIL MEATBALLS

2 pounds ground chuck
1 cup corn flake crumbs
½ cup parsley flakes
2 eggs
2 tablespoons soy sauce
¼ teaspoon pepper
½ teaspoon garlic powder
⅓ cup ketchup
2 tablespoons instant minced onion
1 pound can jellied cranberry sauce
1 12-ounce bottle chili sauce
2 tablespoons brown sugar
1 tablespoon bottled lemon juice

Combine beef, crumbs, parsley flakes, eggs, soy sauce, pepper, garlic powder, ketchup and onion. Form into walnut-size balls and arrange in a 15½x10½x1 inch pan. In a medium saucepan, combine cranberry sauce, chili sauce, brown sugar and lemon juice. Cook over moderate heat (250 degrees) until smooth, stirring occasionally. Pour over meatballs. Bake uncovered for 30 minutes at 350 degrees. Serve in a chafing dish or fondue pot with toothpicks. Even better if made the day before. Makes about 60 meatballs.

Patsy Henderson, Washington University
St. Louis, Missouri

DOTTIE'S SWEDISH MEATBALLS

2 pounds ground meat
1 egg, slightly beaten
1 cup grated onion
Salt to taste
1 12-ounce bottle chili sauce
1 10-ounce jar grape jelly
Juice of 1 lemon

Combine ground meat, egg, grated onion and salt. Shape into small balls (50 to 60). Brown meat. Simmer chili sauce, grape jelly and lemon juice. Add meat balls. Simmer until cooked through.

Cookbook Committee

MELON GINGER COCKTAIL

Use 3 varieties of melon, cantaloupe, watermelon, Casaba, etc. Use apple corer or melon ball cutter to vary shapes.
Cook 6 minutes and cool
1½ cups sugar
¼ cup white corn syrup
Add 2 tablespoons lime or lemon juice
½ cup water
2 tablespoons grated fresh ginger

Pour sauce over melon balls and chill at least 1 hour. Garnish with mint leaves. Enough for six servings.

Connie Spanier, Oregon State University
San Francisco, California

MUSHROOM APPETIZERS

1 8-ounce box fresh mushrooms, chopped and sauteed
1 tablespoon butter
1 small grated onion
1 8-ounce package cream cheese
1 egg yolk
Salt and pepper to taste

Mix all ingredients. Spread on small bun halves or snack rye bread and broil until golden brown.

Sharon Rowland Zurawski, University of Wisconsin-Milwaukee
Milwaukee, Wisconsin

BACON STUFFED MUSHROOMS

2 dozen large mushrooms, fresh
  or canned
Butter or margarine
Salt
Nutmeg
1 tablespoon butter or margarine
2 teaspoons dried chives
1 egg
1 tablespoon lemon juice
1 teaspoon minced parsley
Salt and pepper
5 slices bacon, cooked and
  crumbled
Dry bread crumbs

Clean and stem mushrooms. Pat caps dry, chop stems. Place mushroom caps close together in shallow baking dish. Dot with butter, season with salt and nutmeg. Bake 10 minutes at 400 degrees. Sauté stems and chives in 1 tablespoon butter. Beat egg until foamy. Add lemon juice, parsley, dash of salt and pepper. Blend in sautéd mixture, bacon and enough crumbs to form a filling which holds together. Stuff into caps. Refrigerate until ready to heat and serve. To serve, broil 5 minutes.

Nancy Willis Litzinger, University of Missouri
St. Louis, Missouri

MARINATED MUSHROOMS I

1 pound fresh mushrooms
1 cup cooking oil
1 cup red wine garlic vinegar
1 tablespoon salt
1 tablespoon lemon pepper
1 tablespoon sugar
1 clove garlic, chopped
1 tablespoon parsley, crushed

Fill quart jar with washed mushrooms. Mix other ingredients together and pour over mushrooms. Let stand for a minimum of three days, tipping jar occasionally. Keep refrigerated. Drain before serving.

Chris Loveberg Montgomery,
California State University-San Diego
Orange County, California

MARINATED MUSHROOMS II

1 package Good Seasons Garlic
  Dressing
1 pound fresh mushrooms

Wash mushrooms. Prepare dressing according to directions on package. Bring dressing to boil. Drop in mushrooms. Boil for one (1) minute. Remove from heat. Store in covered container in refrigerator. Wait at least 24 hours before tasting.

Nancy Buell Renton, University of Oregon
Eugene, Oregon

MEAT BALLS IN SAUCE

Meatballs:
1 pound ground chuck
½ pound ground veal
2 cups bread bits
½ cup milk
1 teaspoon onion powder
½ teaspoon garlic salt
1½ teaspoon soy sauce
1 teaspoon hot pepper sauce
1 teaspoon Accent
Sauce:
¼ cup brown sugar
¼ cup vinegar
½ cup Worcestershire sauce
1 cup ketchup
Tabasco sauce
1 teaspoon chili powder
1 teaspoon celery salt
1 cup water
Garlic

To make meatballs: place bread bits in milk and squeeze out as much milk as possible. Add to meat. Add onion powder, garlic salt, soy sauce, hot pepper sauce and Accent. Shape into small balls. Brown lightly, then place in 350 degree oven for about 20 minutes. These may then be frozen.

To make sauce: mix all ingredients, bring to a boil and simmer for 2 hours. Pour sauce over baked meat balls and serve in a chafing dish with toothpicks or cocktail forks.

Evelyn Gooding Dippell, Past Grand President,
University of Illinois
Washington, D.C.

OLIVE CHEESE PUFFS

½ cup butter
2 cups grated strong cheddar
  cheese
½ teaspoon salt
1 teaspoon paprika
Dash cayenne
50 (approximately) small stuffed
  green olives
1 cup flour

Mix softened butter, cheese and spices. Stir in flour, mixing well. Mold 1 teaspoon of this mixture around each olive, covering it completely. Arrange on a baking sheet and chill until firm. Bake in 400 degree oven for 15 minutes. Serve hot. These freeze very well. Make ahead, freeze on a cookie sheet and then store in a plastic bag. Bake as needed. Served to the campers at Sechelt Camp.

Deb Berto, Former Cook, Gamma Phi Beta Camp
North Vancouver, British Columbia

PARMESAN CHEESE SANDWICH

Mayonnaise
Grated Parmesan cheese
1 inch bread rounds
1 onion, peeled and chopped

Mix mayonnaise and cheese to consistency of softened butter. Place a little chopped onion in center of each round of bread. Cover with mayonnaise-cheese mixture. Put under broiler until puffed and brown. Serve immediately. These may be prepared the day before, covered with waxed paper and refrigerated. Broil just before serving.

Connie Lynne Brandon, Vanderbilt University
Nashville, Tennessee

PEANUT STICKS

1 loaf Sandwich bread
1 cup vegetable oil
1 12-ounce jar smooth peanut butter

Cut crusts off of the bread. Cut bread into finger slices — about 5 "fingers" per slice. Toast finger strips in a 275 degree oven about 40 minutes or until very lightly browned. The time will depend on the oven. Toast the crusts also until very light brown and well dried. Put crusts into blender and make fine crumbs. Put vegetable oil and peanut butter into sauce pan and heat just enough to meld when stirred. Cool slightly. Dip finger strips into peanut butter — oil mixture then roll slightly in toasted bread crumbs. Freeze; defrost about 1 hour before serving. DO NOT HEAT. Note: These can be made quickly if one person dips the strips and a second person rolls them in the bread crumbs. Enlist the help of your husband! These are popular as "something" with drinks and at morning coffees.

Doris Erwin Hawkins, Iowa State University
Washington, D.C.

SANDRA'S SALTED PECANS

1 pound pecan halves
¼ pound butter
Dash of salt

Place butter in shallow baking dish or cookie sheet in 300 degree oven. Add pecan halves. After 10 minutes in the oven, remove and sprinkle evenly with salt. Drain on absorbent paper. Stir several times during the time the pecans are in the oven.

Latane Jordan Graham, Memphis State University
Dallas, Texas

HOT SPICED PECANS

2 cups pecan halves
1½ tablespoon melted butter
½ teaspoon Tabasco sauce
3 teaspoons soy sauce
1 teaspoon salt

Melt butter and toss pecans in it. Bake in pan 30 minutes at 300 degrees. Remove from oven and toss in the sauces and salt. Stir. Can be refrigerated for later use.

Arthetta White Swafford, Oklahoma University
Tulsa, Oklahoma

GALA PECAN SPREAD

1 8-ounce package cream cheese, softened
2 tablespoons milk
1 package sliced dried beef
¼ cup finely chopped green pepper
2 tablespoons dried minced onion
½ teaspoon garlic salt
¼ teaspoon pepper
½ cup sour cream
½ cup coarsely chopped pecans
2 tablespoons butter
⅛ teaspoon salt

Combine cream cheese and milk, mixing well until blended. Stir in dried beef which has been cut in small pieces, green pepper, onion and seasonings. Mix well, fold in sour cream. Spoon into baking dish. Heat and crisp pecans in butter and salt. Use slotted spoon to remove nuts from butter and salt mixture and sprinkle over cream cheese mixture. Serve hot with wheat thins and knife. (Crackers will break if dipped into casserole.) Serves 8-10.

Betty Russell Baker, U.C.L.A.
Riverside Area, California

GARLIC COCKTAIL PICKLES

1 gallon large, firm sour pickles
   (commercial)
5 pounds sugar
1 box stick cinnamon
1 small box celery seed
1 small box mustard seed
1 small box whole cloves
5 pods (large) garlic — peeled
   and sliced

Drain pickles very dry. Cut off both ends, then cut in slices ¼ inch thick. Put sliced pickles in large pan. Sprinkle all spices and garlic over pickles, then add sugar. Cover and let stand for 3-4 days (until sugar is dissolved). Stir at least once a day. Pack in glass jars, and pour sugar syrup over pickles. Place a garlic pod and a stick of cinnamon in each jar along with other spices. Seal. These keep well.

Pauline Peacock Little, Iowa State University
Greenville, North Carolina

PARTY POPS

24 Spanish green olives, largest
   size
12 slices of bacon
24 wooden toothpicks

Cut bacon slices in half and wrap each olive in one-half strip bacon. Fasten the bacon pieces around the olives, securing with toothpick. Place on sheet with sides on it and put in 400 degree oven for 15 to 20 minutes, or broil 3 to 4 inches from heat until bacon is crisp. Serve hot. Makes 6 servings.

Peggy Larson Stromer, University of Nebraska
Milton, Wisconsin

RYE LOAF DIP

Round rye bread loaf
16 ounces sour cream
16 ounces mayonnaise
2 tablespoons onion flakes
2 tablespoons parsley flakes
2 tablespoons dill seed
1½ teaspoons seasoning salt

Cut top off round rye loaf. Remove the bread from the center to form a bowl. Cut the bread that is removed into bite-sized cubes to be placed around the loaf for dipping. Mix all the dip ingredients thoroughly and place in rye loaf "bowl". Enjoy the dip, "bowl" and all!

Jonette Crowley, University of Colorado
Denver, Colorado

RYE ROUNDS

Rye rounds
2 cups grated sharp cheese
1 small can ripe olives
2 tablespoons chopped onion
1 cup mayonnaise
Crumbled bacon

Mix the cheese, olives (sliced thinly), chopped onion and mayonnaise. Spread on rye rounds. Top with crumbled bacon. Bake at 300 degrees for 15 to 20 minutes. Serve hot. DELICIOUS!

Evelyn Allard Ellis, University of Illinois
Evansville, Indiana

SALAMI

4 pounds lean ground beef
¼ teaspoon onion powder
¼ teaspoon red pepper
¼ teaspoon black pepper
½ teaspoon dry mustard
1 teaspoon garlic powder
2 teaspoons liquid smoke
1 tablespoon peppercorns
    (coarsely ground — I put in
    blender)
4 tablespoons Morton's Tender
    Quick (meat cure — not a
    tenderizer)
2 cups water

Put all ingredients into water except meat. Then work them into meat. Shape into 4 rolls (like ice box cookies). Wrap each in heavy foil. Refrigerate 24 hours. Poke 4 or 5 holes in bottom of each with a fork before baking. Place on broiler rack. Bake at 300 degrees for 3 hours. Can be frozen. This has been very popular with our friends at cocktail parties — I have also used a frozen one as a bridge prize.

Anita B. Curtis, Vanderbilt University
Colorado Springs, Colorado

SALMON BALL

1 8-ounce package cream cheese
2 cups sockeye salmon
1 teaspoon horseradish
1 teaspoon liquid smoke
1 teaspoon lemon juice
2 teaspoons grated onion

Mix well with electric mixer. Form in ball. Roll in chopped nuts and parsley. Refrigerate. Best served with sesame melba rounds.

Karen Wander Kline, Grand President,
Iowa State University
Omaha, Nebraska

Mollie Ellis Ellis, Oklahoma University
Dallas, Texas

SAUSAGE COOKIES

1 pound sausage
2 cups biscuit mix
1 pound sharp cheese

Partially pre-cook sausage and drain away fat. Melt cheese. Add biscuit mix and sausage. Roll into walnut-sized pieces. Bake 15 minutes at 350 degrees. Yields 30 cookies. These can be frozen and used as desired.

Judy Wilkins Schumann, Iowa State University
Greater Kansas City

IOLA'S SHRIMP DIP

1 cup mayonnaise
2 pounds fresh shrimp, cooked
    and cleaned
Juice of 1 lemon
Dash of garlic salt
Dash of Tabasco sauce

Mix all ingredients in a blender and chill. Serve with assorted crackers.

Latane Jordan Graham, Memphis State University
Dallas, Texas

DIP FOR SHRIMP

6 tablespoons chili sauce, bottled
2 tablespoons lemon juice
1½ tablespoons horseradish
¼ teaspoon grated onion
1 tablespoon Worcestershire
sauce
2 drops Tabasco
Dash salt

Combine ingredients and mix well. Serve as a dip for shrimp.

Sylvia Hardy Trewin, Iowa State University
Richardson, Texas

DOTTIE'S SHRIMP BALL

2 tablespoons mayonnaise
1 can shrimp, chopped
8 ounces cream cheese, softened
Season to taste with:
Worcestershire sauce
A-1 Steak Sauce
Garlic salt
Parsley or chopped nuts

Mix all ingredients and form into ball. Chill overnight. Roll in parsley or chopped nuts, if desired.

Cookbook Committee

SHRIMP BUTTER

2 cups diced shrimp
1 stick butter
Juice of one lemon
1 small diced onion
4 tablespoons mayonnaise
1 8-ounce package cream cheese

Mix everything with electric mixer except shrimp. Stir in shrimp and chill.

Barb Tate, Vanderbilt University
Cincinnati, Ohio

JANE NOLAN'S SHRIMP DIP

1 8-ounce package cream cheese,
softened
1 small minced onion (minced
finely)
1 small can shrimp (rinsed and
broken up) or use the
equivalent of frozen or fresh (I
prefer to use the small bags of
frozen "salad" shrimp)
2 eggs
1½ tablespoons vinegar
2 tablespoons sugar

Mix eggs, vinegar and sugar together over heat until it thickens. Stir constantly. Put softened cream cheese, onion and shrimp in a bowl. Pour cooked mixture over and mix well. This should be made a day or so ahead and stored in the refrigerator. Remove from refrigerator one hour or so before serving with Melba toast rounds. This receipe doubles, triples or quadruples easily. It has gotten rave reviews at our parties.

Julia Terry Templeton, Southern Methodist University
Charleston, South Carolina

HONOLULU SHRIMP

Whole shrimp
Bermuda onions
Pickling spices
Dressing:
1 teaspoon salt
½ teaspoon fresh ground pepper
½ teaspoon paprika
⅔ cup olive oil
2 or 3 dashes Tabasco
1 teaspoon Worcestershire sauce
2 lemons, juice only
⅓ cup tarragon or mixed herb
   vinegar, scant

Lay in peasant bowl or jar, whole steamed shrimp, thinly sliced Bermuda onions and whole pickling spices in alternate layers. Repeat layers until container is full. Cover completely with above dressing. Let stand for 6 to 24 hours. Serve with long handled fork, crackers and lots of paper napkins.

Cherie McElhinney Olsen, University of Iowa
Ann Arbor, Michigan

SHRIMP MOUSSE

1½ tablespoon unflavored gelatin
2 small cans shrimp
1 can tomato soup
3 3-ounce packages cream cheese
1 cup mayonnaise
¾ cup chopped celery
½ cup chopped green onions
½ cup chopped green pepper
Dash Worcestershire sauce

Heat tomato soup and melt cream cheese in it. Cool. Dissolve gelatin in ¼ cup of water. Stir gelatin and other ingredients into tomato soup mixture. Turn into mold and chill until set. Unmold and serve with crackers.

Judy Wagner Witcel, St. Louis University
St. Louis, Missouri

SHRIMP ROLL-UPS OR PINWHEELS

2 tablespoons mayonnaise
1 3-ounce package cream cheese
1 tablespoon ketchup
1 teaspoon mustard
Dash garlic
1 can chopped shrimp, mashed
¼ cup chopped cucumber
1 teaspoon chopped onion

Mix all ingredients together. Spread on "Pollman" loaf sliced lengthwise. Dark Russian Rye bread may be used. Roll up each end to the middle. Chill. Then slice each roll into 6 roll-ups each. 1 slice of bread equals 12 to 14 pinwheels.

Peg Walker Thiesen, University of Nebraska-Omaha
Omaha, Nebraska

SHRIMP SPREAD

1 8-ounce package cream cheese
3 tablespoons mayonnaise
½ package small precooked
   shrimp
4 green onions and tops, chopped
1 chicken boullion cube dissolved
   in ¼ cup water
Dash Worcestershire sauce

Mix all ingredients together using approximately ½ of boullion mixture to taste. Serve on baked bread triangles, made by removing crusts from bread, cutting into 4 triangles and baking 20 minutes at 300 degrees.

Kris Brandt Riske, University of Wyoming
Alamogordo, New Mexico

SOMBRERO DIP

¼ pound hamburger
¼ cup chopped onions
1 16-ounce can hot chili beans
¼ cup ketchup
1 teaspoon chili powder
¼ teaspoon salt
½ cup shredded cheese
¼ cup chopped green olives
¼ cup chopped onions

Brown hamburger and onions together. Mash beans and add to meat mixture. Add remaining ingredients and heat through. Pour into flat serving dish. Garnish with cheese, green olives, and onions. Put in oven to melt cheese.

Peg Walker Thiesen, University of Nebraska-Omaha
Omaha, Nebraska

SPINACH BALLS

6 eggs beaten
2 (10-ounce) frozen packages of spinach
2 cups herbed dressing mix
1 cup Parmesan cheese
2 sticks butter — softened

Cook and drain spinach. Add softened butter and mix. Add cheese and herbed dressing mix. Then add eggs and mix. Form into bite-size balls. Bake at 350 degrees for 10-12 minutes. May be frozen before baking. (May need more dressing mix if too loose to form balls.)

Marty Altmin, University of Illinois
Milwaukee, Wisconsin

SPINACH DIP OR LIZA'S MYSTERY DIP

1 package chopped spinach, or 1 package fresh spinach, chopped
1 pint mayonnaise
½ cup parsley
½ cup green onion tops
½ teaspoon salt
½ teaspoon pepper
¼ teaspoon garlic powder
Juice of one lemon

Drain spinach VERY WELL. (Squeezing with hands may be necessary) Assemble ingredients in blender, the more liquid items first. Blend at high speed. Serve with favorite chips.

Carolyn Coe Cole, University of Texas
Dallas, Texas

Georgiana Post McClenaghan, Oregon State University
Nashville, Tennessee

SPINACH DIP

1 10-ounce package frozen chopped spinach
1½ cups mayonnaise
½ cup plain yogurt or sour cream
½ cup chopped parsley
½ cup chopped scallions
Salt and pepper to taste

Cook spinach as package directs and drain *very well*. Mix with other ingredients and refrigerate a few hours to meld flavors. Serve with chips.

Doris Erwin Hawkins, Iowa State University
Washington, D.C.

SPINACH SPREAD

2 package frozen chopped
  spinach
5 tablespoons chopped onion
Salt and pepper
Dash of Tabasco sauce
Mayonnaise to moisten
1 package Hidden Valley dressing
  mix

Thaw (do *not* cook) spinach and drain. Hand squeeze out all moisture. Put into bowl, adding onions, salt, pepper and Tabasco. Add dressing mix. Add enough mayonnaise to make it spreadable but not runny. This is best made early in the day or even the day before. Cover and refrigerate. Serve with mild crackers. Serves 8-10.

Ginny Ellis Ziegler, Miami University
Philadelphia North Suburban

Jean Anderson Allard, University of Washington
Modesto, California

SPINACH-CHEESE APPETIZER SQUARES

1 package frozen chopped
  spinach
3 eggs
3 tablespoons flour
½ pound cottage cheese
½ pound cheddar cheese, grated

Cook spinach and drain very well. Beat eggs slightly and add flour to eggs. Add cheeses and spinach; pour into buttered 9x12 inch pan. Bake at 350 degrees for 45 minutes. Serve hot in squares.

Elaine Pautler McCammon, University of Missouri
St. Louis, Missouri

SPINACH-CHEESE SNACK

1 cup flour
1 teaspoon salt
1 teaspoon baking powder
2 eggs, well beaten
¼ pound melted butter or
  margarine
1 cup milk
1 pound grated cheddar cheese
1 10-ounce package frozen
  chopped spinach

Sift or mix well the dry ingredients. Add the eggs, butter and milk and mix well. Mix together the cheese and the spinach which has been thawed, well chopped and well drained. Add these to the batter. Pour mixture into greased 9x13 inch pan. Bake 30 to 35 minutes at 350 degrees. Cut into 1 inch squares and let cool slightly before serving. This may be frozen and reheated for 20 minutes at 350 degrees.

Doris Erwin Hawkins, Iowa State University
Washington, D.C.

MARGARET'S TAMALE BALLS

Tamales:
1 pound beef
1 pound pork
1½ cup corn meal
½ cup flour
1 tablespoon chili powder
2 teaspoons salt
¾ cup tomato juice
4 medium garlic pods or 1
  teaspoon garlic puree
Sauce:
2 large (number 2) cans tomatoes
2 teaspoons salt
1 tablespoon chili powder

Grind meats together very fine. Mix in other ingredients and form into stiff balls the size of marbles. Place in sauce and simmer. Make sauce by mashing tomatoes and simmering with salt and chili powder. Simmer all ingredients together for about 2 hours. Keep hot in chafing dish. Serve on toothpicks.

Cookbook Committee

STUFFED CHERRY TOMATOES

2 baskets cherry tomatoes
1 medium can sauerkraut
1 8-ounce package cream cheese
½ teaspoon Worcestershire sauce
⅛ teaspoon onion powder
Salt and pepper to taste
Dill weed for garnish

Drain sauerkraut, reserving juice. Chop sauerkraut fine and mix with cheese, Worcestershire sauce, onion powder, salt and pepper. Thin to proper consistency to stuff tomatoes with reserved juice and some lemon juice. Cut tops from tomatoes, remove seeds and center, then drain upside down. Remove a tiny slice of tomato bottom so that it will sit upright. Stuff with cheese mixture and sprinkle top with dill.

You won't believe this recipe till you've tried it. Few people guess what is in the stuffing.

LaVerne A. Strong, U.C.L.A.
Monterey Bay, California

DIP FOR RAW VEGETABLES

1 3-ounce package pimento cream cheese
¼ cup commercial sour cream
2 tablespoons ketchup
¼ teaspoon paprika
¼ teaspoon salt
¼ teaspoon Worcestershire sauce
1 drop Tabasco

Soften cream cheese and blend with sour cream, ketchup and seasonings, until smooth. Chill. Use as a dip for raw carrots, celery, radishes, green onions, green pepper, tomatoes, cauliflower, et cetera. Makes one cup. Keeps well in refrigerator.

Sylvia Hardy Trewin, Iowa State University
Richardson, Texas

VEGETABLE DIP

⅔ cup sour cream
⅔ cup mayonnaise
1 teaspoon dill weed
1 teaspoon Beau Monde
1 tablespoon dry parsley
2 tablespoons grated onion

Combine ingredients and chill.

Cheryl Stoner Myhra, Iowa State University
Dallas, Texas

RAW VEGETABLE DIP

¼ pound blue cheese
8 ounce package cream cheese
3 tablespoons vermouth
1 clove garlic, crushed
12 or 16 ounces sour cream

Combine until smooth. Serve with raw vegetables such as carrots, celery, turnips, red onion slices, green onions, zucchini, cucumbers, cauliflowers, green peppers and jicama.

Carol Lehrer Wilson, Colorado State
Colorado Springs, Colorado

Beverages

OMEGA'S FRENCH CHOCOLATE (The Living End!)

2 half pints whipping cream
½ cup cocoa
½ cup sugar
1 teaspoon vanilla
1½ quart of scalding milk

Sift together the cocoa and sugar. Whip the heavy cream in an electric mixer until firm, then fold in, by hand the mixture of cocoa and sugar, then the vanilla. This chocolate whipping cream is served in a silver bowl, allowing about ⅓ cup full for each serving. The person pouring will then fill the cup with hot milk and each person will "stir" her own.

During my stay at Omega (and maybe they still do it!) there was a "spread" every Saturday night after midnight. Our house mother served French Hot Chocolate, olives and nuts and finger sandwiches. This was followed by much singing.

Mary Sue Lytle Yett, Iowa State University
Mobile, Alabama

EASY HOT CHOCOLATE MIX

1 1-pound box Nestle's Quik
1 9-ounce box instant milk (scant 4 cups)
1 3-ounce jar non-dairy creamer
½ cup powdered sugar

Mix ingredients well and store in a dry place (well-sealed pitcher or pouring canister is most convenient). Fill serving vessel ½ full of dry mixture and add boiling water to fill. Works great by the cup or by the gallon for a large group.

Makes a great gift for college students, bachelors, tired career women at the end of the day!

Judy L. Sennett, University of Illinois
Chicago, Illinois

RUSTIC ALMOND COFFEE

Cinnamon
Sugar
1 tablespoon sugar
⅓ ounce brandy
⅓ ounce Tia Maria
⅓ ounce Amaretto
Hot coffee
Whipped cream
Sliced almonds
Maraschino cherries

Rub the rim of a 12 ounce wine glass with cinnamon and sugar. Pour 1 tablespoon of sugar (or sugar syrup) in the bottom. Add brandy, Tia Maria, Amaretto. Fill with coffee until ¾ full. Top with whipped cream, sliced almonds and cherry.

Jan Peterson, Iowa State University
Des Moines, Iowa

FROZEN FRUIT DAIQUIRIS

6 ounce rum
6 ounce sweet and sour
Dash of milk
Fruit (strawberries, bananas,
   peaches, pineapple)
Ice
Whipped cream

In a blender, place the rum and sweet and sour. Add a dash of milk and the fruit of your choice (1 frozen package of strawberries, OR 2 bananas OR 2 peaches OR 1 small can of sliced pineapple with juice). Pour in small cubed ice to top of blender. Blend until slushy. Pour into glasses and top with whipped cream. You can mix the fruits too!

Rhonda Rawlings, Northern Arizona University
Flagstaff, Arizona

OLD FASHIONED EGG NOG

½ cup sugar
6 eggs, separated
4 cups milk, scalded
¼ teaspoon salt
2 cups heavy cream (whipped)
2 teaspoons vanilla
¼ teaspoon nutmeg

Mix ¼ cup sugar and egg yolks in double boiler. Slowly add milk, cook, stirring constantly, until mixture coats spoon. Chill. Gradually add salt and ¼ cup sugar to egg whites and beat stiff. Fold egg whites and cream into custard separately. Add vanilla, chill. Garnish with nutmeg. Add 1 cup whiskey to egg nog if you like (Rye or Bourbon). Serves 20 — ½ cup portions.

Cookbook Committee

GRAPEFRUIT COOLER

1½ cups sugar
1 cup water
Handful of fresh mint
1 46-ounce can pink grapefruit
   juice

Dissolve sugar in water, add mint and bring to a boil. Remove the mint, add grapefruit juice and freeze. Remove from the freezer 1 hour before serving.

Dorothy Chase Jones, Southern Methodist University
Dallas, Texas

SWEDISH GLOGG
(from Swedish-American Lines)

20 cloves (whole)
1 piece ginger root
1 tablespoon cardamon seeds
(Place all three in spice bag)
½ cup skinned almonds (unsalted)
½ cup raisins
3 bottles red wine
1 small stick of cinnamon
½ bottle Vodka
½ bottle Cognac
½ bottle Port wine

Place raisins, almonds, red wine, spice bag and small stick of cinnamon in saucepan and bring to boil. *Simmer* for a few minutes, take out cinnamon stick. Add port wine, Vodka and Cognac. Heat up, take out spice bag and remove from stove. Pour a little Vodka or Cognac on top, and burn it off — when the flame is out, it is ready to serve. Place some raisins and almonds in each glass or cup.

(This is a real fog-cutter, and is traditionally served by the Lindblad EXPLORER on Christmas Eve from an out-of doors fire somewhere in the Antarctic, and has been pictured in the National Geographic.)

Beth McCallon Wheeler,
Southern Methodist University
Dallas, Texas

FRANCES' AMBER PUNCH

12 ounce can frozen orange juice
¾ cup lemon juice
46 ounces pineapple juice
3 quarts gingerale
1 cup maraschino cherries,
   including juice
2 cups bourbon OR 2 cups rum
   (optional)

Mix all ingredients and serve with ice or ice ring. Excellent served with or without liquor, or prepare a bowl of each to serve all tastes.

Latane Jordan Graham, Memphis State University
Dallas, Texas

Sandra Graham Cude, Memphis State University
Dallas, Texas

Judy Elaine Graham, Oklahoma University
Greater Kansas City

CHAMPAGNE PUNCH

1 bottle champagne
1 bottle pink catawba wine
1 bottle sparkling water

Mix all ingredients in punch bowl. Garnish with ice ring. Serves 10.

Pat O'Connell Mullins, St. Louis University
Dallas, Texas

CHAMPAGNE PUNCH

1 6-ounce can lemonade
   concentrate
1 6-ounce can pineapple juice
   concentrate
1 6-ounce can orange juice
   concentrate
2 cups dry sherry
2 large bottles champagne
2 fifths sauterne

Mix all ingredients and chill well. Makes 50 servings.

Gwen Lankford Rogers, Iowa State University
St. Louis, Missouri

COFFEE PUNCH

2 quarts strong coffee (cold)
1 pint cold milk
1 teaspoon vanilla
½ cup sugar
1 quart vanilla ice cream
½ pint heavy cream (whipped)

Combine coffee, milk, vanilla, sugar and ice cream. At serving time float whipped cream or punch. YIELD: 15 to 20 punch cups; 10 to 12 glasses. Coffee ice cream may be used instead of the vanilla ice cream.

Virginia Forsythe Vint, University of Missouri
Dallas, Texas

FRANCES' FRUIT PUNCH

12 ounces lemon juice
48 ounces orange juice
36 ounces pineapple juice
4 quarts ginger ale
Add 2 quarts vodka or bourbon to
   taste

Mix all together. Decorate with orange and lemon slices and pineapple chunks. Using a salad mold, freeze water and maraschino cherries and juice from cherries. Set frozen ice mold in punch bowl. Serves 80 people.

Cookbook Committee

HOLIDAY PUNCH

Six cups cranberry juice
(approximately)
Two cups apple juice
One cup Curacao (orange liqueur)
One bottle champagne

Chill all of the above ingredients thoroughly. Mix juices and liqueur in the punch bowl, and just before serving, add one or two cups of ice and chilled champagne.

Kathryn Critchfield McCarville, Iowa State University
Dallas, Texas

HOT CRANBERRY PUNCH

2½ cups pineapple juice
2 cups cranberry juice
1 teaspoon cloves
½ teaspoon allspice
½ cup brown sugar
2 sticks cinnamon, broken

Place spices in top of 10 cup percolator. Put juices and sugar in bottom. Fill with water and perk. Super for fall and winter as it tastes great and smells wonderful. It can be doubled or tripled nicely in a party-size percolator.

Sandra Graham Cude, Memphis State University
Dallas, Texas

LINDA'S BUBBLING PINEAPPLE PUNCH

1 can (46 ounce) pineapple juice,
chilled
3 cups apricot nectar
1 quart club soda
1 quart pineapple sherbet

Combine chilled pineapple juice and apricot nectar in a large punch bowl. Add soda and sherbet just before serving. Makes 25 to 30 servings.

Nell Taylor Wolfe, Iowa State University
Westchester County, New York

LINDA'S PINEAPPLE PARTY PUNCH

1 can (46 ounce) pineapple juice,
chilled
3 cups cranberry juice cocktail,
chilled
1 quart ginger ale, chilled
1 lemon, thinly sliced

Combine juices and ginger ale in a large punch bowl. Float lemon slices on top. Makes 25 servings of 4 ounces each.

Nell Taylor Wolfe, Iowa State University
Westchester County, New York

PUNCH

1 large can frozen lemonade and
water to dilute
1 large can frozen orange juice
and water to dilute
1 46-ounce can pineapple juice
1 package Kool-aid if color is
desired
14 bottles of king-size 7-Up
Sugar to taste

Mix all ingredients together. Serves 40 to 50.

Dorothy Chase Jones, Southern Methodist University
Dallas, Texas

HOSPITALITY PUNCH

6 cups (1 46-ounce can)
   pineapple juice
3 6-ounce cans frozen orange
   juice
2 6-ounce cans frozen lemonade
7 cups cold sweetened tea (use 3
   small teabags)
3 quarts ginger ale
1 quart pineapple sherbet or ice

Mix all ingredients and serve. Makes more than 40 servings.

Cookbook Committee

HOT PUNCH

½ gallon frozen apple cider,
   diluted as directed
1 large bottle cranberry juice
1 can apricot nectar
Sugar to taste
2 tablespoons whole allspice

Combine cider, juice and nectar and heat with allspice in a cloth bag. Do not boil.

Dorothy Chase Jones, Southern Methodist University
Dallas, Texas

HOT PUNCH

2 cups cranberry juice
2½ cups unsweetened pineapple
   juice
½ cup water
⅓ cup firmly packed brown sugar
1½ teaspoon whole cloves
1½ teaspoon whole allspice
3 2-inch cinnamon sticks

Heat first four ingredients in a saucepan over low heat. Place in punch bowl. Add remaining ingredients. Serves 8.

Cookbook Committee

MILK PUNCH

1 cup vanilla ice cream
1 cup milk
½ cup bourbon
1 jigger light rum
1 jigger brandy
Nutmeg

Blend first 5 ingredients in blender. Pour over ice, sprinkle with nutmeg and serve, preferably on the patio, before a leisurely breakfast.

Sandra Graham Cude, Memphis State University
Dallas, Texas

BRENDA'S ORANGE COOLER

For each drink:
Orange juice
3 strawberries, sliced
Powdered sugar
Champagne or vodka

In glass, put strawberries and sprinkle with powdered sugar. If drink is to be non-alcoholic, fill glass with orange juice. If drink is to be champagne cooler, add only enough orange juice to cover strawberries and fill glass with champagne. If drink is to be orange cooler, add one ounce vodka to strawberries and powdered sugar and fill glass with orange juice.

Pat O'Connell Mullins, St. Louis University
Dallas, Texas

SUNSHINE PUNCH

1 6-ounce can frozen limeade
1 6-ounce can frozen lemonade
1 6-ounce can frozen orange juice
4 cups water
1 large bottle ginger ale

Combine, ice and serve. Makes 15 to 20 4-ounce servings.

Margaret Godbold Briscoe,
Southern Methodist University
St. Louis, Missouri

HOT BUTTERED RUM

1 pound butter
1 quart vanilla ice cream
1 pound brown sugar
1 teaspoon each cinnamon and
    nutmeg
Dark rum

Allow butter and ice cream to soften at room temperature, then blend the butter, brown sugar, ice cream and spices together with electric mixer. Store in refrigerator. To serve, place 1 heaping tablespoon of mixture and 1 shot dark rum in pre-heated mug. Fill with boiling water, stir.

Jacki Falkenroth, University of Nevada-Reno
Chicago Northwest Surburban, Illinois

DIANE'S RUSSIAN TEA

2 cups sugar
1 teaspoon cloves, ground
½ teaspoon cinnamon
2 small jars of Tang or 2 cans of
    Start
1 package lemonade mix (dry
    powder)
½ cup instant tea

Mix all ingredients together and store in air tight container. 3 rounded teaspoons of the mix should be added to one 8-ounce cup of boiling water. For a less sweet tea use 1 cup sugar.

Cookbook Committee

CHRISTMAS WASSAIL
(Mulled Wine)

¾ pound sugar
1 cup water
2 sticks cinnamon
3 tablespoons lemon juice
3½ cups pineapple juice
3 cups orange juice
5½ cups red wine
1⅛ cups sherry

Make a syrup mixing the sugar, water, cinnamon, lemon juice, pineapple juice and orange juice together. Strain syrup; add red wine; let simmer about 10 minutes. Just before removing from heat, add sherry. Serve piping hot. Makes 1 gallon or 32 punch cup servings. Place a thin slice of lemon atop each cup.

Merry Christmas!

Latane Jordan Graham, Memphis State University
Dallas, Texas

WHISPERIN' SMITH

1 6-ounce can limeade
1 6-ounce can vodka
7-Up

Put limeade and vodka into a 1 quart jar. Fill jar with 7-Up, leaving 'freeze room' at the top of jar. Freeze. Serve 'mushy', with mint leaf.

Betty Boefer Keller, University of Missouri
Bartlesville, Oklahoma

Breads

FRESH APPLE BREAD

½ cup shortening
1 cup sugar
2 eggs
1 cup grated unpeeled apples
2 cups flour
1 teaspoon soda
¼ teaspoon salt
½ teaspoon cinnamon
2 tablespoons sour milk
½ teaspoon vanilla

Grease 9x5x3 inch pan. Cream sugar, shortening, add eggs and continue to cream. Stir in grated apples. Sift all dry ingredients together and mix with creamed mixture using a fork (lightly). Add milk and vanilla, stir with a fork. Bake for about 1 hour at 350 degrees. Cool on wire rack 5 minutes in pan before removing from pan.

Judy Elaine Graham, Oklahoma University
Greater Kansas City

BANANA BREAD

3 ripe or overripe large bananas
¾ cup sugar
1½ cups flour
1 egg
¼ cup melted butter
1 teaspoon soda
1 teaspoon salt

Mash bananas with fork. Stir in other ingredients. Pour into a buttered 8½x4½x2½ inch loaf pan. Bake about one hour in preheated 325 degree oven.

Latane Jordan Graham, Memphis State University
Dallas, Texas

BANANA NUT BREAD

1 cup sugar
1 cup ripe banana puree
¼ pound margarine
2 eggs
3 tablespoons milk
2 cups flour
¼ teaspoon salt
½ teaspoon baking soda
½ teaspoon baking powder
1 teaspoon vanilla
½ cup broken walnut meats or chopped pecans

Blend margarine, sugar, eggs, milk and bananas. Add flour, salt, baking powder, baking soda, flavoring and nuts. Pour into greased and floured loaf pans and bake in a 350 degree oven for about an hour. Makes 2 small or 1 large loaf.

Lynne Ayers, Vanderbilt University
Nashville, Tennessee

Phyllis Armstrong Johnson, University of Illinois
Moline, Illinois

BEER BREAD

3 cups biscuit mix
3 tablespoons sugar
1 can beer

Grease a 9x5 inch bread pan. Mix ingredients. Bake at 350 degrees for about one hour. Serve hot. For Beer Rolls, pour into well greased muffin tins. Bake 25 minutes at 350 degrees. Serve hot. Makes 16 rolls.

Sue Wolfe, Iowa State University
Sioux City, Iowa

Vicki Savageau, Moorhead State University
Fargo-Moorhead, North Dakota

Pam Rutherford, Vanderbilt University
Nashville, Tennessee

Elizabeth Quick, Indiana University
Mt. Pleasant, Michigan

BUTTERMILK BISCUITS

3 cups all purpose flour
1½ teaspoons salt
4 teaspoons baking powder
½ teaspoon soda (dissolve in buttermilk)
6 tablespoons shortening
1½ cups thick buttermilk

Sift the dry ingredients together. Cut in shortening with a pastry blender. Stir in buttermilk, a little at a time, until you have a soft puffy dough (easy to handle). Round up lightly on a floured board and knead with the heel of your hand, 6 to 8 times. Pat out dough to one inch thickness or thinner for thin biscuits. Cut with floured biscuit cutter. Place on baking sheet. Let stand 15 minutes (or more). Bake at 400 degrees for 12 to 15 minutes.

Viola D. Jammer Larson, Iowa State University
Greater Kansas City

Irene Frame, West Virginia University
Bemidji, Minnesota

COUNTRY CRUST BREAD

2 packages active dry yeast
2 cups warm water (105 degrees to 115 degrees)
½ cup sugar
1 tablespoon salt
2 eggs
¼ cup salad oil
6 to 6½ cups flour
Soft butter or margarine

Dissolve yeast in warm water. Stir in sugar, salt, eggs, oil and 3 cups of the flour. Beat until smooth. Mix in enough remaining flour to make dough easy to handle. Turn dough onto lightly floured board; knead until smooth and elastic, 8 to 10 minutes. Place in greased bowl; turn greased side up. (At this point, dough can be refrigerated 3 to 4 days.) Cover; let rise in warm place until double, about 1 hour. (Dough is ready if impression remains.) Punch down dough; divide in half. Roll each half into rectangle, 18x9 inches. Roll up beginning at short side. With side of hand, press each end to seal. Fold ends under loaf. Place seam side down in greased loaf pan 9x5x3 inches. Brush loaves with salad oil. Let rise until double, about 1 hour. Heat oven to 375 degrees. Place loaves on lower oven rack so that tops of pans are in center of oven. Pans should not touch each other or sides of oven. Bake 30 to 35 minutes or until deep golden brown and loaves sound hollow, when tapped. Remove from pans. Brush loaves with butter. Cool on wire rack. Makes 2 loaves.

Kathleen S. Shanahan, University of Nebraska,
University of Colorado
Hastings, Nebraska

SUPER BISCUITS

2 cups flour
4 teaspoons baking powder
½ teaspoon salt
½ teaspoon cream of tarter
2 teaspoons sugar
½ cup shortening
⅔ cup milk

Sift flour, baking powder, salt, cream of tartar and sugar together. Cut in shortening till mixture resembles coarse crumbs. Add milk all at once; stir till dough forms a ball in the mixing bowl. Roll ½ inch thick on floured board; cut with floured biscuit cutter. Bake on ungreased cookie sheet at 450 degrees for 10 to 12 minutes. Makes 16 medium biscuits.

Sara Hess McElhaney, Iowa State University
Dallas, Texas

AUDREY'S STICKY CINNAMON BUNS

½ cup butter or margarine, melted
½ cup brown sugar, packed
2 tablespoons corn syrup
1 cup pecan halves
½ cup granulated sugar
2 tablespoons cinnamon
Roll dough (enough to roll out to an oblong 15x9 inches)

Combine butter, brown sugar, corn syrup, and pecan halves. Pour into greased oblong pan, 13x9x2 inches. Combine granulated sugar and cinnamon. On floured board roll dough into a 15x9 inch oblong and spread with a little melted butter and sugar-cinnamon mixture. Roll up tightly and cut into 15 one-inch slices. Place these in prepared pan, cover, and let rise in warm place approximately 1½ hours — until double in size. Bake 25 to 30 minutes in 375 degree oven. Take out of oven and invert on serving plate immediately and serve warm. *Note:* Use any basic yeast bread recipe for the dough.

Mary Lawrence Engle, Kansas University
Houston, Texas

CINNAMON BREAD

½ cup butter
¾ cup sugar
2 eggs
½ cup milk
Topping
¼ cup butter (melted)
3 tablespoons sugar
½ teaspoon cinnamon
1¼ cups flour
1¼ teaspoons baking powder
¼ teaspoon salt
1 teaspoon cinnamon

Cream butter and sugar, add eggs and beat well. Sift flour, baking powder, cinnamon and salt together and add to creamed mixture alternately with milk. Pour into a well greased loaf pan and bake about 45 minutes at 350 degrees. Pour ¼ cup melted butter over top of loaf while still hot. Spread sugar and cinnamon over loaf while still warm.

Sue Wolfe, Iowa State University
Ames, Iowa

SUGAR LUMP CINNAMON BREAD

1 cup milk
½ cup butter or margarine
½ cup sugar
1 teaspoon salt
2 packages active dry yeast
⅓ cup warm water
1 tablespoon vanilla
1 egg
5½ to 6 cups flour
1 egg, beaten
Filling:
¼ cup butter or margarine, softened
1½ tablespoons cinnamon
50 sugar cubes (about 4 ounces)
Glaze:
1 cup powdered sugar
1 to 2 tablespoons milk
Dash of vanilla

Heat milk and butter; remove from heat. Add sugar and salt. Cool to lukewarm. Dissolve yeast in water. Add yeast, vanilla and 1 egg to milk mixture. Stir. Gradually add flour to form a stiff dough. Knead on floured surface for 3 to 4 minutes till smooth. Place in greased bowl. Cover; let rise in a warm place till doubled in size about 1 hour. Divide dough in half. On floured or oiled surface, roll each half to a 15x12 inch rectangle; brush with beaten egg. Spread each with half of filling. Roll jelly-roll fashion starting with 12 inch end. Pinch edges to seal. Place seam side down in greased 9x5 inch loaf pans. (Ends will roll up over top of loaf slightly.) Cover. Let rise again till doubled in size. Bake at 375 degrees for 30 to 35 minutes. Remove from pans. While warm, drizzle with glaze.
Filling: Blend butter and cinnamon until creamy, stir in sugar cubes, to coat. Crush slightly.
Glaze: Combine powdered sugar with enough milk to make thin enough to drizzle. Add vanilla. Beat till smooth.

Marjorie A. Vogele Kovatch, Northwestern University
Glen Ellyn, Illinois

CINNAMON COFFEE CAKE

2 whole eggs
1 cup milk
1 stick margarine, melted
2 cups flour, sifted
1 cup sugar
3 teaspoons baking powder
1 teaspoon salt
Topping:
½ cup sugar
1 teaspoon cinnamon

Mix dry ingredients together. Then mix all liquids together. Mix all together until smooth. Pour into greased oblong dish (13x9 inch). Put on top before baking: ½ cup sugar and 1 teaspoon cinnamon mixed together. Pecans may be added if desired. Bake at 375 degrees about 25 to 30 minutes. Cut into squares. Delicious when served hot.

Ella Dodds Mistrot, University of Texas
Dallas, Texas

Sara Hess McElhaney, Iowa State University
Dallas, Texas

CINNAMON CRUMB CAKE

1½ cups sugar
½ cup butter
1 egg, beaten
2 cups flour
1 teaspoon cinnamon
¼ teaspoon salt
1 teaspoon soda
1 cup buttermilk

Cream together sugar and butter. Sift together flour, cinnamon and salt. Add and mix until crumbly and save ½ cup for topping. Stir soda into buttermilk and add to crumb mixture. Add beaten egg. Pour into a greased 10x8 inch or 9x3 inch pan. Sprinkle crumbs over top. Bake at 350 degrees for about 40 minutes.

Lynette Martin Chrenka, Bradley University
St. Louis, Missouri

CRESCENT CINNAMON TWISTS

¼ cup firmly packed brown sugar
2 tablespoons softened margarine
1 to 2 teaspoons cinnamon
1 8-ounce can crescent dinner rolls
Glaze:
¾ cup powdered sugar
1 tablespoon melted margarine
1 to 2 tablespoons hot water

Preheat oven to 375 degrees. Grease cookie sheet. In small bowl combine brown sugar, margarine and cinnamon. Separate crescent roll dough into four rectangles; firmly press perforations to seal. Spread two rectangles with butter-sugar mixture. Place remaining two rectangles over sugar mixture; lightly press together. Cut each rectangle into eight strips. Twist each strip several times, sealing ends. Place on cookie sheet. Bake at 375 degrees for 10 to 15 minutes until golden brown. Immediately remove from cookie sheet. In small bowl, combine glaze ingredients. Spread over warm twists. Cool.

Kay Reynolds Bennett, Texas Tech University
Dallas, Texas

GRANDMOTHER'S COFFEE CAKE

2 cups milk
1 cake yeast
2 tablespoons sugar
1 cup sugar
2 eggs, beaten
1 teaspoon salt
6 tablespoons melted butter
Flour to make a soft dough

Scald milk, cool to lukewarm, add yeast and 2 tablespoons sugar and let stand for 5 minutes. Add 2 cups flour to make a soft dough. Let rise to double its size. Add 1 cup sugar, beaten eggs, salt, melted butter and flour to make a soft dough (about 2 cups flour). Let rise again. Form into round cakes and place in round cake pans that have been well buttered. Sprinkle with melted butter, sugar and cinnamon. Let rise and bake at 375 degrees.

Geraldine Epp Smith, University of Missouri
St. Louis, Missouri

RHUBARB COFFEE CAKE

1½ cups brown sugar
½ cup shortening
1 egg
1 cup sour milk or buttermilk
1 teaspoon soda
2 cups flour
1 teaspoon vanilla
1½ to 2 cups rhubarb, cut fine
½ cup brown sugar
1 teaspoon cinnamon

Cream the 1½ cups brown sugar and shortening. Add egg and sour milk. Sift soda and flour together and add. Add vanilla. Stir in the rhubarb. Mix well. Put in a 9 inch by 12 inch cake pan. Mix the ½ cup brown sugar and cinnamon and put on cake just before placing in oven. Bake at 350 degrees for 40 minutes.

Caroline Hardy Howard, Iowa State University
Centerville, South Dakota

SOUR CREAM COFFEE CAKE

2 sticks butter
2 cups granulated sugar
2 eggs
1 cup sour cream
½ teaspoon vanilla
2 cups sifted cake flour
½ teaspoon salt
1 teaspoon baking powder
Filling:
½ cup chopped nuts
¼ cup brown sugar
1 teaspoon cinnamon

Cream butter and sugar. Add eggs. Beat. Fold in sour cream and vanilla. Add sifted dry ingredients. Pour half of batter in bundt pan. Sprinkle filling on top. Pour on rest of batter. Bake at 350 degrees for 50 to 60 minutes. Cool on rack for 20 minutes and turn out of pan.
Filling: Mix all ingredients together.

Lynne Ayers, Vanderbilt University
Nashville, Tennessee

Barb Tate, Vanderbilt University
Cincinnati, Ohio

SUPREME SOUR CREAM COFFEE CAKE

1 teaspoon soda
1 cup sour cream
1 cup granulated sugar
½ cup (1 stick) butter
2 eggs
2 cups flour
¼ teaspoon salt
1 teaspoon baking powder
1½ teaspoons vanilla
Topping:
½ cup dark brown sugar
3 teaspoons powdered cinnamon
Chopped nuts, if desired

Add soda to sour cream and let stand while blending the other ingredients. Beat the sugar and butter until fluffy. Whip the eggs and add to sugar and butter mixture. Add sour cream gradually. Add flour, baking powder, and salt, which have been sifted together. Stir in vanilla. Pour the batter into a well buttered oblong pan approximately 9½ by 12½ by 2 inches. Blend the topping ingredients together and sprinkle on batter. Bake in 350 degree oven about 35 minutes.

Mae Douglas Garrett, Oklahoma City University
Dallas, Texas

CRANBERRY BREAD

2 cups flour
1 cup sugar
1 teaspoon salt
1½ teaspoons baking powder
½ teaspoon baking soda
1 cup pecans
1 cup sliced cranberries
1 egg
1 orange
2 tablespoons cooking oil
Boiling water

Combine juice and grated rind of one orange, 2 tablespoons cooking oil, and enough boiling water to make ¾ cup of liquid. Sift together all dry ingredients, beat egg, and add to liquids. Add other ingredients. Mix well. Bake in 2 loaf pans 7½x4½x2 inches. Bake in a slow oven about 250-300 degrees for 1 to 1½ hours. Test with a toothpick for doneness.

Cookbook Committee

CRANBERRY FRUIT NUT BREAD

2 cups flour
1 cup sugar
1½ teaspoons baking powder
1 teaspoon salt
½ teaspoon baking soda
¼ cup cooking oil
3 tablespoons chopped candied fruit
¾ cup orange juice
1 well beaten egg
1 cup coarsely chopped cranberries
½ cup chopped walnuts

Sift dry ingredients. Add shortening, juice and egg. Mix. Fold in berries, fruit and nuts. Put in 2 greased loaf pans. Bake at 350 degrees for 60 minutes. Cool, wrap, and store.

Dorothy Benotti, Boston University
Boston West Suburban, Massachusetts

CHARLIE'S CORNBREAD

1 cup self-rising corn meal
2 eggs
½ cup cooking oil
2 teaspoons baking powder
1 cup sour cream
1 8½-ounce can creamed corn

Mix and bake in greased skillet or 9x9 inch baking pan in preheated 400 degree oven for thirty minutes. For parties bake in mini-muffin tins at 400 degrees for about 20 minutes.

Elise Berthon, Birmingham-Southern College
Birmingham, Alabama

SOUR CREAM CORN BREAD

1½ cups corn meal
1 teaspoon soda
1 teaspoon salt
½ cup milk
1 cup sour cream
3 tablespoon light brown sugar
1 egg, beaten
2 tablespoons melted butter

Mix the dry ingredients and combine with the mixed liquids. Bake in a greased pan for 20 to 25 minutes at 375 degrees, or until done.

Mary Anne Bryan, Auburn University
Miami, Florida

DATE BREAD

3 cups sifted flour
4 teaspoons baking powder
½ cup sugar
1½ teaspoons salt
1 cup chopped dates
1 egg, well beaten
1½ cups milk
2 tablespoons melted shortening
¼ teaspoons nutmeg

Sift the flour, baking powder, salt, nutmeg, and sugar into a mixing bowl. Add the dates. Mix the beaten eggs, milk and shortening, add to ingredients in bowl, and stir just until blended. Turn into a well-greased bread loaf pan (about 8x4x4 inch) and let stand at kitchen temperature for 20 minutes; then bake at 350 degrees about 1¼ hours. Let stand in pan a few minutes to steam slightly, then loosen sides and turn out on rack to cool. Optional: Ice with a vanilla glaze.

Mary Jo Ringhofer, Memphis State University
Germantown, Tennessee

MOTHER'S DATE-NUT BREAD

1 package (8-ounce) dates (cut up)
2 cups hot water
2 teaspoons baking soda
2 cups brown sugar (light)
2 eggs
2 tablespoons butter
3 cups flour
1 teaspoon salt
1 cup walnuts (chopped)

Put together first 3 ingredients and let cool. Mix butter, brown sugar and eggs. Add at intervals remaining ingredients and bake in *long* loaf tin for 1 hour at 350 degrees. Or bake in three small loaves at 350 degrees for 45 minutes or until done.

Rachel Rice Cook, University of Vermont
Winchester, Massachusetts

Ruth Hawley Sokol, Iowa State University
Iowa City, Iowa

DYNAMITE DILLY CHEESE BREAD

One loaf French bread
Butter
Garlic salt
¾ pounds grated cheddar cheese
½ cup real mayonnaise
Dill weed

Cut one loaf French bread, long ways, into 3 sections. Place on cookie sheet. Lightly butter each slice; sprinkle with garlic salt. Mix together grated cheese and mayonnaise until soft and spreadable. Cover each section with a generous amount of spread. Sprinkle with dill weed. Bake at 350 degrees, 15 minutes or until bread puffs up and turns golden brown. Remove from oven and cut into individual pieces.

Always a favorite at buffets and dinner parties! Excellent with Italian dishes and broiled meats.

Nancy Boza Klopp, Bowling Green State University
Cedar Rapids, Iowa

HERBED AND CHEESEY FRENCH BREAD

½ cup soft butter or margarine
½ cup creamed cottage cheese
¼ cup bleu cheese
2 tablespoons toasted sesame seeds
2 tablespoons chopped parsley
2 finely minced scallions
½ teaspoon basil
¼ teaspoon dill weed
½ teaspoon crushed rosemary
1 loaf French bread or
1 dozen hard rolls

Mix all ingredients, except bread. Blend well. Slice bread on the diagonal in 1½ inch slices, spread generously with the mixture, roll in foil and bake at 350 degrees for 20 minutes.

Irma Nash, Iowa State Univeristy
Hot Springs, Arkansas

GRAPENUT BREAD

1 cup Grapenuts
2 cups sour milk or sweet milk plus 2 tablespoons vinegar)
4 cups flour
1 cup sugar
4 teaspoons baking powder
½ teaspoon salt
2 cups raisins
2 beaten eggs
2 tablespoons melted fat
1 teaspoon soda

Soak Grapenuts in milk while mixing other ingredients. Sift together the flour, sugar, baking powder, and salt. Add raisins. Combine beaten eggs, fat, and soda with the milk-Grapenuts mixture. Add the dry ingredients and stir just long enough to moisten. Pour into two well greased bread pans and bake at 350 degrees for about 1 hour.

Dorothy Heryford Marshall, Iowa State University
Pittsburgh, Pennsylvania

APRICOT MUFFINS

2 cups flour
3 teaspoons baking powder
½ teaspoon salt
½ cup brown sugar
½ cup chopped pecans
2 teaspoons cinnamon
1 egg
1 cup milk
¼ cup oil
1 teaspoon vanilla
4 tablespoons apricot jam or
  preserves

Preheat oven to 400 degrees. Grease 16 muffin cups well. (Spray with Pam). Sift flour, baking powder, salt, and cinnamon into bowl. Add brown sugar and pecans. In a separate bowl beat egg until frothy, stir in milk, oil, vanilla, and jam and mix well. Stir into flour mixture all at once. Stir quickly and lightly (don't beat). Quickly fill muffin cups ⅔ full. Bake 25 minutes or until a toothpick comes out clean. Serve hot with butter. Divine!

Marilyn Krebs Culwell, Southern Methodist University
Dallas, Texas

FRENCH MUFFINS

¼ cup butter
½ cup sugar
1 egg
½ teaspoon salt
3 teaspoons baking powder
1½ cups flour
½ cup milk

Cream butter and sugar. Beat in egg. Sift salt, baking powder and flour together. Add flour mixture to creamed butter mixture, alternately with the milk. Raisins or blueberries may be added. They are especially nice baked in the smallest muffin tins which have been well greased. Bake at 400 degrees for about 15 minutes. Makes 24 small or 12 large muffins.

Patricia Smith Dieterich, University of Iowa
Ridgefield, Connecticut

ONE MEAL, HEALTH MUFFINS

¾ cup buttermilk
1 teaspoon soda
2 eggs
¼ teaspoon salt
1 cup safflower oil
1-2 cups raw sugar
1 cup rye flour
1 cup soya flour
1 cup whole wheat pastry flour
1 cup wheat germ
1 cup dates or raisins and/or nuts

Let buttermilk stand with soda added until mixture is foamy. Then beat in eggs, salt, oil, and sugar. Beat for 3 minutes. Sift flours and add to above mixture along with wheat germ. Add dates, raisins, nuts, as desired. Bake at 375 degrees for 20 minutes or until done.

One of the muffins is guaranteed to be a meal in itself. Great for lunches with beverage, fruit or cheese.

Lynda Slaughter, University of Western Ontario
London, Ontario, Canada

GRANDMA SULLIVAN'S IRISH SODA BREAD

4 cups sifted flour
½ teaspoon salt
1 teaspoon baking powder
1 teaspoon baking soda
½ box raisins (soak, drain, dry)
¼ cup butter
2 eggs, beaten at room
    temperature
1½ cup buttermilk, room
    temperature
2 teaspoons caraway seeds,
    optional

Mix dry ingredients, sift, add caraway seeds if desired. Cut in butter with 2 knives until it resembles coarse corn meal. Combine beaten eggs with 1 cup buttermilk, stir. Add raisins and remainder of buttermilk, stir. Combine dry and wet ingredients. Turn dough onto lightly floured surface. Knead lightly about 1 minute, shaping into round loaf. Bake in a lightly greased black iron frying pan at 375 degrees for 20 minutes, then 350 degrees for 40 minutes. Cool on rack, put glop of butter on top.

Pat O'Connell Mullins, St. Louis University
Dallas, Texas

LEMON BREAD

½ cup shortening
⅔ cup sugar
2 eggs
2¼ cups flour
2 teaspoons baking powder
¼ teaspoon salt
1 cup milk
½ cup chopped nuts
Grated rind and juice of one
    lemon
⅓ cup sugar

Cream shortening and ⅔ cup sugar. Add eggs one at a time beating well. Sift flour, baking powder and salt together. Add dry ingredients alternately with the milk. Stir grated rind and chopped nuts into the mixture. Bake in a buttered and floured loaf pan (8½x4½inches) at 350 degrees for about 1 hour.
Mix juice of lemon and ⅓ cup sugar. Pour over warm loaf. Cool in pan.

This is wonderful for afternoon tea.

Cookbook Committee

KOLACHY

2 cups flour
½ pound butter or margarine
1 package dry yeast
4 tablespoons sour cream
1 egg
Various fillings: jams, jellies, pie
    fillings
Confectioner's sugar frosting

Preheat oven to 425 degrees. Mix flour and butter or margarine until the size of small peas. Beat yeast, sour cream, and egg slightly. Add to flour mixture. Stir until dough forms. Roll on floured surface to ¼ to ½ inch thickness. Cut into rounds (2 inch centers work well). Press center with thumb or ½ inch pill container. Fill hollow with preserves. Bake at 425 degrees for 12 minutes. Don't overbake just until lightly brown. Cool and frost. Freezable before frosting. Yield about 4 dozen.

Kathleen Gorzalski Baker,
University of Wisconsin-River Falls
River Falls, Wisconsin

MAPLE NUT LOAF

3 tablespoons butter, melted
2½ cups flour
1 cup sugar
3 teaspoons baking powder
2 teaspoons maple flavoring (or more, depending on taste)
½ teaspoon salt
1 egg, beaten
1 cup milk
1 cup chopped nuts

Sift dry ingredients together. Add egg, milk, melted butter and flavoring. Mix only until all are moistened. Stir in nuts. Pour into well-greased 9 by 5 by 3 inch loaf pan. Let stand 20 minutes, then put into 350 degree oven. Test after 40 to 45 minutes, it may need to be baked one hour.

Sue Herzog Johnson, William and Mary
Dallas, Texas

MONKEY BREAD

1 cup All-Bran
¾ cup shortening
½ cup sugar
1 cup boiling water
1 cup lukewarm water
2 packages dry yeast
2 teaspoons salt
2 eggs, well beaten
6½ cups flour
¼ pound margarine, melted

Put All-Bran, shortening, and sugar (minus 1 tablespoon) into large bowl. Pour boiling water over mixture. Stir until shortening is melted. Let stand until mixture is lukewarm. Combine lukewarm water, yeast, and the 1 tablespoon sugar. Add the salt to the eggs and beat well. Fold eggs into the All-Bran mixture and add yeast mixture. Blend well with mixer using low speed. Gradually add 3 cups flour and beat thoroughly, still using mixer. Add remaining flour by hand. Turn out about half the dough onto a lightly floured board and knead lightly until smooth (about 1 minute). Roll out to ¼ inch thickness. Cut in 2-inch diamond shaped strips with sharp knife. Dip each strip in warm melted margarine; drain briefly. Stack strips in ring mold or tube cake pan, filling not more than half full. Cover and let rise in warm place until doubled in bulk. (Do the same for other half of dough). Bake in a 300 degree pre-heated oven for 10 minutes; raise temperature to 400 degrees and bake until golden brown, about 15 minutes, or longer. Yield: 2 loaves.

Martha Cates Johnston, Texas Tech University
Lubbock, Texas

OATMEAL BREAD

4½ to 5 cups flour
1 cup quick oats
2 packages yeast
2½ teaspoon salt
¼ cup molasses
2 tablespoons margarine
2 cups milk

In large mixing bowl combine 3 cups flour, oats, yeast and salt. In saucepan heat milk, margarine and molasses until warm, 115 to 130 degrees. Add to dry ingredients in mixing bowl. Beat at low speed for one-half minute to combine, then at high speed for two minutes. Stir in enough remaining flour to make a soft dough. Turn out onto floured board and knead for 5 minutes or until smooth and elastic. Place in greased bowl. Turn, cover, let rise in warm place until double, about one hour. Punch down dough. Divide in half; shape into two loaves. Place in greased loaf pans. Let rise until double, about 45 minutes. Bake at 375 degrees for 35 to 40 minutes. To prevent excessive browning, cover with foil after 20 minutes. Makes 2 loaves.

Nancy Black, University of Maryland
Newark, Delaware

OATMEAL REFRIGERATOR ROLLS

½ cup shortening
3 tablespoons sugar
1 teaspoon salt
½ cup boiling water
1 cup rolled oats (quick or regular, *not* instant)
1 package dry yeast
½ cup lukewarm water
1 egg, beaten
2 to 2½ cups sifted all-purpose flour

Place shortening, sugar, and salt in a mixing bowl; add boiling water and mix. Add rolled oats and cool to lukewarm. Soften yeast in lukewarm water, add egg and beat with a fork. Add to oatmeal mixture along with 1 cup flour and beat hard. Add remaining flour and mix well. Let rise until doubled in bulk, punch down and refrigerate overnight. Divide dough in half. Roll each half into a circle ⅛ inch thick. Brush with melted butter. Cut each circle into 12 wedges. Roll (starting with wide side of wedge) toward the point. Place on greased cookie sheet with point of wedge down, brush tops of rolls with melted butter. Let stand in warm place until doubled in bulk. Bake in 425 degree preheated oven for 15 to 20 minutes. *Note:* Any shortening may be used. I like ½ butter and ½ chicken fat.

Carribelle Conway, Goucher College
Washington, D.C.

HONEY ORANGE BREAD

1 cup bran
1 cup orange juice
½ cup honey
¼ cup sugar
2 tablespoons shortening
1 egg
1½ tablespoons shredded orange peel
2¼ cups all-purpose flour
2½ teaspoons baking powder
½ teaspoon baking soda
½ teaspoon salt

In a bowl combine bran and ½ cup of orange juice. Let stand several minutes. In mixing bowl, blend honey, sugar, and shortening. Add egg and orange peel. Mix well. Stir together flour, baking powder, baking soda, and ½ teaspoon salt. Add to honey mixture alternately with the remaining orange juice, beating after each addition. Stir in bran-orange juice mixture. Pour into 2 greased 7½x3½x2 inch junior loaf pans or 1 greased 9x5x3inch loaf pan. Bake in 325 degree oven for 45 to 50 minutes for small pans and 55 to 60 minutes in large pan. Cool in pans 10 minutes. Remove from pans. Cool on wire rack.

Nancy Jones Claunts, Texas Tech University
Washington, D.C.

SPICY APPLE PANCAKES WITH CIDER SAUCE

Pancakes:
2 cups biscuit mix
½ teaspoon cinnamon
1 egg
1⅓ cups milk
¾ cup grated apple
Cider Sauce:
1 cup sugar
2 tablespoons cornstarch
¼ teaspoon nutmeg
¼ teaspoon cinnamon
2 cups apple cider
2 tablespoons lemon juice
¼ cup butter

Pancakes: Beat biscuit mix, cinnamon, egg, and milk with rotary beater until smooth. Stir in apple. Pour batter by ¼ cupfuls onto hot griddle. Serve with cider sauce and top with sour cream.
Cider Sauce: In saucepan, mix sugar, cornstarch, cinnamon, and nutmeg. Stir in apple cider and lemon juice. Cook, stirring constantly, until mixture thickens and boils. Boil and stir 1 minute. Remove from heat, stir in butter. Can be used also as a dessert.

Sue Williams, Boise State
Boise, Idaho

DAVID EYRE'S PANCAKE

½ cup flour
½ cup milk
2 eggs, lightly beaten
Pinch of nutmeg
4 tablespoons (½ stick) butter
2 tablespoons confectioner's sugar
Juice of ½ lemon

Preheat oven to 425 degrees. Combine first four ingredients and beat lightly. (Leave batter a little lumpy). Melt butter in a 12 inch skillet with ovenproof handle. When very hot, pour in batter. Bake in oven for 15 to 20 minutes or until golden brown. Remove from oven, sprinkle with the sugar, and return to oven for a minute or two. Remove from heat, sprinkle with the lemon juice, and serve with jelly or marmalade. 2 to 4 servings.

"This is our favorite Sunday morning breakfast." In Dallas we call this a "Texas Pancake".

Dorothy Heryford Marshall, Iowa State University
Pittsburgh, Pennsylvania

Mary Lou Hawk, Arizona State University
Dallas, Texas

PARKERHOUSE ROLLS

1 yeast cake dissolved in ½ cup ice cold water
½ cup shortening
1 teaspoon salt
3 cups flour
¼ cup sugar
½ cup boiling water
1 egg

Cream sugar and shortening. Add ½ cup boiling water. Stir. Beat egg and add to above mixture. Add yeast and ice water. Add flour and salt gradually (with spoon stir). Refrigerate for at least 45 minutes covered. Roll out dough and cut out rolls with biscuit cutter. Stretch rolls into oval shape, dot with butter, and fold over. Let rise 45 minutes. Bake in 425 degree oven 10 to 15 minutes.

Lynne Ayers, Vanderbilt University
Nashville, Tennessee

PARMESAN CHEESE BREAD
(French Bread Style)

Bread:
2 cups water (warm) 105-115 degrees
2 packages yeast
2 tablespoons sugar
1 tablespoon salt
2 tablespoons oil
6 cups flour
Filling:
½ cup Parmesan cheese
1 tablespoon parsley flakes
Dash oregano
¼ teaspoon garlic powder
Softened butter

Proof the yeast by mixing it with the 2 cups of water with 1 teaspoon sugar — proof 10 minutes. Combine the rest of the sugar, with the salt, oil, and the yeast. Stir in the flour a little at a time, or enough to make a moderately stiff dough. Turn out on a lightly floured surface and knead 10 to 15 minutes. Place in a greased bowl and turn to grease the surface. Cover with a towel and let rise 1 hour. Punch down. Turn out on a lightly floured surface. Use palm to get the bubbles out. Divide into 2 portions, cover and let rest 10 minutes. Roll each portion into 15x12 inch rectangles. Spread each portion with softened butter; sprinkle with the filling. Roll up tightly, beginning at the long side, sealing well as you roll. Place each loaf seam side down on a greased baking sheet, sprinkled with corn meal. Cover with a towel and let rise 1 hour. Bake at 375 for 35 minutes. Take off the loaves and cool on a rack. Makes 2 loaves.

This is a good basic low cholesterol bread, that can be used for other kinds of bread, cinnamon, plain, twisted and braided. The Parmesan Cheese is one of the variations.

Ann McCune Volker, Jr., Oklahoma University
Odessa, Texas

EASY POP-UP BREAD

3½ cups flour
1 package dry yeast
½ cup milk
½ cup water
½ cup salad oil
¼ cup sugar
¾ teaspoon salt
2 eggs, beaten

Mix the flour and yeast. Heat milk, water, oil, sugar, and salt over low heat to lukewarm temperature. Stir occasionally while heating. Add heated liquid ingredients to flour and yeast mixture. Blend in beaten eggs. Add enough flour to make a stiff batter. Beat or stir briskly for about one minute. Divide into two greased one pound coffee cans. Put lid on. Let rise in warm place about one hour and 15 minutes (or until the dough is about one-half inch below top of can.) Remove lid. Bake in preheated 375 degree oven for 30 minutes. It is best to cool the bread in can about 15 minutes before removing.

Mae Douglas Garrett, Oklahoma City University
Dallas, Texas

COLD OVEN POPOVERS

2 eggs
1 cup milk
1 cup flour
½ teaspoon salt

Stir eggs with fork. Add flour and milk alternately. Add salt last. Excessive beating is unnecessary, slight lumps are unimportant. Fill well oiled muffin cups one half full. Set in cold oven and turn to 450 degrees. Leave ½ hour and DO NOT PEAK.

Ruth Bartlett, Boston University
Kaneohe, Hawaii

PARMESAN POPOVERS

⅓ cup freshly grated Parmesan cheese
1 cup milk
1 cup all purpose flour
1½ tablespoons butter, melted
¼ teaspoon salt
2 large eggs
Dash Worcestershire sauce

Preheat oven to 450 degrees. Grease 6 deep muffin or custard cups and sprinkle with grated Parmesan. Combine milk, flour, butter, salt and Worcestershire in bowl. Beat in eggs just until blended. Fill cups ¾ full and place on oven rack next to the lowest shelf. Bake 15 minutes. Reduce heat to 350 degrees, (do *not* open oven door) and bake 20 minutes more. Remove popovers and serve immediately.

Susan Countner, University of Washington
Marina Del Rey, California

POPPY SEED BREAD I

1 cup sugar
2 eggs
1 cup evaporated milk
1 cup cooking oil
2 cups unsifted flour
2 teaspoons baking powder
¼ teaspoon salt
1 teaspoon vanilla
¼ cup poppy seeds

Combine sugar, eggs, evaporated milk and cooking oil. Mix on medium speed of electric mixer until well blended. Sift together flour, baking powder, and salt. Add flour mixture to egg mixture. Mix a few minutes on low speed. Add vanilla and poppy seeds. Mix until smooth. Pour batter into greased loaf pan, 9 by 5 inches. Bake in oven preheated to 375 degrees about one hour or until wooden toothpick inserted in center comes out clean. Serve plain, spread with butter or softened cream cheese.

Janet R. Smith Sprouse, Colorado College
Coos Bay, Oregon

POPPY SEED BREAD II

1 box Butter Brickle cake mix
1 package instant coconut cream
   pudding
½ cup butter-flavored oil
1 cup hot tap water
¼ cup poppy seeds
4 eggs
1 teaspoon vanilla

Mix all ingredients for 3 minutes. Pour into 2 greased loaf pans. Bake at 300 degrees for 1 hour. Depending on size of loaf pans, there may be extra batter. Use as muffins or tiny "gift" loaf.

Sue Ann Wiltse Fagerberg, Kansas State University
Greater Kansas City

FABULOUS ROLLS

1 cup milk
¾ cup butter or shortening
¼ cup sugar
½ teaspoon salt
1 package active dry yeast
¼ cup warm water (110 degrees)
4 cups flour, lightly measured
2 eggs at room temperature
Oil
Melted butter

Heat milk, butter, sugar and salt in pan until butter melts. Remove from heat and cool slightly. Dissolve yeast in warm water in large bowl of mixer. When milk mixture is lukewarm, beat into yeast. Add 2 cups flour and beat at slow, then medium speed 2 minutes. (This is the secret of fine texture in rolls. There should be no lumps.) Beat in eggs; when well blended, stop mixer and scrape down beaters and bowl. Slowly add 1 cup flour, beating at slow speed 2 minutes. Remove beaters, stir in ¾ cup flour and beat with wooden spoon until dough is smooth and elastic. Oil large bowl and turn dough into it; brush top with oil and cover with plastic wrap, then a towel wrung out in warm water. Set in warm place protected from drafts and let dough rise until double in bulk (about 2 hours). Punch down dough, beat out all air bubbles by kneading. Divide dough into 4 equal pieces. Sprinkle remaining ¼ cup flour on board and roll each piece in circle ⅛ inch thick. Brush with melted butter, then cut each circle in 8 wedges; roll each up from wide to narrow end to form crescent. Arrange crescents on lightly oiled baking sheets. Brush with melted butter, cover with plastic and set in warm place to rise (about one hour). Bake in 400 degree oven about 10 to 12 minutes. When cool, bag tightly and refrigerate or freeze. To serve: remove as needed; arrange on baking sheets and heat in 350 degree oven about 15 minutes. Makes about 32 large rolls. *Note:* Some prefer butter which makes richer rolls. Shortening makes fluffier rolls.

Marilyn Cooke Sullivan, University of Iowa
Dallas, Texas

POTATO ROLLS

1 cup mashed potatoes
1 cup scalded milk
⅔ cup shortening
⅔ cup sugar
1 teaspoon salt
1 cake yeast
½ cup warm water
All-purpose flour, about 7 cups
2 eggs, well-beaten

Soften yeast in warm water. In large bowl, pour milk over shortening. Let cool to lukewarm. Add potatoes, sugar, salt, yeast, and eggs. Mix. Add flour until it forms a ball. Knead. Dough should leave board. Add flour if necessary. Grease large bowl. Put dough in bowl and turn over so that dough is greased all over. Let rise 2 hours. Work down. Form into 1½ inch balls and put in greased cupcake pans. Let rise 2 hours. Bake at 450 degrees for 10 to 15 minutes. Can be kept refrigerated after first rising.

Lynne Ayers, Vanderbilt University
Nashville, Tennessee

PUMPKIN BREAD

3 cups flour
2 cups sugar
1 cup chopped pecans
1 teaspoon cinnamon
1 teaspoon nutmeg
1 teaspoon salt
1 teaspoon soda
1 cup cooking oil
1 cup pumpkin (cooked)
4 eggs
⅔ cup water

Combine dry ingredients. Stir until well blended. In another bowl combine wet ingredients. Pour wet mixture over dry ingredients and beat with a fork until just blended. Pour mixture equally into three one-pound coffee cans which have been heavily coated with shortening. Bake about one hour at 350 degrees. Remove from oven and allow to cool before removing from cans. Or bake in well greased loaf pans at 350 degrees about one hour.

Theresa Romano Foster, Lamar University
Beaumont, Texas

Lynne Ayers, Vanderbilt University
Nashville, Tennessee

CARAMEL ROLLS

2 packages dry yeast
2 cups lukewarm water
1 egg, beaten
1 teaspoon salt
6 tablespoons sugar
3 tablespoons butter, melted
5 to 5½ cups flour
2¼ cups brown sugar
¾ cup whipped cream

Dissolve yeast in water. Mix egg, salt, sugar, melted butter and add to yeast. Mix in flour. Cover. Let rise until double. Punch down. Roll into a 12 inch by 17 inch rectangle. Sprinkle with a trace of butter, cinnamon and sugar. Roll the long way and cut into inch pieces. Spread brown sugar in jelly roll pan. Sprinkle with whipped cream. Arrange rolls on sugar and cream. Let rise for 20 minutes. Bake at 375 degrees for 20 minutes. Let stand 5 minutes, then invert.

Jan Peterson, Iowa State University
Des Moines, Iowa

CHEESE SHORTBREAD

1 pound very sharp cheddar
cheese
½ pound margarine, softened
1 teaspoon salt or seasoned salt
3 cups flour
Several dashes of cayenne pepper
Worcestershire
Parsley flakes

Cream together by hand: cheese, butter, salt, pepper, parsley and Worcestershire. Slowly knead in sifted flour. Form small balls and flatten like cookies. Bake 15 minutes on a cookie sheet. Very crumbly.

Arthetta White Swafford, Oklahoma University
Tulsa, Oklahoma

STRAWBERRY BREAD

1 cup strawberry jam
1 cup sour cream
1 cup butter
1½ cups sugar
4 eggs, beaten
3 cups flour
½ teaspoon soda
¾ teaspoon cream of tartar
1 teaspoon vanilla
1 teaspoon lemon extract.

Fold sour cream into jam. In a separate bowl, cream butter and sugar and add beaten eggs. Add jam mixture alternately with flour, soda, and cream of tartar. Fold in extracts. Bake in 2 greased and floured loaf pans, 325 degrees for 1 hour.

Twila Honea Moore, Oklahoma University
Dallas, Texas

STRAWBERRY BREAD WITH SPREAD

Bread:
3 cups flour
1 teaspoon baking soda
1 teaspoon cinnamon
2 cups sugar
1 teaspoon salt
2 10-ounce packages frozen
strawberries, thawed & sliced
1¼ cups vegetable oil
4 eggs, well beaten
1 cup chopped pecans
Spread:
½ cup strawberry juice
1 8-ounce package cream cheese,
softened

Bread: Reserve ½ cup strawberry juice for spread. Mix all dry ingredients together. Make a hole in the center of mixture. Pour strawberries, oil and eggs into the hole. Mix by hand until all ingredients are thoroughly combined. Stir in the chopped pecans. Pour into 2 greased and floured 9x5x2½ loaf pans or six 3x2 inch pans. Bake in moderate oven (350 degrees) 40 to 60 minutes.

Spread: Place the ½ cup strawberry juice and cream cheese in blender container. Process until spreading consistency. Spread on cooled bread and make sandwiches.

Betty Mae Conner Jones, Oklahoma University
Dallas, Texas

SOURDOUGH BREAD

Starter:
½ cup lukewarm water
1 package yeast
2 cups lukewarm water
1 tablespoon salt
1 tablespoon sugar
2 cups sifted all-purpose flour
Bread:
1 cup starter
½ cup milk
1 tablespoon shortening
2¼ cups sifted all-purpose flour
2 tablespoons sugar

Starter: Sprinkle yeast into ½ cup warm water. Let stand until dissolved (about 10 minutes). Stir. Add 2 cups water, salt, sugar, and flour. Cover and let stand for 3 days at room temperature. Stir the mix down daily.

Bread: Measure 1 cup starter into a bowl. In a saucepan, scald ½ cup milk and add the 2 tablespoons of sugar and 1 tablespoon of shortening. Cool milk mixture to lukewarm and add to the starter. Stir in 2¼ cups flour. Turn dough out onto lightly floured table and knead until smooth and elastic. Place in greased bowl and let rise. Punch down and shape into loaf. Place in greased bread pan 9x5x3inch. Cover with towel and let rise again. Bake in 400 degree oven for 50 minutes. Makes 1 loaf.

To continue Starter: Add 1 cup lukewarm water, ½ cup flour and 1 teaspoon sugar to original starter mixture. Let stand until ready to make bread again.

Jeanne Abbott, University of Missouri
Anchorage, Alaska

WHITE BREAD

8 cups flour
1 cup milk
1½ cups water
2 packages yeast
½ cup sugar
4 teaspoons salt
2 eggs
¼ cup shortening

Scald milk. Melt shortening and cool. Place salt and sugar in large mixing bowl. Pour scalded milk over sugar and salt and let cool to lukewarm. Add ½ cup very warm but not hot water to yeast and let soften for 5 minutes. Add yeast mixture to milk and sugar mixture, along with the remaining cup water which should also be lukewarm. Mix well. Add half the sifted flour to milk mixture and beat one minute. Add eggs (unbeaten). Mix well. Add shortening and beat again. Gradually add remaining flour. Turn dough onto floured board and let rest 10 minutes. Then knead dough 5 to 10 minutes until smooth and satiny. Place in lightly greased bowl. Let rise until light and doubled. Knead again. Let rise again in same fashion. Make 3 loaves and let rise until light. Bake about 35 to 40 minutes — 375 degrees for 20 minutes and 325 for the remainder. *Note:* I use 375 degrees for 10 minutes and 325 for 20 minutes. First rising takes about 1½ to 2 hours, second rising, 1 hour plus, and third rising about 45 minutes.

Marilyn Cooke Sullivan,
University of Iowa
Dallas, Texas

WHOLE WHEAT BREAD

3 cups milk or warm water
2 or 3 packages yeast
¾ cup honey or ½ cup dark molasses
5 cups unsifted stone ground whole wheat flour
¼ cup oil or butter
1 scant tablespoon salt

Combine milk or water, yeast, and honey or molasses in a bowl. When yeast has softened add the rest of the ingredients. Beat about 6 minutes at low speed. Add and mix well, 2 to 3 cups whole wheat flour to make a stiff dough. Knead dough until smooth, on bread board which has an additional cup of flour on it. More flour may be needed to prevent sticking. Place in a greased bowl and cover and let rise in a warm place until double in bulk. Knead again. Divide into 2 or 3 parts and place in greased pans. When dough reaches top of pans bake at 350 degrees for 50 to 70 minutes. Turn out on rack to cool and brush with butter. Serve with honey if desired.

Judy Elaine Graham, Oklahoma University
Greater Kansas City

ZUCCHINI NUT BREAD

3 cups flour
1 teaspoon salt
1 teaspoon baking soda
¼ teaspoon baking powder
3 teaspoons cinnamon
3 eggs
2 cups sugar
1 cup oil
2 cups grated raw zucchini, unpeeled
2 teaspoons vanilla
1 cup walnuts

Combine flour, salt, baking soda, baking powder, and cinnamon. Set aside. Beat eggs until light. Stir in sugar, oil, zucchini, and vanilla. Add dry ingredients and nuts and stir till blended. Pour into two greased loaf pans. Bake in 350 degree oven for 1 hour.

Nancy Wetherwax Furnas,
Bowling Green State University
Fairfield County, Connecticut

Maxine Leverett Trager,
Southern Methodist University
Dallas, Texas

ZUCCHINI BREAD

2½ cups grated zucchini
¾ cup oil
3 eggs, beaten
1 teaspoon vanilla
3 teaspoons cinnamon
3 cups flour
1½ cups sugar
1 teaspoon each baking powder, soda and salt

Mix beaten eggs, oil, sugar, zucchini and vanilla. Beat well. Sift flour, cinnamon, soda, salt, and baking powder and add to zucchini mixture. Pour into 2 large loaf pans which have been greased and floured. Bake at 350 degrees for about 45 minutes, or until bread pulls away from the side of the pan.

Penny Kisslinger, University of Minnesota
Boulder, Colorado

Latane Jordan Graham, Memphis State University
Dallas, Texas

SOURDOUGH ZUCCHINI BREAD

3 cups flour
1½ cups sugar
1 teaspoon cinnamon
1 teaspoon salt
1 teaspoon baking powder
¾ teaspoon baking soda
2 cups shredded, unpeeled
  zucchini
1 cup chopped nuts
1 cup raisins
3 eggs
1 cup oil
1 cup sourdough starter

In large bowl, stir together flour, sugar, cinnamon, salt, baking powder, baking soda, zucchini, nuts and raisins. In another bowl, beat eggs, oil. Pour over flour mixture, add starter and stir until moistened. Turn into greased 9x5x3 inch loaf pan or 2 small pans. Bake at 350 degrees for 1½ hours or until toothpick inserted in center comes out clean. Cool in pan 10 minutes, invert on rack, turn top-side up, and cool completely.

Margaret C. Diessner, Northwestern University
Rochester, Minnesota

Entree

Beef

BEEF AND BACON ROLLS HERBED RICE

Rolls:
1½ pounds round steak, ¼ inch thick
6 slices bacon
1 tablespoon oil
1 cup water
2 tablespoons sherry
1 envelope (¾ ounce) mushroom gravy mix
Herbed Rice:
3 cups hot cooked rice
2 teaspoons packaged minced green onion
⅛ teaspoon each of garlic powder, basil, thyme and savory

Rolls: Cut steak into 6 serving-size pieces. Roll up each piece and wrap each roll in a slice of bacon. Secure rolls with string or toothpicks. Brown rolls in oil, turning to cook bacon. Drain off excess fat. Add water and sherry. Simmer, covered, one hour or until meat is tender. Remove meat. Measure drippings and add enough water to make one cup. Stir in gravy mix and bring to a boil. Makes 4 to 6 servings. Serve on a bed of Herbed Rice.

Rice: Combine rice and seasonings, tossing lightly to mix. Add butter and salt to taste. Serves 4.

Sylvia Hardy Trewin, Iowa State University
Richardson, Texas

BARBECUED-BROILED ROAST

1 round-bone or chuck roast, or Swiss steak, 2½-3 inches thick
2 cloves garlic, minced
2 tablespoons oil
¼ teaspoon dry mustard
½ teaspoon rosemary, crushed
1 tablespoon soy sauce
6 tablespoons wine vinegar
2 tablespoons ketchup
1 tablespoon Worcestershire sauce
1 tablespoon steak sauce

Roast may be sprinkled with meat tenderizer and monosodium glutamate. Sauté garlic in oil. Blend in mustard, rosemary, soy sauce and vinegar. Place roast in large bowl and cover with sauce. Marinate 24 hours, turning frequently. Add ketchup, Worcestershire sauce and steak sauce to marinade. If roast weighs 3-4 pounds, grill with high flame 5 minutes, reduce flame to low and continue cooking 20 to 25 minutes or longer. Turn to second side and repeat. Total cooking time 1 hour or until done. Baste occasionally with remaining sauce. To serve, cut thin slices diagonally across the grain. Yields 6-8 servings from a 4 pound roast.

Margaret Stewart "Peg", Iowa State University
Del Mar, California

BAR-B-Q BEEF

Beef brisket (3 to 5 pounds)
Sauce:
2 medium onions, chopped
2 cups (bottled) chili sauce
1 cup water
½ cup lemon juice
¼ cup vinegar
⅓ cup Worcestershire sauce
1 tablespoon dry mustard
¼ cup brown sugar
1 tablespoon liquid smoke
2 teaspoons salt
Cayenne or Tabasco to taste

Brisket: Trim excess fat, salt and pepper. Using heavy casserole or Dutch oven, bake covered at 275 degrees for 2 to 4 hours; until well done.

Sauce: Combine above ingredients, simmer for 30 minutes.

Shred or slice beef, add to sauce and simmer. You may need to add a bit more water (depending on brisket size) as it simmers. Freezes well, gets better the next day.

Ann Vandemark Butler, Syracuse University
Dumfries, Virginia

BOEUF BOURGUIGNONNE

2 pounds lean beef
2 large onions, chopped
3 tablespoon bacon fat (or vegetable oil)
3 tablespoons flour
1 stalk chopped celery
1 grated carrot
¼ cup chopped parsley
¼ teaspoon marjoram
Salt and pepper
¼ teaspoon thyme
½ teaspoon monosodium glutamate
2 tablespoons ketchup
½ cup hot water with 1 teaspoon beef bouillon
1 cup dry red wine
½ pound sliced fresh mushrooms

Sauté chopped onions in fat until translucent, (using a heavy pan) remove and reserve. Cut beef into 1 inch cubes and sauté in same drippings, separating into two batches for best results. When nicely browned, toss in flour and add everything but the mushrooms. Stir well, let simmer slowly for 3 hours, covered. Add mushrooms and simmer for another hour. The sauce should be fairly thick and dark brown. If not thick enough, remove cover; if too thick add more wine or liquid. Serve over noodles (I prefer Kluska). Like many things, the flavor improves with a day or two of aging.

Irma Paul Nash, Iowa State University
Hot Springs, Arkansas

BRISKET OF BEEF

2 to 3 pound brisket
1 medium onion, sliced
6 ounces chili sauce
6 ounces beer
⅓ cup barbecue sauce
Dash of Worcestershire sauce
Pepper
4 ounces water

To prepare brisket for cooking, place it flat side up in pan. Slice onions and cover meat, add chili sauce, pepper and water. Bake at 225 degrees, covered, for 3 hours. Baste every 30 minutes, adding water if necessary. Add beer and cook 1½ hours longer, covered. Skim grease off liquid and add Worcestershire sauce for glaze. Serves 3-4 hot or 6-10 cold.

Sally Vanderpearl, University of Missouri
St. Louis, Missouri

BAR-B-QUED BRISKET

3 to 4 pound brisket
Celery salt
Onion salt
Brown sugar
Liquid smoke
Favorite bottled bar-b-que sauce
Black pepper

The night before, place brisket in a glass baking dish. Rub generously on both sides with celery salt, onion salt, brown sugar and liquid smoke. Cover with foil and marinate overnight in the refrigerator. Five hours before serving, seal foil and bake for 4 hours at 275 degrees. At the end of four hours, remove the foil; brush with bar-b-que sauce and return to the oven for one hour more. Cool slightly before slicing; slice across the grain in thin slices. Delicious served cold for sandwiches.

Phyllis Donaldson Choat, University of Nebraska
Omaha, Nebraska

Ann Heath, Iowa State University
Dallas, Texas

SMOKE-FLAVORED BEEF BRISKET

Brisket:
1 2½ to 3 pound well-trimmed boneless beef brisket
¼ cup liquid smoke
½ teaspoon onion salt
½ teaspoon garlic salt
Salt to taste
Smoky Sauce:
1 tablespoon liquid smoke
1½ tablespoons dark brown sugar, firmly packed
½ cup ketchup
¼ cup water
1 teaspoon celery seeds
3 tablespoons melted butter or margarine
2 tablespoons Worcestershire sauce
1½ teaspoons dry mustard
Dash of pepper

Brisket: Sprinkle brisket with regular salt and place on a large piece of aluminum foil. Set in shallow dish or pan and pour liquid smoke over meat. Seal foil and refrigerate overnight. Remove brisket from refrigerator, sprinkle with onion and garlic salts. Reseal foil and bake at 325 degrees for 2½ to 3 hours or until done. Slice thin and serve with smoky sauce. Yield: 6 servings.

Sauce: Combine all ingredients in a saucepan and simmer 5 minutes. Yields about 1¼ cups.

Barbara Fort Beasley, Southern Methodist University
Dallas, Texas

LOLLY'S BEEF BURGUNDY

6 slices bacon, diced
¼ cup butter
24 small whole onions
3½ pounds chuck or sirloin cut in cubes
1 tablespoon garlic-parsley salt
Pepper to taste
½ teaspoon thyme
Nutmeg
2 bay leaves
Celery tops
1 cup hearty burgundy
½ cup water
2-3 tomatoes, cut in wedges (or cherry tomatoes)
1 pound fresh mushrooms

Pierce both ends of onions. Saute bacon, butter, and pierced onions in a heavy pot. May need more butter. Add beef cubes and brown with above. Add garlic-parsley salt, pepper, thyme, nutmeg to taste, bay leaves and celery tops. Pour in burgundy and water. Simmer 2½ hours, adding more wine and water as necessary. Add tomato wedges. Saute mushrooms to be added just before it is to be served. This may be thickened with flour if desired. Can flame with heated brandy at the table. Serve with noodles and pole beans. Lemon cake is a good desert.

Laurel Pithoud Elden, Oregon State University
Central New Jersey

BEEF CARBONNADE

4 pounds lean stew beef, cut in 2-inch pieces
½ cup flour
½ cup salad oil
2 pounds onions, sliced (about 4 medium sized)
3 garlic cloves crushed
3 tablespoons brown sugar
1 bay leaf
1 teaspoon dried thyme
½ cup chopped parsley
1 tablespoon salt
2 10½-ounce cans beef consomme
3 cups beer
2 tablespoons red wine vinegar

Dredge the meat in the flour and brown in the salad oil on all sides in a skillet. Do only a few pieces at a time. Put in a casserole dish and add the onions. Brown the garlic in the oil left in the skillet. Add to the meat, with the brown sugar, bay leaf, thyme, parsley, salt, consomme and beer. Cover and bake at 325 degrees for about 2½ hours or until meat is tender. Pour in vinegar and cook on top of stove until bubbling. If you wish, a thicker sauce can be achieved by adding a little Arrowroot or flour mixed with cold water. You could use this as a basis for a beef pie or add mushrooms if you wish.

Irene Braden Loosley, Oklahoma University
Dallas, Texas

EGGPLANT BEEF CASSEROLE

1½ pounds ground beef
1 medium size onion, chopped
1 medium size eggplant
1½ cups cooked rice
(optional, green onion blades)
1 teaspoon salt
1 cup grated sharp cheese

Cut peeled eggplant into small squares and steam in salted water till tender. Saute meat and onion till brown. Drain eggplant and mix with meat and onion. Add ¼ cup water and steam, stirring occasionally till eggplant is done. Toss in cooked rice. Place in casserole dish and top with cheese. Cook at 350 degrees approximately 15 to 20 minutes.

Connie Burkett, Lamar University
Beaumont, Texas

LOUISE'S GROUND BEEF CASSEROLE

1½ pounds ground beef
1 package (8 ounces) cooked
    noodles
1 can cream tomato soup
1 can Rotel tomatoes (16 ounce)
1 can cream style corn (16 ounce)
1 can whole corn (16 ounce)
1 cup grated cheddar cheese
1 small can peas
1 chopped green pepper
1 chopped onion
Season to taste with garlic salt,
    celery salt, chili powder,
    cayenne to taste

Brown and season meat and drain off extra fat. Place it in the bottom of a large casserole. Drain all vegetables and mix together. Blend in soup. Place mixture on top of meat in casserole. Top with cooked noodles. Top with cheese. Bake at 350 degrees for about 30 minutes. Serves 6 to 8. Good served with a crisp green salad.

Cookbook Committee

SHERRIED BEEF

3 pounds stew meat (do not
    brown)
2 cans golden mushroom soup
1 envelope dry onion soup mix
½ cup sherry
¾ cup water

Cut meat into bite size pieces. Trim fat. Mix with other ingredients and pour into a Reynolds Brown-In-Bag. Bake at 300 degrees for 3 hours. Serve over rice.

Sherry Allen Rucker, Oklahoma University
Anaheim, California

SAVORY STUFFED FILET OF BEEF

3 thinly sliced onions
6 tablespoons olive oil
4 tablespoons butter
2 cloves garlic, minced
18 pitted black olives, coarsely
  chopped
1 teaspoon thyme
2 beaten egg yolks
2 tablespoons chopped parsley
1 cup ham, cooked and chopped
  (or cubed)
Salt and pepper to taste
1 beef filet, about 3-4 pounds

Sauté onions in oil and butter until just limp; add garlic, olives, ham, pepper, thyme, salt. Stir until well blended. Stir in beaten egg yolks and parsley; cook for about 3 minutes. Cut the filet, not quite through, in rather thick slices and spoon stuffing between the slices. Either tie filet securely, or run a needle and string through the middle. Place on rack, brush with oil or butter. Bake at 300 degrees for 50 minutes or until internal temperature is 125 degrees. Let stand 10 minutes. For less rare beef, bake for a longer period of time.

Martha Conrad Clark,
University of Wisconsin-Oshkosh
Milwaukee, Wisconsin

STEAK DIANE

2 tablespoons butter
4 4-ounce slices filet mignon
4 large sliced fresh mushrooms
2 long green onions, sliced
Fresh ground pepper
Salt
¼ cup Burgundy wine
¼ cup beef stock

Prepare in a chafing dish. Melt butter in a pan until it simmers. Put the meat in the pan and cook 4 minutes on the first side over medium heat. Turn the meat, add mushrooms and onions. Season to taste with salt and pepper. Stir mushrooms and onions cooking for 4 minutes. Add wine and beef stock. Simmer 4 minutes longer and serve.

Candy Clymer Hill, Texas Tech University
El Paso, Texas

FANTASTIC FLANK STEAK

1 flank steak, scored
¼ cup salad oil
2 tablespoons lemon juice
¼ cup soy sauce
¼ cup water
3 chopped green onions
1 large garlic clove, crushed
1 teaspoon coarse black pepper

Mix last seven ingredients. Marinate flank in mixture at least 3 hours. Turn frequently. Drain, broil or charcoal grill 3 to 4 inches from heat about 4 minutes on each side. Slice diagonally.

Linda Handley Schweikert,
California State University-San Jose
Sylvania, Ohio

JANE'S CRAZY STEW

3 pounds stew meat (beef)
1 envelope onion soup mix
  (sometimes this is a wee bit
  salty — you might want to hold
  back a bit of the soup mix)
1 can cream of mushroom soup
⅓ cup cooking sherry
1 package frozen peas
1 can sliced mushrooms

In a casserole, mix the first 4 ingredients together well. Cover and cook 1 hour in 350 degree oven, then reduce heat to 300 degrees and cook for 2 more hours. Refrigerate over night. Heat, add frozen peas and mushrooms. Cook until vegetables are done. Serve over rice or noodles.

Gloria Swanson Nelson, Oklahoma University
Dallas, Texas

OVEN BEEF STEW OR STROGANOFF

2 pounds beef stew meat
1 can onion soup
1 can cream of celery soup
2 cans cream of mushroom soup
1½ cups water

Place meat in a flat roasting pan. Mix the four cans of soup with the water. Pour over meat. Cover pan with foil. Carrots and onions may be placed around meat. Bake at 250 degrees for 4 to 5 hours. Serve over mashed potatoes, or over noodles or rice.
For Stroganoff: Just before serving, add ½ pint sour cream. Garnish with dill weed or parsley.

Dorothy Tiemann Adam, University of Denver
Bloomington, Indiana

BEEF STROGANOFF

1 pound sirloin tip steak
Cooking oil
1 medium onion, sliced
1 can tomato soup
1 teaspoon Worcestershire sauce
1 teaspoon salt
½ teaspoon pepper
4 ounces mushrooms (fresh or canned)
1 cup sour cream

Trim fat from steak. Slice steak diagonally into ½ inch wide strips. Cover skillet bottom with oil and heat. Add steak and onion and lightly brown. Add tomato soup, Worcestershire sauce, mushrooms, salt and pepper. Simmer one hour, covered. Add sour cream and reheat. Serve over rice or egg noodles. Serves 4.

Jill Maple Wasch Colella, Oregon State University
Eureka, California

BEEF AND RICE CASSEROLE

2 pounds ground beef, browned (drain off fat)
1 package long grain wild rice, cooked
2 cans cream of chicken soup
2 cans cream of mushroom soup
1 large can mushrooms, stems and pieces
½ teaspoons each of onion salt, celery salt and garlic salt
Parmesan cheese
1 onion, chopped
2 tablespoons butter

Sauté onion in butter, and combine with remaining ingredients. Cover and top with Parmesan cheese. Bake one hour uncovered at 350 degrees in a 9x12 inch pan. Serves 8 to 10.

Terry Gallagher, University of Texas
Dallas, Texas

BEEF-ZUCCHINI-CASSEROLE

1 pound ground beef
2 medium onions, chopped
2 tablespoons salad oil
1 16-ounce can tomatoes
1 8-ounce can tomato sauce
1 6-ounce can tomato paste
1 green pepper, chopped
1 cup Cheddar cheese, grated
1 teaspoon salt
¼ teaspoon garlic salt
½ teaspoon oregano
4 medium zucchini, sliced
½ cup Parmesan cheese, grated

Brown onions and beef in salad oil; drain off excess fat. Add tomatoes, sauce, paste and green pepper. Blend in cheddar cheese. Stir in remaining ingredients. Simmer for 5 minutes. Turn into a 12x8x2 inch pan and sprinkle with Parmesan cheese. Bake 45 minutes at 350 degrees.
Less tomato sauce and paste can be used according to personal taste.

Janet Bellinger Holmes, University of Michigan
Westchester County, New York

CHALUPAS

1 pound lean ground meat
1 large can chili (without beans)
1 can red kidney beans (not drained)
1 package regular size Fritos

Mix together meat, chili and beans and cook until meat is done. If you prefer cooked onions, they may be cooked at this time. Put a handful of Fritos on a plate, top with hot meat mixture. Then pile on any or all of the following:

Chopped onions
Diced avocados
Diced tomatoes
Chopped green chiles
Salsa
Diced celery

Sliced olives
Diced green peppers
Shredded lettuce
Sour cream
Grated cheese

Furnished by Flagstaff Alum Chapter. It is great!

Shirley Grounds Duncan, Kansas University
Tucson, Arizona

EAT MORE

1 pound ground round steak
1 small package noodles
2 cups celery (cut up)
1 can tomato juice (8-ounce)
1 small onion
½ green pepper (cut fine)
1 small can mushrooms
2 tablespoons butter

Cook ground beef in frying pan with butter until browned. Season with salt and pepper. Cook celery in salted water for 15 minutes, drain. Cook noodles until done. Drain and add to meat with all other ingredients. Pour into a well greased casserole. Bake in slow oven for 1 hour at 325 degrees. Serves 6.

Bette Crimmins Simcox, Lake Forest College
Hinsdale, Illinois

HOOVER CASSEROLE

1 pound hamburger meat
Potatoes, sliced
Carrots, sliced
Onions, sliced
1 can Golden Mushroom soup mixed with 1 can water or 1 can milk

In large oven bowl, layer: sliced carrots, hamburger, thin sliced potato, thin sliced onion, salt and pepper. Repeat layer, dot with butter, pour soup mixture over, enough to cover. (Use all of the soup mixture.) Bake at 300 degrees for 3 hours, be careful, it may boil over.

Donna L. Sprague, Wittenberg University
Canal Winchester, Ohio

HAMBURGER CASSEROLE

1 pound ground round steak, browned (or plain hamburger)
1 10½-ounce can cream of mushroom soup
1 8-ounce package frozen mixed vegetables
2 pounds Tater Tots
1 cup cubed Cheddar cheese

Combine browned ground meat, cream of mushroom soup, thawed mixed vegetables, and cubed cheddar cheese. Salt and pepper to taste. Pour into a 9x13 inch casserole. Scatter Tater Tots on top. Bake at 350 degrees for 45 minutes or until brown and bubbly. Serves 6.

Pam Rutherford, Vanderbilt University
Nashville, Tennessee

HAMBURGER PARMESAN

1¼ pounds ground beef
2 tablespoons chopped onion
½ to ¾ jar of Hunt's Prima Salsa
4 squares Mozzarella cheese

Mix ground beef and onion. Shape into 4 patties and brown in a skillet. Pour sauce over browned patties. Cover, bake at 325 degrees for 45 minutes. Top each pattie with cheese, cover again until just melted or pop under the broiler a few seconds. Serve with spaghetti on the side. Serves 4.

Theara Kurt Schonberg, Iowa State University
Omaha, Nebraska

HAMBURGER STROGANOFF

2 pounds hamburger
1 large chopped onion
4 tablespoons flour
1 cup mushrooms
1 teaspoon salt
1 teaspoon garlic salt
½ teaspoon pepper
2 cans cream of mushroom soup
1 can cream of chicken soup

Brown the meat, onions and mushrooms. Stir in salt, garlic salt, pepper and flour. Simmer a few minutes. Add the soup and simmer for 5 more minutes. Serve over noodles. (Noodles Romanoff are especially good). This is a quickie that serves 4-6.

Nancy Hogan Henning, University of Michigan
Dunwoody, Georgia

MACARONI SAUTE

1 pound ground beef
2 cups elbow macaroni (uncooked
   8 ounces)
½ cup chopped onion
½ cup chopped green pepper
1 clove garlic, minced
¼ cup vegetable oil
3 cups tomato juice
1½ teaspoons salt
¼ teaspoon pepper
2 teaspoons Worcestershire sauce

Sauté macaroni, onion, green pepper, beef and garlic in hot oil until macaroni turns slightly yellow. Add tomato juice and seasonings; bring to boil. Cover and simmer 20 minutes.

Chris Loveberg Montgomery,
California State University-San Diego
Orange County, California

SKILLET MACARONI DINNER

2 pounds ground chuck
2 tablespoons salad oil
2 medium onions, chopped
1 28-ounce can tomatoes
1 12-ounce can whole kernel corn
1 cup elbow (small) macaroni
1 tablespoon chili powder
2½ teaspoons garlic salt
1 3½-ounce can pitted ripe olives,
   drained and quartered
1 4-ounce package shredded
   cheddar cheese
Salt and pepper

Heat oil in large cook-and-serve skillet over medium heat. Add meat and cook until browned. Drain off excess fat. Add onions, tomatoes, corn and macaroni and cook covered 30 minutes or until macaroni is tender, stirring occasionally. Stir in chili powder, garlic salt and olives. Sprinkle with cheese and heat covered 5 minutes. Serves 8. Great when unexpected guests drop in.

Dorothy Allen Drees, Washington University
St. Louis, Missouri

ROULADEN

6 round steaks, sliced 3/16
   inches thick and about 6 inches
   wide and 10 inches long
12 strips bacon
Prepared mustard
Pickle relish, drained
Croutons
Shortening
1 coarsely chopped onion
1 tablespoon flour (or more)
5½ cups boiling water

Pat steaks dry. Salt and pepper to taste on both sides. Spread about ¾ teaspoon mustard on one side of the steak. Place 2 strips of bacon on the steak. Sprinkle croutons and relish evenly on the steak. Roll steak jelly-roll fashion, tucking in the sides as you go. Secure roll with white thread. Coat roll with flour. Heat shortening in large, heavy pot. Thoroughly brown steaks on all sides. Remove steaks as they are browned. Into remaining fat, add flour and stir in well. Add onion and cook until clear. Add boiling water, gradually, and stir constantly, until mixture thickens. Return steaks to pan and simmer, covered, for 1 hour. Remove pan from heat, cool, and refrigerate overnight. The next day, skim fat from top. Remove thread. Simmer about ½ hour to heat through.

Pat O'Connell Mullins, St. Louis University
Dallas, Texas

LASAGNA

1½ pounds ground beef
1 pound lasagna
¾ cup finely chopped onion
1 clove garlic, crushed
1 teaspoon finely cut parsley
2 cups water
½ cup Parmesan cheese
1 teaspoon oregano
2 6-ounce cans tomato paste
½ teaspoon pepper
1 teaspoon salt
1 pound Mozzarella cheese, sliced
   thin
1 pound large curd cottage
   cheese

Cook the lasagna. Meanwhile, cook the ground beef in a large heavy saucepan until the color just changes. Add the onion, garlic, parsley, water, oregano, tomato paste, pepper and salt. Bring to a boil. Then, turn the heat low and let simmer gently for 30 minutes. In a greased 15½x10½x2½ inch baking pan arrange first a layer of drained lasagna then the alternating layers of the other ingredients. End with a layer of Mozzarella cheese. Over this sprinkle the Parmesan cheese. Bake at 350 degrees for 20 to 25 minutes or until the mozzarella is just melted. Makes 8 to 12 servings.

Lynne Ayers, Vanderbilt University
Nashville, Tennessee

LASAGNA CASSEROLE

1½ pounds ground beef
1 teaspoon oregano
Garlic salt and pepper to taste
1 16-ounce can tomato sauce
1 8-ounce package egg noodles
1 tablespoon parsley, chopped
1 medium onion, chopped
1 cup cottage cheese
1 cup sour cream
Parmesan cheese

Brown meat, drain, and mix with garlic salt and pepper. Add tomato sauce and simmer 5 minutes. Cook noodles and drain. Toss noodles with parsley, oregano, raw onion, sour cream and cottage cheese. In a buttered 2½ quart casserole, place layer of noodles, meat sauce and sprinkling of Parmesan cheese. Repeat. Cover and bake at 325 degrees for 45 minutes. Serves 8.

Betty Lou Wisland, University of Wisconsin-Madison
Milwaukee, Wisconsin

QUICK AND EASY LASAGNA

1 pound hamburger meat
8 ounces lasagna noodles
1 8-ounce jar spaghetti sauce
1 cup small curd cottage cheese
8 ounces Mozzarella cheese
¼ teaspoon oregano

Cook noodles according to directions on box. Simmer hamburger in spaghetti sauce and oregano for 10-15 minutes, or until browned. Layer half the noodles in 11x7 inch greased casserole dish. Layer half cottage cheese, Mozzarella and sauce. Repeat, saving some Mozzarella for top. Bake at 325 degrees for 30 minutes. Serves 4.

Janet McCarraher, Vanderbilt University
Ft. Lauderdale, Florida

ZUCCHINI LASAGNA

3 large zucchini
2 medium onions, sliced
2 sweet Italian sausages
¾ cup water
1 8-ounce package Mozzarella cheese, shredded
¼ pound mushrooms, sliced
½ teaspoon salt
1 teaspoon oregano
½ teaspoon garlic powder
½ teaspoon sugar
¼ teaspoon pepper
1 20-ounce can tomatoes in puree
½ cup Ricotta cheese

Peel zucchini and cut into thin slices lengthwise. Cook onion, sausage, and water in large skillet, stirring until water evaporates and onion is golden. Remove from heat. Cut up sausage. In a 2 quart shallow casserole or lasagna pan, layer ⅓ zucchini slices and ⅓ Mozzarella and ⅓ mushrooms. Combine salt, oregano, garlic powder, sugar, pepper in small bowl; sprinkle part over bottom layer. Add layer of ⅓ onion-meat mixture and ⅓ tomatoes in puree. Repeat to make 3 layers and cover casserole with aluminum foil. Bake at 350 degrees for 40 minutes. Remove foil and bake 20 minutes more or until zucchini is tender and lasagna is bubbly. Spoon ricotta cheese on top. Let stand 10 minutes before serving. Serves 6. This is low in calories, but delicious to eat.

Bonnie Jean Strand, University of Wisconsin
Madison, Wisconsin

MEAT AND CHEESE LOAF

1 pound ground beef
1 cup diced cheese
1 beaten egg
1 chopped small onion
1 chopped small green pepper
Dash celery salt
Dash paprika
1 cup milk
1 cup dry bread crumbs

Combine ingredients in order given. Mix well. Press into greased loaf pan. Bake at 350 degrees about 1 hour.

Nell Taylor Wolfe, Iowa State University
Westchester, New York

1 pound ground chuck
1 medium onion, minced
⅓ cup applesauce
⅓ cup chili sauce
1 egg
Salt and pepper to taste
Ketchup

JUICY MEAT LOAF

Combine and lightly but thoroughly mix all ingredients (except ketchup). Place in small casserole. Frost with ketchup. Cover loosely with foil leaving one end partly open. Bake at 400 degrees for 1 hour.

Avila Polke Lepera, Bowling Green State University
Bowling Green, Ohio

1½ pounds ground beef
¼ to ⅓ pound well-seasoned pork sausage
1 large egg
4 ounce can mushroom bits and pieces, plus liquid
⅓ cup (or 1 envelope) instant oatmeal flakes
2 teaspoons salt
¼ teaspoon pepper
½ teaspoon sage (powdered or rubbed leaves)
2 teaspoons Worcestershire sauce
1 large onion, sliced

PEERLESS PIERCE'S PERFECT MEAT LOAF

Combine the two meats in a large mixing bowl. Slice the mushroom bits and pieces a little smaller than they are and add them to the meats. Put everything else into blender and chop at high speed until onion is minced fine. Pour blender contents into meats and combine thoroughly with your fingers or a pastry blender. Line a loaf pan with waxed paper and pack in the meat loaf. Let stand in refrigerator an hour or so (or overnight). Turn out in baking pan peel off paper and bake one hour at 350 degrees, basting occasionally. Serves 6 to 8. It is really good cold.

Eleanor Britannia Beers Pierce,
University of Wisconsin-Madison
Tampa, Florida

Meatballs:
1 pound ground beef
1 tablespoon sugar
1 medium onion, chopped
2 slices white bread soaked in milk and then crumbled
1 clove garlic or garlic salt
Salt and pepper to taste
Gravy:
1 tablespoon flour
¼ cup vinegar
¾ cup water
½ cup sugar
1 bay leaf
2 cloves garlic
½ teaspoon celery salt
Salt and pepper to taste

GRANDMA KAY'S HAWAIIAN MEATBALLS

Form meat into balls and either roll in flour and brown in skillet, or bake in 350 degree oven for 20 to 30 minutes.
Gravy: Combine all ingredients in saucepan or skillet. When mixture thickens, add meatballs and simmer covered for an hour or more. Add more liquid if necessary. Serve over rice. Serves 4 to 6.

Sharon McFarland Groves,
Southern Methodist University
Richardson, Texas

SWEET 'N SOUR MEATBALLS

Meatballs:
1 pound ground beef
¾ cup rolled oats (uncooked) or
   soft bread crumbs
¼ cup milk
¼ cup onion, finely chopped
1 egg
¾ teaspoon salt
Sauce:
3 tablespoons corn starch
¾ cup vinegar
1 cup brown sugar, firmly packed
1 cup tomato ketchup
2 teaspoons soy sauce
1 8-ounce can pineapple chunks,
   drained
1 small green pepper, diced

Combine all ingredients for meatballs; mix lightly but thoroughly. Shape into small balls, about 1 inch in diameter. Place in baking pan. Brown in moderate oven (375 degrees) 25 to 30 minutes.

For sauce: blend cornstarch and vinegar in skillet. Add brown sugar, ketchup and soy sauce. Cook, stirring constantly, until thickened. Add meatballs. Cover and simmer 20 minutes. Add pineapple and green pepper; continue cooking 10 minutes. Serve over rice. Serves 4-6. If sauce is too thick add water or pineapple juice.

Note: this does well in an electric skillet. The meatball recipe can easily be doubled using the same sauce recipe and adding more pineapple and green pepper to suite your taste.

Geni E. Everett, Florida State University
Tallahassee, Florida

GLORIOUS MEDLEY

4 pounds ground beef
1 quart canned tomatoes
Celery tops from one stalk
2 medium onions, chopped
1 can cream of mushroom soup
2 cans Mexican style chili beans
Salt, oregano, thyme, and pepper
   to taste as for spaghetti

Brown beef, breaking it up as it cooks. Add tomatoes, celery tops, onions and herbs. Simmer 1 hour. Add soup and chili beans 30 minutes before serving.

Place in serving bowl — followed with smaller bowls lined up to sprinkle over meat mixture: 2 13-ounce bags Fritos, 1 pound grated Longhorn cheese, 1 large head lettuce shredded, 6 chopped tomatoes, 3 bunches green onions, chopped.

Jinnie Drake, University of Missouri
N. Little Rock, Arkansas

PIZZA BY THE YARD

1 pound browned, ground beef
1 unsliced loaf French bread
1 6-ounce can tomato paste
⅓ cup grated Parmesan cheese
¼ cup finely chopped green onion
¼ cup finely chopped ripe olives
4 ounces shredded American
   cheese
¼ teaspoon pepper
½ teaspoon crushed dried
   oregano
¾ teaspoon salt
2 sliced tomatoes
1 green pepper in rings

Cut loaf lengthwise. Combine tomato paste, Parmesan cheese, onion, olive, oregano, salt and pepper. Add meat. Mix well. Spread on loaf. Bake at 400 degrees for 20 minutes. Top with green peppers, tomatoes and American cheese. Bake 5 more minutes. Serves 6.

Pam Rutherford, Vanderbilt University
Nashville, Tennessee

TOWERING PIZZA

1 pound ground chuck
1 tablespoon oil
1 teaspoon salt
½ teaspoon pepper
1 teaspoon onion flakes
2 tablespoons Worcestershire
¼ cup chopped parsley
2 cans crescent rolls
4 beaten eggs
2 3-ounce cans Parmesan cheese
½ pound Provolone cheese
½ pound sliced ham
4-ounce package sliced salami
½ pound Mozzarella cheese
3-ounce package sliced chicken

Brown chuck in oil with parsley, onion, seasonings, and set aside to cool. Roll out the rolls, and line a well-greased casserole, leaving some extra to fold back at the top. Combine eggs, Parmesan and Provolone, and pour ⅔ into pastry, add the chuck mixture and ½ of the ham. Then add the remainder of the egg-cheese mixture, then layers of the ham, salami, and Mozzarella, and top with the chicken. Then fold over the rolls and top with any left over. Bake at 350 degrees for one hour. Serves 6-8.

Linda Wheeler, Southern Methodist University
Santa Fe, New Mexico

BEEF QUICHE

1 pound ground beef
1 lightly baked 10-inch pie crust
3 tablespoons butter
1 cup diced, peeled onion
¼ teaspoon pepper
⅛ teaspoon nutmeg
2 eggs
¾ teaspoon salt
1 cup heavy cream
½ cup grated Cheddar cheese

Cook butter and onions; add beef. Drain and discard fat. Mix above with salt, pepper and nutmeg. Beat eggs with cream and stir into meat mixture. Pour into pie shell and sprinkle with cheese. Bake at 375 degrees for 30 minutes. Let stand 10 minutes before serving. This is also good with 1 cup drained zucchini squash added.

Jennifer L. Elden, Rutgers University
Central New Jersey

ALMOST RAVIOLI

1½ pounds lean ground beef
1 small can tomatoes
1 small can tomato sauce
½ teaspoon each basil, oregano,
   and other herbs if desired
2 tablespoons olive oil
½ pound bow-knot macaroni
1 package frozen spinach, thawed
½ cup chopped parsley
½ cup fine bread crumbs
½ cup Parmesan cheese
¼ teaspoon garlic powder or salt
½ cup tomato juice
3 beaten eggs

Brown meat in oil. Add tomato sauce and tomatoes and herbs. Simmer 20 minutes. Cook and drain macaroni. Mix together remaining ingredients. Layer in casserole. Bake covered at 350 degrees for 30 minutes.

Pauline Sawyer Umland, Boston University
Peninsula, California

TERIYAKI TENDERLOIN

1 2 to 3 pound beef tenderloin
½ cup dry sherry
¼ cup soy sauce
2 tablespoons dry onion soup mix
2 tablespoons brown sugar

Combine first four ingredients. Place beef in plastic bag, set in deep bowl. Add marinade and close bag. Chill 8 to 24 hours. Occasionally, press bag against meat to distribute marinade. Bake at 425 degrees for 50 minutes.

Elise Hodges Weed, Oklahoma University
Dallas, Texas

ESCALOPES DE TERNERA
(Pilar's Veal Scallops)

Enough veal scallopini to serve 4
Flour
Salt
Cinnamon
Nutmeg
2 eggs, beaten
Fine, dry seasoned bread crumbs
Spanish olive oil
Butter
Lemon wedges
Broiled tomatoes

Pound each scallopini with a mixture of flour, and a pinch each of salt, cinnamon and nutmeg. Dip in beaten eggs, then in seasoned crumbs. *Chill one hour. To Fry:* Heat olive oil and butter together until butter melts. Add chilled scallopini, cook quickly over moderately high heat until crisp on each side. Serve at once with lemon wedges and broiled tomatoes. Scallopini should have a golden crisp exterior. The mixture of oil with the butter prevents butter from burning.

I ate this recipe first in Madrid when a Spanish friend of mine cooked it very quickly after we had arrived. The veal was so good, I asked her for the recipe. Have the butcher pound the veal fairly thin, and serve it with a pasta, with only butter and grated cheese.

Mary Orr Denham, Syracuse University
New York, New York

MEXICAN BEEF SANDWICH

½ pound lean ground beef
6 rectangular French rolls
1 medium onion, chopped
¼ pound sliced mushrooms
1 can (2¼ ounces) ripe olives, drained
1 can (7 ounces) green chili salsa
¼ teaspoon each — cumin and salt
½ teaspoon chili powder
4 ounce sliced Cheddar cheese
4 ounces sliced Monterey Jack
6 slices bacon, lightly cooked

Cut off top third of roll, scoop out most of the insides. Lightly toast cut sides, set aside. Crumble beef into fry pan over medium heat and cook 2 or 3 minutes, add onion and mushrooms and cook until onion is limp. Stir in olives, chili salsa, cumin, salt and chili powder. Simmer until liquid is evaporated. To assemble, arrange cheddar cheese on lower portion of each roll. Top with 1 slice bacon, cut in half, 1/6 of meat mixture and jack cheese. Add top of roll, wrap each sandwich in foil. (Chill if made ahead). Place wrapped sandwich on baking sheet and bake 12-15 minutes in a 375 degree oven. Bake 30 minutes, if chilled. These also freeze well, just allow more time to heat through.

Ernestine Dobler McDonald, Northwestern University
Greater Kansas City

OPEN FACE HAMBURGERS

1 pound ground beef
1 pound sausage
1 pound Velveeta cheese
1 tablespoon leaf oregano
½ teaspoon garlic salt
½ teaspoon Worcestershire sauce

Brown meats; drain off fat. Slice cheese thin and add to meat. Add spices and melt into meat. Spread thick on one-half bun. Freeze uncovered on cookie sheets, then store in plastic bags. To serve, brown under broiler three minutes, turn off broiler and leave in oven a few minutes to cook through and keep hot. Takes longer if not thawed first. Makes about 18 halves of small buns.

Great for a party after a football game.

Margaret Smoot Kaiser, University of Iowa
Fargo-Moorhead, North Dakota

Jane Kaiser Gordon, North Dakota State University
Fargo-Moorhead, North Dakota

PARTY SANDWICHES

1 pound ground round
1 pound pork sausage
1 pound Velveeta, cubed
1 teaspoon Worcestershire sauce
1 teaspoon oregano
½ teaspoon salt
½ teaspoon garlic salt
Pepper
Party rye bread

Brown ground round and pork sausage. Drain off fat. Add Velveeta, cubed. Heat to melt. Add remaining ingredients. Spread on party rye. Brown under broiler for 2-3 minutes. These may be frozen on a cookie sheet, then stacked and bagged. Broil frozen.

Shirley Derrick, University of Wisconsin
Chicago Northwest Suburban, Illinois

CHILI I

1 pound ground beef
1 medium chopped onion
2 cans kidney beans
2 cans whole tomatoes
1 teaspoon chili powder
Salt to taste (about 1 teaspoon)

Sauté onions in shortening until clear. Brown hamburger and drain. Combine all ingredients except beans in large saucepan. Simmer 30 to 45 minutes. Add beans and simmer until beans are heated.

Lynne Ayers, Vanderbilt University
Nashville, Tennessee

CHILI II

1 pound ground beef
1 medium onion, chopped
1 can red beans with chili gravy
1 can tomato soup

Brown ground beef and onions, drain grease if desired, add soup and beans. Simmer. 1 package of chili seasonings may be added for more flavor.

Barb Tate, Vanderbilt University
Cincinnati, Ohio

TONGUE

1 fresh beef tongue
¼ cup salt
1 bay leaf
½ cup molasses
1 cup vinegar
½ cup raisins
½ teaspoon allspice
1 teaspoon cinnamon
½ teaspoon whole cloves

Cover the tongue, salt, and bay leaf with water and boil until tender (several hours); skin. Add remaining ingredients to the tongue and simmer ¾ of an hour, covered in the oven. Turn once and baste about halfway through the oventime.

I find ½ of this sauce recipe sufficient to make the tongue tasty.

Ruth Buckman Armstrong, Syracuse University
Dallas, Texas

Cheese

BAKED CHEESE FONDUE

½ pound cheddar cheese, grated
11 ½ inch slices French bread
Softened butter
1 medium onion, grated
1 large carrot, grated
Chopped chives
¼ cup chopped parsley
4 eggs
2½ cups milk
2 tablespoons Dijon mustard
1 teaspoon Worcestershire
½ teaspoon salt
⅛ teaspoon paprika

Cube bread slices and spread with softened butter. Place in a 2 quart souffle dish. Mix grated onion, carrot, cheese, chives, and parsley over bread. Beat remaining ingredients together and pour over mixture. Cover dish with plastic wrap and refrigerate overnight. Remove from the refrigerator the next day, and let stand 45 minutes at room temperature. Bake at 350 degrees for 1 hour or until puffed and golden. Let stand 5 minutes before serving. Serve with green vegetables, salad and dessert with white wine. This dish is delicious served as a brunch with fresh fruit, coffee cake and Sangria.

Ruth Deems Cooper, Iowa State University
Charles City, Iowa

CHEESE CHILE CUBES

3 cups (12 ounces) shredded
   Monterrey Jack Cheese
8 eggs
½ cup flour
1 teaspoon baking powder
¾ teaspoon salt
1½ cups cottage cheese
2 4-ounce cans mild green chilies,
   drained, seeded and chopped

In bowl, beat eggs until light (4-5 minutes). Sift flour, salt, baking powder and add to eggs. Fold in cheese and chilies. Put in greased 9x9x2 inch dish. Bake at 350 degrees for 40 minutes. Let stand 10 minutes. Cut into cubes, serve hot.

Sheila Dorn, Colorado State University
Denver, Colorado

CHEESE SOUFFLE

½ pound Velveeta cheese
10 slices white bread
2 cups milk
4 eggs
1 stick margarine

Trim crusts from bread and break into chunks. Place in bowl. Beat eggs and add milk. Melt margarine and cheese together. Blend margarine-cheese mixture and eggs-milk mixture together. Pour over bread chunks and stir all together. Pour into a greased 8x12 inch flat casserole. Let set overnight in the refrigerator. Bake at 375 degrees for 30 minutes.

Latane Jordan Graham, Memphis State University
Dallas, Texas

GREEN CHILI SOUFFLE

8 ounces Cheddar cheese
1 dozen eggs
4 small cans of chopped green chili, or 8-9 fresh chilies, skinned, cooked and chopped
1 teaspoon salt

Beat eggs and grate cheese. Grease the bottom and sides of a 9x13 inch pan or pyrex casserole. Cover bottom of casserole with ¼ inch of cheese and top with a layer of chopped green chili. Continue to alternate cheese and green chili. Add salt to beaten egg mixture and pour over all. Bake at 350 degrees for 45 minutes or until firm and slightly browned. Let stand for 5 minutes before cutting into squares. Delicious for brunch, lunch or whenever.

Joan P. Laney, McGill University
Albuquerque, New Mexico

CHILI RELLENOS I

1 pound Cheddar cheese, sliced
1 pound Jack cheese, sliced
3 7-ounce cans of green chilies (roasted)
1 13-ounce can evaporated milk
3 tablespoons flour
Salt and pepper to taste
4 eggs

Remove seeds, mash and flatten chilies. Place half in bottom of casserole. Cover with all the cheddar cheese. Top with other half of chilies. Put on all the Jack cheese. Beat egg whites until stiff. Beat yolks with milk, flour, salt and pepper and fold into whites. Pour over chilies and cheese. Bake in 325 degree oven for 45 minutes to 1 hour until lightly browned. Casserole size should be 9x13 inch.

Suzanne Knipschild North, University of Missouri
Greater Kansas City

CHILI RELLENOS II

2 pounds Jack cheese
4 small cans green chilies
6 eggs
½ cup milk

Remove seeds and slice green chilies length-wise and place in bottom of 8x12 inch pyrex baking dish. Spread grated cheese over the chilies. Beat eggs with milk and pour over top. Bake in 350 degree oven for 45 minutes or until set.

Pat Strickler Jennings, University of Washington
Seattle, Washington

CHILI RELLENOS CASSEROLE

1 pound Jack or Longhorn cheese (sharp), grated
2 7-ounce cans whole green chilies
1 small can evaporated milk
2 eggs
½ cup milk
2 teaspoons flour
1 8-ounce can tomato sauce

Place green chilies in 9x13 inch pan side by side. Add layer of grated cheese. Add another layer of chilies and another layer of cheese. Beat eggs until lemon-colored, add canned milk and ½ cup milk. Sprinkle flour over chilies and pour liquid over. Bake at 350 degrees for 20 to 25 minutes. Pour tomato sauce over top and add rest of cheese. Bake 15 minutes longer. Let stand 15 to 20 minutes, and cut into squares. If spicier casserole is desired, use ½ hot Mexican-style tomato sauce and ½ regular tomato sauce.

Doris Havercamp Nelson, University of Iowa
Riverside, California

EASY BRUNCH CASSEROLE

2 cups shredded Longhorn cheese
1 package croutons (select the flavor of your choice)
2 pounds breakfast sausage
6 eggs
¾ teaspoon mustard
2½ cups milk
1 can mushroom soup
1 small can mushrooms (optional)

Place croutons in greased 9x13 metal pan. Put grated cheese over croutons. Brown sausage and drain and place on top of cheese. Beat eggs and mix with mustard, milk, soup and mushrooms. Pour mixture over sausage. Bake, covered with foil, in a 300 degree oven for 1½ hours. This recipe may be prepared the night before and refrigerated. Serves 10.

Cheryl Stoner Myhra, Iowa State University
Dallas, Texas

MARY'S "DELICIOUS" QUICHE

1 can (3 ounce) fried onion rings
1 cup sour cream
1 cup grated Swiss cheese
8 slices bacon, fried and crumbled
3 large eggs, beaten
1 9 inch pie shell, baked

Mix eggs and sour cream, and add to remaining ingredients. Pour into pie shell. Bake 40 to 45 minutes or until firmly set at 350 degrees.

Cookbook Committee

QUICHE OVER EASY

2 cups grated Cheddar cheese
1 unbaked pie shell (9 inch)
6 or 7 eggs, beaten (6, if large)
1 small can diced green chilies,
  optional
Salt and pepper to taste.

Pour beaten eggs into pie shell. Add cheese (and chilies if desired). Bake at 350 degrees for 30 minutes. This can be easily baked in tart shells, with cooking time reduced to 15 minutes. Cut into quarters and use as an appetizer or entree.

Sandra Graham Cude, Memphis State University
Dallas, Texas

SPINACH QUICHE

2 cups shredded Cheddar cheese
10 ounce package frozen spinach
2 tablespoons flour
¾ cup milk
3 eggs
3 crisply cooked bacon slices,
  crumbled
½ teaspoon salt
9 inch unbaked pastry shell

Thaw spinach; drain off excess liquid. Shred cheese into a bowl and toss with flour. Combine milk, beaten eggs and salt. Mix into cheese; add spinach and bacon crumbs. Mix well. Pour into pie shell. Bake at 350 degrees 1 hour or until done. Garnish with additional bacon.

Joan Lonnborg DeLaGarza,
University of Wisconsin-Madison
Dallas, Texas

QUICHE SUPREME

2 cups grated Swiss cheese
1 9-inch pie crust
½ pound bacon, cooked and
  crumbled
¾ pound sliced fresh mushrooms
6 eggs
1 cup whipping cream
½ teaspoon salt
1 tablespoon grated fresh onion
1 teaspoon oregano

Put one layer pie crust in quiche pan or 9 inch pie plate. Put grated cheese in pan, followed by sliced mushrooms and crumbled bacon. Make egg mixture in blender. Whip eggs and cream together. Add salt, onion and oregano. Add dash of hot sauce if desired. Pour over cheese, mushrooms and bacon in quiche pan. Bake for 60-70 minutes at 400 degrees or until a knife comes out clean. Top should be golden brown.
Hint: To make sure crust is crisp, place in 350 degree oven for 10 minutes prior to adding quiche mixture.

Catherine Martin Brown, Iowa State University
Milwaukee, Wisconsin

Eggs

GRANDMA'S EGG SOUFFLE

6 eggs
6-8 slices bread
1 pound sharp cheese
3 cups milk
¾ teaspoon salt
¾ teaspoon dry mustard
¼ teaspoon pepper
Garlic salt
Parmesan cheese (optional)

Butter both sides of bread. Sprinkle bread with garlic salt and cube. Crumble sharp cheese. Butter baking dish and layer with bread, cheese, bread, cheese, etc. Combine remaining ingredients. Pour this mixture over bread and cheese. Top with Parmesan cheese (optional) and place in the refrigerator for 24 hours. Bake at 350 degrees for 1 hour.

Mary Jo Ringhofer, Memphis State University
Germantown, Tennessee

Polly Grove Haliday, Northwestern University
Evanston-North Shore, Illinois

EGG-CHEESE CASSEROLE

8 eggs
1¾ cups milk
2 cups soft bread crumbs (no crusts)
4 tablespoons margarine
¼ teaspoon seasoned salt
½ pound Swiss cheese, shredded
Topping:
1 tablespoon margarine
½ cup dry bread crumbs
8 slices bacon, crisp

Soak soft bread crumbs in milk. Drain in colander and reserve milk. Slightly beat eggs. Mix eggs with leftover milk, salt and pepper to taste. Melt margarine in skillet and cook egg milk mixture until *runny* scrambled. Add soaked bread and mix well. Pour into 6x10 inch greased dish. Sprinkle seasoned salt on top. Spread cheese on top. Cover and refrigerate overnight. Next day: Combine margarine with dry bread crumbs and bacon and sprinkle mixture on top of the casserole. Bake at 350 degrees for 20 to 25 minutes.

Sarah Bristor, Michigan State University
Birmingham, Michigan

BRUNCH EGGS

12 eggs
1 cup diced bacon (½ pound)
¼ cup chopped onion
3 tablespoons butter
1 3-ounce can mushrooms
3 tablespoons milk
1 teaspoon salt
1 pound American cheese, grated (Velveeta)
1 can evaporated milk (1 ⅔ cup)
1 cup bread crumbs
⅓ stick butter
Salt and pepper to taste

Sauté bacon and drain off all but 1 tablespoon grease. Add onion and mushrooms. Gradually stir in milk and grated cheese. Cook until sauce is thickened and smooth, stirring constantly. Set aside. Combine eggs with salt and milk and scramble in butter in a large skillet. In a 2 quart rectangular Pyrex dish, alternate layers of scrambled eggs and sauce ending with sauce. Melt ⅓ stick butter and add 1 cup bread crumbs. Top casserole with crumbs and bake 30 minutes at 350 degrees. May be fixed the day before, refrigerated, then baked according to directions. Serves 12.

Irene Braden Loosley, Oklahoma University
Dallas, Texas

BRUNCH EGG CASSEROLE

8 eggs, slightly beaten
4 cups toasted bread cubes (6 slices)
8 ounces natural Cheddar cheese, shredded (2 cups)
4 cups milk
1 teaspoon salt
1 teaspoon prepared mustard
¼ teaspoon onion powder
⅛ teaspoon pepper

Spread 4 cups toasted bread cubes in bottom of greased 13x8 inch baking dish. Sprinkle the shredded cheese over bread. Blend the slightly beaten eggs, milk, salt, mustard, onion powder and pepper. Pour over bread-cheese mixture. Bake at 325 degrees until egg mixture is set, 40 to 45 minutes. Garnish with 10 slices of crumbled, crisp fried bacon during the last 10 minutes of baking.

Karen Rawlings, University of Missouri
Columbia, Missouri

BRUNCH EGGS AND POTATOES

8 well beaten eggs
8 strips bacon
1 green pepper
1 onion
8 grated potatoes
1 cup shredded cheddar cheese

Grind bacon, pepper and onion together. Sauté in skillet until bacon bits are crisp. Add potatoes. Fry until potatoes are brown. Add eggs, lifting mixture until eggs are set. Sprinkle with cheese and let melt. Serves 8.

Theara Kurt Schonberg, Iowa State University
Omaha, Nebraska

CALIFORNIA BUFFET EGGS

9 beaten eggs
3 tablespoons butter
¼ cup chopped green onion tops
4 ounces dried sliced beef, cut in strips
1 cup small curd cottage cheese

Cook onion tops in butter until tender. Blend eggs (slightly beaten), beef and cottage cheese with onion tops. Cook like scrambled eggs. Keep warm in low oven, if necessary. Serves 4-6 people.

Martha Conrad Clark,
University of Wisconsin-Oshkosh
Milwaukee, Wisconsin

EGGS GOLDENROD

Eggs as needed
3 tablespoons butter
3 tablespoons flour
1 cup milk
2 cups grated cheese
Worcestershire sauce, salt, pepper to taste

Hard boil eggs, grate and place on the bottom of a casserole dish. Make a white sauce of the milk, butter and flour. Add the grated cheese, Worcestershire sauce, salt and pepper. Pour over eggs. Bake at 350 degrees, until bubbly. This can be made in large quantities economically.

May be served over toast points for brunch or lunch. Garnish with parsley.

Active Chapter, Southern Methodist University
Dallas, Texas

EGG TORTILLA CASSEROLE

2 dozen large eggs
2 tablespoons butter
6 corn tortillas (cut in eighths)
1½ cups Cheddar cheese grated
⅓ cup chopped onions
1 pint sour cream
2 cans chili salsa
¼ cup chopped green chilies

Sauté tortillas in butter until limp. Scramble eggs until soft. Layer in casserole tortillas, eggs, cheese, onion, sour cream, salsa and chilies. Bake covered at 250 degrees for one hour or until heated through.

Diane Backus Taylor, University of Arizona
Pasadena, California

BAKED OMELET

8 or 9 eggs
8 or 9 slices of bacon
4 green onions, sliced thinly
1 cup milk
½ teaspoon seasoned salt
2½ cups shredded Monterrey
   Jack cheese

Chop and fry bacon until crisp. Take bacon out of pan and drain off most of the grease. Brown onions lightly in the bacon grease. Beat eggs until slightly frothy and add milk and beat well. Add salt, bacon and onions and 2 cups of cheese. Save ½ cup of the cheese. Pour into 9x13 inch greased pan. Bake uncovered at 350 degrees for 35 to 45 minutes. When almost done, add ½ cup cheese to the top. Cut into squares to serve.

Shirley Davis Tompkins, Iowa State University
Ft. Worth, Texas

WOODCOCK

4 hard-boiled eggs, sliced
¾ stick of butter
3 tablespoons flour
1 cup milk
1 can tomato soup
Salt, pepper to taste
1 small can mushrooms, chopped
½ green pepper, chopped
3 or 4 whole pimientoes, chopped
½ pound Velveeta cheese
Holland rusks, toast, or toasted
   English muffins

Make a cream sauce with butter, flour and milk. Add cheese, soup and other ingredients, except rusks. Serve on rusks, toast, or English muffins. Serves 6 to 8.

(This is a "savoury," used in England as a dessert. However, it is great for a brunch, served with a fruit salad and hot coffee cake for a dessert or sweet ... or for a luncheon with a green salad.) Can also be made ahead of time and warmed over, or used as a party "dunk."

Beth McCallon Wheeler,
Southern Methodist University
Dallas, Texas

Chicken

CHICKEN BALL

4-6 pieces of chicken
1 can cream of chicken or
   mushroom soup
½ to 1 can water
¼ teaspoon ginger
1 teaspoon poppy seeds
1 teaspoon cumin
1 teaspoon turmeric
1 teaspoon coriander
2 bay leaves
4 cardamon seeds
5 cloves
Onion
Garlic

Thin soup with water. Mix in the remaining ingredients. Place chicken in pan. Spread mixture over the chicken pieces. Bake covered about two hours at 325 degrees to 350 degrees. Chicken is delicious if cooked at lower temperature for a longer time, but it can be cooked at 350 degrees to 375 degrees for one hour, or until the chicken is done. Serve with rice. For a milder dish, use ½ of the stated amount of each spice.

I generally fix the chicken an hour or two before baking, to enhance the flavor. Flavor is even better the second day. It makes an excellent leftover. Also freezes well, especially in some of the gravy.

Janet H. Callander, University of Texas
Austin, Texas

BAKED CHICKEN BREASTS WITH ALMONDS

Salt and pepper to taste
4-5 chicken breasts
4 tablespoons cooking oil
1 can cream of mushroom soup
½ cup cooking sherry
¼ cup sharp cheddar cheese
3 tablespoons grated onion
2 teaspoons Worcestershire sauce
½ cup slivered almonds

Salt and pepper chicken; brown in oil. Place in baking dish. Combine soup, sherry, cheese, onion and Worcestershire sauce; pour over chicken. Sprinkle almonds on top. Cover with aluminum foil. Bake at 350 degrees for 45 minutes.

Melinda Copley, Oklahoma State University
Broken Arrow, Oklahoma

BAKED CHICKEN BREASTS

6-8 chicken breasts (boneless, if you prefer)
1 can cream of chicken soup
1 can sauterne (measure according to can of soup)
Salt and pepper.

Mix cream of chicken soup and sauterne together. Add salt and pepper. This will be your sauce. Pour sauce over desired number of chicken breasts.

Bake at 250 degrees for two and one-half hours.

Sharon J. Quevreaux, Texas Tech University
Lewisville, Texas

CHICKEN BREAST DIVINE

4 boned chicken breasts
1 chopped large onion
1 cup thinly sliced fresh mushrooms
½ large (chopped) green pepper
6 or 8 pieces of Swiss cheese
1 can cream of mushroom soup
½ can cream of chicken soup
Salt and pepper to taste
3 tablespoons butter

Preheat oven to 350 degrees. Sauté in a little butter for 3 or 4 minutes the onion, mushrooms and green pepper. Flatten chicken breasts and fold them in half. Add sautéed mixture to the middle of the folded breasts and then lay swiss cheese over sautéed mixture. Fold breast over and then pour the cream of mushroom soup and cream of chicken soup over breasts which have been placed in a shallow baking dish. Bake at 350 degrees for 40 minutes basting with the soups, and serve, placing a few sliced mushrooms on top for looks.

Sue Henning Kirkpatrick, Michigan State University
Audubon, Pennsylvania

CREAMY CASHEW CHICKEN

2 tablespoons butter or margarine
¼ cup green pepper, chopped
1 onion, thinly sliced
1 can cream of chicken soup, undiluted
½ cup milk
½ teaspoon Lawry's seasoning salt
¼ cup cashew nuts, coarsely chopped
2 cups cooked chicken
1 cup carrot slices, cooked
1 can (2-4 ounces) mushrooms, chopped
1 package frozen Chinese pea pods
1 can (8-ounces) water chestnuts, chopped

In saucepan or large skillet, sauté green pepper and onion in butter until tender. Stir in soup, milk and seasoning salt; add half the nuts and the rest of the ingredients. Heat thoroughly. Just prior to serving, add rest of the nuts to top the mixture. Serve over rice. Yields six servings.

Chris Loveberg Montgomery,
California State University-San Diego
Orange County, California

CHICKEN CASSEROLE I

2 cups diced cooked chicken
1 small onion, finely chopped
½ teaspoon salt
½ cup mayonnaise
1 cup diced celery
1 cup cream of celery or cream of chicken soup
1 teaspoon lemon juice
1 cup cooked rice
½ cup chopped almonds or 1 4-ounce can sliced mushrooms

Mix all ingredients and pour into a 9x12 inch casserole dish. Cover with buttered crumbs. Bake 30 minutes at 375 degrees.

Judy Elaine Graham, Oklahoma University
Greater Kansas City

Sunshine Hallar Davis, Southern Methodist University
Nashville, Tennessee

CHICKEN CASSEROLE II

4-5 pound hen
½ pound Italian spaghetti
½ pound butter
⅔ cup flour
1 quart milk
½ pound American cheese
½ pound Old English cheese
1 small can mushrooms
1 small can pimientoes
1 medium onion
1 medium green pepper

Cook hen until tender. Remove meat from bone while warm. Cut in cubes. Cook spaghetti in the stock (at least 1 quart). Make a cream sauce of butter, flour and milk. Add cheese. Cut onion and green pepper in small pieces and combine all ingredients. Put in baking dish and bake at 350 degrees — for 30 to 40 minutes. Serves 12-16

Harriet Lishen Baldwin, University of Missouri
Dallas, Texas

CHEESY CHICKEN CASSEROLE

2 #1 cans whole green beans, drained well
4 chicken breasts, cooked, cut into small pieces
2 cans cream of chicken soup
1 cup mayonnaise
2 teaspoons lemon juice
1 small can water chestnuts (sliced)
½ cup shredded sharp cheese

Arrange beans in bottom of greased 2 quart casserole, distribute chicken over beans. Mix chicken soup with mayonnaise and lemon juice; pour over chicken. Sprinkle water chestnut slices and cheese on top. Bake at 350 degrees for 45 minutes. This may be prepared ahead and then refrigerated before cooking.

Sarah R. Bristor, Michigan State University
Birmingham, Michigan

FANNIE BELLE'S CHICKEN CASSEROLE

1 chicken, stewed and boned
1 can cream of chicken soup
1 8-ounce container of sour cream
1½ cups Ritz cracker crumbs
½ stick margarine, melted
Poppy seeds
Cooked broccoli (optional)

Blend cut up chicken, cooked broccoli (optional), soup, sour cream and ½ cup crumbs together. Pour into greased baking dish. Place remaining crumbs on top of chicken mixture and drizzle with melted margarine. Sprinkle with poppy seeds. Put in 350 degree oven until warmed through, about 35 minutes.

Elise Hodges Weed, Oklahoma University
Dallas, Texas

CHICKEN-CRAB VALENTIN

3 cups cooked chicken breasts, broken into bite-sized pieces
1 cup boned canned or frozen crab
8 slices bacon
2 10-ounce packages frozen peas (cooked)
6 tablespoons butter
6 tablespoons flour
1½ teaspoons salt
¾ teaspoon paprika
1 garlic clove, crushed
⅛ teaspoon nutmeg
5 to 6 drops hot red pepper sauce
2 cups commercial sour cream

Melt butter, add flour and stir to make a roux. Add salt, paprika, garlic, nutmeg, hot pepper sauce and sour cream to flour mixture. Cover and cook 10 to 15 minutes. Add chicken and crab to mixture. Mix lightly. Heat 10 to 15 minutes. Put into serving dish and arrange hot peas around the edge. Sprinkle bacon bits on top of the chicken-crab mixture. SERVES 6. Serve with Walnut Rice; the following recipe.

Barbara R. Stapleton, Kansas University
El Cajon, California

WALNUT RICE

6 cups hot cooked rice
1½ cups walnut halves, sliced vertically
2 tablespoons butter
2 tablespoons Worcestershire sauce
1 teaspoon salt
¼ teaspoon pepper

Heat butter and Worcestershire sauce. Add nuts. Toss lightly for 4 to 5 minutes. Add to rice and season with salt and pepper.

Barbara R. Stapleton, Kansas University
El Cajon, California

CRANBERRY CHICKEN FOR TWO

2 full chicken breasts, skinned
  and halved
1 package dry onion soup mix
1 can cream of mushroom soup
1 can whole cranberry sauce

Roll skinned breasts in onion soup mix and bake at 350 degrees for 30 minutes, or until brown. Combine mushroom soup and cranberry sauce and pour half in bottom of baking dish. Place breasts in the dish and pour the remaining mixture on top of breasts. Bake covered for 30 to 40 minutes. Serve with brown or wild rice.

Penny Dumm Wilkes,
University of Southern California
La Jolla, California

EASY CREAMED CHICKEN
(Low Cholesterol)

2 tablespoons margarine
  (polyunsaturated)
¼ pound fresh mushrooms, sliced
½ cup chopped onion
1 small clove garlic, minced
2 tablespoon chopped parsley
3 tablespoons flour
½ teaspoon paprika
1½ cups chicken broth
2 cups cooked chicken, cut up
½ cup plain yogurt
Whole wheat toast points

Melt margarine in medium skillet. Add mushrooms, onion, garlic and parsley and cook until tender. Remove from heat. Stir in flour, chicken broth and paprika. Return to heat and stir until mixture comes to a boil. Cook for 2 minutes. Then add chicken and yogurt. Heat but do not boil. Serve over whole wheat toast points. Serves 4.

Carolie Goniu, University of Wisconsin-Madison
Milwaukee, Wisconsin

CHICKEN CREPES EXCELSIOR

Chicken:
6 chicken breasts
Garlic salt
¼ pound butter
1 teaspoon paprika
3 tablespoons lemon juice
1 carton sour cream (8-ounce)
¼ cup sherry
1 4-ounce can mushrooms
Cayenne pepper
Crepe Batter:
1½ cups pre-sifted flour
½ teaspoon salt
1 cup milk
4 eggs
3 tablespoons butter or
  margarine melted and slightly
  cooled

Chicken: Sprinkle half inch sections of chicken with garlic salt. Melt margarine, add paprika and lemon juice. Roll chicken in mixture and bake at 375 degrees for 1 hour. Make sauce of sour cream, sherry and mushrooms. Pour over chicken and warm for 15 minutes.

Crepes: Combine flour and salt in mixing bowl, add eggs and half the milk; beat with a rotary beater until smooth. Blend in the remainder of the milk and butter. Cover bowl and let "rest" in refrigerator for about 1 hour.

Cooking crepes: Cure your crepe pan by pouring 1 tablespoon cooking oil on and place on medium heat for 2 minutes. Wipe out with paper towel. When pan is heated, lift it and pour in sufficient batter, pour off excess and return pan to heat for 15-30 seconds or until surface of crepe is dry and slightly brown around the edges. Put about 1 tablespoon chicken in each crepe and roll or fold. Pour excess sauce over crepes after all have been prepared.

Judith Focht, University of Texas
Austin, Texas

CHICKEN CRISP CASSEROLE

2 cans mushroom soup
1 cup chicken bouillon
½ cup chopped onion
½ cup diced celery
4 cups cooked, diced chicken
1 large can chow mein noodles
1 package cashews or slivered almonds

Mix all ingredients except noodles and nuts, this may be done ahead and refrigerated until baking. When ready to bake, alternate mixed ingredients with noodles, until all are used, in a 13x9 inch or other ungreased shallow baking dish. Top with nuts. Bake 20-30 minutes at 350 degrees. Serves 6-8 people.

Ann Vandemark Butler, Syracuse University
Dumfries, Virginia

CHICKEN CHILI

2 pounds ground beef or 4 cups diced cooked chicken
3 or 4 ounce can green chilies
1½ pounds cheese
2 cups tomato juice
1 large can evaporated milk
Large bag Doritos

Brown beef and pour off fat. Add green chilies and mix well. Melt cheese in tomato juice over low heat. Add evaporated milk and remove from heat. Line 9x13x3 inch casserole with Doritos and layer meat, cheese liquid, Doritos, meat, cheese, ending with Doritos on top. Bake at 350 degrees for 20 minutes. May be made a day ahead and also freezes well.

Dorothy Holmes McGinnis, Oklahoma University
Greater Kansas City

MADRAS CHICKEN CURRY

2 medium onions, chopped
1 teaspoon mustard seed
2 chicken bouillon cubes
2 cups water
1 teaspoon cumin seed
2 teaspoons curry powder (Madras Brand if available)
½ teaspoon red pepper, crushed
Garlic powder to taste
1 frying chicken, cut up

Put oil in pan with mustard seed, cover pan until the seeds pop over medium high heat. Add chopped onion and sauté. Add the chicken bouillon dissolved in water. Add seasonings and stir, when mixture comes to boil add chicken. Cook over low heat about 50 minutes. May need to remove lid the last few minutes to thicken sauce according to individual taste. Serve over rice.

Beth Simmons Stapor, Florida State University
Charleston, South Carolina

CHICKEN DINNER FROM BALI

1. Chinese noodles (crisp, canned)
2. Steamed rice (about 1 cup raw)
3. Chicken (2 boiled, cut into pieces): Sliced water chestnuts, optional
4. Gravy (made from broth, 8 cups)
5. Tomatoes, diced (optional)
6. Cooked peas (frozen, 2 packages)
7. Celery, diced (1 to 2 cups)
8. Green onion, chopped (2 bunches)
9. Gravy (pass again)
10. Fresh parsley, chopped
11. Crushed pineapple, (drained 1 large ≠2 can)
12. Grated nippy cheese (½ pound)
13. Coconut (1 package)
14. Sliced nuts, almonds, walnuts etc.

Each person gets a large dinner plate and food is placed in a mound on the plate. All dishes must be served in order 1 through 14, placing one on top of the other. Pass the various dishes in sequence in a variety of serving dishes and bowls. Chicken and gravy should be heated before serving. Serves 8 to 10. It can include hot buttered bread and light wine, Hawaiian decor to top it off.

Patti Crepps, Boise State University
Boise, Idaho

CHICKEN AND DRESSING BAKE

1 7 or 8 ounce herb seasoned dressing-stuffing package
1 small pan baked cornbread (I use the amount in a Jiffy Box)
1 can condensed mushroom soup
2 cups chicken broth
2 well beaten eggs
2½ or 3 cups diced chicken
½ cup milk
2 tablespoons chopped pimentoes
(Chopped onion and celery, if desired)

Toss all together and put in casserole or baking dish and cover with foil. Bake 350 degrees for 45 minutes. Take cover or foil off during last 5 minutes. (1 hen makes 2 recipes.) This can be made the night before cooking or the morning before cooking it in the evening and kept in the refrigerator. This is especially good to take to a church social or to a sick friend's family. All you need to add for a complete meal is either a jello or tossed salad, green beans and hot rolls.

Nina Gay Flanagan Ferguson, Oklahoma University
Cleveland, Oklahoma

EASIEST-EVER CHICKEN

One chicken, cut in halves
2 teaspoons salt
2 teaspoons monosodium glutamate
2 teaspoons paprika
¼ teaspoon poultry seasoning
¼ teaspoon nutmeg
⅛ teaspoon pepper
2 tablespoons oil
½ cup water

Wash the chicken and pat dry with paper towels. Mix all the dry ingredients; cover all the surfaces of the chicken with mixture of spices. Place seasoned chicken in baking dish with cover. Dribble about one tablespoon of oil over each half, spreading with fingers. Pour water in bottom of pan. Bake, covered, at 325 degrees for 90 minutes. Variation: substitute Greek seasoning in place of the spices listed above.

Mary Capps Haraden, University of Texas
Canyon, Texas

CHICKEN WITH GARLIC BUTTER

1 stick (¼ pound) sweet butter,
  softened
3-4 crushed garlic cloves
Pinch dried sage
Pinch dried thyme
2 tablespoons finely chopped
  parsley
1 roasting chicken
4 ounces bread crumbs (about 5
  slices worth) or ½ bag
  commercial stuffing
Livers from the chicken, sauteed
Dash salt
½ fresh lemon

Work the crushed garlic into the butter. Add sage, thyme and parsley. Lift skin of chicken, using a knife to saw away any portion that sticks to the carcass, and spread the meat under the skin with ½ the butter mixture. Mix the remaining butter with the bread crumbs, sauteed chicken livers and salt. Insert ½ lemon in the chicken. Stuff the chicken with the bread crumb mixture. Roast at 475 degrees for 20 minutes, then lower the oven temperature to 400 degrees, and roast for another 40 minutes, or until done, basting occasionally with the butter from the chicken which will melt down from the bird. The dressing will be moist, more like an English bread dressing. Serving suggestions: Watercress and endive salad. Bowl of strawberries for dessert.

Julie Winans, Southern Methodist University
Dallas, Texas

BEV'S GOLDEN GLAZED CHICKEN

1 can (6 ounces) orange juice
  concentrate, thawed
1 can (6 ounces) lemonade
  concentrate, thawed
½ cup soy sauce
1 cup light corn syrup
1 teaspoon lemon and pepper
  marinade seasoning
2 broiler-fryers, halved or
  quartered

Combine orange juice and lemonade concentrates with soy sauce, syrup and seasoning. Place chicken in shallow dish and pour marinade over chicken. Refrigerate, covered, about 6 hours, basting occasionally. Place chicken halves or quarters skin side up on grate set 3 to 6 inches from heat. Brush chicken with marinade. Cook until tender, turning and brushing occasionally. Allow 45 minutes to 1¼ hours cooking time, depending upon the size of the piece and distance from heat. To test for doneness, leg should twist easily out of thigh joint and pieces should be fork tender. (*Note:* Instead of lemon and pepper seasoning, salt and pepper may be used.) Makes 4 servings.

Carol Knox, Iowa State University
Plano, Texas

A CHICKEN DISH BY MOTHER

1½ cups raw rice fried out in butter
2 packages frozen broccoli spears, slightly cooked
Chicken breasts and thighs, layered on top
1 can cream of mushroom soup
½ to ⅔ cup mayonnaise
2 tablespoons lemon juice
½ to 1 teaspoon curry powder
1 medium jar Cheese Whiz
2 cups water

In a 9x13 inch pan, place rice, broccoli, and chicken. Pour water over this. Mix the soup, mayonnaise, lemon juice, curry powder and spread over chicken. Daube Cheese Whiz on top. Bake at 325 degrees for 2 hours. Cover after 1½ hours.

Jennifer L. Elden, (Douglass College)
Rutgers University
Princeton, New Jersey

CHICKEN DIVAN

6 to 8 chicken breasts, cooked and cubed
2 packages of broccoli spears, frozen
2 cans cream of chicken soup
1 cup mayonnaise
1 cup shredded sharp cheese
1 cup buttered bread crumbs
1 teaspoon lemon juice
½ teaspoon curry powder

Cook broccoli and drain. Arrange on bottom of buttered baking dish. Place cubed chicken on top. Mix soup, mayonnaise, lemon juice, curry powder, and cheese together; spread over chicken. Sprinkle buttered crumbs over the top. Bake uncovered at 350 degrees for about 35 minutes. Serves 10-12. Great for Bridge Luncheon.

Nancy Kenney Hick, Syracuse University
Philadelphia West, Pennsylvania

Ann Neighbors, Auburn University
Montgomery, Alabama

EASY ELEGANT CHICKEN

1 can of extra long asparagus spears
¼ cup (½ stick) margarine
2 ounces blanched, slivered almonds
½ teaspoon salt
Dash of pepper
¼ cup flour
1 10¼-ounce can chicken rice soup
¾ cup chicken drippings
6 chicken breasts
1 small can mushrooms (optional)

Bake skinned chicken breasts in foil covered pan for 1 hour at 350 degrees. Remove from oven and cool. Debone breasts. Reserve drippings from chicken breasts. Melt margarine and stir in almonds. Cook until light brown. Stir in flour, salt and pepper. Stir in soup and chicken drippings. Cook until thickened. In a 9x13x2 inch glass baking dish, layer drained asparagus spears. Place chicken breasts over asparagus. Pour soup mixture over breasts and asparagus. Sprinkle small, drained can of mushrooms over top. Cover with foil and store in refrigerator until needed. Bake in foiled covered pan for 45 minutes at 350 degrees.

Linda Frantel, University of Wisconsin-Oshkosh
Milwaukee, Wisconsin

CHICKEN KIEV

½-¾ cup butter
1 tablespoon dried chopped chives
1 tablespoon lemon juice
4 chicken breasts, boned, skinned, halved
1 cup dry bread crumbs
2 eggs, slightly beaten
3 tablespoons water
3 tablespoons melted butter
Salt and pepper to taste

Combine butter, chives, lemon juice; cover and chill. Form chicken into 8 pieces. Sprinkle salt and pepper over chicken. Put 1 piece of butter mixture in each halved breast and roll up, securing with toothpicks. Dip in crumbs, then in mixture of egg and water and again in crumbs. Dry 30 minutes on wire rack. Roll breasts in melted butter. Bake at 350 degrees for 30-45 minutes. Makes 8 servings.

Kris Brandt Riske, University of Wyoming
Alamogordo, New Mexico

KUWAIT CHICKEN

2 potatoes, sliced
3 or 4 pounds chicken pieces
1 box frozen cut okra
1 medium-sized onion, finely diced
5 or 6 tomatoes, cut in eighths
Curry powder, garlic powder, ground cumin, black pepper, salt, allspice, cardamom, cinnamon
1 8-ounce can tomato sauce

Line a large baking dish with a layer of sliced potatoes. Add the chicken pieces in a layer, then the okra, then the onions, tomatoes, and the spices — a generous amount of curry and garlic powders, and a moderate sprinkling of cumin, pepper, salt and allspice, and a little cinnamon and cardamom. Pour the tomato sauce over all, and then about 1½ cans of water. Cover with aluminum foil and bake at 350 degrees for 2 hours, removing the foil the last half hour. Serve with rice. Lamb or beef cubes can be substituted for the chicken pieces, green beans for the okra. Serves 4 to 6.

Caroline Armstrong Teaford,
University of California-Los Angeles
Riverside, California

LEMON BAKED CHICKEN

3 whole chicken breasts, halved
½ cup lemon juice
¼ cup olive oil
2 to 3 fresh garlic cloves, minced
1 to 2 bay leaves
Salt and pepper to taste

Rinse chicken parts under cold water and pat dry with paper towels. Set aside. Mix all ingredients. Marinate the chicken in this mixture in the refrigerator at least 4 hours or overnight. Turn chicken occasionally in the marinade so that all sides get coated. Remove chicken, reserve marinade. Bake chicken in a shallow, greased baking pan at 375 degrees, 45 minutes to one hour until golden brown, basting often with the marinade. (This may be broiled also, and is perfect for dieters.) Serves 4 to 6.

Bonne chance and Bon appetit!!!

Christie L. Grossheider Carter, Washington University
St. Louis, Missouri

MACARONI-CHICKEN CASSEROLE

4 hard boiled eggs, sliced
1 1-pound package elbow
   macaroni (uncooked)
½ pound cheese, diced
2 cups (or more) chicken, cooked
   and diced
2 cans mushroom soup
3 cups milk
1 small onion or onion salt
1 can sliced mushrooms

Stir together all the above and store in refrigerator for 24 hours. Warm up in a large flat pan. Bake at 350 degrees for 1 hour.

Evelyn Allard Ellis, University of Illinois
Evansville, Indiana

CHICKEN MAXIMILLIAN

4 chicken breasts or 6 thighs
1½ cups orange juice
2 tablespoons orange rind grated
   (optional)
½ teaspoon ginger
1 chopped onion
½ teaspoon tarragon
Sliced almonds or raisins,
   optional
Rice
3 tablespoons butter
Salt and pepper, to taste

Brown chicken in skillet with butter, salt and pepper. Add onions and cook until soft. Mix together the rest of the ingredients and pour over browned chicken. Cover and simmer for 45 minutes. Serve over any type of rice.

Linda Edwards Haney, Southern Methodist University
Dallas, Texas

CHICKEN MONTE CARLO

2 packages frozen broccoli spears
2 cups chicken breasts, cooked
2 cans cream of chicken soup
1 cup mayonnaise
1 tablespoon lemon juice
½ teaspoon curry powder
1 small can water chestnuts or
   blanched almonds
1 cup buttered bread crumbs

Layer broccoli (cooked until barely done); chicken chunks and water chestnuts. Mix soup, mayonnaise, lemon juice and curry powder together. Pour over chicken and vegetables; sprinkle with buttered crumbs. Use a 13x9 inch pan. Bake at 350 degrees until bubbly. May be made ahead and reheated. Serves 6-8.

Mary Rice Raber, University of Washington
Seattle, Washington

CHICKEN NOEL

6 chicken breasts, split
1 can mushroom soup, undiluted
1 can mushroom crowns
1 small carton sour cream
½ cup cooking sherry
½ stick butter

Place chicken skin side up in a shallow baking dish. Pack chicken closely, but only one layer deep. Combine remaining ingredients and pour over chicken. Sprinkle generously with paprika and dot with ½ stick butter. Bake at 350 degrees for 1½ to 2 hours or until the chicken is tender.

Jinnie Koch Drake, University of Missouri
N. Little Rock, Arkansas

CHICKEN PILLOWS

3 large chicken breasts, skinned,
  boned and halved
3 slices sandwich-sized boiled
  ham
½ cup grated mozzarella cheese
1 tomato slice, diced
⅓ cup dried bread crumbs
2 tablespoons grated Parmesan
  cheese
4 tablespoons margarine, melted

Place chicken breast between 2 pieces of waxed paper and pound gently with mallet. Discard paper. Place ½ ham slice, some grated mozzarella cheese and one or two pieces diced tomato on chicken breast. Carefully fold ham slice around cheese and tomato. Fold the chicken breast to totally enclose the ham slice and seal by sewing with needle and kitchen thread (dental floss works great!) Dip chicken pillow in melted margarine; roll it in bread crumb-Parmesan mixture and place in shallow baking pan. Bake at 350 degrees for 45 minutes. Serves 6.

Lynn Baxter Maguire, Southern Methodist University
Dallas, Texas

POLLO BARCELONA

3 pounds frying chicken pieces
½ teaspoon salt
Dash pepper
3 tablespoons salad oil
1½ cups chicken broth
¼ cup tomato paste
2 tablespoons chopped parsley
1 tablespoon instant minced
  onion
1 bay leaf
1 can (3 ounces) sliced, drained
  mushrooms
2 tablespoons thinly sliced stuffed
  olives
¼ teaspoon thyme

Sprinkle chicken with salt and pepper. Fry in oil in skillet until golden brown. Combine broth, tomato paste, parsley, onion, bay leaf and thyme; pour over chicken in skillet. Cover and simmer, basting occasionally until chicken is tender, about 30 minutes. Add mushrooms and olives; simmer 5 minutes longer. Serves 3 to 4.

Marjorie Ann White Giles,
Southern Methodist University
Dallas, Texas

EASY CHICKEN AND RICE CASSEROLE

1 frying chicken, cut up
1 cup rice, uncooked
Salt
1 can mushroom soup
1 package onion soup mix
3 soup cans of water

Place chicken in large well-greased baking pan. Add rice. Sprinkle with salt. Mix soups and water and pour over chicken and rice. Bake, covered, at 350 degrees for 2 hours. If too moist, uncover the last 30 minutes.

Kay Reynolds Bennett, Texas Tech University
Dallas, Texas

Jinnie Koch Drake, University of Missouri
N. Little Rock, Arkansas

CHICKEN RICE CASSEROLE I

1 stewing chicken (3 to 4 pounds)
3 or 4 cups of water
1 cup sherry
1½ teaspoon salt
½ teaspoon curry powder
½ teaspoon celery salt
1 medium onion
2 6½-ounce packages Uncle
 Ben's wild and regular rice
1 cup sour cream
1 can cream of mushroom soup

Simmer chicken 1 hour or until tender covered with water, sherry, salt, curry powder, onion and celery salt. Strain broth and cook rice in the strained broth. Chop chicken into 2 quart casserole. Add soup, sour cream, and rice. Refrigerate until needed. Bake at 350 degrees about 30 minutes.

Ann Sokol Heath, Iowa State University
Dallas, Texas

CHICKEN-RICE CASSEROLE II

6 chicken breasts
2 tablespoons cooking oil
1 cup uncooked rice
1 envelope onion soup mix
1 4-ounce can sliced mushrooms
 plus liquid
2 tablespoons diced pimento
1 can cream of chicken soup
1½ cups hot water

Slightly brown chicken breasts in oil. Spread uncooked rice in bottom of a 13½x9x2 inch baking dish. Add chicken, pimento, mushrooms and liquid, and chicken soup. Pour hot water over this, and sprinkle onion soup over top. Cover with foil. Bake at 350 degrees for about 45 minutes. Uncover and fluff up rice. Bake for another 5 to 10 minutes if too thin. Serves 6.

Frances Cheatham Burnecke, University of Texas
Dallas, Texas

CHICKEN PARMESAN

1½ cup Italian bread crumbs
½ cup Parmesan cheese
1 tablespoon salt
½ teaspoon pepper
6 chicken breasts
2 sticks butter

Combine bread crumbs, cheese, salt and pepper. Dip chicken breasts in the melted butter and then in the bread crumbs. Place breasts, skin side up in baking dish and bake in a 350 degree oven for 30 to 35 minutes, uncovered. Do not turn chicken.

Dawn Chappell, California-Riverside
Riverside, California

CHICKEN PARMESAN AND RICE

1 can each: cream of celery soup,
 cream of mushroom soup,
 cream of chicken soup
¼ pound melted butter
¼ cup almonds
1¼ cup rice
2 quartered chickens
Parmesan cheese

Mix soups, butter, almonds, and rice. Place in bottom of 9x13 inch baking dish. Place 2 quartered chickens on top of rice mixture. Bake uncovered at 325 degrees for 2 hours. Sprinkle Parmesan cheese on top during the last half hour. Serves 8.

Talie McKenzie, Northwestern University
Chicago Northwest Suburban, Illinois

CHICKEN AND RICE CASSEROLE

3 cups instant rice, uncooked
2 cut up chickens
Salt and pepper
1 can cream of mushroom soup
1 can cream of celery soup
2 cans cream of chicken soup
½ to ⅔ can of water
1 package instant onion soup mix

Place the uncooked instant rice in the bottom of a greased, *big* roasting pan. Lay the cut up chicken parts of top of the rice. Mix the soups and water together and pour over the rice and chicken. Sprinkle the onion soup mix over the soup mixture. Bake at 325 degrees for about 2 hours. Stir twice in the first 30 minutes, as the rice may stick to the pan. When stirring, it is not necessary to keep the chicken on the top of the rice. It may be necessary to add more water.

Kathleen Sullivan, St. Louis University
St. Louis, Missouri

SESAME SEED CHICKEN

1 whole chicken or selected
  chicken pieces, cut up
1½ cups soy sauce
½ cup liquid brown sugar
1 cup sesame seeds

Preheat oven to 350 degrees. Stir soy sauce and brown sugar together in a shallow baking dish. Place chicken in mixture. Let soak 15 minutes on each side. Put chicken in sauce, (bottom of chicken up) in the oven. Cook on this side ½ hour. Turn chicken over. Sprinkle sesame seeds evenly over chicken. Cook ½ hour more. Save sauce to be poured over chicken as a gravy during dinner. Serve with fried rice. Quick, easy and great cold for picnics.

Milo Fay Minnis Keith, University of Oregon
Mercer Island, Washington

CHICKEN WITH SESAME RICE

¼ cup butter (divided)
2 tablespoons sesame seeds
1 cup uncooked regular rice
2 cups chicken broth or stock
  (divided)
1½ teaspoon salt (divided)
1 2½ pound fryer, cut up
⅓ cup flour
1 teaspoon paprika
½ cup dry white wine

Melt 1 tablespoon butter in skillet; add sesame seeds and rice. Cook over moderate heat, stirring frequently until lightly browned. Add 1½ cups chicken broth and ½ teaspoon salt; heat to boiling. Turn into 2 quart casserole and cover. Bake at 300 degrees while browning chicken. Combine flour, remaining salt and paprika in a paper bag. Shake chicken pieces, one or two at a time, in flour mixture until well coated. Brown floured chicken slowly in remaining butter. Remove casserole from oven, place chicken on top. Heat remaining broth in skillet to loosen browned particles from pan and pour over all. Pour wine over chicken and cover. Bake about 40 minutes longer or until chicken is tender. Serves 4 *generously*.

Monica Morse Stallings, University of Arizona
Ventura, California

CHICKEN SOPPA

1 3-pound chicken
1 can cream of chicken soup
1 can cream of celery soup
1 medium size onion, chopped
½ small can green Mexican
  chilies, chopped
½ pound Longhorn cheese, grated
Doritos, plain flavored

Stew chicken. Cut into bite size pieces, save broth and set aside. Combine two cans of soup with a soup can (10 ounces) of the reserved broth, set aside. In bottom of casserole place layer of Doritos, then half the chicken. Sprinkle half of onion and chilies on top, pour half of soup mixture over all. Top with half the cheese. Repeat. Heat thoroughly in a 350 degree oven. Serves 4-6.

Jean Leitzsey Shields, Oklahoma University
Tulsa, Oklahoma

"POOR MAN'S LOBSTER"
(or "Special Chicken")

8 boned and skinned chicken
  breasts
½ cup soy sauce
½ cup pineapple juice
¼ cup oil
1 teaspoon dry mustard
1 tablespoon brown sugar
1 teaspoon ground ginger
1 teaspoon garlic salt
½ teaspoon pepper

Combine all ingredients, marinating breasts for three hours or more. Broil breasts on the second shelf, so as not to be too close to the flame. Broil 10 minutes on each side, or until golden. Be careful that they do not burn, or they will be tough. Serve as you would serve lobster, with melted butter.

Patsy McGahey Henderson,
Washington University
St. Louis, Missouri

CHICKEN SQUARES

2 cans crescent dinner rolls
4 tablespoons melted margarine
6 ounce package cream cheese
2 chickens, boned and cubed or 8
  chicken breast halves, cooked,
  boned and cubed
½ teaspoon salt
¼ teaspoon pepper
8-10 tablespoons milk
1 stick of melted butter
1 box unseasoned croutons,
  crushed
2 tablespoons chives, chopped
2 tablespoons pimientoes,
  chopped.

Melt margarine. Add cream cheese and melt, also. Add chicken, salt, pepper, milk, chives and pimientoes and mix well. Spoon ⅛ of mixture into center of each bisquit square (2 crescent biscuit rolls will form a square). Pull corners of biscuit square to center. Seal edges. Brush all sides and bottom of biscuit dough with melted butter. Roll chicken squares in crushed croutons. Bake on ungreased cookie sheet for 20-25 minutes at 350 degrees. Makes 8.

Katherine Seaborn Portman,
Southern Methodist University
Dallas, Texas

8 slices white bread
2 cups diced cooked chicken
½ cups diced onion
½ cup chopped celery
¼ cup chopped green pepper
1½ cups milk
½ cup mayonnaise
½ teaspoon salt
¼ teaspoon pepper
2 eggs slightly beaten
1 can mushroom soup (undiluted)
½ cup sharp Cheddar cheese,
  grated
1 or 2 teaspoons butter

CHICKEN STRATA

Butter 2 slices bread, cut in 1 inch cubes and set aside. Dice remaining bread and line bottom of baking dish 8x8 inches. Combine chicken, mayonnaise, vegetables, seasonings, milk and eggs, add and pour over bread. Spread buttered cubes on top and place in refrigerator over night. When ready to use, pour soup over the mixture and place in 300 degree oven. Bake one hour, then sprinkle cheese over the top and bake 3 to 4 minutes. Serves 5 to 6.

Katherine L. Gasser, Iowa State University
Interlochen, Michigan

4 cups diced, cooked chicken
¼ pound butter
½ pound canned, sliced
  mushrooms
2 pints cream
4 tablespoons flour
4 tablespoons margarine
2 tablespoons sherry
2 tablespoons dry white wine
½ pound medium noodles
6 tablespoons Parmesan cheese
Salt and pepper to taste

CHICKEN TETRAZINI

Melt butter; sauté mushrooms in butter. Add chicken, cream, both wines, salt and pepper. Bring almost to boiling. Make a paste of the flour and margarine. Stir into mixture. Cook noodles according to package directions. Put noodles into a greased baking pan (large (11x9) lasagna pan). Put chicken mixture over. Sprinkle Parmesan cheese over the top. Bake at 350 degrees for 30-40 minutes.

This is best if made the day before and refrigerated overnight. In that event, sprinkle the Parmesan on just before baking. And be sure to let the dish come to room temperature if it is not a refirgerator-to-oven type. Serves 8 to 10.

Elaine Dennison Pinholster, University of Maryland
Northern Virginia

¼ pound butter or margarine
3 chicken breasts, split and
  skinned
1 cup seedless grapes, halved
1 cup sherry
Lemon juice
Salt and pepper

CHICKEN VERONIQUE

Rub chicken breasts generously with lemon juice, salt and pepper. Melt butter, brown chicken, add wine and simmer (covered) for about 40 minutes. Turn and baste occasionally, and if necessary, add chicken stock or water. Add grapes and simmer 5 or 10 minutes more. Serve with rice.

This is marvelous, and so simple — one of my favorite recipes. Actually, a whole chicken, quartered, can be used, but breasts make it more gourmet.

Linda Wheeler, Southern Methodist University
Santa Fe, New Mexico

CHICKEN ON THE VINE

6 whole boned chicken breasts
Flour, salt, pepper, butter
2 tablespoons grape juice
1 cup seedless grapes
8 ounces mushrooms
1 cup chicken broth
Paprika
½ cup sherry or white wine (or less, according to taste)

Dust chicken with flour, salt and pepper mixture and sauté in butter. Remove chicken. Stir mushrooms into drippings, add two tablespoons flour mixture and grape juice. Continue to stir while adding broth and spices. Stir, simmer, for 10 minutes. Pour in wine and grapes, immediately pour mixture over chicken in baking pan. Cover and bake at 350 degrees for 30 minutes. Remove cover for last 5 minutes of baking.

Nancy E. Lubamersky, University of California
Berkeley, California

VIVA LA CHICKEN!

4 whole chicken breasts
1 dozen corn tortillas
1 can cream of chicken soup
1 can cream of mushroom soup
1 cup of milk
2 tablespoons chopped onion
1 can green chili salsa
½ cup sour cream
½ pound grated sharp cheddar cheese

Cook chicken breasts. When cool bone and cut up in large pieces. Cut tortillas in 1 inch strips. Mix soups, milk, onion and salsa. Butter a shallow baking dish. Add 1 tablespoon of broth from boiled chicken. Arrange strips of tortillas, then place a layer of chicken on tortilla strips, and cover with some of soup mixture. Repeat the layer of tortillas, chicken and soup mixture. Dot with sour cream, and sprinkle cheese on top. Let stand in refrigerator for 24 hours (at least long enough for flavors to blend). Bake at 300 degrees for about one hour or until bubbly hot. (Use a pyrex baking dish that measures 9x13 inches.) Serves 8 to 10.

Beatrice Hill Wittenberg, Past Grand President,
Stanford University
Pasadena, California

Chris Loveberg Montgomery,
California State-San Diego
Orange County, California

ANN'S SWISS ENCHILADAS

1 chopped red onion
2 tablespoons oil
1 garlic clove, crushed
2 cans chopped green chilies
2 cups cooked, diced chicken
Salt to taste
2 cups tomato puree
4 chicken bouillon cubes
2 cups cream
12 corn tortillas
Oil
¼ pound grated Cheddar cheese
¼ pound Monterrey Jack cheese

Sauté onion in oil until transparent. Rinse chilies and add to onions. Add garlic, tomato puree, chicken and salt, simmer uncovered 10 minutes. Put cream in pan and heat, but do not boil. Add bouillon to cream and dissolve. Put ¼ inch oil in another saucepan and heat. Dip first tortilla into hot oil just to coat, then dip into hot cream mixture. Fill tortilla with chicken mixture, roll up and place in baking dish. Repeat with remaining tortillas, pour remaining cream over tops of tortillas. Sprinkle cheeses on top. Bake at 350 degrees for 30 minutes. Serves 12.

Cookbook Committee

BEV'S CHICKEN CREAM ENCHILADAS

Salad oil
1 package (12) corn tortillas
Chicken Filling (directions follow)
⅔ cup whipping cream
2 cups shredded jack cheese
Radishes, pitted ripe olives, and
    fresh coriander (optional) to
    garnish
Lime wedges

In a small frying pan, heat about ¼ inch salad oil over moderate heat. Fry one tortilla at a time, turning once, just until limp but not crisp. Drain on paper towels. Add oil to pan as needed. Spoon about ⅓ cup of the chicken filling down the center of each tortilla and roll to enclose. Set enchiladas seam side down in a 9x12 inch casserole, side by side. (Cover and refrigerate the dish at this point, if you have made it ahead.) Moisten tops of the enchiladas with the cream, then sprinkle cheese evenly over them. Bake uncovered in a 375 degree oven for 20 minutes to heat through. (If chilled, bake for 30 minutes; cover the casserole for the first 15 minutes). Garnish with radishes, olives, and coriander before serving. Pass lime wedges to squeeze on individual servings. Makes 6 main dish serving.

Carol Knox, Iowa State University
Plano, Texas

CHICKEN FILLING FOR ENCHILADAS

2 large onions, thinly sliced
2 tablespoons butter or
    margarine
2 cups diced, cooked chicken,
    skin removed
½ cup canned, roasted sweet red
    pepper or pimientos, chopped
2 small packages (3 ounces each)
    cream cheese, diced
Salt to taste

In a large frying pan, cook onions in butter or margarine, over moderate heat, stirring occasionally, for about 20 minutes, until limp and just beginning to brown. Remove from heat and add 2 cups diced, cooked chicken, red pepper or pimientos and cream cheese. Mix lightly with 2 forks to blend, then season with salt to taste.

Carol Knox, Iowa State University
Plano, Texas

CALIFORNIA GREEN CHILI ENCHILADAS

2 cans of mushroom soup
1 4-ounce can green chilies,
    whole
1 package 12 tortillas
¾ pound Jack cheese
Sour cream
1 cup Cheddar cheese

Wash to remove seeds from chilies. Chop fine. Mix with soup. Pour ½ of sauce into bottom of a baking dish. Dip tortillas in hot oil to soften, but do not fry. Cut Jack cheese into 12 fingers. Place these in tortillas, roll up, place in dish seam side down, and cover with remaining sauce. Top with 1 cup cheese, grated. Bake at 350 degrees for 35 minutes, or in microwave oven, roast setting, 12 to 15 minutes. Before serving, top with sour cream. Serve with refried beans. Ole!

Mavis Schutz, San Diego State University
Orange County, California

CHICKEN ENCHILADAS

1 can mushroom soup
1 large can evaporated milk
1½ cup grated cheese
2 cans (6½-ounces) boned
  chicken
1 medium chopped onions
1 small can green chilies,
  chopped
1 dozen tortillas, quartered

Sauté onions and chilies. Mix soup, milk and ½ cup of the cheese over low heat until cheese melts. Add cut-up chicken and sauteed onion and chilies. Put layer of tortillas, layer of sauce in large pan (9x13 inch) or deep casserole dish; repeat layers. Sprinkle 1 cup cheese and paprika on top. Bake at 350 degrees for 30 to 40 minutes.

Cindy Blanton, Southern Methodist University
Dallas, Texas

SOUR CREAM CHICKEN ENCHILADAS

4 chicken breasts
1 6-ounce carton sour cream
1 medium onion
8 ounces Monterrey Jack cheese,
  shredded
½ jar, or 4 ounces, "La Victoria
  Green Tomatilla Sauce"
8 flour tortillas
1 cup shredded Cheddar cheese

Place chicken in pot, add 2 cups of water and simmer until done. Cool and cut up into small chunks. Set aside. Sauté onion and add to cheese, sour cream and "Tomatilla" sauce. Stir all together. Now take a flour tortilla and add a small helping of chicken and roll it up and place it in a 13x9½ inch baking pan (crosswise). Repeat with each tortilla. Pour sauce over tortillas. Cover with foil and bake at 350 degrees for 30 minutes. Serve with shredded Cheddar cheese on top.

Joan Lonnborg DeLaGarza,
University of Wisconsin-Madison
Dallas, Texas

SOUR CREAM CHEESE ENCHILADAS

12 corn tortillas
Hot lard
1 pound grated Jack cheese
  (reserve 1 cup for top)
1 can (4 ounces) peeled green
  chilies
1½ cup salsa or canned tomatoes
2 cups chopped cooked chicken
2½ cups dairy sour cream
  (reserve 1 cup for top)

Filling: Use 1½ cup of sour cream, all of chicken, season with salt and pepper.
Dip tortillas in hot lard. On each one put ¼ cup cheese, ⅓ of a chili strip and 1/12 of filling; top with 2 tablespoons tomatoes. Roll and put in baking dish, seam side down. Pour remaining sour cream over all and sprinkle with reserved cheese. Bake in moderate oven (350 degrees) 20 to 25 minutes. Makes six servings.

Shirley Grounds Duncan, Kansas University
Tucson, Arizona

SWISS ENCHILADA

4 chicken breasts, boned
2 tablespoons onion, chopped
2 tomatoes, chopped
10 corn tortillas
1 pint whipping cream
4 chicken bouillon cubes
1 pound Jack cheese
Salt and pepper
2 tablespoons butter

Brown onion in butter, simmer for 5 minutes. Add tomatoes, simmer 5 minutes. Bake chicken in foil, seasoned with Lawry's seasoned salt for 1 hour. Bone and shred. Add to tomato mixture and simmer 20 minutes. Fry tortillas for 8 to 10 seconds on each side, then drain on paper towel. Grate Jack cheese. Fill tortillas with chicken mixture and roll. Place in lightly greased pan and cover with grated cheese. Dissolve bouillon cubes in whipping cream, then pour over enchiladas. Cover with foil. Bake at 350 degrees for 30 minutes, then remove foil and bake 15 minutes.

Leslie A. Northrup, Northern Arizona University
Flagstaff, Arizona

TURKEY A LA ENDI

¼ pound butter
1 cup cream
½ cup flour
½ pound sliced mushrooms
1½ teaspoons salt
3 tablespoons pimiento
1 cup milk
1 green pepper, diced
1 cup consommé or bouillon
3-4 cups diced turkey
½ cup sherry (optional)

Cook diced green pepper in consommé and sauté mushrooms in 2 tablespoons butter. Make cream sauce of remaining butter, flour, cream and milk in double boiler. Add salt, turkey, mushrooms, pimiento, green pepper and consommé and heat to blend flavors. Add sherry before serving, but do not boil after wine is added. Serve on toast points, over rice, or any favorite base.

Gloria Swanson Nelson, Oklahoma University
Dallas, Texas

TURKEY HOT BROWN

1 10 pound turkey roll, sliced and thawed
20 tomatoes, sliced
2 loaves sandwich bread (1½ pound size)
Cheese Sauce:
8 cups grated American cheese (about 4 pounds)
2 sticks butter or margarine
1 cup flour
8 cups milk
2 teaspoons salt
½ teaspoon pepper
(Makes 12 cups)

Cheese Sauce: Melt the butter in a double boiler (or set LARGE pan inside of another pan filled with a little water.) Add flour, salt and pepper. Stir until creamy smooth (3 to 5 minutes on medium high.) Add milk, stir until thickened. Add grated cheese a cup at a time. Pour into a crock pot. Turn on low. Will keep to serve for up to 6 hours if necessary.
Bake thawed turkey roll 45 minutes at 350 degrees in foil.
To Serve: Toast bread. Put 1 slice of toast on plate, top with 1 turkey slice, 1 slice tomato and cover with hot cheese sauce. (Fix as company arrives, NOT before.) This works SUPER after a football game, as turkey and baked beans can be baked 45 minutes, at 350 degrees; right before leaving, turn off and leave in oven. Make sauce ahead and leave in crock pot on low.
Smaller amounts of cheese sauce (1½ cup): 2 tablespoon butter, 2 tablespoons flour, ¼ teaspoon salt, dash pepper, 1 cup milk, 1 cup cheese.
Follow above directions, not necessary to put in crock pot, may serve immediately.

Sharon Overton, Indiana State University
Evansville, Indiana

TURKEY TETRAZZINI

2 4-ounce jars sliced mushrooms
1 tablespoon lemon juice
1 teaspoon grated onion
3 tablespoons butter or
    margarine
3 tablespoons flour
1½ teaspoon salt
¼ teaspoon each, pepper, nutmeg
2 cups chicken broth
1⅓ cups milk or half and half
1 green pepper, chopped
1 2-ounce jar pimiento, chopped
½ pound spaghetti, cooked,
    drained
4 ounces diced cooked turkey (or
    chicken)
½ cup grated Parmesan or Swiss
    cheese

Add lemon juice and onion to drained mushrooms. Melt butter in saucepan, blend in flour. Add salt, pepper and nutmeg. Gradually add chicken broth and milk. Cook and stir until thickened. Add mushrooms, green pepper, pimento and cooked spagetti to half of the sauce. Pour half of this mixture into a greased, shallow (9x13x2 inch) baking dish. Mix turkey (or chicken) with the remaining half of the sauce. Spoon over spaghetti mixture and top with remaining spaghetti mixture. Sprinkle cheese over all. Bake at 375 degrees for 25 minutes. Serves 8.

Polly Grove Haliday, Northwestern University
Evanston-North Shore, Illinois

DIRTY RICE

1 cup raw rice
4 ounce can mushrooms (or fresh)
1-2 bell peppers, chopped
Garlic
Soy sauce
Tabasco
2-3 tablespoons oil
¼-½ pound chicken livers
1 medium onion, chopped
(Water chestnuts, green beans or
    peas may be substituted for
    chicken livers)

Prepare rice according to package directions. Heat oil in a large pot and sauté livers. When they are nearly done, add mushrooms, peppers, onion and sauté until done. Add the cooked rice, stir well to mix, and add a bit more oil if necessary. Season with garlic, Tabasco, and soy sauce to taste. This will taste better if prepared in advance and reheated before serving.

Elizabeth Sloan Phillips (Kiki), Washington University
State College, Pennsylvania

BAKED CHICKEN SANDWICHES

3 cups cut up cooked chicken
1 can cream of mushroom soup
1 can Franco American Chicken
    Gravy
2 tablespoons chopped green
    pepper
2 tablespoons chopped onion
1 can thinly sliced water
    chestnuts
White bread
3 eggs
2 tablespoons milk
Potato chips

Mix chicken, soup, gravy, green pepper, water chestnuts and onion together. Cut crusts from bread. Spread bottom slice of bread as thickly as possible. Place top on sandwich — do not press down. Wrap sandwiches, individually, and freeze for at least 24 hours. (Keeps much longer.) When ready to bake and serve, beat eggs and milk together. Dip whole frozen sandwiches in egg mixture, then roll in finely crushed potato chips until all sides are coated. Place on slightly greased cookie sheet. Bake at 300 degrees for 1 hour or until slightly brown and crispy. Makes 6-8 sandwiches.

Jeannette Collins Sicks, Iowa State University
Ames, Iowa

Seafood

CLAMS CASINO

2 dozen clams, raw, opened
6 slices bacon
½ diced green pepper
½ diced onion
Garlic powder to taste
½ stick melted butter
4-5 diced pimientoes
Dash celery salt

Cook bacon strips. Mix together pepper, onion, garlic powder, butter, pimientoes, and celery salt. Put teaspoon of mixture on each clam. Place ¼ strip of bacon on top. Bake at 350 degrees for 15 minutes.

Kathryn Hart, Lehigh University
Philadelphia North Suburban, Pennsylvania

SPAGHETTI WITH WHITE CLAM SAUCE

2 cans (7½-ounces) minced clams
4 medium cloves garlic, minced
4 tablespoons chopped parsley
4 tablespoons butter or margarine
2 cans (10½-ounce) cream of mushroom soup
½ cup milk or light cream
3-4 tablespoons grated Parmesan cheese
½ pound spaghetti, cooked and drained

Drain clams; reserve liquid. In saucepan, cook clams, garlic and parsley in butter for a few minutes. Stir in soup, milk, clam liquid and cheese. Cook over low heat 10 minutes. Stir now and then. Serve over spaghetti, with garlic bread and a tossed green salad. Serves 4.

Betty Bussey Demarke, San Diego State
Aiea, Hawaii

CHARLIE'S COQUILLE ST. JACQUES

6 tablespoons butter
3 tablespoons flour
1 teaspoon salt
⅛ teaspoon white pepper
¼ cup onion, finely chopped
2 tablespoons Madiera or sweet sherry
3 tablespoons bread crumbs
½ pound scallops, sliced
½ pound shrimp, cooked and cleaned
¼ pound crab meat
½ pound mushrooms, sliced
2 cups light cream

Melt 4 tablespoons butter in saucepan, blend in flour, salt, pepper. Gradually add cream, stirring steadily to boiling point. Cook over low heat five minutes. Melt remaining butter in skillet; sauté scallops, onion and mushrooms in it. Combine sauce, shrimp, scallops, mushrooms, crab meat and wine. Mix lightly and taste for seasoning. Spoon into 6 scallop shells (or casserole) and sprinkle with bread crumbs. Bake at 400 degrees until browned.

Bory Reid, Past Grand President,
University of Michigan
Landrum, South Carolina

COQUILLE ST. JACQUES

2 pounds scallops
2 cups dry sherry
1 bay leaf
1 pound fresh mushrooms
1 chopped onion
½ cup butter
3 tablespoons flour
2 tablespoons lemon juice
1 teaspoon salt
½ chopped green pepper
½ teaspoon paprika
⅛ teaspoon cayenne pepper
Grated Parmesan cheese

Simmer scallops 10 minutes in sherry with bay leaf. Drain, but reserve broth. Preheat oven to 325 degrees. Saute mushrooms, onions, green pepper in butter until lightly brown. Add flour. Stir in wine broth and lemon juice. Cook, stirring until thickened. If too thick add water. Add seasonings and scallops. Pour into buttered casserole. Sprinkle with cheese. Bake at 325 degrees for 20 minutes. Serve over rice.

Arline Ely Chafey, University of Michigan
Ft. Lauderdale, Florida

BAKED AVOCADOS WITH CRAB MEAT

3 avocados
1 can crab meat
4 tablespoons butter
6 tablespoons flour
1½ cups milk
⅜ teaspoon salt
Few grains pepper
1 tablespoons minced onion
3 tablespoons lemon juice
½ cup grated American cheese

Melt butter in saucepan, blend in flour and seasonings. Add milk gradually, stirring constantly. Cook until thickened. Add crab meat and minced onion. Peel avocados and cut in half lengthwise. Rub the insides with lemon juice — about 1 teaspoon for each half. Fill with creamed crab meat and sprinkle with grated cheese. Place in baking pan and pour in water to ½ inch in depth. Bake at 350 degrees for 15 minutes. Serves 6.

Lois McBride Dehn, Past Grand President,
University of Washington
Seattle, Washington

CRAB AND CHEESE BAKE

3 slices of bread without crusts
½ pound (or can) of crab meat
1 cup grated cheese
3 eggs
2 cups milk
Season to taste

Butter the bread and cut into strips. Place in the bottom of a greased casserole. Over the bread, spread the crab meat, and ½ of the grated cheese. Season to taste. Beat the eggs and milk together and pour over the crab, cheese, and bread. Sprinkle remainder of cheese on top. Let stand at least one hour before baking. Bake at 325 degrees for 1 hour.

Virginia Gray Douglas, Washington University
Seattle, Washington

CRAB SELDOVIA

1 cup fresh bread crumbs
2 tablespoons melted butter
1 tablespoon capers
1 teaspoon salt
1 teaspoon English mustard
1 cup mayonnaise
1 pound lump crabmeat
2 tablespoons chopped parsley
2 tablespoons dry sherry
⅛ teaspoon cayenne

Mix crumbs with butter, capers, salt, mustard and sherry. Mix with mayonnaise. Fold carefully into crabmeat. Crab should be stirred as little as possible so as not to shred. Pile lightly into crab shells or ramekins. Dust with cayenne and top with additional mayonnaise. Heat in 375 degree oven for 15 minutes. Brown under broiler. Garnish with chopped parsley. Serves 6.

With sourdough bread and a salad, this is a terrific dinner for an impromptu dinner party — thirty minutes of work!

Jeanne Abbott, University of Missouri
Anchorage, Alaska

DEVILED CRAB

1 tablespoon butter
3 tablespoons onion, chopped finely
2 tablespoons green pepper, chopped finely
1 cup crab meat
¼ teaspoon dry mustard
1 teaspoon Worcestershire sauce
2 dashes cayenne
1 tablespoon bread crumbs
2 tablespoons mayonnaise

Sauté the onion and green pepper in the 1 tablespoon butter. Add and mix remaining ingredients together. Fill 4 seafood scallop shells with the crab mixture. Sprinkle lightly with additional bread crumbs. Dot with butter. Place shells on a cookie sheet. Bake at 350 degrees for 20 minutes.

Mrs. John L. Strong, U.C.L.A.
Monterey Bay, California

MARYLAND LADY CRAB CAKES

1 pound crabmeat
1 cup Italian seasoned breadcrumbs
1 large egg or 2 small
About ¼ cup mayonnaise
½ teaspoon salt
¼ teaspoon pepper
1 teaspoon Worcestershire sauce
1 teaspoon dry mustard

Remove all cartilage from crabmeat. In a bowl, mix breadcrumbs, egg, mayonnaise and seasonings. Add crabmeat and mix gently but thoroughly. If mixture is too dry, add a bit more mayonnaise. Shape into 6 cakes. Cook cakes in frying pan with just enough fat to prevent sticking until browned or 5 minutes to each side. If desired, crab cakes may be deep fried at 350 degrees for 2 to 3 minutes.

Barbara Harding White, Western Maryland College
Washington, D.C.

MARYLAND SEASHORE CRAB

1 pound fresh or canned
  crabmeat
½ cup mayonnaise
1½ cups sharp Cheddar cheese,
  shredded

Flake crabmeat and mix with mayonnaise. Fill buttered ramekins and cover with shredded cheese. Bake at 350 degrees for 25 minutes. Makes 4 servings. Also can be served on toast. (Broil until the cheese melts) Great for lunch. Very easy recipe.

Mary Anne Youngwood, Pennsylvania State University
Washington, D.C.

CRAB MEAT AU GRATIN I

4 tablespoons butter
5 tablespoons flour
1 cup heavy cream
1 cup milk
1 cup freshly-grated Parmesan
  cheese
1 pound all lump crab meat
  (fresh)
Salt and pepper to taste

Melt butter, add flour to make smooth roux. Add cream and milk slowly until cream sauce is thick and smooth. Add cheese, except for three heaping tablespoons. Since the cheese is salty, now is the time to add salt and pepper to taste. Mix in the crab meat lightly, being careful to preserve it in lump form. Turn into a casserole, sprinkling the remaining Parmesan on top. If you expect the dinner will be delayed either by late arrivals or the hostess' enjoyment of the conversation over the hors d'oeuvres, brown the casserole lingeringly at 325 degrees. If you want to hurry the serving, bake at 400 degrees until brown and bubbling. Supposedly this dish serves six. However, in our family, it serves three (uncomfortably, I might add).

Hon. Helen Meyner, U.S. House of Representatives,
Colorado College
Washington, D.C.

CRAB MEAT AU GRATIN II

4 tablespoons butter
1 tablespoon chopped onion
1 tablespoon chopped green
  pepper
2 tablespoons flour
1 cup milk
½ teaspoon salt
Dash cayenne pepper
12 ounces crabmeat (frozen or
  canned)
¾ cup shredded Cheddar cheese
Dash Worcestershire sauce
1 drop Tabasco
2 tablespoons sherry

Sauté onion and green pepper in the butter. Stir in the flour. Add milk, salt and cayenne pepper. Stir and simmer. Add crabmeat, cheese, Worcestershire sauce, Tabasco and sherry. Stir and simmer. Top with more cheese and brown under broiler. This recipe is from the Virgin Islands.

Sylvia Hardy Trewin, Iowa State University
Richardson, Texas

CRABMEAT SHERRY CASSEROLE

½ pound fresh mushrooms, sliced
5 tablespoons butter
3 tablespoons flour
1½ cup milk
1½ cup grated Cheddar cheese
¼ cup sherry
Fresh bread crumbs
½ teaspoon salt
⅛ teaspoon pepper
1½ cups crabmeat, cut into
   pieces
4 hard boiled eggs, sliced
¾ cup chopped walnuts

Sauté mushrooms in 2 tablespoons butter until lightly browned. Set aside. In saucepan, melt remaining 3 tablespoons butter; stir in flour and milk. Bring to boil, cook, stirring until thickened. Add cheese, sherry, salt and pepper. Simmer, stirring occasionally, about ten minutes. In a buttered, baking dish, arrange in alternate layers: crabmeat, mushrooms, eggs and walnuts. Pour on cheese sauce. Sprinkle with fresh bread crumbs. Bake 20 minutes in a 350 degree oven until hot and bubbly and crumbs are lightly browned.

Victoria Beach, Gettysburg College
Wyckoff, New Jersey

CRAB-SHRIMP CASSEROLE

½ cup chopped green pepper
¼ cup minced onion
1 cup chopped celery
1 can crabmeat
1 can small shrimp
1 teaspoon Worcestershire sauce
1 cup mayonnaise
½ teaspoon salt
2 cups crushed cornflakes
Butter

Combine all the ingredients and mix lightly. Place in a baking dish; cover with 2 cups crushed cornflakes. Dot with butter; sprinkle with paprika. Bake at 350 degrees for 30 minutes. Serves 6.

Jean Hervey, University of Missouri
Shawnee Mission, Kansas

CASSIE'S CRAB SOUFFLE

12 slices bread, trim crust
2 cans crab meat (or 1 can crab
   and 1 can shrimp)
½ cup mayonnaise
1 small chopped onion
1 chopped green pepper
1 cup chopped celery
3 cups milk
4 eggs
1 can cream of mushroom soup
Paprika
Grated Parmesan cheese

Cut 6 slices bread and line the pan. Beat eggs with milk. Mix crab, mayonnaise, onion, celery, green pepper and add to egg and milk mixture. Pour over bread. Top with remaining bread. Put in refrigerator overnight. Next day, put in oven at 325 degrees for 15 minutes. Take out and let set. Spoon *undiluted* cream of mushroom soup over, sprinkle with cheese and paprika. Return to oven at 325 degrees for 1 hour. Wonderful luncheon dish.

Latane Jordan Graham, Memphis State University
Dallas, Texas

BAMBI'S CRAB CASSEROLE

2 cans crabmeat
6 hard boiled eggs
2 cups half & half
1 cup mayonnaise
2 teaspoons finely chopped onion
Salt and pepper
1 can thinly sliced water
chestnuts
3 cups Pepperidge Farm dressing
mix (the original kind)
1 stick margarine
2 tablespoons parsley
Dash curry

Melt butter and sauté parsley and bread crumbs — reserving 1 cup for topping. Add to other ingredients. Pour into 2 small or 1 large casserole. Top with crumbs. Bake at 350 degrees till bubbly and brown. Serve with green salad and French bread. Serves 8. Really delicious!

Julia Terry Templeton, Southern Methodist University
Charleston, South Carolina Crescent Circle

CREOLE CRAB-RICE CASSEROLE

⅔ cup uncooked rice
1 small onion, minced
1 small green pepper, chopped
2 tablespoons butter
1 large can tomatoes, about 20
ounces
1 teaspoon seasoned salt
¼ cup Parmesan cheese
¼ teaspoon seasoned pepper
1 teaspoon sugar
½ teaspoon Worcestershire
1 bay leaf
6 whole peppercorns
2 whole cloves
1 7-ounce can crab meat
Salt and pepper

Cook rice according to package instructions. Sauté onion and green pepper in butter for 2 or 3 minutes. Add tomatoes, seasoned salt and pepper, sugar and Worcestershire. Tie whole spices in small piece of cheesecloth and add to tomatoes. Simmer uncovered for 10 minutes. Add crabmeat, rice and salt and pepper to taste. Put in 1½ quart casserole and sprinkle with cheese. Bake at 375 degrees for 30 minutes. Serves 4 to 6.

Jacki Falkenroth, University of Nevada-Reno
Chicago Northwest Suburban, Illinois

BEER BATTER FOR FISH

2 10-inch halibut fillets or other
white fish
2 cups biscuit mix
2 beaten eggs
1 can beer
Dash garlic salt and pepper
Corn oil, enough to cover bottom
of electric fry pan

Cut fish into serving chunks. Measure biscuit mix; add garlic salt and pepper, eggs and beer to consistency of thin pancake batter. Place chunks of fish in batter for 10 minutes. Deep fry in corn oil heated to 370 degrees about 10 to 15 minutes. Also may be fried in electric fry pan by turning until lightly browned all around. Serves 6 to 8.

Mary Rice Raber, Washington University
Seattle, Washington

FABULOUS FISH FILLETS

5 small or 3 medium fillets of
snapper or other fish
2 tablespoons butter
2 tablespoons white wine
3 diced shallots
4 tablespoons diced mushrooms
Salt and pepper
1 can crabmeat or 1 package
frozen crab
½ cup mayonnaise
1½ tablespoons prepared
mustard
1½ tablespoons lemon juice
2 tablespoons Vermouth or white
wine

Melt the butter; add the 2 tablespoons white wine, diced shallots, diced mushrooms. Salt and pepper the fillets. Lay them in the bottom of a shallow pan. Cover with the crabmeat. Pour the above mixture over them. Bake at 350 degrees for 10 minutes depending upon thickness of fish. Then combine mayonnaise, prepared mustard, lemon juice and Vermouth or wine. Pour over fish and crab and broil until bubbly and beginning to brown. Crumbs may be then added for a bit more interest.

Estelle Lindow Pfeifer, University of Wisconsin
Ft. Lauderdale, Florida

STUFFED FLOUNDER

1 pound flounder fillets
1 can cream of potato soup
1 cup white wine
1 small can mushroom caps
¾ cup fresh bread crumbs
Salt and pepper
1 or 2 teaspoons dill seed (to
taste)

Dilute soup with ½ cup water and white wine. Add mushrooms. Salt and pepper fillets. Sprinkle bread crumbs over fillets and roll up jelly-roll style. Place fillets in baking dish, sprinkle with dill. Pour soup-mushroom mixture over fillets. Bake at 350 degrees for 30-35 minutes. Serves 4.

Christie L. Grossheider Carter, Washington University
St. Louis, Missouri

SALMON CROQUETTES I

2 cups or 1 can salmon
½ cup flour
1 cup self-rising meal
1 teaspoon salt
2 eggs
1 teaspoon Worcestershire sauce
Onion to taste (optional)

Mix ingredients well. If mixture seems dry, add enough milk to get to consistency for rolling into small balls. Roll into small balls, then flatten to patties. Fry in HOT vegetable oil until brown, turn and brown on other side. Drain on paper towel. Serve hot.
Variation: Add a can of cream of celery soup instead of milk.

Margaret Gatlin 'Meg' Smith, Florida State University
Minneapolis-St. Paul, Minnesota

SALMON CROQUETTES II

1 can red salmon (16-ounce)
1 small green pepper, chopped
1 small onion, chopped
1 or 2 eggs, beaten
Salt and pepper

Debone salmon, mix with other ingredients. Quantities of other ingredients can be varied according to taste. Mold into patties, brown in margarine. Serve with white sauce and drained boiled peas. Serves 6.

Barb Tate, Vanderbilt University
Cincinnati, Ohio

COLD POACHED SALMON WITH LEMON SAUCE OR CUCUMBER MAYONNAISE

Salmon:
1 onion
2 stalks celery
1 cup water
¼ teaspoon salt
3 pound piece fresh salmon
Sauce:
3 beaten egg yolks
3½ tablespoons sugar
½ tablespoon salt
Juice of 1½ lemons
1 cup strained fish broth
2 teaspoons cornstarch

Simmer ingredients for the salmon together ½ hour. Cool. Prepare sauce by combining yolks, sugar, salt, lemons. Add 1 cup fish broth. Cook until thick. If more sauce is desired, add corn starch and ½ cup more broth. Serve over cold salmon.

Cucumber Mayonnaise: Combine 1 cup mayonnaise, 3 tablespoons lemon juice, dash Tabasco, ½ cup cucumbers chopped and drained. Serve over cold salmon.

This is first-rate to serve guests in summer.

Jeanne Abbott, University of Missouri
Anchorage, Alaska

SALMON LOAF WITH SHRIMP SAUCE

2 1-pound cans salmon
¼ cup finely minced onion
¼ cup chopped parsley
¼ cup lemon juice
½ teaspoon salt
½ teaspoon pepper
½ to 1 teaspoon thyme
2 cups course cracker crumbs
About ½ cup milk
4 eggs, well beaten
¼ cup melted butter

Drain salmon, saving liquid. Flake salmon into bowl. Add next 7 ingredients. Mix lightly. Add salmon liquid plus enough milk to make 1 cup. Add eggs and butter. Mix lightly. Spoon into greased 2 quart loaf pan or casserole. Bake at 350 degrees for 1 hour or until loaf is set in center. Serves 8 to 10.

Shrimp Sauce: Heat a can of frozen condensed cream of shrimp soup according to directions on label. Add ¼ cup milk. Stir until smooth. Spoon onto hot salmon loaf.

Sue Bireline, Iowa State University
Newell, Iowa

SALMON SOUFFLE

3 tablespoons melted butter
3 tablespoons flour
1½ cup milk
2 eggs, separated
½ teaspoon salt
¼ teaspoon nutmeg
Dash pepper
1 1-pound can red salmon

Melt butter in top of double boiler. Add flour and stir until smooth. Add milk slowly, while stirring. Cook over boiling water until smooth and thickened. Beat egg yolks, then add sauce slowly while stirring. Add seasonings; fold in salmon in coarse flakes. Beat egg whites stiff; fold into salmon. Turn into greased 1½ quart casserole. Bake at 350 degrees for 45 minutes. Garnish (and use on top of individual servings) with lemon. Serves 4-6.

Lorraine Forester Grigsby, University of Wyoming
Cheyenne, Wyoming

1½ cups cooked Uncle Ben's wild
  rice mix
1 cup chopped green pepper
½ cup chopped onion
1 cup mayonnaise
1 can sliced drained water
  chestnuts
12 ounces crabmeat
½ cup chopped celery
12 ounce package cooked shrimp
1 cup tomato juice
Salt and pepper

SEA FOOD CASSEROLE

Mix the above ingredients except for topping. Place in 2½ quart greased casserole. Cover with topping mixture. Sprinkle paprika on top. Bake at 350 degrees for 35 minutes.
Topping:
¾ cup sliced almonds, toasted in butter
¾ cup fresh shredded Cheddar cheese
Sue Ward Ragsdale, Southern Methodist University
Dallas, Texas

1 small onion, minced
⅓ cup green pepper, chopped
⅓ cup celery chopped
1 pound crabmeat (about 2 cups)
2 pounds shrimp (about 3 cups),
  cooked
Dash salt
¾ cups mayonnaise
¾ cups Durkee's salad dressing

SHRIMP/CRAB CASSEROLE

Cook onion, pepper, and celery slowly in butter or margarine until tender but not brown. Mix all ingredients together and place in buttered casserole. Top with buttered bread or cracker crumbs or crushed corn flakes. Bake at 350 degrees for 30 minutes. Serves 8.
Mary Alice Betts, William and Mary
Orlando-Winter Park, Florida

1 cup uncooked rice
1 pound shrimp (cooked and
  cleaned)
1 can cream of mushroom soup
1 can evaporated milk
½ pound grated Swiss cheese
½ green pepper, chopped
1 medium onion, chopped
Lemon

SHRIMP CASSEROLE A LA STOCKTON

Sauté onion and green pepper until soft. Cook rice as directed. (You will have two cups). Combine all ingredients. Add a bit of lemon juice or grated lemon rind on top. Bake ½ hour at 350 degrees. Cooking time critical; if allowed to stand, it will dry out. This recipe makes a lot, so use a large bowl.
Connie Spanier, Oregon State University
San Francisco, California

1 pound shrimp (16-18)
¼ cup milk
1 egg
½ cup bread crumbs
½ teaspoon paprika, salt and
  pepper
1 pound crabmeat
2 tablespoons mayonnaise
⅛ teaspoon Tabasco sauce
1 teaspoon prepared mustard
2 slices fresh bread, cubed with
  crusts removed
1 teaspoon Worcestershire sauce
1 medium onion, minced
½ green pepper, finely chopped
½ cup melted butter or margarine

BAKED STUFFED SHRIMP

Peel uncooked shrimp, leaving tail shells on. Split shrimp and spread apart, butterfly fashion. Dip uncooked shrimp into milk and egg mixture, then in bread crumbs which have been combined with paprika. Combine crabmeat and next five ingredients. Saute onion and green pepper in 2 tablespoons butter or margarine. Firmly stuff shrimp with combined crabmeat, onion, and green pepper mixture. Place shrimp tail side up on a greased, shallow baking dish. Baste with melted butter. Bake at 400 degrees about 15 minutes or until brown. Serve piping hot. Serves 4.
Carol Coe Cole, University of Denver
Montgomery, Alabama

KATHARINE'S SHRIMP AND CHEESE CASSEROLE

6 slices bread
2 cans shrimp
½ pound Old English cheese, sliced
¼ cup butter or margarine, melted
½ teaspoon dry mustard
3 whole eggs
2 cups milk

Break bread in pieces about the size of a quarter, Break cheese into bite sized pieces. Arrange shrimp, bread and cheese in several layers in greased casserole. Pour melted butter over this. Beat eggs. Add mustard and then milk. Pour this over casserole and let stand covered in the refrigerator overnight, or a minimum of 3½ hours. Bake 1 hour at 350 degrees covered — may be uncovered the last 10 minutes to brown.

Jocelyn Birch Burdick, Northwestern University
Fargo-Moorhead, North Dakota

SHRIMP CURRY

1 cup mayonnaise or salad dressing
1 teaspoon curry powder
⅔ cup evaporated milk
Dash paprika
1½ cups cooked shrimp
2 tablespoons chopped pimento, drained
1 tablespoon chopped onion
3 tablespoons ketchup
2½-ounce can mushrooms
¼ cup white wine

Blend curry powder into mayonnaise. Gradually add evaporated milk and dash paprika. Heat over low heat, in skillet. Add remaining ingredients except wine. Heat thoroughly, stirring occasionally. Add wine. Serve over rice. Serves 4.

Diane Gay Winterhalter, Michigan State University
Columbus, Ohio

SOUR CREAM SHRIMP CURRY

⅓ cup butter
½ cup chopped onion
¼ cup chopped green pepper
2 cloves garlic, minced
2 cups sour cream
2 teaspoons lemon juice
2 teaspoons curry
¾ teaspoon salt
½ teaspoon ginger
⅛ teaspoon chili pepper
3 cups cooked shrimp
4 cups cooked rice
½ cup slivered almonds

Melt butter, add onion, garlic and green pepper. Cook until tender but not brown. Stir in sour cream, lemon juice, seasonings, and shrimp. Cook over *low* heat, stirring constantly, just until hot. (Sauce is thin). Serve immediately over hot rice with slivered almonds. Serves 6.

Carolyn Coe Cole, University of Texas
Dallas, Texas

SHRIMP WITH DILL AND LEMON SAUCE

2 pounds shrimp
¼ pound sweet butter
Salt and pepper to taste
1 tablespoon chopped fresh dill or 2 teaspoons dried dill weed
Juice of one lemon
6 drops Tabasco sauce
1 teaspoon Worcestershire sauce

With a pair of kitchen shears, cut the shell of the shrimp down the back and discard. Wash shrimp under cold running water to remove intestinal tract. Dry the shrimp. Melt the butter in a skillet. When hot, add shrimp. Shake skillet occasionally so shrimp will cook on both sides. When shrimp are red in color and cooked through, about 3 or 4 minutes, sprinkle with remaining ingredients and serve immediately.

Nell Taylor Wolfe, Iowa State University
Westchester, New York

SHRIMP MARSEILLAISE

20 large shrimp
¾ teaspoon salt
¼ teaspoon freshly ground black pepper
½ teaspoon leaf saffron or ¼ teaspoon powdered
1 large shallot, chopped
1 tablespoon chopped parsley
½ tablespoon thyme (fresh) or ¼ teaspoon dried
3 tablespoons olive oil
juice of two lemons
¼ pound butter
2 small cloves garlic, chopped

Peel shrimp, but leave on last tail segment. Devein. Rinse and dry. Place salt, pepper, saffron, shallot, garlic, thyme, olive oil and lemon juice in a bowl. Cover the shrimp with the marinade and let stand in the refrigerator 1-2 hours. Turn once or twice. Melt butter in a small pan and set aside. Broil shrimp 2-3 minutes a side. Arrange on warm platter and sprinkle with parsley. Pour pan drippings and extra marinade into butter. Heat sauce to boiling and serve separately with the shrimp. 4-6 servings.
Delicious!

Susan K. Sismondo, University of Michigan
Westchester County, New York

SHRIMP VIENNESE

1 pound cooked, shelled and deveined shrimp (takes 2 pounds if not cleaned)
8 large fresh mushrooms, including stems, sliced
1 tablespoon minced fresh onion
½ cup margarine (save 2 tablespoons for dotting)
1 tablespoon flour
1 tablespoon fresh dill (1 teaspoon if dried)
½ cup chicken broth (may be canned)
½ cup light cream
1 tablespoon white wine
½ large lemon, juiced
2 cups cooked rice

Sauté mushrooms and onions in margarine. Stir in flour and simmer a minute; then stir in chicken broth, cream, wine and lemon juice, stirring constantly; cook until sauce thickens. Add dill, then salt and pepper to taste. Place rice in casserole dish, fold all but 9 shrimp into sauce and spoon over rice. Use the 9 shrimp to decorate the top and dot with the remaining margarine. Use a 1½ quart casserole. Bake at 325 degrees for about 15 minutes. Serves 4 generously.

Gladys Hecker Myles, Washington University
St. Louis, Missouri

TUNA CASSEROLE

1 can tuna
1 can chinese noodles
1 can water chestnuts
1 cup chopped celery
3 green onions, chopped
1 can mushroom soup
¼ cup cold water
¼ cup cashews, chopped

Mix together and pour into a well greased casserole. Bake for 30 minutes at 325 degrees.

Bette Crimmins Simcox, Lake Forest College
Hinsdale, Illinois

SUPER EASY TUNA CURRY

1 can cream of mushroom soup
1 can cream of celery soup
1 large can chunk tuna
Curry powder
1 can cocktail peanuts
1 package shredded coconut
1 box raisins
Cooked rice

Combine mushroom soup, celery soup, tuna and curry to taste. Heat thoroughly. Serve on bed of hot cooked rice. Allow each person to add peanuts, coconut and raisins. Sprinkle on top as condiments.

Judy Hubbard White, Kansas State University
Overland Park, Kansas

HOT TUNA DELIGHTS

1 7-ounce can tuna
3 hard boiled eggs, chopped
1 cup Velveeta, cubed
8 pitted ripe olives, chopped
3 tablespoons green pepper, chopped
2 tablespoons sweet pickles
1 tablespoon chopped onion
1 cup mayonnaise
Hamburger buns

Mix first 8 ingredients. Divide mixture between 6 or 8 hamburger buns. Wrap in foil and bake at 350 degrees for 30 minutes.

Sharon Rowland Zurawski,
University of Wisconsin-Milwaukee
Milwaukee, Wisconsin

Lamb

CURRY IN A HURRY

½ stick butter or margarine
3 stalks celery, diced
2 small onions, diced
1 large apple, peeled, cored, and diced
2 tablespoons flour (use 3 if leftover gravy is not available)
2 cups cold roast lamb, diced
Hot water
Leftover lamb gravy (or 1 teaspoon Kitchen Bouquet for color)
½ teaspoon salt
⅛ teaspoon pepper
2 teaspoon curry powder (less if desired)
½ cup seedless raisins
⅛ teaspoon ground cloves (optional)

Melt butter in large skillet. Add celery, onion, and apple and sauté until golden. Add flour, stirring well. Add lamb. Add hot water and gravy to cover, stirring well; add remaining ingredients. Bring to a boil, cover and reduce heat to simmer. Cook ½ hour or until liquid assumes consistency of gravy. Serve with steamed rice. Pass chutney, chopped toasted cashews, seived egg yolk, etc. Serves 6.

Barbara Apple Keffer, Iowa State University
Tryon, North Carolina

EAST INDIA CURRIED LAMB

1 pound boneless lamb, loin cut
2 tablespoons oil
1 cup uncooked rice
2 teaspoons turmeric
⅓ stick whipped margarine or
   butter
2 heaping tablespoons flour
1 cup beef stock
1 teaspoon onion flakes
½ teaspoon ground ginger
2 teaspoons curry powder
½ teaspoon ground coriander
½ teaspoon ground cummin seed
1 tablespoon curry sauce or paste
1 tart apple, pared and cubed
⅛ cup white raisins
1 generous tablespoon lemon
   juice

Cut lamb into ¾ inch cubes, removing any gristle. Brown meat over medium heat. Place rice in top of double broiler. Cover with 1 cup of water and one drop of oil. Use 1 teaspoon turmeric to color rice. Cook about 45 minutes, or until rice has absorbed water and grains are fluffy. Melt butter or margarine in top of second double boiler, or a sturdy saucepan. Add 2 heaping tablespoons of flour. Mix thoroughly. Slowly add the beef stock, stirring constantly. After sauce is medium thick and smooth, add the rest of the turmeric, onion flakes, coriander, curry powder, curry sauce or paste, white raisins, cumin and ginger. Cook for about 10 minutes. Check sauce for flavor. Add meat and cubed apple. Cook over low heat for 30 minutes or more. Add tablespoon of lemon juice just before serving. Serve over rice, or serve rice on the side. Dress individual servings with the following condiments: ½ cup chopped cashews or dry roasted peanuts; ¼ cup bacon bits, ¼ cup dried shredded coconut; 4 tablespoons mango chutney; candied ginger, if available; preserved kumquats, if available. This is an excellent one-dish meal that can be prepared in advance and held for 45 minutes or longer. If the rice becomes too dry, add a droplet of boiling water. This recipe can be doubled or tripled to accomodate a large group.

Eleanor G. Hemminger, Northwestern University
St. Louis, Missouri

LEG OF LAMB WITH COFFEE GRAVY

5 pound leg of lamb
2 cups coffee (liquid)
¼ teaspoon allspice
½ teaspoon cinnamon
⅔ cup honey

Combine coffee, allspice, cinnamon and honey; mix well. Place lamb on rack in shallow roasting pan. Roast at 325 degrees for 2½ to 3 hours or until meat thermometer registers 175 to 180 degree of doneness. Baste lamb with coffee mixture frequently during cooking period.
Gravy: Reserve drippings in roasting pan. Combine 4 tablespoons flour and ¼ cup water; mix well. Blend flour mixture into drippings in pan. Cook over low heat, stirring constantly until thickened. Pour over lamb and slice.
Cooked butternut squash is good with this dish.

Carolyn Kelly, Southern Methodist University
Dallas, Texas

LAMB SHANKS

4 to 6 lamb shanks
Salt
Pepper
Dry dill weed
¾ to 1 cup white wine

Season lamb shanks with salt, pepper, and dill. Place on rack of roaster in oven at 400 degrees for 20 minutes; reduce heat to 350 degrees for 40 minutes. Turn shanks during this time to brown. Pour white wine over shanks, and add water to cover bottom of pan about ¼ inch deep. Cover. Cook in the oven at 350 degrees for 1½ more hours, checking occasionally. Transfer to platter and serve with gravy from the bottom of the pan. Mint sauce also is a delicious accompaniment. This dish is good with roasted new potatoes or parsnips. Quarter new potatoes; season with salt, pepper, paprika, and butter. Place in covered dish with a small amount of water. Bake at 350 degrees about 1 hour. Allow one lamb shank per person.

Kay Reynolds Bennett, Texas Tech University
Dallas, Texas

LAMB STEW WITH ARTICHOKES

1½ pounds boneless lamb
  shoulder, cubed
Seasoned flour
2 tablespoons olive oil
1 clove garlic
1 tablespoon finely minced
  parsley
1 teaspoon paprika
Juice of ½ lemon
1 teaspoon salt
1 cup water
1 package frozen artichoke hearts

Dredge lamb in seasoned flour and brown in hot oil until well browned on all sides. Push meat to one side of pan, add the whole peeled garlic clove and cook until brown, then remove. Add minced parsley, paprika, lemon juice, salt and water, cover and simmer gently 45 minutes or one hour, or until meat is tender. During the last 10 minutes of cooking, add artichoke hearts and continue to cook until tender. Thicken juices, if necessary and serve piping hot with hot steamed rice.

Dorothy Cooley Thompson, Iowa State University
Milwaukee, Wisconsin

YAPRAK SARMA

1 jar canned grape leaves
1 pound ground lamb
½ pound raw rice
1 medium onion, chopped
¼ cup chopped fresh mint, if
  available
¼ cup chopped parsley
2 teaspoons salt
½ teaspoon pepper
½ cup lemon juice
1 teaspoon powdered cinnamon

Rinse and drain grape leaves. Mix other ingredients, using hands. Flatten each leaf and place a large teaspoon of lamb mixture on veined side. Cut off stem of leaf. Fold sides and roll up the leaves. Place in a flat casserole one layer deep. Add water to cover. Bake covered at 350 degrees for one hour. Remove cover during last 10 minutes. Tomato sauce may be used with water if desired.

Pauline Sawyer Umland, Boston University
Peninsula, California

Pork

HAM FILLING FOR CREPES

2 tablespoons margarine
1 cup sliced mushrooms
3 tablespoons chopped green
   onions
¼ cup diced green pepper
3 hard cooked eggs
2 cups ham, cooked and cubed
1 package frozen peas
½ teaspoon salt
¼ teaspoon dry mustard
White Sauce:
¼ cup melted margarine
¼ cup flour
2 cups milk
¼ teaspoon salt
Dash of pepper

Prepare peas as per package. Drain. Melt margarine and saute mushrooms, onions, green pepper. Prepare white sauce. When thick, add vegetables and the rest of the ingredients. Heat thoroughly. Spoon ⅓ cup or less into each crepe. Roll. Top with a little additional sauce.

This was given to me by Sue Kellar — a Gamma Phi Beta in Moline, Illinois.

Sue Bireline, Iowa State University
Newell, Iowa

HAM LOAF

Ham Loaf:
1½ pounds lean ham
1½ pounds lean pork
1½ cups dry bread crumbs
1½ cups milk
1 teaspoon salt
1 small onion, grated
1 egg
Basting Sauce:
6 tablespoons brown sugar
2 tablespoons water
2 tablespoons vinegar
1 teaspoon dry mustard, optional

Have ham and pork ground together. Add crumbs, milk, salt, onion and egg and mix well. Pack into a 9x5x3 inch loaf pan. Bake at 350 degrees for 2 hours, basting with the sauce during the last half hour of baking.

Dorothy Cooley Thompson, Iowa State University
Milwaukee, Wisconsin

Gloria Swanson Nelson, Okalhoma University
Dallas, Texas

HAM LOAF SUPREME

2 pounds fresh pork (end of loin
   bone)
1 pound raw smoked ham (lean)
2 beaten eggs
1½ cups milk
1 cup cracker crumbs
1 tablespoon sugar
1 teaspoon salt
Pepper
1 can tomato soup

Have butcher grind pork and ham. Mix first eight ingredients, form into loaf, place in baking pan and pour soup over all. Bake at 300-350 degrees for 2 hours. Serve with horseradish sauce made with whipped cream, horseradish, and a dash of salt.

Jane Thurman Leonard, Washington University
St. Louis, Missouri

LAKE SHORE CASSEROLE

1 pound pork
1 pound veal
1 package boiled noodles (8 ounce)
2 cans cream of chicken soup
1 cup water
1 finely chopped green pepper
1 pound diced American cheese
1 can mushrooms
1 small can pimientos, cut fine

Dice and simmer pork and veal in ¼ cup butter for 10 minutes or until brown. Combine all ingredients in buttered casserole and bake one hour at 350 degrees. Top with buttered crumbs for last 15 minutes of baking.

Gladys A. McKahin, Iowa State University
Tri City

BAKED PORK CHOPS

One T-bone pork chop per person, ½ to ¾ inch thick
1 or 2 beaten eggs, depending on number of chops
½ to 1 cup crushed corn flakes
Salt and pepper to taste

Cut fat off pork chops, Use fat to grease baking dish. Dip salt and peppered pork chops into beaten egg, then into corn flakes. Bake at 350 degrees for 35 to 45 minutes depending on the thickness of the chops. Cover during baking time.

Margaret Miller Browne, Oregon State University
Dallas, Texas

PORK CHOP CASSEROLE

4 thick lean pork chops
Salt and pepper
6 ounces long-grain rice
1 #2 can sliced baby tomatoes
1 large onion
1 medium-large green pepper
¼ teaspoon oregano
3 slices bacon
½ cup chicken broth

Grease bottom of large skillet. Salt and pepper chops. Cook until brown on both sides. Put RAW rice in a well greased casserole. Sprinkle with salt. Layer the chops over rice. Pour undrained tomatoes over chops and rice. Slice green pepper into ½ inch rounds. Slice onions into ½ inch rounds. Cut bacon strips in half and form into curls. Place a green pepper ring on a chop and top with an onion slice. Top onion slice with bacon curl. Pour broth over all. (This can all be done the day before). To serve, preheat oven to 375 degrees. Bake in the covered casserole 45 minutes. At end of 45 minutes if dish looks a bit dry, add a bit of water and cook few more minutes. Serves 4.

Mae Douglas Garrett, Oklahoma City University
Dallas, Texas

PORK CHOPS NEW ORLEANS

4 thick pork chops
2 tomatoes, sliced
1 large onion, sliced
1 green pepper, chopped
¼ teaspoon thyme
¼ teaspoon sage
Salt, pepper
⅔ cup raw rice
1 cup chicken broth (made with
    bouillon cube)
½ cup white wine

Brown the chops on both sides in a skillet and place in a buttered casserole. Arrange sliced tomatoes, onion and green pepper on top of chops and season with salt, pepper, thyme and sage. Heat broth and wine together in a separate pan, sprinkle raw rice into casserole and pour the hot broth and wine over it. Cover the casserole and bake in a 350-degree oven for 45 minutes or until all liquid is gone and rice is tender.

Alyce Anne Martin Chism, Texas Tech University
Lubbock, Texas

PORK CHOPS WITH RICE

6 pork chops
2 tablespoons oil or drippings
1½ cups uncooked rice
1 can cream of mushroom soup
1½ cups hot water
1 4-ounce can sliced mushrooms
    and liquid
2 tablespoons diced pimiento
    (optional)
1 package onion soup mix

Slightly brown pork chops in oil or drippings. Spread uncooked rice in bottom of baking dish (13½x9x2 inch). Add chops, pimiento (optional), mushrooms with liquid, soup and water. Sprinkle with onion soup mix. Cover with foil. Bake at 350 degrees for 45 minutes. Uncover and fluff up rice. Bake uncovered an additional 5 to 10 minutes if too thin. Serves 6.

Frances Cheatham Burnecke, University of Texas
Dallas, Texas

Margaret Gatlin "Meg" Smith, Florida State University
Minneapolis, Minnesota

ROAST PORK WITH SOUR CREAM GRAVY

Pork butt roast
Salad oil
2 teaspoon salt
1 teaspoon salt
1 teaspoon pepper
¼ teaspoon each: thyme,
    oregano, ground fennel
Flour
¾ cup chicken broth
1⅓ cup white port wine
2 cloves garlic, minced (or ¼-½
    teaspoon garlic powder)
½ teaspoon nutmeg
1 cup sour cream

Brush roast with oil. Mix seasonings and rub into meat. Dredge with flour, rubbing in well. Heat 2 teaspoons oil in electric frying pan. Brown roast on all sides. Add broth, wine, garlic and nutmeg. Cover and simmer 2-3 hours, turning meat occasionally. Lift onto platter and keep warm in low oven. Skim fat off gravy and strain out spices. Thicken with flour and water blended to smooth paste. Heat sour cream and stir into gravy.

Nancy Willis Litzinger, University of Missouri
St. Louis, Missouri

JAN'S SAUSAGE AND LENTILS

2 pounds Polish sausage
1 16-ounce can tomatoes
(chopped)
1 cup washed lentils
2 medium onions (chopped)
3 cloves garlic (crushed)
2 tablespoons vegetable oil
1 teaspoon sugar
1 bay leaf
½ teaspoon pepper and salt to
taste

Slice sausage into ½ inch slices. Cook lentils in salted water to cover 20 minutes. Sauté onions in oil in 2 quart casserole, add garlic, tomatoes, salt and pepper, sugar, bay leaf and sausage. Simmer until liquid is almost gone. Add lentils and bake 30 minutes at 350 degrees. Serves 4 to 6.

Margo Twiss Heegeman, University of Wisconsin
Alexandria, Virginia

SAUSAGE RING

2 pounds bulk pork sausage (hot
or mild)
2 well beaten eggs
1 tablespoon grated onion
1½ cups Pepperidge Farm
stuffing, slightly crumbled
¼ cup chopped parsley

Preheat oven to 350 degrees. Grease a 9-inch ring mold. Mix all ingredients and pack into the mold. Bake 20 minutes and then pour off any fat which has accumulated. The amount will depend on the kind of sausage used. Bake 15 minutes more and pour off any fat. Unmold onto large serving plate. Fill the center with scrambled eggs, or fried apples, or parsley. This is very popular at brunches. It may be made a day in advance; it freezes well. Serves 10.

Doris Erwin Hawkins, Iowa State University
Washington, D.C.

WILD RICE CASSEROLE

1 pound pork sausage
1 cup wild rice
2 cups chopped onions
1 4-ounce can mushrooms
2 tablespoons butter
¼ cup flour
2½ cups bouillon
¼ teaspoon salt

Boil rice in 1 quart water until tender, drain. Brown sausage and onions. Drain. Combine all ingredients. Bake at 350 degrees for 1 hour.

Emily Jammer Fisher, Iowa State University
Rock Rapids, Iowa

WILD RICE AND SAUSAGE

1 pound bulk pork sausage
2 cups uncooked wild rice (or use
    packaged mixture of wild rice
    and long grained rice, if
    preferred)
2 4-ounce cans mushrooms
½ cup half & half
4 tablespoons flour
½ cup onion, chopped
2½ cups chicken broth
½ teaspoon Accent
¼ teaspoon oregano
⅛ teaspoon thyme
⅛ teaspoon marjoram
1 teaspoon salt
¼ teaspoon pepper
½ cup almonds, slivered

Cook rice, following directions on package. Break up sausage in skillet with fork and fry until lightly browned. Drain off excess fat. Add mushrooms, onions, and saute until onions are slightly yellow. Stir in flour. Stir in half and half and broth. Cook, stirring constantly until thickened. Add seasonings. Mix with rice and slivered almonds. Pur in oiled casserole. Bake at 350 degrees for about 30 minutes. Makes 12-15 servings.

May be made ahead and refrigerated until time to be baked. Add 15 minutes to baking time if refrigerated.

Margaret Stewart "Peg", Iowa State University
Del Mar, California

BARBECUED RIBS

4 pounds back ribs or 4 center cut
    pork chops (rather thick)
1 14-ounce bottle ketchup
4 tablespoons cider vinegar
2 tablespoons sugar
2 teaspoons prepared mustard

Mix ketchup, vinegar, sugar and mustard and stir until smooth. Pour over meat. Bake at 300 degrees for 2 to 3 hours.

Gladys McKahin, Iowa State University
Tri-City

BARBECUED SPARERIBS

1 cup of beer
2 tablespoons vinegar
1 tablespoon Worcestershire
    sauce
2 tablespoons lemon or lime juice
2 tablespoons brown sugar
½ cup chili sauce
Spareribs

Combine, then heat mixture, stirring until sugar is dissolved. Baste spareribs frequently with sauce while baking. Bake at 425 degrees for 30 minutes, then reduce heat to 350 degrees and bake for about 2 more hours.

Bette Crimmins Simcox, Lake Forest College
Hinsdale, Illinois

CHINESE SPARERIBS

3½ pounds spareribs
Accent
Ginger and garlic powder
Salt and pepper
Ketchup
Molasses
Soy sauce

Cut spareribs into strips. Place in pan, edge up, side by side. Cover with a coating of ketchup. Sprinkle with salt and pepper to suit taste. Sprinkle with Accent. Sprinkle with small amounts of ginger powder and garlic powder. Shake soy sauce generously over ingredients. Thread dark molasses back and forth over pan (do not use too much, to avoid being over-sweet.) Bake in a 350 degree oven for 1 to 1¼ hours, watching carefully after one hour to avoid burning. Serves 4.

Barbara A. Myhre, Gettysburg College
Gettysburg, Pennsylvania

½ cup cooked ham or bacon cut
  into small pieces or 1 cup
  seafood (shrimp or crab)
3 eggs
½ cup biscuit mix
¼ pound melted butter or
  margarine, cooled
1½ cups whole milk
¼ teaspoon salt
Dash of pepper
1 cup shredded Swiss cheese

IMPOSSIBLE QUICHE

Place all ingredients, except the cheese and meat or seafood in a blender. Mix for a few seconds to blend. Sprinkle cheese and meat or seafood in well greased 9 inch pie pan. Pour egg mixture over cheese and meat. Pan will be very full. Bake at 350 degrees for about 45 minutes or until set. Allow quiche to "sit" about 10 minutes before cutting.

Doris Erwin Hawkins, Iowa State University
Washington, D.C.

Salads

Salads

CHEESY APRICOT SALAD

2 16-ounce cans peeled apricots
1 16-ounce can crushed pineapple
2 small packages orange jello
2 cups hot water
1½ cups syrup drained from fruit
½ cup chopped nuts
1 cup marshmallows
½ cup sugar
3 tablespoons flour
1 egg, slightly beaten
1 cup syrup from fruit or canned
    apricot nectar
2 tablespoons butter
1 cup cream (whipping)
¼ cup grated Longhorn cheese

Drain fruits, reserving syrup. Cut apricots into small pieces. Dissolve gelatin in hot water; add 1½ cups syrup from fruits. Cool. Add fruit, nuts and marshmallows. Pour into lightly oiled dish (9x13 inches). Chill until firm. Combine flour, sugar, egg, and 1 cup syrup from fruit. Cook, stirring constantly until thickened. Add butter; cool. Whip cream, fold into custard mixture. Spread over gelatin layer and sprinkle with cheese. Refrigerate. Serves 12 to 14. For a more tart salad omit the sugar, and reduce the marshmallows.

Kay Johnson Marovich, Kansas State University
South Bay, California

ASPARAGUS SALAD

1 small package lime gelatin,
    dissolved in ½ cup hot water
8 ounces cream cheese
¾ cup finely chopped celery
⅓ cup chopped green pepper
1 to 2 tablespoons chopped onion
1 can asparagus soup
½ cup mayonnaise
1 small jar pimento, optional

To dissolved gelatin, add cream cheese and soup and blend thoroughly. Add celery, green pepper and onions, stir. Add mayonnaise and blend. Chill in mold until firm.

Cookbook Committee

AVOCADO IN ASPIC

2 envelopes unflavored gelatin
½ cup cold water
2 cups tomato juice
1 medium onion, chopped
4 sprigs parsley, chopped
2 tablespoons vinegar
1 tablespoon lemon juice
4 whole cloves
2 teaspoons sugar
½ teaspoon salt
1 cup diced avocado
½ cup chopped celery

Soften gelatin in cold water. Combine remaining ingredients, except avocado and celery in saucepan. Simmer over low heat about 15 minutes. Strain, discarding onion, parsley and cloves. Add gelatin to hot liquid. Mix well and chill until slightly thick. Add avocado and celery. Pour into mold and chill until firm. Serves 4 to 6.

Cookbook Committee

CHICKEN STUFFED AVOCADO

1-2½ to 3 pounds chicken
3 cups water
1 stalk (rib) celery
1 teaspoon salt
½ teaspoon pepper
2 tablespoons lemon juice
½ cup chopped celery
½ cup chopped green pepper
1 teaspoon salt, ½ teaspoon pepper
½ cup chopped onion
½ cup mayonnaise
1 teaspoon Worcestershire sauce
4 avocados — 1 lemon
1 teaspoon onion salt or sprinkle with garlic salt
1 cup bread crumbs
2 teaspoons melted butter
½ cup chopped almonds

Stew chicken in water to which celery, salt, pepper and lemon juice have been added. Remove chicken from bone, cut in bite size pieces and mix well with the celery, green pepper, mayonnaise and Worcestershire sauce. Cut avocados in two and peel. Cut a small slice from the rounded side so that they sit firmly. Rub with juice from lemon and fill each with a mound of chicken salad. Put in a 400 degree oven for ten minutes. In the meantime, brown bread crumbs in melted butter. Remove stuffed avocados from oven and add buttered crumbs to top, then chopped almonds and return to oven for five minutes. The salad may be made the day before serving. The avocados may be prepared a few hours in advance of serving if they are well rubbed with lemon juice.

These are delicious. You'll want to eat two, but you'll feel stuffed if you do.

Kathryn Critchfield McCarville, Iowa State University
Dallas, Texas

AVOCADO-CRANBERRY SALAD

1 3-ounce package lemon gelatin
3 tablespoons sugar
1½ cups boiling water
1 cup fresh cranberries, ground
1½ teaspoons prepared horseradish
1 3-ounce package lime gelatin
½ teaspoon salt
1 tablespoon lemon juice
1 ripe avocado, peeled and mashed
3 tablespoons sour cream

Dissolve lemon gelatin and sugar in 1 cup of boiling water. Add ¼ cup cold water. Chill until thickened. Fold in cranberries and horseradish. Pour into 1½ quart mold. Chill until set but not firm.
Dissolve lime gelatin and salt in 1 cup of boiling water. Add ¾ cup cold water. Blend in mashed avocado, lemon juice and sour cream. Chill until slightly thickened. Spoon over lemon mixture in mold. Chill until firm. Serves 8 to 10.

Pat O'Connell Mullins, St. Louis University
Dallas, Texas

AVOCADO MOUSSE

1 tablespoon (1 envelope) plain gelatin
¼ cup cold water
3 medium, fully ripened avocados (about 1½ pounds)
2 tablespoons lemon juice
1½ tablespoons onion juice
¾ teaspoon salt
¾ cup mayonnaise
¾ cup heavy cream, whipped
Water cress
Sliced oranges
Grapefruit sections

Soften gelatin in water for five minutes, then set over hot water until dissolved. Meanwhile, puree the avocados (there should be about 2 cups). Add the next four ingredients. Add dissolved gelatin slowly, stirring constantly. Fold in the whipped cream thoroughly, but gently, and pour into a 6-cup mold or individual molds that have been rinsed with cold water. Chill until firm; unmold onto a flat platter and garnish with water cress, thick slices of orange, and grapefruit sections.
Variation: Omit onion juice. Steep one teaspoon grated lime rind in two tablespoons lime juice for one minute. Press out juice, discard rind and substitute the lime juice for the lemon juice in the above recipe.

Frances Johnston Harmon,
Southern Methodist University
Dallas, Texas

8 large tomatoes
1 large onion
1 bunch celery
Juice from 1 to 2 lemons
²⁄₃ cup olive oil
1¹⁄₂ tablespoons salt
2 green peppers

BARBECUE SALAD

Dice tomatoes, onion, celery and peppers. Add lemon juice, olive oil and salt. Let stand at room temperature for an hour or two, then refrigerate. Will keep for several days. More tomatoes can be added if there's juice left. Serve in small bowls. Serves 15. Great for cook-outs.

Ann Bronsing, Indiana State University
St. Louis, Missouri

1 can cut green beans
1 can cut wax beans
1 can kidney beans
1 can garbanzo (Ceci) beans
  (optional)
1 chopped green pepper
1 cup chopped celery
1 chopped onion
³⁄₄ cup sugar
¹⁄₃ cup vinegar
¹⁄₂ cup salad oil
1 teaspoon salt
¹⁄₂ teaspoon pepper

THREE BEAN SALAD

Drain beans; add green pepper, celery and onion. Mix together other ingredients. Cover bean mixture with "dressing"; let stand at least 24 hours. Leftover "dressing" can be used for marinade, salad dressing, etc.

Chris Loveberg Montgomery,
California State University-San Diego
Orange County, California

Katherine Kruger Scott, Indiana State University
Winamac, Indiana

1 package lime gelatin
9 marshmallows cut into small
  pieces (or about 36 miniature
  marshmallows)
1 3-ounce package cream cheese
2 cups boiling water
1 cup crushed pineapple, drained
1 cup whipped cream
Chopped nuts

BEST EVER SALAD

Stir cheese, marshmallows and gelatin into boiling water until dissolved. Chill until mixture starts to set. Add thoroughly drained pineapple, whipped cream and nuts. Chill until firm. Serves 12.

Lorraine Forester Grigsby, University of Wyoming
Cheyenne, Wyoming

1 small package lemon gelatin
1 cup hot water
1 cup blueberry juice, or
  pineapple juice, or half and half
1 cup blueberries
1 small can drained pineapple
  (crushed)
Topping:
¹⁄₄ cup mayonnaise
3 ounces cream cheese
¹⁄₂ teaspoon vanilla
¹⁄₂ cup marshmallows (broken in
  small pieces)

BLUEBERRY AND PINEAPPLE SALAD

Dissolve gelatin in hot water, mix with fruit ingredients and chill. Beat topping ingredients together (marshmallows can still be in pieces) and spread over hardened salad.

Sally Vanderpearl, University of Missouri-Columbia
St. Louis, Missouri

CAESAR SALAD

3 cloves garlic
¼ cup salad oil or olive oil
1 head leaf lettuce (romaine or
  other)
1 cup croutons
2 tomatoes, diced or wedges
Dressing:
1 beaten egg
½ cup grated Parmesan cheese
¼ cup fresh lemon juice
1 teaspoon Worcestershire sauce
½ teaspoon pepper
½ teaspoon salt

Mash garlic and add to salad oil; let stand while mixing remaining ingredients. Break lettuce in bowl. Add tomatoes. Strain salad oil to remove garlic. Pour over vegetables and toss until oil coats all vegetables. Combine dressing ingredients and mix well. Pour over salad and toss lightly. Garnish with croutons.
Optional: Garnish with anchovy fillets or tomato wedges.
Note: This may be too much garlic for some tastes.

Gayle Howard Young,
University of Texas
Dallas, Texas

CALIFORNIA SALAD

2-3 cups diced cooked chicken or
  turkey
1 cup diced celery
1 cup sliced and quartered
  hothouse cucumber
1 green onion, minced
1 tart red or yellow apple, diced,
  skin on
½ pound Thomson seedless
  grapes
1 pound can pineapple chunks,
  well drained (save juice)
½-¾ cup sliced almonds, toasted
  (optional)
Lettuce cups or wedges of
  honeydew melon
Dressing:
1 cup mayonnaise
2-4 teaspoons curry powder to
  taste
¼ cup reserved pineapple juice
⅛ teaspoon nutmeg

Combine all ingredients through the pineapple chunks in a large bowl. Mix the dressing, pour over the salad in the bowl and stir gently but thoroughly to coat all the pieces. Divide the salad among 4-6 plates with lettuce cups or wedges of honeydew melon, and mound the salad attractively. Sprinkle the toasted almonds over the top if desired, or garnish as desired. This is an excellent bridge luncheon or light summer supper served with San Francisco style sour dough rolls and iced tea or a good white wine.

Katherine Blight Chituras, U.C.L.A.
Modesto, California

JOANIE'S CARROTS

2 pounds carrots = 6-8 servings,
  peeled
1 green pepper, chopped
1 medium onion, chopped
1 can tomato soup
½ cup sugar
½ cup vinegar
½ cup oil

Cut carrots into bite size chunks. Partially cook for 10 minutes. Remove from heat, drain. Heat soup, dissolve sugar in it. Add vinegar. Add oil, slowly; stir well with wire whisk as it might separate. Pour over carrots, onion, green pepper — while carrots are still warm. Serve warm or chill in refrigerator and serve cold. Lasts for weeks in refrigerator and always tastes fresh.
Children and adults love this salad.

Joanie Johnson Maines, California State University
Fresno, California

COLD CARROT SALAD

2 pounds carrots, cut in wheels,
  cooked tender and cooled
2 medium onions, sliced thin
1 medium green pepper, sliced
  thin
Marinade:
1 can tomato soup
½ cup salad oil
¾ cup sugar
¾ cup white vinegar
1 tablespoon prepared mustard
1 teaspoon salt
1 teaspoon celery salt
1 teaspoon basil
1 teaspoon Worcestershire sauce

Add cooked, cooled carrots, onions and green pepper to marinade. Refrigerate for 48 hours. Keeps 2 to 4 weeks. Great for barbecues.

Kay Johnson Marovich, Kansas State University
South Bay, California
Karen Diehl Greening, Washington University
St. Louis, Missouri
Mary Jane Chamberlain Howard, William and Mary
Richmond, Virginia

CABBAGE SALAD

4 cups shredded cabbage
½ to 1 cup shredded carrot
1 peeled and diced orange
Approximately ¾ cup mayonnaise
  or salad dressing
1 teaspoon curry powder

Mix all above ingredients. Chill. Serve.

Sharon Green, Colorado State University
Denver, Colorado

COLESLAW

1 head of chopped cabbage
1 green pepper, chopped
4 stalks of celery, chopped
½ bermuda onion, chopped
1 tablespoon sugar
1 tablespoon salt
1 teaspoon pepper
4 tablespoons vegetable oil or
  corn oil
3 tablespoons cider vinegar
½ cup mayonnaise

Mix all ingredients. Refrigerate 3 to 24 hours before serving.

Sylvia Hardy Trewin, Iowa State University
Richardson, Texas

EASY COLESLAW

2-2½ pound head of cabbage,
  shredded
1 onion, chopped fine
1 small green pepper, slivered
⅓ cup white vinegar
1 cup sugar
1 teaspoon salt
1 teaspoon celery seed
1 teaspoon mustard seed

Mix together and let marinate at least 24 hours. Stir occasionally. This will keep for a week.

Ruth Johnson, University of Illinois
Arlington Heights, Illinois

CHINESE COLESLAW

8 cups chopped Savoy cabbage
2 tablespoons chopped onion
4 ounce can sliced mushrooms
Chinese noodles
Dressing:
2 tablespoons soy sauce
1 cup Hellman's mayonnaise

Toss cabbage, onion and mushrooms and put in covered bowl in refrigerator. Mix dressing ingredients. Toss dressing and cabbage mixture well and top with Chinese noodles. Serve at once.

Dorothy Chase Jones, Southern Methodist University
Dallas, Texas

HOT CELERY SALAD

1 stalk fresh celery
6 slices bacon
1 cup onion, sliced
1 cup thinly sliced carrots
1½ teaspoons salt
¼ teaspoon powdered mustard
1½ teaspoons sugar
¼ teaspoon pepper
1 chicken bouillon cube
¾ cup boiling water
1 tablespoon cornstarch
1 tablespoon cold water
2 tablespoons vinegar

Trim celery and cut into thin diagonal slices (about 6 cups). Set aside. In large skillet, cook bacon crisp. Crumble and set aside. Pour off all but 3 tablespoons of bacon fat and add onions, carrots and celery. Cook and stir 5 minutes. Stir in sugar, salt, mustard and pepper. Cook and stir 3 more minutes. Dissolve bouillon in boiling water. Blend cornstarch with cold water and vinegar. Stir into skillet with bouillon. Cook until mixture thickens. Sprinkle bacon on top. Makes 8 ½-cup portions.

Dorothy Holmes McGinnis, Oklahoma University
Greater Kansas City

CHERRY SALAD

1 can dark cherries (pitted) and juice
¼ cup sugar
1 cup orange juice
2 packages lemon gelatin
½ cup nuts
½ cup celery, chopped
1 small can crushed pineapple
Juice of one lemon

Combine cherries, juice and sugar; bring to a boil. Add gelatin and cool until slightly thickened. Add all other ingredients. Pour into mold and chill until firm. Serves 10.

Allys Field Boyle, University of Denver
Dallas, Texas

CHERRY AND COKE MOLD

1 large 8-ounce Philadelphia cream cheese
1 large can pitted dark red cherries
1 small 6-ounce bottle Coke
3½ ounces of pecans
1 small package cherry gelatin

Drain juice from cherries. Heat juice and dissolve gelatin in juice from cherries. Allow to thicken in refrigerator until soupy. Form cheese into small balls and mix with refrigerated gelatin. Blend cherries and pecans into mixture. Last add Coke. Do not add water! Place mixture in mold and chill in refrigerator.

Mavis Schutz, San Diego State University
Orange County, California

CHERRY FRUIT SALAD

1 can cherry pie filling
1 medium size can crushed pineapple
1 small can coconut
1 can sweetened condensed milk
1 cup chopped pecans
1 small container (pint size) Cool Whip, thawed somewhat

Mix together in large bowl. Chill and serve. Serves 12 to 15.

Virginia Forsythe Vint, University of Missouri
Dallas, Texas

HOT CURRIED FRUIT

One number 2½ size can each:
cling peach halves, pear halves,
pineapple chunks
½ cup Maraschino cherries
¾ cup brown sugar
2 teaspoons curry powder
1 teaspoon cinnamon
½ teaspoon nutmeg
½-¾ cup butter

Melt butter. Add sugar and spices. *Drain Fruits*. Put in layer in large rectangular baking dish. Pour butter mixture over all. Bake at 325 degrees for 30 minutes. Make a day ahead — reheat to serve.

Patricia Smith Dieterich, University of Iowa
Ridgefield, Connecticut

CHICKEN MOUSSE

1 can cream of mushroom soup
3 cups diced cooked chicken
1 small package cream cheese
2 tablespoons horseradish
2 cups diced celery
1 cup mayonnaise
2 envelopes plain gelatin
½ cup water

Heat mushroom soup with ¼ cup water. Dissolve gelatin in other ¼ cup water. When soup is heated, add gelatin, cream cheese and mayonnaise. Let cool, add chicken, horseradish, diced celery and salt to taste. Turn into mold and chill until firm. Serves 12.

Allys Field Boyle, University of Denver
Dallas, Texas

CURRIED CHICKEN SALAD

6 cups cooked chicken breast
2 6-ounce cans water chestnuts,
sliced
1 pound seedless grapes
2 cups sliced celery
½ cup toasted slivered almonds
1 cup mayonnaise (1 tablespoon
curry powder and ½ teaspoon
salt may be mixed in)
Bibb or Boston lettuce
Pineapple chunks or cantaloupe
rings for garnish

Toss together first six ingredients. Serve on lettuce with fruit garnish. Serves 12. For a more tart salad add 1 tablespoon lemon juice to mayonnaise.

Mary Jane Brown Monnig, Washington University
St. Louis, Missouri

Elaine Pinholster, University of Maryland
Northern Virginia

CHICKEN SALAD

2-3 cups cubed cooked chicken
½ cup diced celery
¼ cup green pepper
1 hard boiled egg for garnish
½ cup mayonnaise
½ teaspoon seasoned salt
½ teaspoon salt
½ teaspoon poultry seasoning
Dash pepper

Mix in all ingredients except chicken. Mix in chicken. Serve on lettuce leaf. Garnish with sliced egg.

Harriet Lishen Baldwin, University of Missouri
Dallas, Texas

CHICKEN ALMOND SALAD

1 envelope plain gelatin
¼ cup cold water and ½ cup *hot*
water
¼ cup slivered almonds (toasted)
1 cup mayonnaise
1 cup whipping cream
½ teaspoon salt
1½ cups cooked diced chicken
1 cup seedless green grapes,
halved

Put mayonnaise in large bowl. In small bowl, sprinkle cold water over gelatin to soften, let stand a minute and then completely dissolve with ½ cup hot water. Whip cream until stiff. Combine gelatin with mayonnaise, whipped cream and salt. (Combine well.) Fold in diced chicken, almonds and grapes. Put in oblong pyrex dish which has been lightly buttered. Refrigerate. Delectable! Veal or tuna may be substituted for the chicken.

Gene White Joyce, University of Texas
Dallas, Texas

HOT CHICKEN SALAD I

2 cups cooked light meat of
 chicken (about 2 large whole
 breasts)
1 can (10¾-ounce) cream of
 chicken soup
¾ cup mayonnaise
1 cup grated sharp cheddar
 cheese
1 tablespoon lemon juice
3 hard cooked eggs, diced
1 cup chopped celery
1½ cups crushed potato chips,
 divided

Slowly heat soup, mayonnaise and cheese until cheese is melted. Add lemon juice and remove from heat. Add chicken, eggs, celery and 1 cup of potato chip crumbs. Turn into a lightly buttered baking dish. Top with remaining crumbs. Bake in a 350 degree oven about 25 minutes, or until heated through. 6 servings.

Dorothy Cooley Thompson, Iowa State University
Milwaukee, Wisconsin

HOT CHICKEN SALAD II

1 can chicken (or 2 cooked
 breasts)
4 hard cooked eggs, chopped
1 can mushroom soup
1 package potato chips
¼ cup onion or 1½ tablespoons
 onion flakes
1 cup chopped celery
½ cup mayonnaise

Toss lightly, all except chips. Alternate mixture with layers of crushed chips in baking dish. Top with chips and slivered almonds (optional). Bake 35 minutes at 350 degrees or 9 minutes in microwave oven turning dish several times during cooking.

Janet Shelby, Southwestern State University
Weatherford, Oklahoma

HOT CHICKEN SALAD III

1 pound almonds
4 pounds diced celery
6 tablespoons chopped onions
6 pounds cooked chicken
1 quart mayonnaise
¾ cup lemon juice
¾ teaspoon lemon rind
Pepper

Combine all ingredients. Top with shredded cheese and crushed chips. Bake at 350 degrees for 30 minutes. Makes enough salad for 50 people.

Peg Walker Thiesen, University of Nebraska-Omaha
Omaha, Nebraska

SUMMER CHICKEN SALAD

4 chicken breasts
¼ cup sherry
2 tablespoons chopped onion
½ cup almonds
¼ cup celery
¼ cup sweet pickles
1 8-ounce can pineapple chunks,
 drained
½ cup mayonnaise
1 teaspoon lemon juice
1 teaspoon curry powder
Salt and pepper to taste

Simmer chicken breasts in water and ¼ cup sherry until tender. Cool, drain, debone and cube chicken. Add onions, almonds, celery, pickles, unsweetened pineapple chunks, mayonnaise and lemon juice. Blend and season with curry, salt and pepper as needed. Chill 1 hour before serving.

Sandra Graham Cude, Memphis State University
Dallas, Texas

2 envelopes plain gelatin
1 cup cold water
1 can (10½ ounces) cream of
   celery soup
¼ teaspoon salt
2 tablespoons lemon juice
1 cup salad dressing or
   mayonnaise
2 tablespoons diced pimento
1 cup diced celery
2 cups cooked chicken (diced)

MOLDED CHICKEN SALAD

Sprinkle gelatin over water in saucepan. Place over low heat; stir until gelatin dissolves. Remove from heat, stir in celery soup, salt, lemon juice and salad dressing; beat with a rotary beater until smooth. Add pimento, celery and chicken. Turn into a 6-cup loaf pan or mold. Chill until firm. Serves 6 to 8.

Sara Hess McElhaney, Iowa State University
Dallas, Texas

3 envelopes plain gelatin
½ cup cold water
2 cups mayonnaise
2 cups Cool Whip
4 cups diced, cooked chicken
¾ cup chopped stuffed olives
¾ cup chopped celery
⅓ cup chopped green pepper
¾ cup chopped toasted almonds

SUPER CHICKEN MOLD

Place the gelatin in the cold water, dissolve by holding over hot water. Blend into it, the mayonnaise, Cool Whip, chicken, olives, celery, green pepper and almonds. Pour into greased mold. Serve on crisp greens and enjoy! Will serve 12.

Anne Gross Hayes, Ohio Wesleyan
Columbus, Ohio

5 cups chopped cooked chicken
2 tablespoons each salad oil,
   orange juice, and vinegar
1 teaspoon salt
3 cups cooked rice
1½ cups small seedless grapes
1 cup chopped celery
1 15-ounce can pineapple chunks,
   drained
1 11-ounce can Mandarin
   oranges, drained
¾ cup toasted slivered almonds
½ cup mayonnaise

SUPER CHICKEN SALAD

Combine chicken, salad oil, orange juice, vinegar and salt; let stand 30 minutes. Add remaining ingredients and toss lightly. Garnish with parsley sprigs. Serves 10 to 12.

The Cookbook Committee

1 quart cranberries
2 apples, cored
1 unpeeled orange
2 cups sugar
1 3-ounce package lemon flavored
   gelatin
1 cup walnut meats

CRANBERRY SALAD

Grind cranberries, apples and orange. Add the sugar and mix. Drain in colander one hour or more. To the juice that drained out, add enough water to make 2 cups. Heat and add lemon gelatin. Stir to dissolve and add cranberry mixture and nuts. Put into a flat pan (7½ by 12 inch) or other mold and refrigerate until congealed. Serve on lettuce leaves, with mayonnaise, or as desired.

Sylvia Hardy Trewin, Iowa State University
Richardson, Texas

1 jar cran-orange relish
1 3-ounce package strawberry
   gelatin
1 8-ounce package cream cheese
1 small can crushed pineapple,
   drained
1 cup hot water

MOLDED CRANBERRY SALAD

Dissolve gelatin in 1 cup of hot water. Add cream cheese and beat together. Add relish and pineapple. Chill until firm.

Anne Yeager, Southern Methodist University
Dallas, Texas

CRANBERRY NUT SALAD

1 can cranberry sauce
1 tablespoon lemon juice
1 pint whipping cream or whipped topping
¼ cup salad dressing or mayonnaise
¼ cup confectioners sugar if using fresh whipping cream
1 teaspoon vanilla
1 cup chopped nuts

Put cranberry sauce in regular ice cube pan (without ice cube frame). Break up the sauce with a fork and spread evenly over pan bottom. Add lemon juice and mix into cranberry sauce. Whip cream with electric mixer. Do not over whip. With spoon stir salad dressing, confectioners sugar, vanilla and nuts into whipped cream. Spread this mixture over top of cranberry mixture. Place pan in freezer for overnight or day before serving. When frozen, cover with plastic wrap. Keeps for months in freezer. Serve on lettuce.

Lillian Brighton Spaid, Pennsylvania State University
Letitz, Pennsylvania

CRANBERRY ORANGE SALAD

9-ounce package raspberry gelatin
3 cups hot water
1½ cups cold water
3 14-ounce jars cranberry orange relish
3 unpeeled red tart apples, finely diced

Dissolve gelatin in hot water, add cold water, chill in 9x13x2 inch pyrex dish until partially set. Then fold in relish and apples. Chill until firm. Serves 20.

Barbara Apple Keffer, Iowa State University
Tryon, North Carolina

CRANBERRY-RASPBERRY MOLD

3 cups boiling water
9 ounce package raspberry flavored gelatin
2 cups sour cream
1 can (1 pound) whole cranberry sauce

Pour boiling water over gelatin in a bowl, stirring until gelatin is dissolved. Chill until very thick but not set. With rotary beater, beat in sour cream and cranberry sauce. Pour into 13x9x2 baking dish or mold. Chill until firm.

Cookbook Committee

CRANBERRY SOUR CREAM SALAD

1 3-ounce package cherry gelatin
1 cup hot water
1 1-pound can whole cranberry sauce
½ cup diced celery
¼ cup chopped nuts (pecans or walnuts)
1 cup sour cream

Dissolve gelatin in hot water, chill until slightly thickened. Break up cranberry sauce and stir into gelatin. Add nuts and celery. Pour half of mixture into mold, spread evenly with sour cream. Pour remaining cranberry sauce mixture on top and chill. Makes 1 quart, 6-8 servings.

Mary Jane Chamberlain Howard, William and Mary
Richmond, Virginia

COTTAGE CHEESE-CUCUMBER MOLD

1 3-ounce package lime gelatin
1 cup boiling water
1 cup cottage cheese
½ cup salad dressing
1 cup finely chopped cucumber
¼ cup chopped ripe olives
1 tablespoon finely chopped onion

Dissolve gelatin in boiling water. Combine cottage cheese and salad dressing. Stir in gelatin. Chill until slightly thickened. Fold in remaining ingredients. Pour into one quart mold. Chill until firm.

Sharon Rowland Zurawski,
University of Wisconsin-Milwaukee
Milwaukee, Wisconsin

CREAMY CUCUMBER ASPIC

2 cups tomato juice
2 tablespoons gelatin
1 8-ounce package cream cheese,
  cubed
½ teaspoon salt
1 cup mayonnaise
1 cup coarsely shredded, peeled
  cucumber, well drained
1 cup minced celery
1 tablespoon grated onion

Mix ½ cup tomato juice and gelatin; let stand to soften. Put remaining juice in saucepan, add cheese and heat, stirring until well blended and smooth. Stir in softened gelatin and salt. Heat until gelatin dissolves. Remove from heat. Beat in mayonnaise. Chill mixture until partly set. Fold in vegetables. Pour into 5-cup ring mold. Chill until firm. Black olives in center is a nice garnish.

Beverly Vandervoort, Washington University
Mt. Prospect, Illinois

ENDIVE AND HEARTS OF PALM

Salad:
3 heads Belgian endive, cut
  crosswise in ¼ inch slices
2 bunches watercress, well
  trimmed
1 14-ounce can hearts of palm,
  drained and julienned
¾ cup sliced fresh mushrooms
1 bunch radishes, sliced
¼ cup chopped parsley
Dressing:
¾ cup oil
¼ cup tarragon vinegar
1 egg yolk
1 tablespoon Dijon mustard
2 shallots, minced
1 teaspoon salt, ¼ teaspoon
  pepper

Combine all salad ingredients in large bowl and chill. Combine all dressing ingredients in a jar with a lid. Shake well and pour over salad. Toss and serve.

Susan Countner, University of Washington
Marina Del Rey, California

ENGLISH PEA SALAD

1 small head lettuce
1 small cucumber, peeled
4 green onions with tops
1 ripe avocado
1 hard-boiled egg
1 8½-ounce can English peas,
  well drained
½ cup ranch-style dressing

Hand-tear lettuce and place in large salad bowl. Add diced cucumber, diced onion, avocado and egg. Sprinkle in peas. Toss with dressing and serve immediately. Tastes best *without* salt and pepper! Serves 6.

Carolyn Coe Cole, University of Texas
Dallas, Texas

FIVE CUP SALAD I

1 pint sour cream
1 6-ounce can fruit cocktail,
  drained
1 medium can mandarin oranges,
  drained
½ cup miniature marshmallows
½ cup walnuts

Mix all ingredients together. Chill 2 hours before serving.

Barbara Kenney Fortenbaugh, Syracuse University
Arlington, Texas

FIVE CUP SALAD II

1 cup miniature marshmallows
1 cup crushed pineapple
1 cup mandarin oranges
1 cup coconut
1 cup whipped topping

Drain fruits. Mix all ingredients well. Keep chilled. Serves 6-8.

Pam Rutherford, Vanderbilt University
Nashville, Tennessee

FRITO SALAD

1½ pounds ground beef, cooked
  and drained
1 chopped onion
1 teaspoon chili powder
1 teaspoon salt
4 ounces cubed cheddar cheese
4 ounces cubed Monterey Jack
1 8-ounce bottle Green Goddess
  dressing
1 can kidney beans, drained
1 can chick peas
2 tomatoes
1 small package Fritos (9 ounce-
  regulars)
Pepper (optional)
½ head lettuce

Toss all ingredients together for a fabulous summer salad. Add lettuce and fritos last.

Shirley Bibbings, Michigan State University
Northern Virginia

FROSTED SALAD

Salad:
2 boxes lemon gelatin
2 cups boiling water
2 cups Seven-Up
1 large can crushed pineapple,
  drained
1 cup miniature marshmallows
2 large bananas, sliced
Topping:
½ cup sugar
2 tablespoons flour
1 cup pineapple juice
9 ounce carton whipped topping

Dissolve gelatin in boiling water, then add Seven-Up. When nearly set, add all other ingredients and refrigerate until firm.

For topping: cook sugar, flour and pineapple juice until thick, then let cool. Fold whipped topping into mixture. Spread on top of congealed salad. Top may be sprinkled with grated cheese.

Theresa Romano Foster, Lamar University
Beaumont, Texas

EASY FRUIT SALAD

1 medium size can pear halves,
  sliced (or can sliced pears)
1 medium size can pineapple
  chunks
3 or 4 average size bananas
1 medium size can grapes (or use
  fresh grapes)
1 package (3¾-ounce size)
  instant vanilla pudding

Drain fruit, saving 1 cup of juice. Mix fruits. Add juice to package of instant vanilla pudding; add to fruit just before serving. *Note:* a can of chunky mixed fruit or fruit cocktail can be used instead of some of the above fruits.

Virginia Forsythe Vint, University of Missouri
Dallas, Texas

FALL FRUIT SALAD

3 delicious apples
1 cup miniature marshmallows
⅓ cup English walnuts
Small bunch Tokay grapes
2 or 3 bananas
1 can chunk pineapple
2 tablespoons flour
¼ cup sugar
1 cup pineapple juice
1 egg

Diced unpeeled apples. Half and seed grapes. Combine apples, marshmallows, nuts, grapes, drained pineapple and sliced bananas. In saucepan, mix flour and sugar, then pineapple juice and beaten egg. Cook, stirring until it comes to a boil and is thick. Pour sauce over mixed fruit. Refrigerate until serving time. Can be made in the morning and served in the evening. *Note:* You won't have enough pineapple juice reserved from the can of chunks to make 1 cup. So if you don't have more pineapple juice, just add orange juice to fill out the cup of fluid needed. It gives it a nice tangy taste.

Evie Bane, University of Illinois
North Virginia

HOT CURRIED FRUIT

1 pound can sliced pears
6 maraschino cherries
1 pound can cling peaches OR
   apricots OR half and half
1 pound 4 ounce can pineapple
   chunks or slices
⅓ cup melted butter
¾ cup brown sugar, packed
4 teaspoons curry powder

Heat oven to 325 degrees. Drain fruit and arrange in 9x13 inch oblong pan. Pour mixture of other ingredients over fruit. Bake 15 minutes. Baste with drippings. Bake 15 minutes more.

Sue Ward Ragsdale, Southern Methodist University
Dallas, Texas

HOT FRUIT SALAD

1 cup sliced peaches
1 cup sliced pears
1 cup pineapple chunks
½ cup cherries
1 cup apricots
1 cup apricot juice
2 tablespoons brown sugar
1 tablespoon cornstarch

Drain all fruit; reserve 1 cup apricot juice. Mix fruit. Pour into baking dish. To 1 cup apricot juice, add brown sugar and cornstarch. Pour apricot juice mixture over fruit. Bake at 350 degrees until fruit is heated.

Cookbook Committee

CREAMY FROZEN FRUIT SALAD

2 cups sour cream
2 tablespoons lemon juice
¾ cup sugar
⅛ teaspoon salt
1 banana, sliced
1 can (8½-ounces) crushed
   pineapple, drained
¼ cup sliced maraschino cherries
¼ cup chopped pecans

Blend sour cream, lemon juice, sugar and salt. Stir in remaining ingredients. Pour into one-quart mold, or 12 cup cake papers in muffin tins. Place in freezer until firm. Serve on lettuce.

Barbara Callander Davis, Vanderbilt University
Amarillo, Texas

EASY FROZEN FRUIT SALAD

1 cup whipping cream
1 envelope unflavored gelatin
2 tablespoons lemon juice
¼ cup boiling water
½ cup mayonnaise
1 large can fruit cocktail, drained

Whip cream and set aside. Into blender container put gelatin, lemon juice, and boiling water. Cover and blend on medium speed for 30 seconds. Add mayonnaise and fruit. Cover and blend on high speed for 15 seconds. Fold into whipped cream. Pour into ice tray or salad ring mold and freeze. Cut into bars or slices to serve. Serves 6-8.

Sharon McFarland Groves,
Southern Methodist University
Richardson, Texas

1 can (number 303) coconut
1 cup white cherries, pitted
1 cup mandarin oranges
1 cup miniature marshmallows
1 cup crushed pineapple, drained
1 cup peaches, diced
1 cup cream, whipped
½ cup mayonnaise
Fruit Juice Dressing:
2 eggs
½ cup sugar
1 tablespoon cornstarch
½ cup pineapple juice
¼ cup orange juice
¼ cup lemon juice

FROZEN FRUIT SALAD

Chill fruit. Combine whipped cream and mayonnaise. Fold in fruit. Freeze. Serves 8.
Serve with fruit juice dressing, as follows: Beat eggs. Add sugar-cornstarch mixture. Add fruit juices and cook until thickened.

Gwen Lankford Rogers, Iowa State University
St. Louis, Missouri

3 large cucumbers
3 large tomatoes
2 green peppers
6 ribs celery
1 large bunch green onions
1 10-ounce can consommé
1 5-ounce can Snappy Tom
  (tomato juice)
¼ cup vegetable oil
½ teaspoon each salt and pepper
¼ teaspoon each dill, thyme,
  oregano
½ teaspoon garlic powder
1 tablespoon parsley

CRUNCHY GAZPACHO

Cut vegetables into bite-sized pieces, place in large mixing serving bowl. Pour liquids and spices into blender; blend quickly at high speed. Pour liquid mixture over vegetables, let set 4-5 hours in refrigerator before serving. Serves 10-12.

Carolyn Coe Cole, University of Texas
Dallas, Texas

4 cans grapefruit, drained,
  reserving juice
4 tablespoons gelatin dissolved in
1 cup cold water
1½ cup boiling water
1 cup sugar
½ teaspoon salt
Juice of ½ lemon
1 tart, unpared red apple
  (Jonathan), diced
2 avocados, sliced
½ cup blanched almonds

GRAPEFRUIT SALAD MOLD

Dissolve gelatin in cold water, add boiling water, sugar, salt and lemon juice. To this, add 1½ pints of the grapefruit juice or add water to make this amount. Cool to a syrupy stage. Put about one third of the gelatin mixture in a very large ring mold. Alternately lay in segments of grapefruit and avocado and refrigerate until set. Apple can be thinly sliced and laid in also — tedious, but very pretty when unmolded. Otherwise, add remaining ingredients to set mixture and refrigerate. Unmold on watercress or endive and serve with a light mayonnaise.

Irma Paul Nash, Iowa State University
Hot Springs, Arkansas

SALAD KEY ROYALE

1 can mushroom soup
3 3-ounce packages cream cheese
2 tablespoons unflavored gelatin
½ cup cold water
1 cup mayonnaise
1 cup celery, diced
½ green pepper, diced
1 small onion, diced
1 small can pimentos, diced
1 can water chestnuts, sliced thin
1 pound grouper OR snook OR
  cobia OR flounder OR halibut
  cooked and flaked (Red
  snapper is also delicious)

Soak gelatin in cold water. Heat soup to boiling. Add cheese and gelatin, stir until dissolved. Add vegetables, mayonnaise and fish (which must be well-cooked, preferably boiled). Mix well. Mold in fish mold if possible. Place in refrigerator for 12 hours. For serving, unmold carefully, and decorate platter with watercress, roses of radishes, and thin slices of cucumber. May be made the day before, and may be served with warm garlic bread or crackers. Serves 8.

Janet M. Heaton, University of Denver
Sarasota-Manatee County, Florida

MANDARIN ORANGE SALAD

Salad:
½ head shredded lettuce
1 cup chopped celery
1 tablespoon minced fresh parsley
2 green onions (and tips) chopped
1 11-ounce can mandarin
  oranges, drained
Dressing:
½ cup salad oil
¼ cup tarragon vinegar
½ teaspoon Tabasco sauce
1 teaspoon salt
¼ cup sugar
¼ cup toasted sliced almonds

Mix salad ingredients and chill. Combine dressing ingredients in jar and blend well. Add to salad as needed. Add toasted almonds before serving.

Ruth Stoufer, Iowa State University
Beverly Hills and Los Angeles

TRIPLE ORANGE MOLDED SALAD

1 package unflavored gelatin
1 package orange jello
1 pint orange sherbet
2 number 7 cans mandarin
  oranges

Dissolve unflavored gelatin in ¼ cup water. Add 2 cups boiling water to orange jello and gelatin mixture. Dissolve and cool slightly. Gradually beat in the sherbet. Add mandarin oranges with their juices. Mixture is frothy looking. Put into an extra large pyrex serving dish. Chill until firm.

Kay Mensing Teitgen,
University of Wisconsin-Madison
Milwaukee, Wisconsin

MARINATED SALAD

3 cans green beans
1 can wax beans
2 cans artichokes, quartered
1 4-ounce can mushrooms, sliced
1 large onion, thinly sliced
½ cup black olives, sliced
  (optional)
16 or 18 cherry tomatoes, cut in
  halves
½ cup grated Parmesan cheese
2 recipes Good Seasons Italian
  Dressing (made as directed)

Drain all canned vegetables. Combine all ingredients except cherry tomatoes and Parmesan cheese. Add dressing, toss and let stand in refrigerator 24 to 48 hours. Toss from time to time. Just before serving, add tomatoes and cheese. Toss. Serves 12.

Sue Dorsey Durrett, University of Missouri
Greater Kansas City

MEXICAN CHEF SALAD

Salad:
2½ pounds ground beef
2 cans kidney beans
1 package taco seasoning
1 teaspoon chili powder
1 head lettuce, shredded
½ cup celery, diced
2 tomatoes, chopped
½ cup green pepper, chopped
½ cup cucumbers, diced
1 cup grated Mozzarella cheese
Taco chips
Dressing:
1 cup sugar
1 cup oil
1 cup catsup
⅓ cup vinegar
Salt

Brown meat, add beans and seasonings. Prepare dressing in a blender. Make a tossed salad of the lettuce, celery, cucumbers, tomatoes and green pepper. Add cheese. To serve, put salad on dinner plates, add hot meat and beans, cover with salad dressings and crumble taco chips on top. Makes a one dish meal. Serves 6.

Anita Andrews Threlfall, Iowa State University
Sun City, Arizona

MIGUEL'S SALADA

Salad:
1 dozen corn tortillas
1 medium size head of lettuce
3 medium tomatoes
¼ pound Longhorn and Jack
  cheese
2 medium avocados
3 chicken breasts, cooked
1 large can refried beans
Ripe olives
Dressing:
½ cup white vinegar
½ cup salad oil
¼ cup oil from jar of jalapeño
  peppers
1 medium onion, thinly sliced

Fry corn tortillas until crisp. Heat refried beans until hot. Finely chop lettuce and cut tomatoes into wedges. Slice avocados into long strips. Cut Longhorn and Jack cheese into finger strips. Tear cooked chicken into thin strips. Place 1½ fried tortillas in the center of each plate. Smooth hot beans over tortillas. Pile chopped lettuce on top of this to make a mound. Next, alternate strips of chicken, cheese, avocado and tomato around the lettuce. Top with a few ripe olives.

Make dressing by mixing vinegar, salad oil, jalapeño oil together. Let stand with thin slices of onion in refrigerator until ready to use. If this is too hot, use less jalapeño oil. Let each person pour salad dressing over the tortillas according to their taste. Serves 4.

Melora "Petey" Dietz, Northern Arizona University
Escondido, California

MOSTLY MUSHROOM SALAD

1 pound fresh mushrooms
1 cup chopped celery
1 cup chopped green pepper
2 tablespoons chopped onions
2 tablespoons salad oil
1 tablespoon wine vinegar
2 tablespoons lemon juice
2 teaspoons salt
Pinch of pepper

Rinse, pat dry and slice mushrooms (makes about 5 cups). In a salad bowl place mushrooms, celery, green pepper and onions. Combine remaining ingredients and pour over vegetables, toss gently and serve. Vegetables may be prepared early in the day, adding dressing at serving time. Serves 6-8.

Julia Lynn Baldwin, Wittenberg University
Pittsburg, Kansas

BETTY'S FRESH MUSHROOM SALAD

½ pound thin sliced fresh
  mushrooms
1 cup water
1 tablespoon lemon juice
¼ cup sour cream (more if
  desired)
2 tablespoons green onion (finely
  chopped)
½ teaspoon salt
Dash of black pepper

Combine and cook the mushrooms, water and lemon juice until tender (2-3 minutes). Drain and cool and add the sauce of sour cream, green onion, salt and black pepper. Toss gently and serve on lettuce leaves.

Betty Kathryn Jones, Oklahoma University
Irving, Texas

SPICED PEACH SALAD

1 package lemon gelatin
1 package orange gelatin
1 large can white cherries
1 large can crushed pineapple
1 large can pickled peaches
½ cup pecans

Drain juice from cherries and discard. Pit cherries. Drain juice from pineapple and peaches and add enough water to make 4 cups. Heat. Combine gelatin and hot liquid. Stir until dissolved. When cool fold in fruit. Refrigerate to set gelatin.

Sunshine Hollar Davis, Southern Methodist University
Nashville, Tennessee

PINEAPPLE CREAM CHEESE BLOCKS

1 3-ounce package cream cheese
1 envelope plain gelatin softened
  in ½ cup cold water
1 cup boiling water
1 3-ounce package lemon gelatin
1 small can crushed pineapple
½ cup chopped nuts
1 cup cold water

Soften plain gelatin in ½ cup cold water. Combine cream cheese, lemon gelatin and boiling water and dissolve. Add softened plain gelatin. Add remaining cold water and cool slightly. Add pineapple and nuts. Pour into flat pan or mold and chill until firm. Cut into blocks and serve on lettuce leaves. Serves 6.

Linda Speckmann, Southern Methodist University
Dallas, Texas

PINEAPPLE MINT FREEZE SALAD

1 20-ounce can crushed pineapple
1 envelope unflavored gelatin
1 10-ounce jar mint jelly
1 cup whipping cream
1 tablespoon confectioners' sugar
Dash of salt

Drain pineapple and reserve syrup. In small saucepan, soften gelatin in syrup. Add jelly and dash of salt. Heat mixture and stir until gelatin and jelly are dissolved. Stir in pineapple. Chill until mixture is cool. Fold sugar into whipped cream and mix gently into gelatin mixture. Add few drops of green coloring. Spoon into freezer pan, 8½x4½x2½ (or 8 molds). Freeze until firm. Let stand at room temperature 15 minutes before serving.

Ann Sokol Heath, Iowa State University
Dallas, Texas

PINK SALAD

1 3-ounce package strawberry
gelatin
1 3-ounce package cream cheese
1 cup hot water
1 small can crushed pineapple
(not drained)
½ cup nuts, chopped
½ pint cream, whipped

Cream gelatin and cheese together. Add water and beat until gelatin dissolves. Add pineapple. When mixture starts to set, add nuts and cream. Pour into mold and let set.

Ernestine Dobler McDonald, Northwestern University
Greater Kansas City

PISTACHIO SALAD

1 pint sour cream
1 small package pistachio instant
pudding
1½ cups coconut
1 small can crushed pineapple
with juice

Mix all ingredients together in small bowl. Refrigerate. Ready to serve in 1 hour.

"Beautiful to see, and delicious to taste. Sweet enough to be a dessert. Serve in chilled stem glasses with whipped cream."

Ann Neighbors, Auburn University
Montgomery, Alabama

POTATO SALAD FOR A CROWD

6 pounds new potatoes
2 tablespoons salt
2 tablespoons celery seed
¾ cup minced onion
1 cup diced dill pickle
5 hard boiled eggs (diced)
¼ cup pickle juice
2 cups salad dressing or
mayonnaise
½ cup chopped pimento

Cook potatoes, peel and dice. Sprinkle with salt and celery seed and refrigerate. Combine with other ingredients and add enough salad dressing to blend. Chill before serving. Serves about 25.

Gayle Howard Young, University of Texas
Dallas, Texas

MOM'S POTATO SALAD

2 pounds red potatoes, cooked
and diced
4 to 6 hard boiled eggs, diced
1 to 2 cups mayonnaise or salad
dressing
3 to 6 medium onions, chopped
1 tablespoon celery seed
2 tablespoons parsley
1 green pepper, diced
4 tablespoons chives
2 shakes from jar of onion powder
1 teaspoon mustard seed
1 shake from jar of garlic powder
3-4 tablespoons prepared
mustard
Salt and pepper to taste

Mix all ingredients thoroughly. Chill overnight.

Pat O'Connell Mullins, St. Louis University
Dallas, Texas

HOT GERMAN POTATO SALAD

10 medium red potatoes, cooked,
   sliced (with jackets left on)
6 slices bacon, cooked, crumbled
1½ cups onions, chopped
4 tablespoons flour
4 tablespoons sugar
2½ teaspoons salt
1 teaspoon celery seed
Pepper to taste
1½ cups water
⅔ cup vinegar

In bacon drippings, cook onions until tender and browned. Stir in flour, sugar, salt, celery seed and pepper. Cook over low heat, stirring constantly until mixture is bubbly. Remove from heat and gradually stir in water and vinegar. Return to heat and cook over medium heat until mixture boils. Boil and stir about 2 minutes. Stir potatoes and bacon into this mixture. Heat thoroughly. Serves 8 generously.

Cookbook Committee

ELEGANT WISCONSIN HOT POTATO SALAD

2 cups diced cooked potatoes
6 hard boiled eggs
1 small onion, diced
Dash of Worcestershire sauce
¼ cup crumbled Roquefort or
   Bleu cheese
4 tablespoons mayonnaise
Salt and pepper to taste
Few bacon bits and sliced stuffed
   green olives for garné

Mix ingredients, placing diced bacon and stuffed olive slices on top. Heat through at 400 degrees for about 20 minutes. Bleu cheese gives an unusual flavor!

Virginia Anderson Wells, Northwestern University
Milwaukee, Wisconsin

RED, WHITE, AND BLUE SALAD

1 3-ounce package strawberry
   jello
2 cups hot water
½ teaspoon strawberry flavoring
   (optional)
1 envelope unflavored gelatin
½ cup cold water
1 cup half and half cream
1 cup sugar
1 teaspoon vanilla
2 cups dairy sour cream
1 package raspberry jello
1 cup hot water
1 can blueberries, reserve liquid

Dissolve strawberry jello in 2 cups hot water. Add flavoring and pour into oiled mold. Dissolve gelatin in ½ cup cold water. Heat cream and sugar until dissolved and add to softened gelatin. Cool and add vanilla and sour cream. Pour over first layer when set. Dissolve raspberry jello in 1 cup hot water. Add liquid from blueberry can and enough water to make 1 cup. Add blueberries. Congeal and pour over second layer. Refrigerate overnight.

"A favorite at 4th of July picnics."

Lynne Barnett, University of Colorado
Boulder, Colorado

SALINAS SALAD BOWL

1 cup cauliflower flowerets
1 cup mushroom slices
1 cup celery slices
1 cup broccoli flowerets
1 cup cherry tomato halves
1 cup green pepper strips
½ cup radish slices
Dressing:
½ cup salad oil
3 tablespoons lemon juice
3 tablespoons wine vinegar
2 teaspoons salt
½ teaspoon sugar
¼ teaspoon pepper

Combine vegetables with dressing and serve.

Cheryl Stoner Myhra, Iowa State University
Dallas, Texas

SAUERKRAUT SALAD

1 large can sauerkraut, drained
1 cup celery (cut crosswise)
1 bell pepper (slivered)
1 *red* onion, cut in rings
1 small jar pimento, drained
   (chopped)
½ cup vinegar
1 cup sugar
1 cup oil

Mix vinegar and sugar. Heat and then let cool. Add oil to make dressing. Mix vegetables and kraut. Pour on dressing, mixing well. Marinate for at least 2 hours.

Connie Spanier, Oregon State University
San Francisco, California

SHRIMP AND AVOCADO SALAD

12 ounces shrimp (frozen,
   cleaned, cooked)
1 cup chopped celery
⅓ cup thousand island dressing
1 teaspoon lemon juice
2 avocados
Salt and pepper

Defrost shrimp under cold, running water. Chop celery and cut avocados in half, removing the pits and skins. Combine shrimp, celery, salad dressing, lemon juice, and salt and pepper. Place avocado halves on bed of lettuce and fill with the shrimp mixture. 4 servings.

Melanie Purdy, Southern Methodist University
Englewood, Colorado

SHRIMP ASPIC

2 cups V-8 juice
2 cups chili sauce
Juice of 1 lemon
1 tablespoon horseradish
2 envelopes unflavored gelatin
4 tablespoons water
½ cup chopped onion
½ cup chopped celery
1 6-ounce package shrimp

Heat V-8 juice, chili sauce, lemon juice, horseradish in saucepan. Dissolve gelatin in water. Add hot mixture. Set until slightly congealed. Add celery, onion, shrimp, Pour into greased mold.

Carol Cole, University of Denver
Montgomery, Alabama

SHRIMP MOLD

1 can undiluted tomato soup
1 8-ounce package cream cheese
¾ cup chopped onions
¾ cup chopped celery
2 envelopes Knox gelatin
2½ cups small shrimp
1 cup mayonnaise
Salt and pepper

Heat soup. Soften gelatin in ¼ cup cold water. Pour into soup. Mix in all remaining ingredients, adding shrimp last. Pour into greased mold and refrigerate at least half day.

Jane Thurman Leonard, Washington University
St. Louis, Missouri

Victoria S. Beach, Gettysburg College
Wyckoff, New Jersey

Rosemary Morel Stafford, Gettysburg College
Central New Jersey

Nellie Weston Ullrick, Northwestern University
Moline, Illinois

Julia Terry Templeton, Southern Methodist University
Charleston, South Carolina

SKILLET SALAD

¼ cup chopped green onion
¼ cup chopped green pepper
1 12-ounce can Spam
1 tablespoon oil
3 medium potatoes, cooked and diced
¼ cup salad dressing or mayonnaise
½ pound cheddar cheese, diced

Sauté onions, green pepper and meat in oil until meat is brown. Add potatoes, salad dressing and seasonings to taste. Heat, mixing lightly. Stir in cheese, heat until it begins to melt. Serves 4.

Jacki Falkenroth, University of Nevada-Reno
Chicago Northwest Suburban, Illinois

NINE DAY SLAW

1 medium cabbage, shredded
2 stalks celery, diced
2 medium onions, diced
1 green pepper, diced
2 cups sugar
1 cup salad oil
1 cup cider vinegar
2 tablespoons salt
2 tablespoons sugar
Pimento optional

Combine cabbage, celery, onion and green pepper. Add two cups sugar and blend well. Combine remaining ingredients. Bring to a boil, stirring constantly. Pour dressing over cabbage mixture immediately and allow to cool. Cover and store in refrigerator at least one day before serving. Slaw will stay crisp and fresh for nine days!

Cathy Guthrie Lindauer, Iowa State University
Denver, Colorado

COLD SPAGHETTI SALAD

½ pound spaghetti, broken into
small pieces and cooked
1 medium-sized onion, chopped
½ pound cooked, cleaned and
deveined shrimp
Salt and pepper
Mayonnaise

Combine cooked spaghetti and onion. Add mayonnaise to moisten spaghetti. Add shrimp. Salt and pepper to taste. Chill. Better if made a day ahead. Serve on lettuce leaf with hot rolls.

Elizabeth Mullare Messenger, University of Denver
Denver, Colorado

SPINACH SALAD FLAMBE

Salad:
1 pound fresh spinach
3-4 hard boiled eggs
½ cup shredded Mozzarella
cheese
½ teaspoon szechuan pepper,
coarsely ground
Dressing:
6 strips bacon, fried crisp and
broken up
½ cup strained bacon drippings
¼ cup tarragon vinegar
2 tablespoons lemon juice
1 tablespoon sugar
¼ teaspoon Worcestershire sauce
½ cup brandy or cognac

Into a large bowl, tear spinach. Add sliced eggs, cheese, salt and pepper. Add bacon just before serving. Heat dressing ingredients, except for brandy, in a small saucepan. Warm brandy in a ladle, ignite, and pour into dressing gently. When flaming is done, add to salad and toss well. Dressing should be warm enough to wilt spinach slightly.

Barbara A. Clark, University of Texas
Nashua, New Hampshire

ORIENTAL SPINACH SALAD

2 bags fresh spinach
1 can water chestnuts, sliced
1 can bean sprouts
6 green onions, diced
4 hard cooked eggs
8 slices bacon, fried crisp and
crumbled
Dressing:
1 cup salad oil
¾ cup sugar
½ cup white vinegar
2 teaspoons salt
½ cup ketchup

For dressing: Combine all ingredients in jar, bowl, or bottle. Shake or beat till blended; or mix in electric blender.
For salad: Wash and tear spinach leaves to bite size. Remove hard stem part. Mix first four salad ingredients. Just before serving, slice eggs on top and crumble bacon. Pour dressing over all. Serves 8 to 10.

Evelyn Allard Ellis, University of Illinois
Evansville, Indiana

Margaret Miller Browne, Oregon State
Dallas, Texas

Ardis Decamp Moriarty, Colorado State University
Mountain View, California

SPINACH-DILL SALAD BOWL

½ cup corn oil
⅓ cup white wine vinegar
1 teaspoon dried dillweed
8 cups fresh spinach
1 cup sliced fresh mushrooms
1 cup sliced cucumber
1 cup cherry tomatoes, halved
1 small red onion, thinly sliced
4 hard cooked eggs, sliced
1 can sardines, drained

Combine oil, vinegar and dill weed. Chill. Tear spinach into bite size pieces. Add remaining ingredients. Toss gently with chilled dressing. Serves 8.

Carolie Goniu, University of Wisconsin-Madison
Milwaukee, Wisconsin

KATHRYN'S UNUSUAL SPINACH SALAD

2 packages frozen chopped
   spinach (Don't cook. Thaw and
   squeeze by hand.)
½ cup finely chopped onion
½ cup finely chopped celery
1 cup sharp cheddar cheese,
   grated
1 cup mayonnaise
½ teaspoon salt
2 tablespoons horseradish
4 hard boiled eggs, chopped
½ teaspoon Tabasco sauce
1½ teaspoon vinegar

Mix all ingredients, adding spinach last. If serving as individual salad, add a dab of horseradish on lettuce leaf next to spinach. Serves 8.

Talie McKenzie, Northwestern University
Arlington Heights, Illinois

MOLDED STRAWBERRY SALAD

2 3-ounce packages strawberry
   gelatin
1 can (15 ounce) crushed
   pineapple, drained
2 packages frozen strawberries
1 12-ounce carton sour cream
2 cups hot water
2 bananas, sliced (optional)

Dissolve gelatin in hot water. Add strawberries, pineapple and bananas. Put half of this mixture in a 8x13 inch dish or mold, and refrigerate. When thoroughly congealed, spread on sour cream and then remaining gelatin mixture. Chill.

Holly Wilcox Eastman, Miami University
Bartlesville, Oklahoma

Dorothy S. Kenney, Syracuse University
Syracuse, New York

Shirley Von Ruden, Kansas State University
Hutchinson, Kansas

Patrice Allen Hainzinger, Auburn University
Bartlesville, Oklahoma

STRAWBERRY SALAD SUPREME

2 packages strawberry jello
1 16-ounce package frozen strawberries
2½ cups boiling water
2 sliced bananas
1 small can crushed pineapple (drain and reserve liquid)
Topping:
⅔ cup pineapple juice
1 egg, well beaten
1 cup whipped cream or whipped topping
½ cup sugar
2 tablespoons flour

Combine ingredients and chill until completely set. A few hours before salad is to be served, make the topping by cooking juice, egg, sugar and flour together until thick. When cool, fold in 1 cup whipped cream or whipped topping and spread over top of gelatin salad.

Cindy Drevo, University of Nebraska
Lincoln, Nebraska

SUNSHINE SALAD

2 small packages lemon gelatin
1½ cups boiling water
1½ cups cold water
2 tablespoons vinegar
1 9-ounce can crushed pineapple
2 cups shredded cabbage
2 medium carrots, shredded
1 stalk celery, finely chopped
A few sliced olives (optional)

Dissolve gelatin with water and add vegetables and fruit. Pour it into mold. When set, turn upside down on large plate.

Mary M. Crannell, St. Louis University
Fenton, Missouri

SWEDISH VEGETABLE SALAD

2 packages frozen peas and carrots
1 package French style green beans
1½ cups raw cauliflower
1 cup canned artichoke hearts, quartered
½ cup chopped onion
½ cup chopped celery
⅔ cup French dressing
Dressing:
¾ cup mayonnaise
¼ cup bottled chili sauce
2 teaspoons dry ground dill
1 teaspoon salt
⅛ teaspoon pepper
1 teaspoon lemon juice

Cook the first two ingredients until tender; drain, cool, then mix with the next four ingredients. Marinate in ⅔ cup of very sharp French dressing overnight. Before serving, drain and add above dressing. Serves 12.

Betty Lou Wisland, University of Wisconsin-Madison
Milwaukee, Wisconsin

TABOULI

1 cup cracked wheat
3 cups water
3 tomatoes, diced
2 cucumbers, diced
1 large bunch green onions diced
¼ cup parsley, chopped fine
Juice of 3 lemons
3 tablespoons dried mint
½ cup olive oil
1 tablespoon pepper
1 tablespoon salt

Soak cracked wheat overnight in water. Drain well, squeeze out excess water with hands. Mix remaining ingredients together with wheat. Let set in refrigerator 3 hours or more before serving. Serves 8-10.

Carolyn Coe Cole, University of Texas
Dallas, Texas

MEATLESS TACO SALAD

1 large head lettuce
1 cup chopped celery
1 cup chopped carrots
¼ cup chopped onion
¼ cup chopped green pepper
1 can chili beans — drained but
   not washed
1 6-ounce package shredded
   Cheddar cheese
1 small bottle Green Goddess
   salad dressing
1 package — small frito chips

Mix all ingredients except dressing and fritos. Chill — right before serving toss with dressing and fritos.

Holly Wible Deeg, Indiana University
Evansville, Indiana

TACO SALAD

Amounts vary depending on
   number to be served:
Chopped lettuce
Shredded cheese
Tomatoes
Kidney beans, drained
Ground beef
Red wine vinegar and oil dressing
Taco sauce
Doritos chips

Brown ground beef and add small amount of taco sauce to taste. Toss with lettuce, tomatoes and kidney beans. Add salad dressing and let sit up to 1½ hours in refrigerator. Before serving, top with cheese and crushed Doritos.

Cathy Frost, Michigan State University
Birmingham, Michigan

TEA GARDEN SALAD

Salad:
1 package orange gelatin
1 cup hot tea
1 11-ounce can mandarin oranges
1 9-ounce can crushed pineapple
1 can water chestnuts (optional)
Dressing:
1 cup whipped cream
½ cup mayonnaise
Grated orange rind
Dash of nutmeg

Dissolve gelatin in cup of hot tea, add 1 cup syrup obtained from draining can of oranges and can of crushed pineapple. Chill gelatin until slightly thickened. Add drained oranges, drained pineapple and sliced water chestnuts. Chill.

To make the dressing, whip cream until stiff, fold in mayonnaise, add grated rind of orange, dash nutmeg and spread on top of gelatin mixture.

Jeannette Collins Sicks, Iowa State University
Ames, Iowa

Elaine Campbell Simpson, University of Iowa
Washington, DC

TOMATO SALAD RING FOR FRUIT

1 can tomato soup
½ pound cream cheese
1 cup water
1½ tablespoons plain gelatin
1 cup mayonnaise
1 cup diced celery
1 medium size onion, minced
1 green pepper, minced
2 tablespoons lemon juice

Heat soup. Add cheese, stir until dissolved. Add gelatin dissolved in water. Chill. Add remaining ingredients. Place in ring mold and chill.

In serving, center mold with melon balls — cantaloupe, watermelon, honeydew. Surround ring with 1 can of sliced pineapple, bananas cut in long quarters, canned or fresh peach halves, Bing cherries, grapes (seeded and halved) and halved apricots. Orange and grapefruit segments may also be used.

Edmee Moellman Moore, Washington University
St. Louis, Missouri

EASY TOMATO ASPIC

1 can tomato soup, heated
1½ tablespoon gelatin (1 packet)
1 package lemon gelatin
1 cup hot water to melt gelatin
1 cup chopped celery
2 tablespoons green pepper
2 3-ounce packages cream cheese
1 cup mayonnaise
1 cup chopped walnuts

Melt cream cheese into heated soup. Cool. Add remaining ingredients. Turn into molds to chill. Serve on lettuce.

Variations: Omit walnuts and add shrimp, salmon or chicken, 2 hard-boiled eggs, chopped pimentos, sliced olives, green onions.

Tippy Briley Timm, Iowa State University
Ames, Iowa

MICHELLE'S ITALIAN TOMATO SALAD

3 firm, ripe, tomatoes, cored,
   sliced into wedges
2 stalks celery, chopped
1 small cucumber, sliced thin
½ cup olive oil
2 teaspoons oregano
4 cloves garlic, chopped
Salt and pepper to taste

Mix all ingredients together and marinate ½ hour before serving.

Cookbook Committee

MOLDED TOMATO SALAD

1 16-ounce can stewed tomatoes,
   cut up
1 3-ounce package lemon jello
½ cup mayonnaise or salad
   dressing
1 small bottle stuffed olives,
   thinly sliced

Heat stewed tomatoes and add jello. Cool slightly then add mayonnaise and mix well with electric mixer. Add sliced olives.

Very attractive made in flower molds with a dab of dressing and an olive on top. Makes 6 molds.

Jeannette Collins Sicks, Iowa State University
Ames, Iowa

TOMATO-RASPBERRY MOLD

1 large package raspberry gelatin
3 cans stewed tomatoes (16 ounce size)
1 small can crushed pineapple

Put stewed tomatoes in blender for 30 seconds. Pour tomato liquid into sauce pan and add raspberry gelatin. Heat over medium heat. Cool and add pineapple chunks and juice. Put in mold and chill until set. Serves 10.

Mollie Ellis Ellis, Oklahoma University
Dallas, Texas

TUNA SALAD

2 6½-ounce cans water pack tuna, drained
11 ounces frozen peas
1 cup chopped celery
¾ cup mayonnaise
1 tablespoon lemon juice
½ teaspoon curry powder
⅛ teaspoon garlic salt
1 cup Chinese chow mein noodles (canned)
½ cup toasted almonds

Mix tuna, peas and celery and chill. Combine mayonnaise, lemon juice, curry powder and garlic salt. Add to chilled ingredients. Just before serving add noodles and almonds.

Ruth Hendrix Stoufer, Iowa State University
Los Angeles and Beverly Hills, California

DEL MAR TUNA SALAD

2 6½-ounce cans white tuna, drained
1 can water chestnuts, sliced
2 13¼-ounce cans pineapple tidbits, drain and cut in half
½ cup chopped celery
½ cup diced green onions
1 #303 can Chinese noodles
Dressing:
1 cup sour cream
1 cup mayonnaise
1 teaspoon curry powder

For the tuna salad, mix all ingredients together, except Chinese noodles. Mix all ingredients for the dressing, blend into tuna mixture and chill. Just prior to serving, add the Chinese noodles. Serves 8.

Margaret Stewart, Iowa State University
Del Mar, California

TUNA FISH SALAD

1 envelope plain gelatin
¼ cup cold water
1 can tuna (6½-ounce), rinsed
½ cup celery, diced
½ cup green pepper, diced
¾ cup mayonnaise
Small jar stuffed olives, sliced
½ teaspoon salt
¼ teaspoon paprika
1 tablespoon vinegar
1 small jar pimientos (diced)

Soften gelatin in cold water. Place over boiling water until dissolved. Cool. Mix vinegar, gelatin, salt and paprika in mayonnaise. Mix all ingredients together. Place in a glass dish to set. Cut into serving pieces. Serve on lettuce.

Virginia Docking, Kansas University
Topeka, Kansas

COTTOI'S TUNA SALAD

1 3-ounce package lime jello
1 3-ounce package lemon jello
2 cups hot water
2 6½-ounce cans white tuna, drained
2 tablespoons sliced stuffed olives
1 cup celery, cut fine
2 tablespoons chopped green pepper
6 ounces of cream cheese, softened
1 cup mayonnaise
1 cup half and half
8 hard boiled eggs, cut up, not too fine

Dissolve lemon and lime jellos with hot water, stir. Let cool. Carefully mix all ingredients together except tuna. Lastly, stir in tuna lightly, then chill. Use a 8x12 inch casserole dish or 9x12 inch loaf pan. Serves 15 to 18 people.
This is real Ladyfood!

Latane Jordan Graham, Memphis State University
Dallas, Texas

CURRIED TUNA

2 6½-ounce cans tuna
2 cups cooked minute rice
1 cup diced celery
1½ teaspoons curry
1 teaspoon lemon juice
½ cup mayonnaise
½ teaspoon salt
⅛ teaspoon pepper

Mix all ingredients together, serve immediately at room temperature. Curry flavor best when neither too hot nor too cold. Serves 4-6.

Carolyn Coe Cole, University of Texas
Dallas, Texas

TUNA-MACARONI SALAD

½ package shell macaroni (6 ounces), cooked
2 to 3 hard boiled eggs, chopped
4 sweet pickles, diced
½ small onion, diced
1 fresh tomato, peeled and diced
1 small can LeSeuer peas, drained
2 small, or 1 large, can tuna, drained
Mayonnaise

Drain cooked macaroni well. Add next 6 ingredients; mix. Moisten well with mayonnaise, and season to taste with salt and pepper. Chill thoroughly. Serve on lettuce leaves.

Kay Reynolds Bennett, Texas Tech University
Dallas, Texas

TUNA SALAD SUPREME

2 envelopes plain gelatin
½ cup cold water
1 (8 ounce) package cream cheese
1 can cream of mushroom soup
1 cup mayonnaise
2 (6½ ounce) cans tuna
1 cup chopped celery
1 small jar red pimiento, chopped

Heat mushroom soup over low heat, add gelatin which has been softened in water. Add cream cheese and stir until melted. Remove mixture from heat and add mayonnaise. Add chopped celery, chopped pimiento, and tuna that has been drained and flaked.
Pour into 8 by 11 inch pan and chill several hours or over night. Cut in squares and serve on lettuce leaves. Serves 8 to 10.

Sara Hess McElhaney, Iowa State University
Dallas, Texas

TURKEY FRUIT SALAD

2½ cups cold, cooked turkey, cubed
1 cup celery, chopped
1 can mandarin orange slices, drained
½ cup slivered almonds, toasted
½ teaspoon salt
1 cup mayonnaise
½ cup whipping cream, whipped
½ to 1 teaspoon grated orange rind
½ to 1 teaspoon candied ginger, chopped fine
1 fresh pineapple, cored and sliced in rings*

Mix first 5 ingredients. Mix together mayonnaise and whipped cream and stir into turkey mixture with ginger and orange rind. Place 1 slice pineapple on lettuce leaf and spoon one serving of chilled salad on each. Garnish with parsley or fresh mint leaves.

*Cantaloupe rings or canned pineapple slices may be substituted. Serves 6 to 8.

Nancy Worten, University of Denver
Bartlesville, Oklahoma

SEVEN LAYER SALAD

½ large head lettuce, broken into pieces
2 small cans LeSeuer peas, drained
5 stalks celery, diced
1 small red onion, ringed
3 teaspoons sugar
2 cups mayonnaise
Parmesan cheese
8-10 slices fried bacon

Arrange in layers in large salad bowl. Then sprinkle on sugar and cheese. Spread mayonnaise evenly on top. Cover tightly and store in refrigerator 8-10 hours, or overnight. Just before serving, crumble bacon and toss with salad. A great meal all by itself — add hot cornbread and it's pure Southern!

Bonnie Allen Gregory, Oklahoma University
Simpsonville, South Carolina

Jill Tennis Heiteman, St. Louis University
Rolla, Missouri

Phyllis Donaldson Choat, University of Nebraska
Omaha, Nebraska

TWENTY-FOUR HOUR SALAD

1 medium head lettuce
1 cup thinly sliced onions
1 cup thinly sliced celery
1 6-ounce can water chestnuts
1 10-ounce package frozen peas
2 cups mayonnaise
1 teaspoon sugar
½ teaspoon salt
¼ teaspoon pepper
1 cup shredded Mozzarella cheese
½ cup grated Parmesan cheese
Cherry tomatoes
Bacon bits
Parsley

Shred lettuce and place in bottom of glass dish. Layer onions, celery, water chestnuts and frozen peas. Spread with layer of mayonnaise. Sprinkle with mixture of sugar, salt and pepper. Top with cheese. Cover tightly with foil and refrigerate 24 hours. Garnish with tomatoes, bacon bits and parsley before serving.

Terry Gallagher, University of Texas
Dallas, Texas

UNTOSSED SALAD

Torn lettuce (½-1 small head)
Green pepper, chopped
Fresh mushrooms, sliced
Frozen peas
Celery, chopped
2 cups mayonnaise
2 tablespoons sugar
Cheddar cheese, grated
Bacon, crumbled
(Amounts depend on number
being served.)

Fill *straight sided* bowl half full with torn lettuce. Add a layer of celery, a layer of green pepper, a layer of fresh mushrooms, a layer of separated frozen peas (do *not* cook). Top with mayonnaise and sugar mixed — go all the way to edges of bowl so vegetables are sealed. Top with cheddar cheese. Cover and refrigerate for 8 to 10 hours. Before serving, top with crumbled bacon.

Connie Baker, University of Minnesota
Atlanta, Georgia

VIRGINIA'S TWENTY-FOUR HOUR SALAD

1 pound Tokay grapes, seeded
1 large can crushed pineapple, drained
1 pint whipping cream, whipped
Sauce:
4 egg yolks, beaten
½ cup sugar
Juice of two lemons

Cook custard sauce over low heat until thickened. Cool. Combine sauce with fruit and whipped cream. Chill 24 hours. So sweet and rich it could be used as a dessert.

Diana Veenkant Owen, University of Michigan
Dallas, Texas

CURRIED VEGETABLE SALAD

⅓ cup mayonnaise
1 package Chicken Flavored Rice-a-Roni
4 green onions sliced thin
½ chopped green pepper
12 pimento olives sliced thin
2 6-ounce jars of marinated artichoke hearts or bottoms
¾ teaspoon of curry powder

Cook rice omitting the browning process directed on box. Cool. Add green onions, pepper and olives. Drain artichokes, reserving oil. Combine marinade oil with curry and mayonnaise. Add hearts to rice and toss with dressing. Chill. Serve on lettuce cup. Serves 6 to 8.

Barbara M. Charles Merz,
University of California-Berkeley
La Jolla, California

VEGETABLE SALAD

1 envelope plain gelatin
1 package lemon gelatin
1 cup hot water
2 tablespoons lemon juice
1 tablespoon sugar
½ teaspoon salt
½ cup mayonnaise
½ cup sour cream
1 tablespoon mustard
1½ cups chopped cabbage
½ cup grated carrot
½ cup diced celery
2 tablespoons grated onion
1 tablespoon parsley, chopped

Soften plain gelatin in lemon juice. Dissolve gelatin in hot water. Add lemon juice with plain gelatin, sugar and salt. Chill until syrupy. Fold in mayonnaise, sour cream and mustard. Chill until slightly thick. Stir in cabbage, carrots, celery, onion and parsley. Makes 4 to 6 servings, may be easily doubled.

Grace Pitchford Killingsworth, Oklahoma University
Dallas, Texas

PICKLED VEGETABLES

⅔ cup tarragon vinegar
½ cup salad oil
2 tablespoons water
1 tablespoon sugar
1 clove garlic crushed
1½ teaspoon salt
Dash each of pepper, hot pepper
  sauce
Fresh onions, sliced
Fresh mushrooms
Hearts of palm
Small carrots
Artichoke hearts
Broccoli
Zucchini, etc.

Blend all ingredients except vegetables. Place vegetables in bowl. Top with marinade; cover; store in refrigerator at least 24 hours, stirring occasionally. Drain before serving. Serve as a salad or appetizer. Multiply marinade for larger quantity.

Barbara Baverle Glanz, Kansas University
Western Springs, Illinois

MOTHER'S WATERGATE SALAD

1 small package Pistachio jello
  pudding
1 (9 ounce) package Cool Whip
1 cup miniature marshmallows
½ cup maraschino cherries
1 (15½ ounce) can crushed
  pineapple
½ cup nuts, chopped
½ cup chopped dates

Mix jello pudding with Cool Whip. Add marshmallows, cherries, pineapple, juice and all, nuts and dates.

Gloria Swanson Nelson, Oklahoma University
Dallas, Texas

Salad Dressing

CELERY SEED DRESSING

1½ cups sugar
1 tablespoon paprika
1½ teaspoon dry mustard
½ teaspoon salt
½ cup vinegar
¼ cup grated onion (less for
  milder flavor)
1 cup salad oil
1 tablespoon celery seed

Combine first five ingredients in sauce pan and boil for 1 minute. Stir constantly. Remove from heat and cool to lukewarm. Mixture will thicken. Place in blender or mixer, gradually blend in onion and salad oil. Fold in celery seed. Wonderful on citrus or any fruit.

Beatrice Brown Freeman, Iowa State University
Aiken, South Carolina

AUNT SUSIE'S COLE SLAW DRESSING

½ cup sugar
1 teaspoon dry mustard
1 teaspoon salt
1 tablespoon flour
1 well beaten egg
¼ cup white vinegar
2 tablespoons butter or
  margarine

Mix dry ingredients. Add egg and vinegar. Cook over slow heat. Stir constantly. When thick, add butter. Cool.

Ethel Bate, University of Arizona
Phoenix, Arizona

FRENCH SALAD DRESSING

2 cups salad oil
¾ cup sugar
½ cup cider vinegar
2 tablespoons minced onion
2 teaspoons salt
2 teaspoons paprika
2 teaspoons dry mustard
2 teaspoons celery seed

Mix thoroughly. Place in top of double boiler and heat just to body temperature. Remove quickly and beat mixture with electric mixer. Shake well before using. (Dressing will be fairly thick.)

Patricia Smith Dieterich, University of Iowa
Ridgefield, Connecticut

FRENCH DRESSING

1⅓ cups sugar
⅔ cup ketchup
1 cup vegetable oil
½ cup white vinegar
1½ teaspoons salt
Juice of 1 lemon
2 to 3 green onions sliced fine

Put in quart jar and shake well.

This is an old tried and true favorite from Ruth's home town of Farmington, Illinois.

Ruth Johnson, University of Illinois
Arlington Heights, Illinois

ADAH'S SWEET FRENCH DRESSING

1 can tomato soup
1½ cup oil
¾ cup vinegar
½ cup sugar
½ teaspoon each: basil, oregano,
  parsley, tarragon, chervil, salt,
  and pepper

Place all ingredients in blender. Blend well. Let stand 2 hours before serving.

Pat O'Connell Mullins, St. Louis University
Dallas, Texas

FLUFFY FRENCH DRESSING

2 egg whites, beaten quite stiffly
⅛ cup sugar
1 tablespoon paprika
⅛ teaspoon pepper
¼ teaspoon salt
1 cup oil
1 cup ketchup
1 tablespoon Worcestershire
  sauce
½ cup tomato juice
⅛ cup salad vinegar
1 small garlic clove, grated
1 small onion, grated
Juice of ½ lemon

Beat egg whites in mixer, then slowly add all ingredients. Store in glass container. Shake before using.

Harriett Trippe Benz
University of Wisconsin-Madison
Sullivan, Wisconsin

WALNUT OIL FRENCH DRESSING

1 teaspoon salt seasoned with 1
  clove of garlic for 24 hours
1 teaspoon dry mustard
Fresh-ground black pepper
½ cup wine vinegar with tarragon
1¼ cups walnut oil, or ¾ cup
  walnut oil and ½ cup peanut oil

Season 1 teaspoon salt with 1 clove of garlic for 24 hours, add other ingredients and shake briskly.

Elizabeth Fee Arnold, Past Grand President,
Colorado State University
Los Angeles, California

OMAR'S DRESSING

2 eggs
1 tablespoon sugar
1 teaspoon salt
½ teaspoon paprika
½ teaspoon dry mustard
1 teaspoon Worcestershire sauce
½ cup ketchup
2 cups salad oil
½ cup vinegar
⅔ cup warm water

Mix all ingredients except oil, vinegar and water in mixing bowl that has been rubbed with garlic clove. Stir them into a smooth paste. Add oil slowly, alternating with vinegar. Beat in electric mixer into a thick dressing, add the warm water slowly. Keep refrigerated. Makes slightly more than a quart. Excellent on spinach salad, — spinach, red onion slices and sliced mushrooms.

Sylvia Hardy Trewin, Iowa State University
Dallas, Texas

FRUIT DRESSING

½ cup sugar
1 teaspoon dry mustard
1 teaspoon paprika
1 teaspoon salt
¼ cup vinegar
1 teaspoon poppy seed (or celery
  seed)
1 teaspoon onion juice
1 cup salad oil

Combine all ingredients except oil in small mixer bowl. Add oil 2 teaspoons at a time while beating. If the oil is added slowly the dressing will remain mixed and thick for several weeks. Very good over fresh fruits, and can be used on vegetable salads.

Barbara B. Derrick, Iowa State University
Ft. Worth, Texas

POPPY SEED DRESSING I

1½ cups sugar
2 teaspoons dry mustard
2 teaspoons salt
⅔ cup vinegar
2 tablespoons onion juice
2 cups salad oil
2 tablespoons poppy seeds

Mix together sugar, mustard, salt and vinegar in blender. Add onion juice and blend thoroughly. With blender running, add oil slowly, and continue blending until thick. Add poppy seeds and whirl for a few more seconds. Store covered in a cool place or keep in refrigerator. Serve over fruit or any salad.

Lynne Ayers, Vanderbilt University
Nashville, Tennessee

POPPY SEED DRESSING II

¾ cup sugar
1 teaspoon dry mustard
1 teaspoon salt
⅓ cup red wine vinegar
1 tablespoon instant minced
onion
1 cup corn oil
1 teaspoon poppy seed
1 teaspoon sesame seed

Blend first 5 ingredients throughly in blender. Gradually add oil, blending well. Last, blend in seeds. Chill. Makes 1½ cups. Good on salad, fruits or slaw.

Nita Waninger Steck, Washington University
St. Louis, Missouri

BASIC MAYONNAISE AND SOUR CREAM BLEU CHEESE VARIATION

Mayonnaise:
1 egg
¾ teaspoon salt
½ teaspoon dry mustard
¼ teaspoon paprika
2 tablespoons lemon juice
1 cup salad oil
Sour Cream Bleu Cheese
Variation:
1 cup sour cream
1 cup crumbled bleu cheese (less
for milder flavor)
½ teaspoon garlic salt
½ teaspoon Worcestershire

Put the egg, lemon juice and ¼ of oil in a blender, cover and process at High. Immediately remove feeder cap and pour remaining oil in a steady stream. All the oil should be added in less that 30 seconds. Yield: 1¼ cups.
Variation: Sour Cream Bleu Cheese, Add all ingredients except the cheese to mayonnaise, cover and process at High until smooth. Stop blender and add cheese, cover and process at High only until cheese is mixed throughout. For a smoother dressing process longer. Yield: 3 cups.

Suzanne Schwantes Coil, Kansas University
Lawrence, Kansas

SWEET AND SOUR DRESSING

1 egg
¾ cup apple cider vinegar
¼ cup honey
¼ cup salad oil
½ teaspoon garlic salt

Beat egg white until stiff. Add beaten egg yolk. Beat separately or shake remaining ingredients. Add to egg and beat until well mixed.

Joan Lonnborg DelaGarza,
University of Wisconsin-Madison
Dallas, Texas

HOMEMADE YOGURT

2 cups of nonfat dry milk powder
3 cups tepid water
1 can evaporated milk
3 tablespoons of yogurt

Beat together, 2 cups of nonfat dry milk powder, 3 cups tepid water and 1 can evaporated milk. Heat to a warm, not hot temperature; add yogurt. Mix well. Pour into clean glass jars and cover loosely. Set in a pan of water in a 225 degree oven. Turn oven off immediately and leave overnight. Do not disturb mixture. Refrigerate in the morning. If you desire a sweeter taste, add sugar or honey or artifical sweetener. Fruit, both fresh or frozen may also be added if desired. Makes a delicious topping for fruit, and is a real party food when served in parfait glasses.

Judy Elaine Graham, Oklahoma University
Greater Kansas City

Soups

COLD AVOCADO SOUP

1 ripe avocado
1½ cups chicken broth
1 tablespoon lemon juice
1 cup milk
½ teaspoon salt
Dash of Tabasco sauce
Chopped parsley (optional)

Peel and cut avocado into small pieces, place in container of electric blender. Add chicken broth and lemon juice. Process until smooth. Add milk, salt and Tabasco. Stir until well mixed. Chill. Sprinkle with chopped parsley. Makes about 4 cups. This is so-o-o delicious; wonderful for a summer luncheon, or to start a dinner party.

Sara Hess McElhaney, Iowa State University
Dallas, Texas

AVOGOLEMONO SOUP
(Greek Egg and Lemon Soup)

6 cups chicken stock or broth
¼ cup long-grain converted rice
1 teaspoon salt
3 eggs
⅓ cup lemon juice
¾ cup cooked, diced chicken
Parsley, chopped

Combine rice, stock and salt in large saucepan. Bring to a boil. Reduce heat, cover and simmer for 20 minutes. Beat eggs until frothy and pale yellow. Gradually add lemon juice, in a steady, slow stream while beating, so eggs will not curdle. Stir 2 cups of the hot rice mixture into eggs, whisking constantly. Slowly pour back into remaining soup. Place over medium heat and cook until slightly thickened, about 8 minutes, stir frequently. Remove from heat and add chicken and parsley. Cool, cover and refrigerate several hours or overnight. Serve in individual bowls, garnish with lemon slices and parsley.

Susan Countner, University of Washington
Marina Del Rey, California

CHEDDAR CHEESE SOUP

2 teaspoons arrowroot
2 cups chicken stock
2 tablespoons chopped onion
¼ cup diced carrots
¼ cup diced celery
1 cup water
¼ cup butter
½ cup flour
3 cups hot milk
½ pound sharp soft cheddar
   cheese, diced
½ teaspoon salt
⅛ teaspoon soda
¼ teaspoon paprika
1 teaspoon chopped fresh parsley
⅛ teaspoon yellow food coloring

Dissolve arrowroot in ½ cup stock. Cook onion, carrots, and celery in 1 cup water until tender. Melt butter, and add flour, stir in hot milk and cook until thick. Heat 1½ cups chicken stock, arrowroot mixture and cheese. Stir until cheese melts. Add hot milk mixture, salt, soda, paprika, parsley, coloring, vegetables and water in which vegetables were cooked. Do not boil.

Dorothy Chase Jones, Southern Methodist University
Dallas, Texas

CLAM CHOWDER — NEW ENGLAND STYLE

1 quart clams
Salt pork or bacon
4 potatoes, diced
2 cups milk
2 cups light cream
Salt and pepper to taste
3 tablespoons butter
1 tablespoon chopped onion

Saute bacon and onion. Add clams, simmer. Add potatoes, salt and pepper to taste. Cook 10 minutes. Add milk and simmer. Do not boil. Add cream and butter a few minutes before serving. Serve with oyster crackers. Enjoy!! This clam chowder is just delicious!

Cynthia Townsend Colway, Syracuse University
Oneida, New York

BEAN SOUP

Ham bone or pork fat
1 bag Great Northern or navy
   beans
Celery, chopped
Carrot, chopped
Onion, chopped
Green pepper, chopped
Salt and ground pepper

Simmer ham bone or pork fat in water. Clean beans before adding to water. Add celery, carrot, onion, and green pepper. Salt and pepper to taste. Simmer for several hours.

Barb Tate, Vanderbilt University
Cincinnati, Ohio

BAGHDAD BISQUE

¼ cup chopped celery
¼ cup chopped onion
1 teaspoon curry powder
2 tablespoons butter
1 can cream of chicken soup
1 can tomato bisque soup
1½ cans water
Slivered almonds, toasted

In saucepan, cook celery, onion and curry powder in butter until vegetables are tender. Blend in soups and water. Heat, stirring now and then. Serve with almonds. Serves 4 to 6. Easy but excellent!

Anne Reese Cline, Pennsylvania State University
Philadelphia North Suburban, Pennsylvania

SAVORY SUMMER BISQUE (COLD GREEN BEAN SOUP)

1 medium onion, chopped
1 clove garlic, minced
4-5 cups green beans, cut in small pieces
3 cups chicken bouillon (strong)
¼ teaspoon savory leaves
Salt and pepper to taste
Sour cream
¼ cup slivered almonds (toasted or sautéed until golden)

Saute onion and garlic in 2 tablespoons butter or margarine until limp. Stir in beans and bouillon, cover, and simmer about 10 minutes, or until beans are tender. Put mixture into blender container and whirl until smooth. Add salt, pepper and savory. Chill well.
To serve, pour into mugs and garnish with a dollup of sour cream and a sprinkling of almonds.

Susan Doornek, University of Wisconsin-Milwaukee
Milwaukee, Wisconsin

NEW ENGLAND CLAM CHOWDER

3 strips bacon, diced
1 medium onion, chopped
1 can cream of potato soup
1 8-ounce can minced clams
1 teaspoon minced parsley
1 teaspoon thyme
Pinch of rosemary
Salt and pepper
⅓ cup milk
½ cup sour cream

Brown bacon; add onion, then soup. Drain clams. Add juice only. Blend and simmer briefly. Add clams and seasonings. Simmer two minutes. Just before serving, add milk and sour cream. Heat to boiling and stir. Serve hot.

Jan Shockley, Washington University
St. Louis, Missouri

EASY CREAM OF CORN SOUP

2 cans corn, drained
4 cups milk
2 tablespoons dried onion
2 or 3 slices of bread
Salt and pepper to taste

Cut crust off bread and pulverize in blender. Remove. Put drained corn and 1 cup milk in blender, cover and blend on medium speed. Place corn, bread, salt, pepper, onion and rest of milk in saucepan. Heat and serve. Serves 4.

Carolyn Coe Cole, University of Texas
Dallas, Texas

CHILLED CUCUMBER SOUP

3 medium cucumbers, chopped
  (about 4 cups)
⅔ cup sliced scallions or green
  onions
3 tablespoons margarine
3 tablespoons flour
2 13¾-ounce cans chicken broth
1 teaspoon salt (taste first)
⅛ teaspoon ground black pepper
1 teaspoon dill week OR 1
  tablespoon snipped fresh dill
1½ cups buttermilk
1 tablespoon lemon juice
Dill sprigs, optional
Cheese Parmesan snack crackers

Sauté the chopped cucumbers and scallions or green onions in margarine until soft; stir in flour. Gradually add chicken broth, stirring constantly until mixture thickens slightly and comes to a boil. Add salt, pepper and dill weed. Simmer, covered for 10 minutes. Chill thoroughly. (May be prepared up to this point and refrigerated overnight.) Puree in blender. Stir in buttermilk and lemon juice. Garnish with dill sprigs, if desired. Serve with cheese Parmesan snack crackers. Makes six 1-cup servings.

Joan Thompson, University of Denver
Dallas, Texas

COLD CUCUMBER SOUP

1 10¾-ounce can cream of celery
  soup
1 cup milk
¼ cup cottage cheese
½ cup cucumber, peeled and
  coarsely chopped
1 tablespoon coarsely chopped
  onion

Combine all ingredients in the container of electric blender; process until smooth. Chill. Makes 4 servings. Sprinkle with chopped parsley or chopped chives.

Cookbook Committee

LINDA'S COLD CUCUMBER SOUP

2 cucumbers, seeded and cut in
  pieces
⅔ cup sour cream or 1 cup plain
  yogurt
Dill weed, chopped fresh sweet
  basil
Salt and pepper to taste

Put in blender and blend. Serve in cold dishes.
This is very rich. Serve small portions or add ⅓ cup milk.

Nell Taylor Wolfe, Iowa State University
Westchester County, New York

CHICKEN AND SPINACH SOUP

4 chicken breasts, boned and
  skinned
1 pound spinach leaves, washed
  and stemmed
2 tablespoons flour
2 tablespoons butter
3 cups chicken broth
½ cup sour cream
2 scallions, chopped
Salt and pepper
Lime wedges

Simmer the chicken breasts in about a cup of water until cooked. Remove breasts and cool. Save liquid for stock. Melt butter in a saucepan, add the flour and cook for a few minutes. Add one cup of chicken broth at a time, stirring constantly, using your liquid saved from cooked chicken breasts. Add chopped scallions, dash of salt and pepper and fresh spinach. Simmer. Cut chicken up or leave whole and add to soup mixture. Simmer for about 15 minutes more. Serve with a dollup of sour cream in each bowl and if using whole breasts, serve with a breast in each bowl. Serves four. Also serve with lime wedges, squeezing a few to add a zingy flavor. Wonderful!

Joan Lonnborg DeLaGarza,
University of Wisconsin-Madison
Dallas, Texas

ICED GAZPACHO

1 small clove garlic
1 46-ounce can tomato juice
¼ cup olive oil
1 teaspoon Worcestershire sauce
1 cucumber, finely diced (1½
  cups)
1 cup shredded carrots
1 tablespoon sugar
1½ teaspoon salt
2 tablespoons lemon juice
3 tomatoes, finely diced (2 cups)
1 green pepper, finely diced
1 cup thinly sliced green onions

Put garlic through a press; combine with sugar, salt, tomato juice, olive oil, lemon juice, Worcestershire sauce in large bowl. Beat with rotary blender to blend in olive oil. Cover and chill while preparing vegetables. Stir in vegetables; chill again for at least one hour; pour into serving bowls.

Laurel Pithoud Elden, Oregon State University
Central New Jersey

BOB'S GASPACHO

2 cups canned jellied beef
  consomme
½ cup finely diced cucumbers,
  peeled
1 cup finely diced, peeled, seeded
  tomatoes (push out ¼ slice
  with thumb)
2 tablespoons red wine vinegar
2 teaspoons olive oil
¼ cup thinly sliced green onion
½ cup finely diced celery
¼ teaspoon Tabasco

Mix all ingredients lightly; refrigerate. Serve from punch bowl or in individual soup cups, with or without sour cream. Caviar is a nice addition, but expensive. Serves 8.

Frances Kirk Cranfill, University of Tulsa
Washington University
Dallas, Texas

LINDA'S GAZPACHO

4 large tomatoes, peeled, seeded
and diced
2 large cucumbers, peeled,
seeded and diced
2 green peppers, seeded and
diced
10 green onions, sliced
½ cup minced parsley
1 teaspoon salt
4 cups tomato or V-8 juice
4 cups canned beef or chicken
consomme
¼ teaspoon Tabasco sauce
3 tablespoons olive oil
6 tablespoons lemon juice or 2 of
red wine vinegar
Optional: 1 tablespoon fresh
basil, ½ teaspoon each ground
coriander, cumin, chili powder

Put first 5 ingredients through blender or food processor. Mix with remaining ingredients. Add fresh diced vegetables. Serve very cold with croutons. Serves 10.

Nell Taylor Wolfe, Iowa State University
Westchester County, New York

SIMPLE YET SUPREMELY DELICIOUS LEEK SOUP

2 leeks, washed well
4 tablespoons butter
1 large potato, peeled
2 cups milk
Salt, pepper to taste

Slice leeks and potato. Sauté in butter. Then add milk and cook until soft. Blend 3 minutes in a blender. Reheat and serve. This mixture turns out so fantastically thick and creamy it may be necessary to add water or milk to reach the desired consistency.

Lynda Slaughter, University of Western Ontario
London, Ontario

SAILOR MOKU SOUP

1 can black bean soup
3 cans Manhandler's vegetable
soup
4 cans water
1 number 2 can Mexican chili
beans
1 number 2 can peas
1 5-ounce jar dried beef, chopped
4-5 large stalks celery
½ head cabbage, coarsely
chopped
1 large onion, chopped
½ teaspoon grated garlic
1 pound hot Linguisa or Italian
sausage, peeled and chopped
2 or 3 dashes Tabasco sauce
2 teaspoons chili powder
Salt and pepper to taste
(2 or 3 more cups of water may be
added)

Sauté chopped sausage and onions until onions are clear. Add all other ingredients and cook until cabbage is done. (About 1 hour.) Yields about 6 quarts. Freezes well. Serves 24.

Gretchen W. Winston, Indiana University
Bloomington, Indiana

MUSHROOM SOUP

½ white onion, chopped
4 green onions, chopped
1 cup sliced mushrooms
2 cans cream of mushroom soup
1 can beef broth (or equivalent in bouillon)
1 teaspoon nutmeg

Sauté onions and mushrooms in butter. Combine onions and mushrooms with the three cans of soup in saucepan; add water or broth (bouillon) as needed for consistency. Add nutmeg to soup. Stir. Add more nutmeg to taste by ½ teaspoons.
Excellent with toasted French bread and a white semi-soft cheese.

Julie Winans, Southern Methodist University
Dallas, Texas

ONION SOUP

6 10½-ounce cans condensed beef bouillon
3 cans water
30 onions, sliced
2 sticks margarine or butter

Sauté onions in butter. Add liquid and simmer 2 hours. Serve with buttered French bread and grated Parmesan cheese. Serves 18 to 20.

Sylvia Hardy Trewin, Iowa State University
Richardson, Texas

FRENCH ONION SOUP

2 large onions, sliced
3 tablespoons butter
1½ tablespoons flour
4 large fresh mushrooms
2 French bread rounds
1 can beef consomme
1 cup beef bouillon
Jack cheese, shredded
Parmesan cheese, shredded

Sauté onions in butter until transluscent, add flour, stirring, add consomme, bouillon, and mushrooms. Simmer 15 minutes. Dip bread rounds in soup and place on top of soup in 2 individual casseroles. Top with shredded cheese and place under boiler until cheese is bubbly and slightly browned. Serves 2.

Ruth Deems Cooper, Iowa State University
Charles City, Iowa

PARTY SOUP

1 can cream of chicken soup
1 can cream of mushroom soup
1 (10.5-ounce) can water from shrimp
½ pound frozen shrimp
¼ cup sherry

Cook shrimp according to package directions. Drain, saving water, and cool. Dice. Combine canned soups, water, sherry, and diced shrimp. Heat through until blended. Serves 4.
If using pre-cooked shrimp, use plain water, but add salt to soup to taste.

Talie McKenzie, Northwestern University
Chicago N.W. Suburban, Illinois

3-DAY PEA SOUP

1 package dried split peas
1 ham bone (cooked and left-over
    from butt or shank)
1 medium onion, diced
1 clove garlic
1 bay leaf
2 tablespoons flour
2 tablespoons margarine
Salt and pepper

Soak split peas in water to cover overnight. Discard water. Place peas, *10 cups* water, and ham bone in large pot and simmer, covered, for 3 hours. Add onions, garlic, and bay leaf and simmer additional 1 hour. Remove ham bone, pick off the meat and reserve it for adding later. Put the soup through sieve or Foley food mill. Chill overnight and remove grease.

To Serve: Melt margarine. Blend in flour and a little of the soup mixture. Bring to a boil and slowly add remaining soup, the reserved ham, and salt and pepper to taste. Thin with milk if desired. Serve with a dab of margarine and toasted croutons.

Lynn Baxter Maguire, Southern Methodist University
Dallas, Texas

SHRIMP CHOWDER

1 cup shrimp, cooked and
    deveined
1 can cream of shrimp soup
1 can cream of potato soup
3 cups water
¾ cup chopped onion
¼ cup chopped parsley
2 tablespoons butter

Sauté onions in butter until tender. Pour shrimp soup, potato soup, water, sautéed onion and cooked shrimp into large saucepan. Heat well. Add chopped parsley and serve. Serves 6.

Penny Kisslinger, University of Minnesota
Boulder, Colorado

HOMEMADE TOMATO SOUP

3 fresh ripe tomatoes
1 clove garlic
¼ onion
1 teaspoon oregano
1 teaspoon salt
¼ cup barley
Fresh parsley
Mozerella cheese
Lime wedges

Cut tomatoes up in quarters and place in blender. Add onion and garlic. Add water to fill half your blender. Liquify, press button on and off, repeatedly, just enough to make a liquid. Pour into saucepan. Add oregano and salt, barley and fresh chopped parsley (to taste). Simmer 20 minutes or until barley is cooked. Serve with a thick slice of Mozeralla cheese in bowl. Also serve with lime wedges for squeezing into soup. Delicious!

Joan Loonborg DeLaGarza,
University of Wisconsin-Madison
Dallas, Texas

Sauces

CHOCOLATE SAUCE

3 squares bitter chocolate
1¼ cup hot water
½ cup light corn syrup
1 cup sugar
1 cup canned milk (evaporated)
1 teaspoon vanilla
¼ teaspoon salt

Melt chocolate over very slow heat. Add the hot water and stir well. Slowly add the sugar and syrup. Cook until it forms a soft ball (about 235 degrees). Add milk, vanilla and salt. Stir until smooth. May be frozen; recipe may be multiplied as much as three times.

Viola D. Jammer Larson, Iowa State University
Greater Kansas City

D-LISH VELVET HOT FUDGE

½ cup butter or margarine
4 squares unsweetened chocolate
3 cups sugar
½ teaspoon salt
1 13-ounce can evaporated milk

Melt margarine and chocolate in top of double boiler. Gradually stir in sugar. Mixture becomes very thick and dry. Add salt. Slowly add evaporated milk. Store in refrigerator — can be reheated many times.

Jan Peterson, Iowa State University
Des Moines, Iowa

Margaret K. Dega, Lake Forest College
Madison, Wisconsin

CHOCOLATE TOPPING FOR ICE CREAM

1 cup miniature marshmallows
1 cup evaporated milk
1 cup chocolate morsels
Dash of salt

Combine all ingredients in a saucepan. Stir until marshmallows and chocolate morsels have dissolved (over medium-low heat). Serve warm or cold over ice cream. Store in refrigerator.

Genevieve E. Everett (Geni), Florida State University
Tallahassee, Florida

MOM'S HOT FUDGE SAUCE

2 tablespoons cocoa
2 tablespoons water
½ cup sugar
2 tablespoons butter or
   margarine
1 teaspoon vanilla

Blend cocoa with water in saucepan over medium heat. Add sugar. Cook to soft ball stage. Add butter and vanilla. Stir until blended. Delicious over ice cream.

Lynne Ayers, Vanderbilt University
Nashville, Tennessee

SISSY'S FRUIT SAUCE

2 cans salad fruit
1 cinnamon stick
4 tablespoons brown sugar
½ cup cognac
3 tablespoons butter
3 teaspoons corn starch
2 bananas, sliced

Drain fruit, set aside. In juice, add all other ingredients except bananas and simmer three hours over *very low* heat. Thicken with corn starch. Add fruit and fresh sliced bananas. Heat. Serve warm with dab of ice cream or whipped cream.

Jean Brooks Oliver, Northwestern University
Atlanta, Georgia

BRENNAN'S PRALINE PARFAIT SAUCE

2 cups dark corn syrup
⅓ cup sugar
⅓ cup boiling water
1 cup chopped pecans

Combine all ingredients in saucepan and bring to boil over medium heat. As soon as you reach boiling, *remove immediately.* Cool and store in covered jar in the refrigerator. Serve on vanilla ice cream.

Barbara Small, Michigan State University
Chicago Northwest Suburban, Illinois

CANDIED BRANDIED CRANBERRIES

4 cups fresh or frozen
   cranberries; washed
2 cups sugar
4 tablespoons brandy or cognac

Place cranberries in shallow baking pan, large enough so fruit can lie absolutely flat. Sprinkle sugar over berries; cover tightly with foil (double strength) and bake in preheated over, 350 degrees, 1 hour. Cool, then mix in brandy or cognac to taste. Sprinkle lightly with a little sugar. Spoon into handsome glass bowl. Berries will be whole and shiny. Makes about 2 cups.

Connie Spanier, Oregon State University
San Francisco, California

FREEZER STRAWBERRY JAM

1 quart strawberries
4 cups (1¾ pounds) sugar
2 tablespoons orange juice
1 1¾-ounces package fruit pectin

Mash berries with potato masher, add sugar and orange juice. Set aside. In small saucepan over medium heat, heat pectin with ¾ cup water until boiling; boil 1 minute, stirring constantly. Stir into fruit mixture and ladle into freezer containers. Let set at room temperature about 24 hours, then freeze. Store in refrigerator after opening. Makes 6 8-ounce jars.

Cathy Frost, Michigan State University
Birmingham, Michigan

PICKLED PEACHES

1 number 2½ can Cling peaches,
   whole or halves
¾ cup brown sugar
1 teaspoon whole allspice
½ cup vinegar
2 3-inch cinnamon sticks
1 teaspoon whole cloves

Drain peach syrup into saucepan. Add sugar, vinegar and spices. Boil 5 minutes. Add peaches and simmer for 5 minutes. Chill peaches in pickling syrup for several hours or overnight. Serve cold with cold leftover turkey or other cold meats.

Margaret Stewart, Iowa State University
Del Mar, California

MIXED VEGETABLE RELISH

2 10-ounce packages frozen
   mixed vegetables
1½ cups sugar
2 tablespoons flour
1 cup vinegar
2 tablespoons prepared mustard
8 stalks diced celery
1 small green pepper chopped
1 small onion chopped
1 cup red kidney beans (rinsed)

Cook the mixed vegetables — not too done. Drain. Cool. Cook the sauce mixture (sugar, flour, vinegar) until clear. Cool. Add sauce to vegetables. Then add the remaining five ingredients. Keep in refrigerator.

Caroline Hardy Howard, Iowa State University
Centerville, South Dakota

SACK POSSET

¾ cup sugar
2 tablespoons flour
½ teaspoon nutmeg
3 eggs, beaten
4 cups milk
¾ cup sherry

Mix sugar, flour and nutmeg in double boiler top; gradually add milk and eggs. Cook, stirring constantly, until slightly thickened. Slowly add sherry. Serve warm. Serves 10 — ½ cup servings. Chill and serve over ice cream.

Latane Jordan Graham, Memphis State University
Dallas, Texas

TARTAR SAUCE

½ cup chopped dill pickles
¼ cup chopped onions
¼ cup capers
Mayonnaise for consistency

Mix pickles, onions, and capers in blender. Drain off excess fluid. Measure and add less than equal amount of mayonnaise.

Lucy Crimmins Eichorn,
Southern Methodist University
Dallas, Texas

MUSTARD SAUCE

½ cup cream of tomato soup
(undiluted)
½ cup mustard (not dry)
½ cup vinegar
½ cup sugar
½ cup margarine
3 egg whites, lightly beaten

Combine all ingredients in top of double boiler and cook until thick. Excellent served hot or cold with ham. Also good cold as spread on sandwiches.

Doris Havercamp Nelson, University of Iowa
Riverside, California

SWEET AND SPICY MUSTARD

½ cup cider vinegar
½ cup sugar
1 egg (beaten with 3 tablespoons
cold water)
1 2-ounce can dry mustard

Add all ingredients together in a double-boiler and cook until thickened over a medium heat. Delicious with cheese and crackers.

Kerry Lavine, Southwest Texas State University
Fort Worth, Texas

FRUIT SAUCE FOR HAM

1 pound can sliced peaches, diced
8 ¾-ounce can crushed pineapple
2 tablespoons cornstarch
½ teaspoon cinnamon
Dash cloves
⅓ cup frozen orange juice
concentrate, thawed
½ cup whole maraschino cherries
¼ cup white raisins
½ cup pecans, optional
1 cup water

Drain peaches and pineapple and reserve syrup. Combine cornstarch and spices. Stir in all reserved syrup, orange juice and water. Cook and stir until thickened and bubbly. Spoon some over ham last half hour. Simmer fruit in remaining sauce for 10 minutes before serving.

Margaret Godbold Briscoe,
Southern Methodist University
St. Louis, Missouri

BAKED PINEAPPLE DRESSING FOR HAM

½ cup (1 stick) butter or
margarine
1 cup sugar
4 eggs
1 can (1 pound, 4 ounces)
crushed pineapple, drained
5 slices white bread, cubed

Cream together butter and sugar. Beat in eggs one at a time. Stir in pineapple. Fold in bread cubes. Turn into greased 1½ quart casserole. Bake, uncovered at 350 degrees for 1 hour. Serve with ham. Makes 6 servings.

This with baked ham makes a delightful Easter dinner. I usually don't serve potatoes when we have pineapple stuffing. I think everyone to who I've served this has asked for the recipe.

Anne Olson McCoy, University of Nebraska
Greater Kansas City

HOMEMADE STEAK SAUCE

1 tablespoon Kitchen Bouquet
½ cup ketchup
1 teaspoon Worcestershire sauce
1 teaspoon Angostura bitters
2 tablespoons wine vinegar
½ teaspoon garlic powder

Mix all ingredients in a bottle and shake well. Refrigerate. A considerable saving over commercial steak sauces.

Barbara Clark, University of Texas
Nashua, New Hampshire

NEVER-FAIL QUICK SPAGHETTI SAUCE

1 pound ground beef
12 ounces tomato paste
3 cups of water
1 package onion soup mix
1 can sliced mushrooms
1-1½ tablespoons Italian
    seasonings

In a large skillet, brown ground beef. Drain. Add tomato paste and water and stir in well. Add onion soup mix and stir well until dissolved. Add mushrooms and seasonings and simmer one hour. Serve over spaghetti. Serves 4.

Susan N. Gilkey, William and Mary
Winchester, Virginia

BARBECUE SAUCE

1 cup water
1 6-ounce can tomato paste
5 teaspoons chili powder
3 teaspoons black pepper
32 ounce bottle ketchup
½ teaspoon garlic powder
4 tablespoons Worcestershire
    sauce
½ cup lemon juice
1 cup vinegar
32-ounce bottle ketchup
1 teaspoon salt
½ stick butter
½ stick margarine
¼ teaspoon red pepper
½ cup brown sugar
2 tablespoons honey

To the water, add tomato paste and chili powder. Mix well over a medium heat. Add the remaining ingredients to this mixture one at a time as each is blended in. Bring mixture to a boil. Boil 2 minutes. Simmer till desired thickness (about 3 hours). Store in refrigerator 3 months.

Pat O'Connell Mullins, St. Louis University
Dallas, Texas

TART B-B-Q SAUCE

1 small onion, chopped
2 tablespoons oil
2 tablespoons vinegar
2 tablespoons brown sugar
¼ cup lemon juice
1 cup tomato ketchup
3 tablespoons Worcestershire
  sauce
½ teaspoon prepared mustard
½ cup water
Pinch salt
Dash cayenne

Brown onion in fat. Add remaining ingredients. Simmer for 30 minutes. Makes 2 cups. For less tangy sauce, add more catsup.

Audrey Johnson Nelson, Mankato State College
Chicago NW Suburban, Illinois

TERIYAKI MARINADE

1 cup pineapple juice
1 cup soy sauce
½ cup brown sugar
2 cloves garlic
2 teaspoons ginger
2 bay leaves

Combine and marinate any meat in a large bowl for 2 hours or over night. Especially good with flank steak to be barbecued.

Janet Bellinger Holmes, University of Michigan
Westchester County, New York

SAUCE FOR VEGETABLES

1 cup mayonnaise
1 bouillon cube
2 tablespoons hot water
1 cup sour cream
¼ to ½ teaspoon curry powder

Dissolve bouillon cube in hot water, and mix with mayonnaise, sour cream and curry powder. This is delicious served over cooked asparagus, broccoli, green beans or spinach. It can be stored in the refrigerator in a closed glass jar.

Margaret Miller Browne, Oregon State University
Dallas, Texas

Vegetables

HOT ARTICHOKE-CHEESE BARS

2 tablespoons oil
⅓ cup finely chopped onion
1 clove garlic, minced
4 eggs
1 14-ounce can artichoke hearts, drained
¼ cup dry bread crumbs
8 ounces Swiss or Cheddar cheese, shredded
2 tablespoons minced parsley
¼ teaspoon oregano
Salt and pepper to taste

Grease an 11x7 inch baking dish. Preheat oven to 350 degrees. In small skillet heat oil and saute onion and garlic until limp. Beat eggs to a froth in mixing bowl. Chop artichokes into small pieces and add to bowl. Stir in onion and garlic, bread crumbs, cheese, parsley, and seasonings. Turn into baking pan and bake at 325 degrees for 25 to 30 minutes, until set when touched lightly. Let cool a bit before cutting into bars.

Gay Pettinato Hammitt, Northwestern University
Pasadena, California

ARTICHOKE HEARTS AND SPINACH AU GRATIN

1 can artichoke hearts (10 or 12 hearts)
1 tablespoon butter
3 packages frozen chopped spinach
1 8-ounce package cream cheese, softened in 2 tablespoons milk
Salt and pepper
1 cup grated Swiss cheese or ½ cup Parmesan cheese

Sauté artichoke hearts in butter. Set aside. Cook spinach according to package directions and drain *well*. (No moisture should remain.) Mix in softened cream cheese; salt and pepper to taste. Arrange artichoke hearts in casserole and put spinach mixture over that. Spread cheese over all. Cook uncovered in preheated 350 degree oven for 15 minutes, until cheese melts and browns. Serves 6-8.

Jan Duccilli, Miami University
Cincinnati, Ohio

Jodie Ganz, Indiana University
Birmingham, Michigan

ASPARAGUS PARMESAN CHEESE CASSEROLE

1 can asparagus
¼ cup margarine or butter
¼ cup dry bread crumbs
¼ cup Parmesan cheese

Drain and arrange asparagus in baking dish, sprinkle top with mixture of ¼ cup margarine or butter with the same amount of dry bread crumbs, and same amount of Parmesan cheese. Bake at 375 degrees for 10 to 12 minutes. Serves 4.

Lucy Crimmins Eichorn,
Southern Methodist University
Dallas, Texas

LOUISE'S SCALLOPED ASPARAGUS

⅓ cup margarine
¼ cup flour
1 teaspoon salt
¼ teaspoon pepper
2 cans asparagus
Crackers
2 hard boiled eggs
Milk
Cheese
Pimento

Melt margarine and add flour, salt and pepper. Blend well. Drain asparagus, reserving liquid. Add milk to the asparagus liquid to make 2 cups. Stir into flour mixture until thick. Chop pimentos and add to sauce. Grease casserole with margarine. Put thin layer of broken crackers in casserole then layers of asparagus, egg slices, and enough grated cheese to cover. Pour half of the sauce and repeat the layers. Pour remainder of the sauce over this last layer. Trim with asparagus and pimento in spoke-like fashion. Bake at 375 degrees for 20 minutes.

Cookbook Committee

SPICY BARLEY CASSEROLE

1 stick butter
1 cup diced celery
2 chopped onions
1 cup quick barley
1 tablespoon basil
2 cups chicken stock
1 8-ounce can sliced mushrooms
1½ tablespoons parsley
1 tablespoon Worcestershire
   sauce
Salt and pepper to taste

Sauté celery and onions in butter. Add all other ingredients. Mix well and bake at 300 degrees for 2 hours, stirring occasionally.

Gretchen Youse Rein, University of Kansas
Greater Kansas City

BARLEY CASSEROLE

¼ pound butter
1 medium onion, chopped
¼ pound fresh or canned
   mushrooms
1 cup barley (quick)
2 cups consomme or broth
½ teaspoon salt

Cook onion, mushrooms and barley in butter over medium heat. Stir frequently until barley is light brown. Turn into casserole and add consomme which has been brought to boil. Season. Cover and bake at 350 degrees for 60 to 90 minutes. Add more broth if it's absorbing too much in cooking. Serves 4.

Helen Harris Thompson,
Southern Methodist University
Mt. Vernon, Iowa

JULIE'S BAKED BEANS

6 1-pound cans baked beans
½ cup dark molasses
½ pound salt pork
¾ cup brown sugar
1 bottle catsup or chili sauce
Salt, pepper to taste

Cut salt pork in small pieces and brown in skillet. In a large bean pot or oven dish, combine beans, salt pork pieces, molasses, brown sugar, seasonings and catsup. Mix thoroughly, and bake in a 350 degree oven for about 2½ to 3 hours until the liquid is thick and delicious. Serves 18-20.

Gloria Swanson Nelson, Oklahoma University
Dallas, Texas

CALICO BEANS

⅓ pound bacon
1 onion, chopped
16 ounce can baby lima beans, drained
16 ounce can red kidney beans, drained
16 ounce can red beans, drained
16 ounce can pork and beans, undrained
½ cup ketchup
½ cup brown sugar
¼ cup red wine
1 tablespoon mustard
½ teaspoon salt

Chop bacon, fry, and drain. Sauté onion in 2 tablespoons bacon grease. Combine all ingredients. Bake in 2 quart casserole at 300 degrees for 1 to 2 hours. Serves 12.

Diane Walter Prah, Miami University
Milwaukee, Wisconsin

JENNIEBELLE'S FIVE BEAN CASSEROLE

1 pound can large dark red kidney beans
1 pound can Garbanzo beans
1 pound can butter beans
1 pound can small green lima beans
1½ pound can B&M pork & beans
½ pound lean bacon, diced
1 cup sliced celery
¼ cup chopped green pepper
½ cup chopped onions
½ cup light brown sugar
½ cup cider vinegar
2 tablespoons dark molasses
1 teaspoon thyme
1 teaspoon pepper

Mix all together, including bean liquids, in casserole. Bake uncovered in 350 degree oven for 2 hours. Watch toward end of cooking time. If too dry, add more water. Stir gently. Serves 18 to 20.

Cherie McElhinney Olsen, University of Iowa
Ann Arbor, Michigan

DILLED GREEN BEANS

2 cans cut green beans
2 (or more) slices bacon
1 tablespoon dill seeds OR dill weed
4 tablespoons flour
4 tablespoons butter
1 cup bean juice
1 cup milk
2 teaspoons grated onion
1 teaspoon cracked pepper
2 teaspoons mei yen seasoning
3 dashes Tabasco

Simmer beans, bacon, and dill 30 minutes. Make sauce of last 8 ingredients. Mix with beans in casserole. Top with buttered bread crumbs. Bake at 350 degrees for 20 to 30 minutes.

Lynn Lady, Michigan State University
Alexandria, Virginia

GREEN BEANS WITH HERBED BUTTER

1 pound green beans (I use 1 can French-style green beans)
¼ cup butter or margarine
¾ cup minced onions (I use instant minced onions)
1 clove garlic, minced
¼ cup minced celery
¼ cup snipped parsley
¼ teaspoon dried rosemary
¼ teaspoon dried basil
¾ teaspoon salt

Wash beans; remove ends. Cut crosswise into thin, slanted slices. Cook them, covered, in ½ inch boiling salted water about 15 minutes, or until tender; drain. (Obviously, the use of canned beans eliminates this step.) Meanwhile, melt butter in saucepan. Add onions, garlic, celery; sauté 5 minutes. Add rest of ingredients; simmer, covered, 10 minutes. Toss well with beans. This recipe adapts well to quantity cooking for parties. The proportions hold true no matter how many "4's" you prepare.

Marjorie White Giles, Southern Methodist University
Dallas, Texas

PEPPER BEAN CASSEROLE

1½ cups water
1 teaspoon salt
3 10-ounce packages frozen lima beans
3 green peppers, cut in julienne strips
¼ to ½ pound bacon, cut in ½ inch pieces
1 tablespoon packed brown sugar
1 teaspoon dry mustard
1 tablespoon molasses
1 16-ounce can stewed tomatoes

Heat water and salt to boiling. Add beans and green pepper strips. Heat to boiling; reduce heat. Cover and simmer till tender about 8 minutes. Drain and set aside.
Cook bacon pieces in medium skillet until limp but not brown. Stir in brown sugar, mustard, molasses and stewed tomatoes. Cook 5 minutes over low heat.
Mix tomato and vegetable mixtures. Pour into buttered 2 quart casserole. Cover and bake at 350 degrees for about 40 minutes.

Lynette Martin Chrenka, St. Louis University
Manchester, Missouri

SWEET AND SOUR BEANS

6 slices chopped bacon
2 chopped green peppers
3 medium onions, chopped
2 teaspoons oil
2 teaspoons brown sugar
1 teaspoon dry mustard
½ cup vinegar
Dash Worcestershire sauce
2 cans kidney beans, drained
2 cans lima beans, drained
1 large (2½) can baked beans

Sauté together bacon, green pepper and onions. Add oil, sugar, mustard, vinegar and sauce. Mix all ingredients together in a 4 quart casserole. Bake at 325 degrees for at least 1 hour in a covered casserole.

Mary Rice Raber, University of Washington
Seattle, Washington

BROCCOLI CASSEROLE I

2 10-ounce packages frozen broccoli, chopped
1 can cream of mushroom soup
¾ cup sour cream
½ cup chopped celery
1 2-ounce can chopped pimentos
¾ cup shredded sharp cheese
1 teaspoon salt
¼ teaspoon pepper
⅓ cup chopped onion
½ cup chopped green pepper

Preheat oven to 350 degrees. Cook broccoli according to package directions; drain well. Combine all ingredients; pour into a greased 1½ quart casserole. Bake for 20-30 minutes. Serves 6.

Phyliss Donaldson Choat, University of Nebraska
Omaha, Nebraska

BROCCOLI CASSEROLE II

2 packages frozen, chopped
  broccoli
1 can cream of mushroom soup
½ cup mayonnaise
1 tablespoon lemon juice
½ cup grated sharp cheese
1 jar chopped pimento
1 cup crushed cheese crackers
¼ cup slivered almonds

Cook broccoli according to the package directions and drain. Arrange broccoli in buttered casserole. Mix soup, mayonnaise, lemon juice and cheese. Pour over broccoli. Top with pimento, crackers and almonds. Bake at 350 degrees for about 30 minutes.

Sharon Fitzgerald Thompson, University of Missouri
St. Louis, Missouri

BROCCOLI CASSEROLE III

2 packages frozen chopped
  broccoli (or 1 broccoli and 1
  cauliflower)
1 can cream chicken soup —
  undiluted
Small onion chopped
6 tablespoons butter
Small jar Cheez Whiz
2½ cups cooked rice
Small can mushrooms — drained

Cook broccoli as directed on package until thawed — don't cook completely. Drain. Cook rice. Sauté onion in the butter. Combine all ingredients and bake at 350 degrees for 30 minutes in uncovered casserole dish.

Victoria Friede, University of Wisconsin-Milwaukee
Lawrence, Kansas

BEST BROCCOLI CASSEROLE

2 10-ounce packages frozen
  broccoli pieces
1 11-ounce package frozen rice
  pilaf (rice, mushrooms, onions)
1 8-ounce jar pasteurized process
  cheese spread
1 10¾ ounce can cream of
  mushroom soup
1 8-ounce can sliced water
  chestnuts, drained

Cook broccoli according to package directions; drain. Cook rice pilaf according to package directions; place in buttered 2 quart casserole. Add cheese spread; stir until melted. Add soup and water chestnuts. Fold in broccoli. Bake at 325 degrees for 40 minutes. Serves 8. Can be made a day ahead of serving, refrigerated covered; allow longer cooking time the following day. A yummy combination of flavors!

Elise Bossort Bell, University of Wisconsin
Milwaukee, Wisconsin

BROCCOLI-RICE CASSEROLE

1 10-ounce package frozen
  chopped broccoli
1 medium chopped onion
¾ stick butter
1 cup uncooked rice
1 can cream of mushroom soup
½ cup milk
1 cup shredded cheese

Cook rice and broccoli as directed on boxes. Cook onion in butter. Mix milk with the can of soup. Drain broccoli and combine ingredients in casserole dish. Cover dish and bake at 350 degrees for 20 to 30 minutes.

Linda Speckmann, Southern Methodist University
Dallas, Texas

Ann Sokol Heath, Iowa State University
Dallas, Texas

Susan Lippincott Hayes, Indiana State University
Edinburgh, Indiana

JANE'S BROCCOLI-RICE CASSEROLE

1½ cups long grain rice
1 package frozen chopped broccoli
1 large onion, chopped fine
4 stalks celery, chopped
¼ pound butter
1 can mushroom soup
1 can cream of chicken soup
1 16-ounce jar Cheez Whiz

Cook rice according to directions on package. Cook broccoli according to directions on package. Sauté onion and celery in the butter. Add soups and Cheez Whiz. Add rice and broccoli and mix well. Put in large casserole or two or three smaller ones. Bake in 350 degree oven until bubbly. Serves 12. Freezes well.

Gloria Swanson Nelson, Oklahoma University
Dallas, Texas

BROCCOLI SUPREME

1 10-ounce package frozen chopped broccoli, partially thawed
1 can (small) cream style corn
1 cup herb seasoned stuffing mix
1 slightly beaten egg
1 tablespoon grated onion
¼ teaspoon salt
Pepper
3 tablespoons butter

Combine egg, broccoli, corn, onion, salt and pepper in a mixing bowl. Melt butter in a small sauce pan. Add stuffing mix and toss to coat. Stir ¾ cup of stuffing mix into vegetable mixture. Turn into greased 1 quart casserole. Sprinkle with remaining stuffing mix. Bake uncovered at 350 degrees for 35-40 minutes. Serves 4-6.

Key Mensing Teitgen, University of Wisconsin-Madison

Milwaukee, Wisconsin

WALNUT BROCCOLI CASSEROLE

3 packages frozen chopped broccoli, barely cooked
1 stick butter
4 tablespoons flour
1½ tablespoons chicken base
2 cups milk
⅔ cup water
6 tablespoons butter
⅔ package herb stuffing mix
⅔ cup coarsely chopped English walnuts

Use 1 stick butter, flour, chicken base and milk to make white sauce. Heat water with 6 tablespoons butter, and add stuffing mix and walnuts. Place broccoli in buttered 9x13 inch casserole, and pour white sauce over broccoli. Top with crumb mixture. Bake at 400 degrees for 20 minutes. Serves 12.

Gwen Lankford Rogers, Iowa State University
St. Louis, Missouri

BROCCOLI ZITI

10 ounces ziti, shells or other pasta
Boiling, salted water
1½ sticks butter
¼ cup oil
2½ large onions, chopped
4 garlic cloves, minced
4 cups broccoli florets
1 cup chopped parsley
Salt and freshly ground pepper

Cook ziti or shells in boiling salted water for about 10 to 12 minutes. Drain and place in large bowl. In large skillet, combine butter and oil. Place over medium heat until butter has melted, then add onion and garlic and cook until onion is soft. Remove from heat and add to ziti. Parboil broccoli for about 3 minutes; rinse with cold water and drain. Stir into ziti mixture. Add parsley, salt and pepper to taste. Pour mixture into a well greased 3 quart casserole dish. Cover and bake for 20 minutes at 350 degrees. Serve hot.

Susan Countner, University of Washington
Marina Del Rey, California

MOTHER'S RED CABBAGE

1 head red cabbage, shredded
1 large apple, grated
Accent, salt to taste
1 tablespoon bacon fat
Dash of sugar
1 tablespoon vinegar

Place cabbage in skillet and cover with water. Add Accent and salt. Cook slowly until water is nearly gone. Add apple. Cook down slowly; then add bacon fat and a little sugar. Just before removing from fire, add vinegar.

Gloria Swanson Nelson, Oklahoma University
Dallas, Texas

CARROT CASSEROLE

3 cups cooked mashed carrots or
(4 jars baby food carrots)
1 cup white sugar
½ stick butter, melted
1 cup milk
2 heaping tablespoons flour
4 teaspoons cinnamon
3 eggs, beaten
1 teaspoon baking powder
1 cup chopped nuts

Mix dry ingredients, add other ingredients. Bake at 350 degrees until set, about 1½ hours. Serves 6-8.

Maxine Leverett Trager,
Southern Methodist University
Dallas, Texas

HORSERADISH CARROTS

6 to 8 carrots, cut in chunks
¼ cup saved cooking water
1 tablespoon horseradish
1 teaspoon grated onion
½ cup mayonnaise

Cook carrots and save water. Combine ¼ cup of the water with horseradish, onions and mayonnaise. Pour over hot carrots. (Do not cook.) Garnish with paprika or chopped parsley.

Elaine Pautler McCammon, University of Missouri
St. Louis, Missouri

LUSCIOUS CARROTS

6 cups cooked carrots, slice on
  slant
½ cup water
2 tablespoons butter
1 cup milk
1 cup grated cheese
1 can onion rings
½ teaspoon salt
2 tablespoons flour

Cook carrots. Make cheese sauce in normal manner. Layer carrots in buttered dish; layer of sauce, sprinkle with onion rings; repeat process until used except save some onion rings for the top. Put these onion rings on top during the last 5 minutes of cooking. Bake at 350 degrees for 15 minutes.

Carolyn Williams, Denver University
San Francisco, California

WINTER CARROT CASSEROLE

1½ pounds carrots (7 or 8 medium sized)
½ cup mayonnaise
2 tablespoons chopped onion
¼ cup crushed saltines (7 crackers)
2 teaspoons oleo (melted)
2 tablespoons prepared horseradish
¼ teaspoon salt
Dash pepper

In saucepan cook carrots, covered in boiling salted water for 10 minutes or till tender. Drain. Place in 1 quart casserole. Combine mayonnaise, onion, horseradish, salt and pepper. Spoon over carrots. Mix crumbs and oleo; sprinkle atop. Bake uncovered in a 350 degree oven for 30 minutes or till hot.

Ann Fisher Gardner, Southern Methodist University
Dallas, Texas

GLAZED CARROTS

6-8 carrots
2 tablespoons butter
Salt
½ teaspoon thyme
1 tablespoon sugar (white or brown)

Clean carrots, cut into fairly thin rounds. Place in large saucepan and barely cover with water. Place butter on top. Add salt, thyme, sugar. Do not put lid on. Boil. Then reduce heat to medium and cook until carrots are tender, water evaporates, and glaze has formed. About 15 minutes.

Mary Jean Lauvetz Hart, University of Nebraska
Philadelphia North Suburban, Pennsylvania

EVA'S CAULIFLOWER

1 medium head cauliflower
½ cup butter
2 cups milk
8 ounces sliced mushrooms
Paprika
¼ cup green pepper
¼ cup flour
1 teaspoon salt
6 slices pimento cheese

Separate cauliflower in medium pieces and cook covered in boiling salted water until just tender, 10-15 minutes. Drain.
Cook green pepper in butter until tender. Blend in flour and milk. Cook until thick. Add salt, mushrooms and cheese.
Place ½ cauliflower in 1½ quart casserole. Cover with ½ cheese sauce. Repeat layers. Sprinkle top with paprika.
Brown lightly in 350 degrees for 15 minutes.

Karen Wander Kline, Grand President,
Iowa State University
Omaha, Nebraska

MOLLY'S SCALLOPED CELERY

4 cups coarsely chopped celery
¼ cup slivered, blanched almonds
1 6-ounce can water chestnuts
½ cup mushroom pieces
5 tablespoons margarine
3 tablespoons flour
½ cup half and half
1 cup chicken broth
½ cup dried bread crumbs
½ cup Parmesan cheese

Boil celery 5 minutes. Drain. Make white sauce from the margarine, flour, half and half, and broth. Combine celery and white sauce. Add water chestnuts and mushrooms. Put in buttered baking dish, top with bread crumbs, cheese and almonds. Bake at 375 degrees until bubbly (about 20 to 25 minutes.)

Cookbook Committee

CHEESE CORN CASSEROLE

3 well beaten eggs
¼ cup flour
2 tablespoons sugar
1½ cups sharp cheese, cut up (if you like "cheezy dishes", use more)
2 16½ ounce cans whole kernel corn, drained
8 slices bacon, cooked and diced

Combine eggs, flour and sugar. Beat well. Add cheese and corn. Put into casserole. Sprinkle with diced bacon. Bake at 350 degrees for 30 minutes or until a knife comes out clean. Serves 6.

Audrey Shafer, Past Grand President,
University of Missouri-Columbia
Greater Kansas City

LOUISE'S BAKED CORN IN SOUR CREAM

6 slices bacon
2 tablespoons margarine
½ teaspoon salt
2 12-ounce cans whole kernel corn, drained
1 tablespoon parsley
2 tablespoons onion, chopped
2 tablespoons all-purpose flour
1 cup sour cream

Fry bacon, drain and crumble. Set aside. Saute onion in margarine for 5 minutes. Blend in flour and salt. Gradually add sour cream, stirring until mixture is smooth. Heat just to boiling. Add corn, and heat thoroughly 2 minutes. Fold in half the bacon. Spoon into a greased 2 quart casserole. Bake at 350 degrees for 30 minutes. In a microwave oven, heat at high setting for 7-8 minutes. Top with parsley and remaining bacon.

Cookbook Committee

CORN PUDDING

3 eggs
2 tablespoons sugar
1 teaspoon salt
4 tablespoons flour
2 cups milk
2 cups *whole kernel* corn
1 tablespoon butter

Heat butter in bottom of casserole pan. Beat eggs in blender. Add sugar, salt, and flour. Blend again. Add milk. Blend well. Add corn into mixture in blender. Turn blender on for just a slow five-count; enough to be thoroughly mixed but not enough to disintegrate the corn kernels. Pour in pan and cover. Bake at 350 degrees for 1 hour. Stir often for the first 30 minutes so corn won't settle to the bottom. Remove lid after first 30 minutes for the pudding to brown.

Pam Rutherford, Vanderbilt University
Nashville, Tennessee

Sunshine Hollar Davis, Southern Methodist University
Nashville, Tennessee

HARTWELL FARM CORN PUDDING

2 cans creamed corn
1 or more cup frozen corn
1½ cups cracker crumbs
3 eggs, beaten
1 jar chopped pimento with juice
½ green pepper, chopped
½ chopped onion
Salt and pepper to taste
1 cup milk

Combine all ingredients. Place in 9x13 inch buttered baking dish. Cover with a checkered pattern of cheddar cheese and bacon. Bake 30 to 40 minutes at 350 degrees. Serves 8.

Gwen Lankford Rogers, Iowa State University
St. Louis, Missouri

CORN AND BROCCOLI CASSEROLE

1 can cream corn
1 package broccoli, chopped
¼ cup cracker crumbs
1 beaten egg
2 tablespoons melted butter
2 tablespoons minced onion
(or onion salt as substitute)
½ teaspoon salt
Dash of pepper
Topping:
¼ cup cracker crumbs
2 tablespoons melted butter

Pre-cook broccoli and drain. Combine corn, cooked broccoli, ¼ cup cracker crumbs, egg, butter, onion, salt and pepper. Put in a 1½ quart casserole. For topping, mix melted butter and cracker crumbs. Spread over mixture in the casserole. Bake at 350 degrees for 45 minutes.

Cindy Drevo, University of Nebraska
Lincoln, Nebraska

Sue Keller, University of Illinois
Quad Cities

TAMALE CORN

2 cans cream style corn
¾ cups corn meal
¾ teaspoons garlic salt
½ teaspoon baking powder
2 eggs (beaten)
½ cup cooking oil
2 cans green chilies
¼ pound (grated) Cheddar cheese

Sift dry ingredients, add to corn. Stir in eggs, oil, chilies, and cheese. Bake until firm (45 minutes) at 350 degrees.

Kay Conrad, University of Idaho
Corvallis, Oregon

BROCCOLI, CAULIFLOWER, BRUSSEL SPROUT, CHEESE CASSEROLE

1 box broccoli spears, frozen
1 box cauliflower, frozen
1 box brussels sprouts, frozen
1 8-ounce jar Cheez Whiz
1 can cream of mushroom soup
Buttered bread crumbs

Cook vegetables according to package directions. Drain and put in a greased 1½ quart casserole dish. Blend soup and cheese. Pour on top. Top with buttered crumbs. Heat in 350 degree oven for ½ hour. Serves 6.

Carolyn Schwem, Northwestern University
Chicago Northwest Suburban, Illinois

LOUISE'S EGGPLANT CASSEROLE

⅓ cup olive oil
¾ cup thinly sliced onions
2 cloves garlic, sliced
4 green peppers, cut into strips
2½ cups eggplant, peeled, diced
3 cups zucchini, sliced into ½
    inch slices
2 cups tomatoes, peeled, seeded,
    quartered
Salt and pepper to taste.

In deep skillet or heavy casserole, sauté onions and garlic in olive oil. Add green peppers, eggplant, zucchini and tomatoes. Salt and pepper to taste. Simmer, covered, over very low heat 35 to 45 minutes. Uncover and continue to simmer to reduce the amount of liquid. Serve hot or cold.

Cookbook Committee

CHEESE GRITS

4 cups water
1 teaspoon salt
1 cup grits
3 beaten eggs
1¼ cups grated sharp cheese
1 cup milk
½ cup margarine
Few drops Tabasco
Dash of Worcestershire sauce

Preheat oven to 350 degrees. Grease 2 quart casserole pan. Bring water to boil. Slowly stir in grits. Cook 4-5 minutes after brought back to a boil. Remove from heat and stir in eggs, one cup of cheese, milk and butter. Pour mixture in casserole. Sprinkle remaining cheese on top. Bake 1 hour.

Pam Rutherford, Vanderbilt University
Nashville, Tennessee

Judy Elaine Graham, Oklahoma University
Greater Kansas City

Martha Klerekoper Harris, University of Texas
Hobbs, New Mexico

KASHA

1 cup bulgar wheat
1 egg, beaten
2 cups chicken or beef broth
¼ teaspoon pepper
½ cup butter
1 teaspoon salt

Mix wheat and egg until coated; heat in large pan until dry, not brown. Add remaining ingredients, simmer (about 20 minutes) until liquid is absorbed. Sauté 1 medium onion in 2½ tablespoons butter for 10 minutes. Add with ½ cup coarsely chopped walnuts to kasha, bake in 350 degree oven for ½ hour.

Terry Hughes, William and Mary
Williamsburg, Virginia

GLORIA'S MUSHROOMS AU GRATIN

1 pound fresh mushrooms, sliced
    ¼ inch thick
2 tablespoons butter
⅓ cup sour cream
1 egg yolk
Salt and pepper
⅓ cup parsley
½ cup grated Swiss cheese

Sauté mushrooms in butter in large skillet until lightly browned. Simmer 2 minutes. Blend sour cream, egg yolk, salt and pepper until smooth. Pour into skillet. Heat mixture over medium flame, stirring constantly. Remove from heat, pour into a shallow round baking pan. Sprinkle with parsley and Swiss cheese. Bake 20 to 30 minutes or until mixture is firmly set at 350 degrees.

Cookbook Committee

NOLA'S WEST TEXAS OKRA

Fresh okra
Salt
Yellow cornmeal
Flour
Oil

Slice okra into ½ inch slices. Salt it and roll it in the cornmeal. Then roll it in flour. Fry in ½ inch, or deeper, hot oil. Take out as soon as crispy and light brown.

Sylvia Hardy Trewin, Iowa State University
Richardson, Texas

ONION CASSEROLE

1 can cream of mushroom soup
2 tablespoons milk
2 or 3 cups sliced onion
1 cup grated Cheddar cheese
1½ cups crushed potato chips

Dilute cream of mushroom soup with 2 tablespoons milk. Layer onions, cheese and potato chips in an oven proof dish or casserole. Pour soup and milk mixture over all. Bake uncovered at 350 degrees for about 1 hour. This is a simple but delicious casserole. It always gets raves!

Twila Honea Moore, Oklahoma University
Dallas, Texas

WANDA'S PEA THING

2 packages frozen peas
2 cans sliced water chesnuts
1 can cream of mushroom soup
1 onion, minced
2 tablespoons chopped green
  pepper
1 cup sliced celery
2 pimentoes, diced
1 stick butter

Sauté onions, green pepper and celery over moderate heat in the stick of butter, stirring until barely soft. Remove from heat and stir in the peas, chesnuts and pimentoes. Alternate layers of the vegetable mix and the mushroom soup in a two-quart greased casserole. Top with buttered cracker crumbs and bake in a 350 degree oven for 30 minutes.

Patsy McGahey Henderson, Washington University
St. Louis, Missouri

EASY AU GRATIN POTATOES

2 pounds package hash browns,
  thawed
2 cups sour cream
1 can cream of chicken soup
½ cup melted butter
½ cup chopped onion
8 ounces grated Cheddar cheese
  or 1 can Cheddar soup
Topping:
2 cups crushed corn flakes
¼ cup butter melted

Mix topping ingredients. Combine ingredients. Sprinkle with topping. Bake at 350 degrees for 45 minutes or until brown and bubbly. Can be put in any casserole dish or 13x9 pan.

Gail Pludeman, University of Wisconsin-Oshkosh
Milwaukee, Wisconsin

POTATOES ROMANOFF

6 cups cooked potatoes
2 cups large curd creamed
  cottage cheese
1 cup sour cream
1 clove garlic, minced
1 teaspoon salt
2 tablespoons chopped chives or
  green onions with tops
Grated Cheddar cheese and
  paprika

Mix all ingredients except grated cheese and paprika. Pour into oblong pyrex baking dish. Top with cheese and paprika. Bake at 350 degrees for 25 to 30 minutes. Serves 6 to 8. Delicious with ham or roast.

Carole Stokes Hines, Florida State University
Atlanta, Georgia

Dee Baldwin Crane, Pennsylvania State University
Omaha, Nebraska

PARTY POTATO CASSEROLE

6 medium red potatoes
2 cups shredded Cheddar cheese
½ cup margarine or butter
1 teaspoon salt
¼ teaspoon pepper
1½ cups sour cream
½ cup chopped green onions
(include some tops)
Salt and pepper

Boil potatoes in their skins. Cool, peel and shred coarsely. Melt cheese and butter or margarine over low heat until melted, stirring constantly. Remove from heat and add sour cream, green onions, salt and pepper. Fold into potatoes and bake in a greased casserole at 350 degrees for 25 minutes. This can be made a day ahead and refrigerated. Bring to room temperature and bake as noted above, or increase baking time to about 1 hour.

Susan Doornek, University of Wisconsin-Milwaukee
Milwaukee, Wisconsin

SWEET POTATO CASSEROLE

2 cups cooked hot mashed sweet
potatoes
½ cup sugar
½ cup milk
½ teaspoon cinnamon
2 eggs
¾ stick butter, melted
½ teaspoon nutmeg
¼ cup bourbon or rum

Whip all together. Place in casserole. Mixture thickens as it cooks. Bake 45 minutes at 350 degrees. Serve with toasted pecans or coconut.

Lynne Ayers, Vanderbilt University
Nashville, Tennesse

RATATOUILLE

2 medium onions, sliced
2 cloves garlic, minced
¼ cup olive oil
2 small zucchini, cut in ½ inch
slices
3 tomatoes, peeled and diced
1 small eggplant, peeled and cut
in 1 inch cubes
1 large green pepper, cut in strips
2 tablespoons chopped parsley
2 teaspoons salt
½ teaspoon basil leaves
⅛ teaspoon pepper

Cook onions and garlic in hot olive oil in bottom of Dutch oven. Add remaining ingredients. Cover and cook 15 minutes. Uncover and continue cooking until vegetables are tender and juice is thickened. Stir occasionally. Serves 8.

Sylvia Hardy Trewin, Iowa State University
Richardson, Texas

Jane Rowan Mott, Iowa State University
Dayton, Ohio

GREEN RICE

2 tablespoons chopped onion
2 tablespoons chopped celery
2 tablespoons parsley
4 tablespoons butter
1 can cream of mushroom soup
1 can beef bouillon broth
1 can evaporated milk
1 10-ounce package frozen
chopped spinach, cooked and
drained
1 cup grated Cheddar cheese
1 cup raw rice

Sauté onions, celery and parsley in butter. Add remaining ingredients together and mix well. Season to taste with salt and pepper. Bake at 350 degrees for 45-60 minutes or until rice is cooked. Serves 6.

Georgiana Post McClenaghan, Oregon State University
Nashville, Tennessee

Betty Russell Baker,
University of California-Los Angeles
Riverside Area, California

GREEN RICE CASSEROLE

2 10-ounce packages frozen
  chopped broccoli, thawed
2 cans cream of mushroom soup
1¾ cups instant rice
1 pound Velveeta
1 large onion, chopped
1 stick margarine
Salt and pepper to taste

Melt cheese and margarine, stir in onion; mix with rice, soup and broccoli. Bake in 3 quart casserole at 350 degrees for 1 hour. Serves 6.

Anne Coulson, University of Kansas
Greater Kansas City

JALAPENO RICE

2 cups raw rice, cooked
2 cups mild Cheddar cheese
1 pint sour cream
2 cans cream of celery soup
1 can chopped and seeded green
  chilies
3 finely chopped jalapenos

Mix all ingredients. Put into shallow casserole dish and heat at 350 degrees until bubbly, approximately 30-35 minutes. Top with additional cheese and let melt on casserole. Serve.

Katherine Seaborn Portman,
Southern Methodist University
Dallas, Texas

MOM'S RICE

1 cup rice
1 pint sour cream
¾ pounds grated Jack cheese
1 small can chopped ortega
  chilies

Boil rice in 2 cups water. Add sour cream, cheese (reserve some for topping), and chilies. Season with Accent and garlic salt to taste. Sprinkle with remaining cheese. Bake uncovered 25 minutes at 350 degrees.

Patricia Metzger Trujillo,
California State University-Long Beach
Pasadena, California

TALLAHASSEE RICE

1 cup rice
1 can condensed onion soup
  (made with beef stock)
1 can beef consommé or bouillon
1 3-ounce can mushrooms in
  butter
1 stick of butter or margarine,
  melted

Combine all ingredients in a casserole dish and bake at 350 degrees for 1 hour.

Genevieve E. Everett, Florida State University
Tallahassee, Florida

SPINACH CASSEROLE I

4 packages frozen chopped
  spinach
1 pint sour cream
2 packages onion soup mix
1¼ cups cornflakes crumbs or
  bread crumbs
4 tablespoons melted butter

Cook and drain spinach. Add sour cream and soup mix. Put in buttered 2 quart casserole. Toss melted buttered crumbs on top. Bake at 325 degrees for 30 minutes. Serves 12.

Dorothy S. Kenney, Syracuse University
Syracuse, New York

Gayle Maryl Hurst, Texas Tech University
Dallas, Texas

SPINACH CASSEROLE II

2 packaged chopped frozen
 spinach
1 medium chopped onion
1/4 pound longhorn cheese, grated
1 can cream of mushroom soup
2 to 3 tablespoons lemon juice
28 finely crushed saltines
2 to 4 slices bacon, sautéed and
 crumbled

Cook and drain spinach. In bowl mix soup, cheese, lemon juice, chopped onion, and cracker crumbs. Add drained spinach. Mix thoroughly. Put in casserole dish. Crumble bacon on top. Freeze at this point or bake at 350 to 375 degrees for 25 to 40 minutes. (If frozen, thaw before baking.)

Talie McKenzie, Northwestern University
Chicago Northwest Suburban, Illinois

SPINACH CASSEROLE III

2 packages spinach
1 stick margarine
1 pound fresh mushrooms
1/4 cup sliced onions
1 teaspoon garlic salt
1 cup grated cheese

Cook spinach according to package directions. Sauté fresh mushrooms, onions and garlic salt with margarine. Add this margarine mixture to spinach. Sprinkle grated cheese on top of casserole and bake at 350 degrees for 20 minutes.

Elaine Campbell Simpson, University of Iowa
Washington D.C.

SPINACH MILANESE

2 packaged chopped frozen
 spinach
1/2 cup chopped onion
8 pieces bacon, fried and
 crumbled
4 egg yolks
1/2 cup Parmesan cheese
1/4 teaspoon nutmeg

Thaw and drain spinach. Brown onions and combine with other ingredients. Place mixture in a well-greased ring mold. Place the ring mold into a pan containing cold water. Bake at 350 degrees for 45 minutes to 1 hour, until set. Serve with cheese sauce, if desired.

Donna Berra Cutler, Washington University
St. Louis, Missouri

SPINACH RICE CASSEROLE

2 10-ounce packages chopped
 frozen spinach
1 cup uncooked converted rice
1 16-ounce jar Cheez Whiz
1 package frozen chopped onion,
 or 3 raw chopped onions

Cook spinach until thawed, drain thoroughly, pressing water out. Add onion, Cheez Whiz and rice that has been cooked according to directions on package. Mix together well and put in greased casserole (can use oblong casserole or square deep one — Rice will be more moist in deeper dish). Sprinkle top generously with Parmesan cheese. Bake at 325 degrees for 35-40 minutes, or until cheese melts and casserole is bubbly.

Martha Conrad Clark,
University of Wisconsin-Oshkosh
Milwaukee, Wisconsin

SPINACH RISLEY

2 packaged frozen chopped
  spinach
4 tablespoons margarine
2 tablespoons flour
2 tablespoons chopped onion
½ cup evaporated milk
½ cup vegetable liquid
½ teaspoon pepper
¾ teaspoon celery salt
¾ teaspoon garlic salt
6 ounces Jalapeno cheese
1 teaspoon Worcestershire sauce
Red pepper to taste

Cook spinach. Save liquid. Melt margarine. Add flour to blend, not brown. Add onion until it become tender. Add liquid and milk slowly, cooking until smooth and thick. Add seasonings and cheese, stirring until melted. Combine with cooked spinach. Put in a casserole and top with buttered bread crumbs if desired. May be heated through again before serving. Serves 5 to 6.

Joanne Risley Artz, University of Vermont
Statesboro, Georgia

SQUASH OR GREEN BEAN CASSEROLE

1 green pepper, finely chopped
Small onion, finely chopped
4 strips bacon, fried crisp and
  then crumbled
1 cup drained tomatoes, chopped
2 cans green beans or squash
1 teaspoon Worcestershire sauce
¼ cup mayonnaise
Salt and pepper to taste
½ cup buttered bread crumbs

Cook onion, pepper and bacon together until onion and pepper are soft. Add tomatoes and simmer 5 minutes. Add green beans or cooked squash. Do not cook, but add mayonnaise and seasonings. Place in a greased casserole. Top with crumbs. Bake uncovered at 350 degrees for 20 minutes. Serves 8.

Janet Werner Harris, Oklahoma University
Dallas, Texas

SQUASH SOUFFLE

2 or 3 pounds of yellow summer
  squash
2 eggs well beaten
¼ cup finely chopped onion
  sauted in ¼ cup butter
½ cup cracker crumbs
2 cups grated Cheddar cheese
Salt and pepper to taste

Cook squash in covered saucepan with small amount of water until tender. Drain and mash. Add eggs, crumbs, onions and ½ of cheese. Mix well and put into casserole. Cover with more cracker crumbs and rest of cheese. Bake at 350 degrees for 20 minutes.

Linda Edwards Haney, Southern Methodist University
Dallas, Texas

SQUASH CASSEROLE

2 packaged frozen squash or 3-4
  fresh squash
8-10 pieces bacon, crumbled
12-15 Ritz crackers, crumbled
1 small onion, chopped
Grated Cheddar cheese

Boil squash until done, drain, mash. Add all other ingredients except cheese, and stir. Pour into greased casserole. Sprinkle cheese over top. Bake at 350 degrees until cheese is melted. Serves 6.

Kerry Lavine, Southwest Texas State University
Fort Worth, Texas

SUMMER SQUASH CASSEROLE

2 pounds yellow summer squash,
  sliced (6 cups)
¼ cup chopped onion
1 can condensed cream of
  chicken soup or mushroom
1 cup dairy sour cream
1 cup shredded carrot
1 8-ounce package herb-seasoned
  stuffing mix
½ cup butter or margarine,
  melted
Salt and pepper to taste

In saucepan, cook sliced squash and chopped onion in boiling salted water for 5 minutes; drain. Combine cream of chicken soup and sour cream. Stir in shredded carrot. Fold in drained squash and onion. Combine stuffing mix and butter or margarine. Spread half of stuffing mixture in bottom of 12x7½x2-inch baking dish. Spoon vegetable mixture atop. Sprinkle remaining stuffing over vegetables. Bake at 350 degrees for about 30 minutes or until heated through. Makes 6 to 8 servings.

Genevieve E. Everett, Florida State University
Tallahassee, Florida

Elise Berthon, Birmingham-Southern College
Birmingham, Alabama

STUFFED SQUASH

6 yellow summer squash
4 tablespoons melted butter
1 medium onion, chopped
1 tablespoon sugar
⅛ teaspoon black pepper
1 teaspoon salt
1 cup (or more) cracker crumbs

Wash and scrub squash. Place in just enough water to cover and allow to cook for about 20 minutes, or until just tender. Drain, cool and slice off the top. Take spoon and scoop out pulp. Add the remaining ingredients to the pulp, using enough cracker crumbs to make mixture fill squash cavities. Place stuffed squash on greased baking pan. Bake in preheated 325 degree oven for 20-30 minutes, or until tops are light brown.

Connie Brandon, Vanderbilt
Nashville, Tennessee

SQUASH-TOMATO-CHEESE CASSEROLE

4 large zucchini
1 small onion (I use instant
  minced onion)
2 slices bread
2 cups cooked or canned
  tomatoes
1 teaspoon salt
Pepper, as you like
1 cup thin strips of cheese

Slice squash. Finely chop onion. Cut bread in small pieces. Put tomatoes in greased baking pan; (cut in large pieces). Sprinkle onion, bread, salt and pepper over tomatoes. Put squash on top. Put cheese over squash. Cover and bake at 375 degrees (moderate oven) about 45 minutes, until squash is tender. Yield: 6 servings, about 1 cup each.

Marjorie Ann White Giles,
Southern Methodist University
Dallas, Texas

MOM'S NEW ENGLAND SUCCOTASH

Salt pork (approx. 2 inches x 1
  inch) cut into small cubes
1 medium onion, chopped
1 can pinto beans
1 can corn
3 medium potatoes (raw), peeled
  and cut into cubes

Brown salt pork in saucepan. Add rest of ingredients and cover. Cook until potatoes are done.

Lynne Ayers, Vanderbilt University
Nashville, Tennessee

BAKED SLICED TOMATOES

¼ cup butter or margarine
¼ cup chopped green onions
1½ cup fresh bread crumbs
(about 3 slices put in blender
or food processor)
2 tablespoons chopped parsley
1 teaspoon salt
Dash pepper
6 large, firm ripe tomatoes
1 to 2 teaspoons sugar

Heat oven to 350 degrees. Melt butter or margarine in saucepan, over medium heat. Add green onions and cook until tender. Stir in crumbs, parsley, salt and pepper. Remove from heat. Dip tomatoes in boiling water for 30 to 40 seconds; remove skins. Core tomatoes; cut into ½ inch slices. Arrange some slices around sides of a buttered 1½ quart ovenproof dish. Put layer of slices in bottom of dish. Sprinkle with a little sugar and some crumb mixture. Repeat layering 2 more times, ending with crumbs. Cover dish with foil. Bake 25 minutes or until bubbly. Makes 6 servings. This dish is good with almost any kind of meat.

Kay Reynolds Bennett, Texas Tech University
Dallas, Texas

LOUISE'S STUFFED TOMATO

8 tomatoes
2 packages frozen spinach
1 cup bread crumbs
1 cup grated Parmesan cheese
3 green onions, chopped
2 eggs, beaten
3 tablespoons margarine, melted
½ teaspoon thyme
¼ teaspoon garlic salt
Dash hot pepper
Salt and pepper to taste

Scoop out tomato and save. Season inside of tomato with salt. Cook spinach according to package directions. Drain well. Combine spinach with remaining ingredients. Spoon into tomato. Bake 30 minutes at 350 degrees. Serves 8.

Pat O'Connell Mullins, St. Louis University
Dallas, Texas

VEGETABLE MEDLEY

2 or 3 packages frozen broccoli
(or fresh)
1 package baby limas
2 cups carrots
1 can water chestnuts, sliced
1 4-ounce can mushrooms
2 cans mushroom soup
1 cup grated cheese
1 tablespoon minced onion
1½ teaspoon salt
1 teaspoon dry mustard
Dash of pepper
Slivered almonds

Cook broccoli, limas and carrots until just tender. (Canned carrots and limas can be used.) Drain everything well. Combine all ingredients but the almonds, tossing lightly and mixing well. Turn into shallow casserole, sprinkle nuts over top and bake at 350 degrees for 35 to 40 minutes.

Marcia McKee Lyons, Nebraska University
Cedar Falls, Iowa

BAKED VEGETABLE MEDLEY

1 cup small onions, or sliced
  onions
1½ cups carrots, sliced or in thin
  strips
¾ cup green pepper, in thin strips
2 teaspoons salt
⅛ teaspoon pepper
3 tablespoons minute tapioca
2 cups sliced celery
2 cups frozen green beans,
  separated, or 2 cups asparagus
  pieces
2 cups canned tomatoes, broken
  up
2 tablespoons butter, melted

Combine ingredients and place in a casserole; cover tightly. Bake in a 350 degree oven 1½ hours to 2 hours. If necessary, uncover toward the end of the baking period to get rid of excess liquid. 8-10 servings.

Mildred Hawkins, Iowa State University
Rock Rapids, Iowa

Ruth Deems Cooper, Iowa State University
Charles City, Iowa

VEGETABLE CASSEROLE

1 package frozen whole kernel
  corn, defrosted
1 package frozen baby limas,
  defrosted
1 package frozen peas and
  carrots, defrosted
2½ cups cooked rice
1½ cups consomme
Butter
Seasonings (onion juice, optional)

Place a layer of cooked rice in bottom of an electric skillet. Sprinkle peas and carrots next layer; then whole kernel corn; another layer of rice, and place lima beans on top. Pour consomme over vegetables, dot with butter and season with salt and pepper (and onion juice, if desired). Cover and turn temperature control to 300 degrees. Simmer for about 20 minutes.

Paulette S. Justice, West Virginia University
Charlton Heights, West Virginia

GREEN VEGETABLE CASSEROLE

1 can each: asparagus, green
  beans, green peas, water
  chestnuts, mushrooms
½ pound grated mild Cheddar
  cheese
¼ pound butter, melted
1 can cream of mushroom soup
3 slices white bread — in crumbs

Drain vegetables *very* well. Slice water chestnuts and mushrooms. Layer in 2 quart buttered casserole: asparagus, beans, peas, chestnuts, mushrooms, soup and cheese. Toss bread crumbs in the melted butter, spread on top of casserole. Bake uncovered at 350 degrees for 40-45 minutes. Serves 6 to 8 as side dish.

Carolyn Coe Cole, University of Texas
Dallas, Texas

BROILED ZUCCHINI

Zucchini, as many as you wish to
  serve, but be sure they are
  small and slender
Minced garlic or garlic powder
Fresh ground pepper
Minced chives
Grated Parmesan cheese
Margarine

Trim off ends of zucchini and split lengthwise. Do not peel. Place in buttered shallow pan or spray pan with vegetable spray-on. Sprinkle each with a little minced garlic or garlic powder, the pepper and chives. Then add a generous coating of Parmesan cheese and dot with margarine. Broil for 10 to 15 minutes or until lightly browned but still crisp.

Carolie Goniu, University of Wisconsin-Madison
Mequon, Wisconsin

ZUCCHINI CASSEROLE I

½ pound bacon
½ onion minced
2 cups herb stuffing
6 medium tomatoes, sliced
2 pounds zucchini, sliced
4 ounces Cheddar cheese,
  shredded

Cut bacon in half and fry. Brown onion in bacon grease. Mix with stuffing mix (including grease). Arrange ingredients in layers with the final topping of crumb mixture and cheese. Bake uncovered at 350 degrees for 1 hour. Serves 4 to 6.

Carolyn Kelly, Southern Methodist University
Dallas, Texas

ZUCCHINI CASSEROLE II

4 medium zucchini
1 large onion
2 tablespoons soy sauce
1 16-ounce carton cottage cheese
2 eggs
2 tablespoons mayonnaise
Parmesan cheese
2 tablespoons butter
½ teaspoon oregano
2 tablespoons flour
1 tablespoon parsley
1 1-pound can tomatoes, drained
1 cup shredded Cheddar cheese

Sauté sliced zucchini and sliced onion in butter until tender. Stir in soy sauce and oregano. Remove from stove and reserve. Whip cottage cheese, eggs, flour and mayonnaise together. Place ½ of zucchini mix in buttered 2 quart casserole. Add ½ of cottage cheese mix. Add ½ of the tomatoes, cut in pieces. Add ½ of shredded cheese. Repeat layers. Top with Parmesan cheese. Bake 1 hour at 350 degrees. Serves 6-8.

Theara Kurt Schonberg, Iowa State University
Omaha, Nebraska

ZUCCHINI CHEESE PUFF

6 medium zucchini
1 cup cottage cheese
1 cup shredded Jack cheese
2 beaten eggs
¾ teaspoon dill weed
¾ teaspoon salt
½ cup soft bread crumbs
1 tablespoon melted butter

Cut zucchini into ½ inch slices. Simmer in salted water 5 minutes. Drain. Turn into a shallow 1½ quart casserole. Mix eggs, cottage cheese, Jack cheese, dill weed and salt. Pour over zucchini and bake uncovered at 350 degrees for 15 minutes. Mix bread crumbs and butter and sprinkle over zucchini mixture. Bake 15 minutes longer.

Marion Benshaw, University of Minnesota
Riverside, California

ITALIAN ZUCCHINI CASSEROLE

2½ pounds zucchini, cut in ⅜
   inch slices (8 cups)
½ cup chopped onion
½ cup chopped green pepper
4 tablespoons butter or
   margarine
1 3-ounce can sliced mushrooms,
   drained
1 package dry spaghetti sauce
   mix
1 cup water
1 6-ounce can tomato paste
4-ounce package shredded
   Mozzarella cheese (1 cup)
2 tablespoons grated Parmesan
   cheese

In large saucepan, cook zucchini covered in boiling salted water till crisp-tender, about 4-5 minutes. Drain well; set aside. In same saucepan cook onion and green pepper in butter or margarine till tender but not brown. Remove from heat. Stir in mushrooms, dry sauce mix, water and tomato paste; mix well. Gently stir in zucchini and Mozzarella cheese. Turn into 10x6x2 inch baking dish or 1½ quart shallow casserole. Sprinkle with Parmesan cheese. Bake at 350 degrees for 30 to 35 minutes. Serves 6-8.

Nancy Hines Burton, University of Colorado
Boulder, Colorado

ZUCCHINI MICHELE

6 pounds of zucchini
1 tablespoon butter
8 ounces sour cream
½ pound grated Swiss cheese
Salt and pepper to taste

Peel zucchini. Slice finely. Put in large saucepan with butter, salt and ground pepper to taste. Cover. Let melt on moderate fire, stirring frequently. When everything has turned into a sort of rough puree, drain excess water in a colander. Mix in the sour cream, most of the grated cheese, and pour mixture into a low baking dish (a lasagna pan will do). Top with rest of grated cheese and with little pats of butter. Bake at 350 degrees for 30 minutes or until golden brown.

Version With Eggs: Beat 3 eggs lightly and mix in sour cream, grated cheese, a pinch of grated nutmeg, salt and pepper. Pour this mixture over cooked zucchini, fold in and bake at 450 degrees for 15 to 20 minutes, or until golden brown. Serves 6.

Kathleen Benson, Syracuse University
Floral Park, New York

STUFFED ZUCCHINI

1½ pounds zucchini
1½ cups bread crumbs
¾ cup grated Cheddar cheese
¼ cup minced onion
2 tablespoons chopped parsley
1¼ teaspoons salt
⅛ teaspoon pepper
2 eggs, beaten
2 tablespoons margarine

Scrub zucchini and cut off ends. Cook in salt water for 5-7 minutes. Cut in half lengthwise. Remove squash from shell and cut in small pieces. Combine rest of ingredients with squash and pile into shells. Arrange in oblong baking dish. Bake 30 minutes, uncovered at 350 degrees. (Add extra cheese if desired — tops should be browned)

Karen Diehl Greening, Washington University
St. Louis, Missouri

Sweets

Cakes

APPLE CAKE

¼ cup milk
2 teaspoon vanilla
3 eggs
1½ cup salad oil
2 cups sugar
3 cups flour
1 teaspoon baking soda
1 teaspoon salt
1 tablespoon cinnamon
3 cups chopped, peeled apples
1 cup slivered almonds

Combine milk, vanilla, eggs, oil and sugar in large mixing bowl, blend well. Add flour, salt, cinnamon and soda. Mix well. Stir in apples and nuts. Pour into greased 13x9x2 pan. Bake at 350 degrees for 60 minutes. Delicious when served warm with ice cream.

Karen Garrelts Hammer, Kansas State University
Dover, Delaware

ADAH'S APPLE CAKE

3 cups flour
1 cup vegetable oil
¼ cup water
3 teaspoons baking powder
3 cups sugar
4 eggs
2½ teaspoons vanilla
1 teaspoon salt
½ cup sour cream
4 large apples, pared and diced
Mixture:
¼ cup sugar
2 teaspoons cinnamon
¼ cup pecans
¼ cup raisins

Preheat oven to 350 degrees. Place all ingredients except apples and mixture in a large bowl and beat until smooth. Pour ½ of batter into a greased and floured tube pan. Spread ½ of apples and ½ of mixture over batter. Repeat layers. Take knife and slice through pan from top once. Bake at 350 degrees for 1½ hours.

Cookbook Committee

PAL'S COCOA APPLE CAKE

3 cups all purpose flour
3 tablespoons cocoa
1 teaspoon each cinnamon and allspice
1 teaspoon baking soda
1 cup butter or margarine
2 cups sugar
3 eggs
¾ cups sour cream
2 cups grated apple
1 cup chopped nuts
1 tablespoon vanilla

Preheat oven to 325 degrees. Grease and flour bundt pan. Mix together flour, cocoa, soda, cinnamon, and allspice. Set aside. Beat together margarine, sugar and eggs until fluffy. Add vanilla and sour cream, beating until smooth. Mix in dry ingredients. Fold in apples and nuts. Spoon batter into prepared pan. Bake 60 to 70 minutes, or until cake tests done. Cool in pan 10 minutes. Turn out and continue cooling on rack. Place on cake plate and dust top with powdered sugar. Decorate with pieces of candied cherries. Extraordinarily good eating.

Connie Spanier, Oregon State University
San Francisco, California

APPLE SAUCE CAKE

½ cup shortening
1½ cups sugar
2 eggs, unbeaten
2 cups all purpose flour
1½ teaspoons baking soda
¾ teaspoon salt
½ teaspoon cinnamon
½ teaspoon nutmeg
½ teaspoon cloves
½ teaspoon allspice
2 tablespoons cocoa
¾ cup each — raisins, chopped
   dates and nuts
½ cup apple sauce

Sift ½ cup of the flour over the fruit and nuts. Cream shortening and sugar. Add eggs and mix well. Sift together all dry ingredients and add to shortening, sugar and eggs. Mix well. Add apple sauce, and floured fruit and nuts. Bake 1 hour at 350 degrees in a greased 9 inch tube pan.

Margaret Miller Browne, Oregon State University
Dallas, Texas

APPLE PUDDING CAKE

Cake:
¼ cup butter
1 cup sugar
1 beaten egg
1 cup flour
1 teaspoon cinnamon
1 teaspoon soda
¼ teaspoon salt
3 grated apples
½ cup chopped nuts
Butterscotch Sauce:
½ cup brown sugar
½ cup white sugar
¼ cup butter or margarine
½ cup cream or half and half
Pinch of salt
1 teaspoon vanilla

Cake: Cream butter, sugar. Add egg. Sift flour, cinnamon, soda and salt together. Add to creamed ingredients. Add apples and nuts. Bake in 8 inch square pan at 350 degrees for 50 minutes.
Sauce: Cook all ingredients over low heat until smooth and creamy. Serve warm over cake. Whipped cream topping is also good.

Audrey Johnson Nelson, Mankato State College
Chicago NW Suburban, Illinois

BANANA CAKE & TOPPING

½ cup shortening
1½ cups sugar
2 beaten eggs
2¼ cups cake flour or 2 cups
   regular flour, sifted
¼ teaspoon baking powder
¾ teaspoon baking soda
1 teaspoon salt
¼ cup buttermilk
1 cup mashed bananas (ripe)
½ cup nuts (optional)
½ cup coconut or raisins
   (optional)
Frosting:
8 ounces cream cheese
½ cup margarine
1 teaspoon vanilla
1 package powdered sugar
Nuts (optional)

Cream shortening and sugar. Beat in eggs. Sift together flour, baking powder, baking soda, and salt. Add alternately with buttermilk, bananas, and nut mixture. Bake at 350 degrees for 25-30 minutes. Ice with cream cheese frosting.

Barb Tate, Vanderbilt University
Cincinnati, Ohio

ETHEL DRAKE'S GERMAN BERRY CAKE

Cake:
1½ cups all purpose flour
½ cup sugar
2 teaspoons baking powder
¼ teaspoon salt
1 egg in measuring cup
milk to fill cup
2 tablespoons melted shortening
Topping:
2-3 cups fresh boysenberries or
　blackberries
1-1½ cups sugar (Depending on
　tartness and amount of fruit)

Preheat oven to 375 degrees. Grease 8x12 inch or 8x14 inch baking pan. Sift dry ingredients into mixing bowl. With spoon, make a well in the center. Break egg into measuring cup; beat with fork or whisk. Add milk to fill cup and pour into well in dry ingredients. Add melted shortening. Beat until well blended. Spread mixture in baking pan. It should be about ½ inch thick. Sprinkle berries evenly over cake surface. Then sprinkle surface with sugar. Place cake in oven and bake 30 to 40 minutes (or longer, if necessary) until top is golden brown. Serve warm or cold with or without cream or vanilla ice cream.

This has been a family favorite for more than 40 years, especially when made with our own home-grown, fresh picked boysenberries. Probably other fresh fruits could be used, but we like this so well "as is" we've never tried anything else.

Penelope Murdoch Simonson,
University of California-Berkeley

BROWN STONE FRONT CAKE

Cake:
1½ cup sugar
½ cup butter
1 cup milk
2 cup cake flour
3 teaspoons baking powder
3 eggs (separated)
2½ squares unsweetened
　chocolate
Frosting:
3 squares unsweetened chocolate
3 tablespoons butter
3 cups powdered sugar, sifted
⅛ teaspoon salt
7 tablespoons milk
1 teaspoon vanilla

Cake: Cream butter and sugar. Add melted chocolate. Sift cake flour 5 times, then sift with baking powder. Add beaten egg yolks to butter and sugar mixture. Add milk alternately with dry ingredients. Lastly, fold in stiffly beaten egg whites. Bake at 350 degrees for ½ hour or until done. Makes 2 layers.
Frosting: Blend together butter, sugar, salt, milk, and vanilla. Melt chocolate and add to mixture. Mix well. Let stand, stirring occasionally until right consistency to spread. Spread between layers and around sides and top of cake.

Gladys McKahin, Iowa State University
Tri-City

BUTTERMILK CAKE

1 cup shortening
3 cups sugar
4 well beaten eggs
1 cup buttermilk
3 cups flour
½ teaspoon soda
½ teaspoon salt
1 teaspoon vanilla

Cream shortening and sugar together. Add eggs. Sift flour, soda and salt together and add alternately to first mixture with 1 cup buttermilk. Add vanilla. Bake at 325 degrees for 1 hour, 20 minutes in a large tube pan or fluted Bundt pan.

Marilyn Cooke Sullivan,
University of Iowa
Dallas, Texas

BUTTER PECAN BUNDT CAKE

1 package butter pecan cake mix
1 cup water
½ cup liquid shortening
4 eggs
1 package instant vanilla pudding
  mix
1 teaspoon butter flavoring
Glaze:
1 cup powdered sugar
3 tablespoons milk
½ teaspoon vanilla
½ teaspoon butter flavoring
½ cup chopped pecans

Mix together dry ingredients, add water and liquid shortening. Add eggs, one at a time beating well after each addition. Add flavoring. Pour batter into a well greased and floured bundt pan. Bake at 350 degrees for 45 minutes. Allow cake to cool for 15 minutes, then remove from pan. While warm drizzle glaze over cake and sprinkle chopped pecans on top.

Twila Larson Voss, Kearney State College
North Platte, Nebraska

ANN'S PINEAPPLE-CARROT CAKE

Cake:
3 cups flour
2 cups sugar
2 teaspoons cinnamon
1½ teaspoons salt
1 teaspoon baking powder
1½ teaspoon baking soda
1 can (8¾ ounce) crushed
  pineapple
2 cups raw grated carrots
3 eggs, beaten
1½ cups salad oil
2 teaspoons vanilla
1½ to 2 cups finely chopped nuts
Frosting:
3 ounces of cream cheese
1 stick margarine, softened
2 cups powdered sugar
1 teaspoon vanilla
Drops of water as needed

Cake: Mix dry ingredients together. Drain pineapple, saving syrup. Add pineapple syrup to the dry ingredients. Combine eggs, oil and vanilla, beating at least 3 minutes. Stir in pineapple, carrots and nuts. Add to flour mixture. Pour into greased and floured 9x16 inch pan. Bake at 325 degrees for 45 minutes.
Frosting: Cream all ingredients together. Spread on cooled cake.

Pat O'Connell Mullins, St. Louis University
Dallas, Texas

SUSIE'S CARROT CAKE

Cake:
1½ cups salad oil
2 cups sugar
4 eggs
2 cups sifted flour
2 teaspoons baking soda
2 teaspoons cinnamon
1 teaspoon salt
3 cups raw grated carrots
1 cup chopped nuts
Frosting:
1 8-ounce package cream cheese
½ stick melted margarine
2 teaspoons vanilla
1 box powdered sugar

Cake: Blend oil and sugar together. Add eggs, one at a time, beating well after each addition. Sift dry ingredients and add to sugar, egg, and oil mixture. Add carrots and nuts. Bake in 3 greased and floured 8 or 9 inch layer cake pans at 300 degrees for 40 to 50 minutes.
Frosting: Blend together and spread between layers and top and sides of cake.

Jean Brooks Oliver, Northwestern University
Atlanta, Georgia

CHESS CAKE

1 package Duncan Hines butter cake mix
4 eggs, room temperature
1 stick butter (NOT margarine), room temperature
1 8-ounce package cream cheese, room temperature
1 pound box powdered sugar

Squeeze with hands until well-mixed, the cake mix, butter and one egg. Pack with fingers into bottom of greased 13x9x2 inch pan. Mix other three eggs, cream cheese and sugar with a mixer and pour over the first mixture. Bake at 350 degrees for about 45 minutes. Cool and cut like brownies.
Very rich and very good.

Janie Bowles Means, Texas Tech University
Dallas, Texas

CHEESE CAKE

1¾ cup graham cracker crumbs
1½ cup sugar
1 teaspoon cinnamon
⅓ cup soft butter
4 eggs
2 pounds softened cream cheese
1 tablespoon lemon juice
Dash of salt
1 teaspoon vanilla
2 cups cultured sour cream

Mix well the graham cracker crumbs, ¼ cup of sugar, cinnamon and butter. Press into bottom of a 10 inch spring form pan, reserving ¾ cup for topping. Beat eggs and 1 cup of sugar until thick and lemon-colored. Without washing beaters, beat cheese until fluffy and smooth. Add beaten eggs to cheese with lemon juice and salt; beat well. Pour into crumb lined pan. Bake at 375 degrees for 30 minutes. Remove from oven. Fold remaining ¼ cup of sugar and vanilla into the sour cream. Spread over cake. Sprinkle with reserved crumb mixture. Return to 475 degree oven for 10 minutes. Cool and refrigerate 2-3 hours. Allow to stand at room temperature 1 hour before serving. Unbuckle pan just before serving.

Suzanne Young Brayer, Arizona State University
Phoenix, Arizona

Karen Lee Kendall, Vanderbilt University
Nashville, Tennessee

BLUEBERRY CHEESECAKE

Crust:
½ cup butter or margarine
⅓ cup sugar
1½ cups corn flake crumbs
Filling:
1 envelope unflavored gelatin
2 8-ounce packages cream cheese
1 can sweetened condensed milk
2 tablespoons lemon juice
4½ ounces non-dairy whipped topping
Glaze:
1 cup sugar
2 tablespoons cornstarch
1 cup water
1 pint fresh blueberries

Crust: Cook butter and sugar until mixture boils; remove. Mix in crumbs. Reserve 2 tablespoons for garnish; press remainder in 9 inch spring form pan. Chill.
Filling: Prepare gelatin mixture; set aside. Beat cheese until smooth. Add condensed milk and lemon juice; mix well. Fold in whipped topping. Spoon into prepared pan. Spoon blueberry glaze over top. Sprinkle the 2 tablespoons of crumbs around outer edge of cake. Chill 3 hours.
Glaze: Combine sugar and cornstarch in a small sauce pan; blend. Stir in water. Cook over medium heat, stirring constantly, until mixture thickens and boils. Boil about 2 minutes or until clear. Cool. Add blueberries.

Violet Baswell Mahaffey,
Birmingham-Southern College
Birmingham, Alabama

FRUIT CHEESECAKE

Crust:
1 cup graham cracker crumbs
3 tablespoons sugar
⅓ stick melted butter
Cake:
2 8-ounce packages cream cheese
¾ cup sugar
¼ cup flour
2 eggs
1 cup light cream
1½ teaspoon vanilla

To make the crust, combine cracker crumbs, sugar and butter. Pat into square cake pan. Bake at 325 degrees for 10 minutes. Take out and let cool.
To make the cake, combine softened cream cheese, sugar and flour. Mix well. Blend in eggs one at a time. Stir in cream and vanilla. Pour over crumbs. Bake at 350 degrees for 35-45 minutes. Check center for doneness — it should spring back to a soft touch. Top with canned pie filling of choice. Blueberries, cherries or other. A sure hit with everyone!

Connie Baker, University of Minnesota
Atlanta, Georgia

CHEESE CAKE

Graham Cracker Crust:
1⅔ cups crumbs
3 tablespoons sugar
6 tablespoons melted butter
½ teaspoon cinnamon
Filling:
2 large packages cream cheese
⅔ cup sugar
½ teaspoon vanilla
2 whole eggs
Topping:
3 tablespoons sugar
1 carton sour cream
½ teaspoon vanilla

For crust, mix all ingredients together and press in a ten inch spring form pan.
For filling, soften cheese and beat thoroughly. Add sugar gradually then vanilla and then the eggs one by one, beating thoroughly. Bake at 375 degrees for 20 minutes. Partially cool, then continue with topping.
For topping, mix all ingredients together and spread over cake. Bake at 500 degrees for 5 minutes. Cool and chill.

Suzanne Knipschild North, University of Missouri
Greater Kansas City

Rhonda Reed Russell, East Texas State University
Dallas, Texas

CHOCOLATE CHEESE CAKE I

1 cup flour
1 stick margarine
1 cup chopped pecans
1 8-ounce package cream cheese
1 cup powdered sugar
1 cup Cool Whip
1 large package instant chocolate
  pudding
1 small package instant vanilla
  pudding
3 cups milk

Combine first three ingredients and place them into the bottom of a 13x9 inch pan. Bake at 350 degrees for 15 minutes. Cool completely. With an electric mixer, mix well the cream cheese, powdered sugar. Add the Cool Whip. Pour over the crust. Beat the pudding mixes with the milk. Beat until thick and pour over cheese layer. Top with more Cool Whip, then garnish with chipped pecans and shaved sweet chocolate.

Karen Boyer Croley, Oklahoma State University
Bartlesville, Oklahoma

CHOCOLATE CHEESECAKE II

1 box thin chocolate wafers,
  crushed
¾ cup butter, melted
¼ teaspoon cinnamon
1 12-ounce package semi-sweet
  chocolate chips
1 tablespoon cocoa
2 pounds cream cheese, softened
2 cups sugar
4 eggs
2 teaspoons vanilla
1 cup sour cream

Combined crushed wafers, butter and cinnamon; press into pan. Chill. Melt chocolate chips in double boiler. Beat cream cheese in large bowl until fluffy and smooth. Gradually beat in sugar, then eggs, one at a time, beating after each addition. Add melted chocolate, cocoa and vanilla. Blend thoroughly. Stir in sour cream and pour into chilled crust. Bake at 350 degrees for 1 hour and 10 minutes. Cool at room temperature. Chill at least 5 hours. Freezes well.

Nancye Joan Tucker Duhon,
Louisiana State University
Gueydan, Louisiana

PUMPKIN CHEESE CAKE

¼ to ½ cup graham cracker
  crumbs
4 8-ounce packages cream
  cheese, softened
1½ cups sugar
5 large eggs
¼ cup all-purpose flour
¼ teaspoon salt
1 1-pound can pumpkin
2½ teaspoons pumpkin pie spice
1 cup heavy cream, whipped

Butter bottom and sides of a 9½ inch spring-form pan generously. Sprinkle with cracker crumbs. Shake pan to coat all sides and let excess crumbs remain on bottom. Heat oven to 325 degrees. Beat cream cheese in large bowl until fluffy. Beat in sugar gradually. Add eggs, one at a time, beating well after each addition. Beat in flour, salt, pumpkin and spice. Pour into prepared pan. Bake at 325 degrees for 1½ hours, or until firm around sides but soft in center. Turn off heat. Open oven door and let cake cool in oven for 30 minutes. Remove from oven and cool completely on wire rack. Remove sides of pan. Chill cake. Ice with whipped cream and serve. Serves 10-12.

Barbara Read Stapleton, Kansas University
Memphis, Tennessee

MOTHER'S PETITE CHERRY CHEESECAKES (STRAWBERRY)

2 8-ounce packages cream cheese
¾ cup sugar
2 eggs
1 tablespoon lemon juice
1 teaspoon vanilla
24 vanilla wafers (Sunshine)
1 21-ounce can cherry pie filling
  or fresh strawberries

Beat cream cheese, sugar, eggs, lemon juice and vanilla until light and fluffy. Line small muffin pans with paper bake cups. Place a vanilla wafer in each cup. Fill cups ⅔ full with cream cheese mixture. Bake at 375 degrees for 15 minutes or until set. Top each with pie filling. (In strawberry season, top with whipped cream and a fresh strawberry.)

Alice Jane Herr, Pennsylvania State University
Elizabethtown, Pennsylvania

Margaret McGill Kunkel, Texas Tech University
Dallas, Texas

CHOCOLATE CAKE

Cake:
2 cups sugar
2 cups flour
½ cup shortening
1 stick butter or margarine
1 cup water (or coffee)
4 tablespoons cocoa
1 teaspoon salt
½ cup buttermilk
2 beaten eggs
1 teaspoon soda
1 teaspoon vanilla
1 teaspoon red cake coloring
Icing:
1 stick butter or margarine
4 tablespoons cocoa
6 tablespoons milk
1 box powdered sugar
1 teaspoon vanilla
1 cup chopped nuts

Cake: Sift together sugar, salt and flour. In a saucepan, bring to boil the shortening, butter, water and cocoa. Pour over flour mixture while still hot. Add the buttermilk, beaten eggs, soda, vanilla and coloring. Bake in a large greased cookie sheet with sides or two 8x8 inch cake pans. Bake at 400 degrees for 20-25 minutes. (It is better baked as a sheet cake.)
Icing: Bring to a boil the butter, cocoa and milk. Add the powdered sugar, vanilla and nuts. Spread over cake while both are hot.

Betty Hodnett, Oklahoma State University
Stillwater, Oklahoma

Judy Tonning Price, Southern Methodist University
Dallas, Texas

CHOCOLATE CAKE

One package cake mix (Double
  Dutch Chocolate or Devils Food
  or any other chocolate or fudge
  mix, 18.5 ounce size)
2 eggs
1 can of applesauce (size 303
  can) 1¾ cup
Frosting:
One package of chocolate bits (6
  ounce package)
½ of a small carton of sour cream
  (8-ounce)

Mix together in a mixing bowl. Grease and flour a 13x9x2 inch pan. Bake at the temperature on the cake mix, sometimes it is 350 degrees and others are 375 degrees. Bake for 25 to 30 minutes or till done when tested with a straw.
Frosting: Melt the bits in a small pan, (over hot water) when completely melted, take pan off fire and mix with the cream. Spread over cake.
Quick and foolproof.

Ruth E. Irma Havens, University of Illinois
San Pedro, California

CHOCOLATE BUNDT CAKE

1 package chocolate fudge cake
   mix
1 small package chocolate instant
   pudding mix
1 cup sour cream
½ cup oil
½ cup warm water
4 eggs
1 small package chocolate chips

Place first 6 ingredients in large bowl of mixer, and beat about 10 minutes. Stir in the chocolate chips. Grease and flour a bundt pan and pour in chocolate mixture. Bake at 350 degrees for 50 or 60 minutes, or until done. Let set in pan for about 30 minutes then invert on large plate.

Sue Wolfe, Iowa State University
Sioux City, Iowa

DOTTIE'S CHOCOLATE BUTTERMILK CAKE

1 cup water
1 cup butter
¼ cup cocoa
2 cups flour
2 cups sugar
1 tablespoon baking soda
2 eggs
½ cup buttermilk
Icing:
⅓ cup buttermilk
½ cup butter
1 box powdered sugar
¼ cup cocoa
½ cup nuts (optional)

Blend water, butter, and cocoa in a saucepan and heat to boiling. Sift flour, sugar, and baking soda. Combine both mixtures. Blend well. Stir in eggs and buttermilk. Pour into greased jelly roll pan. Bake at 400 degrees for 20 minutes.
Icing: Heat buttermilk and butter to boiling. Add remaining ingredients.

Cookbook Committee

CHOCOLATE CHERRY CAKE

Cake:
1 box chocolate cake mix
3 eggs
1 can cherry pie filling
½ teaspoon almond extract
   (optional)
Frosting:
5 tablespoons butter or
   margarine
⅓ cup milk
1 cup sugar
1 6-ounce bag chocolate chips

Mix all ingredients for the cake and beat according to package directions. Bake in a greased and floured pan (9½x13½ inches) at 350 degrees for about 30 minutes or until done. Cool.
For frosting, mix butter or margarine, milk and sugar in sauce pan. Boil for 1 minute. Remove from heat and add chocolate chips. Stir until chips are melted and well blended. Spread over cooled cake.

Carmel Streeter, Syracuse University
Syracuse, New York

CHOCOLATE CHIP CAKE

1 package yellow cake mix
4 eggs
1 package 3¾ ounces vanilla
 instant pudding
1 cup corn oil
1 cup milk
1 4-ounce package German sweet
 cooking chocolate, grated
1 package 6 ounces chocolate
 chips
¼ cup 10X sugar (powdered)

In mixing bowl, combine cake mix, eggs, pudding, corn oil and milk. Mix for 5 minutes at medium speed. Set aside 2 tablespoons of the grated chocolate for topping. Add remaining grated chocolate and chocolate chips to the batter and mix gently. Put mixture into a greased and floured tube pan. Bake in preheated 350 degrees for 1 hour. Let cool in pan. Remove cake from pan and sprinkle 10X sugar and reserved chocolate over the top.

Connie Brandon, Vanderbilt University
Nashville, Tennessee

CHRISTMAS CAKE

1 pound candied cherries
1 pound pineapple rings (all
 colors)
1 pound pitted dates
1 pound shelled pecans
1 package (8 or 10 ounces)
 shredded coconut
1 can sweetened condensed milk
(Pour brandy or whiskey over
 cooked cake if desired)

Cut all ingredients coarsely. Place ingredients in a bowl. Pour condensed milk over and mix thoroughly until it is evenly divided into the mixture. Grease small loaf pans and line with waxed paper. Pack firmly with hands. Bake at 350 degrees about 1 hour. Remove from pans and waxed paper. Cool and then re-wrap in wax paper. Then wrap in foil. Freeze or refrigerate.

Arthetta White Swafford, Oklahoma University
Tulsa, Oklahoma

MARGARET'S CHRISTMAS CAKE

½ pound butter
1 cup sugar
3 egg yolks
1½ tablespoons lemon extract
1½ tablespoons vanilla
1½ cups flour
1 teaspoon baking powder
3 egg whites, beaten stiff but not
 dry
½ pound chopped pecans
½ pound white raisins

Cream butter and sugar, add egg yolks and beat. Add lemon extract and vanilla. Sift flour and baking powder together and add to mixture. Fold in beaten egg whites. Add nuts and raisins. Pour into bundt or tube pan that has been buttered and floured. Bake at 325 degrees for about 1 hour or until cake tester comes out clean.

"This is so delicious, don't wait for Christmas."

Sara Hess McElhaney, Iowa State University
Dallas, Texas

CHRISTMAS CHERRY CAKES

¼ pound butter or margarine
1 cup sugar
3 eggs, beaten one at a time into butter & sugar
1¾ cups flour sifted
¼ teaspoon baking powder
Pinch of salt
½ cup walnuts, or almonds, cut up slightly
1 8-ounce package candied cherries, cut up

Have butter at room temperature; mix very well with sugar. Add eggs, one at a time and beat thoroughly. Add dry ingredients, nuts, and cherries. Bake 350 degrees for 50-60 minutes in loaf pan. Can also be made in small loaf pans — (makes 3). Test with toothpick for doneness.

Margaret Sawyer, Oregon State University
San Francisco, California

COCOA COLA CAKE

1 cup margarine
1¾ cups sugar
2 eggs, slightly beaten
1 teaspoon vanilla
2 cups flour
1 teaspoon baking soda
3 tablespoons cocoa
½ cup buttermilk
1 cup cola beverage
1½ cups mini-marshmallows
Frosting:
½ cup soft margarine
3 tablespoons cocoa
⅓ cup cola
4 cups powdered sugar

For the cake, measure first 8 ingredients and mix well. Add cola. Mix again. Fold in mini-marshmallows. Pour in greased and floured 9x13 inch pan. Bake at 350 degrees for 35 minutes.
For the frosting, combine ingredients and beat until smooth. Spread on cooled cake.

Susan Roberts Redpath, University of Minnesota
Wayzata, Minnesota

Becky Mason, Wichita State University
Wichita, Kansas

CRANBERRY CAKE WITH BUTTER SAUCE

1 cup sugar
4 tablespoons margarine or butter
2 cups flour
2 teaspoons baking powder
¼ teaspoon salt
1 cup milk
2 cups whole raw cranberries
Butter Sauce:
¼ cup butter or margarine
1 cup sugar
½ cup cream or evaporated milk
1 teaspoon vanilla

Cream butter or margarine and sugar. Sift dry ingredients and add alternately with milk to creamed mixture. Add whole cranberries. Bake at 350 degrees for 40 minutes in an 8x8 inch or 8x10 inch pan. Melt butter and add sugar and cream or evaporated milk to a boil. Add 1 teaspoon vanilla. Serve hot on cake.

Nancy Price Lilly, Syracuse University
Canterbury, New Hampshire

Zo Karlstad, University of North Dakota
Grand Forks, North Dakota

CRUMB CAKE

3¼ cups whole wheat or white
  flour
1 cup butter
1 cup brown sugar (packed)
2 eggs
1 cup brown sugar (packed)
½ teaspoon baking powder
1½ teaspoon cinnamon
¼ teaspoon salt
1 teaspoon baking soda
½ teaspoon cloves
1½ teaspoons nutmeg
⅔ cup sour milk

Mix first three ingredients together to fine crumbs then remove 1 cup and set aside. Add 2 eggs to the remaining crumbs. Mix the remaining ingredients well. Grease and flour bundt pan. Sprinkle ½ cup crumbs in pan then ½ of the batter and then the remaining crumbs and batter. Bake at 375 degrees for 25 minutes in high altitudes. Other areas, bake at 350 degrees for 35 to 40 minutes.

Ann Clapp Scott, Southern Methodist University
Denver, Colorado

DATE AND NUT CAKE

⅔ cup butter
1½ cup sugar
1 teaspoon vanilla
1 egg
2¾ cups flour
1 teaspoon baking soda
½ teaspoon salt
⅓ cup milk
1 cup chopped dates
½ cup chopped nuts
Icing:
2 tablespoons *browned* butter
1½ cups powdered sugar
Hot water

Cream butter and sugar. Add vanilla and the egg. Mix the flour, baking soda and salt. Add flour mixture alternately with the milk. Coat with a little of the flour and add the dates and nuts. Bake at 350 degrees for about 25 minutes in a 9x13 inch greased pan. For the icing, mix the browned butter and powdered sugar with enough hot water to spread easily. Frost the cake. Cut into squares.

Mynnette Lomas Sheller, Iowa State University
Milwaukee, Wisconsin

FRUIT CAKE

1 pound whole candied cherries
½ pound candied pineapple,
  cubed
½ pound candied citron
½ pound candied orange peel,
  diced
1 pound candied lemon peel,
  diced
1 pound pitted dates, sliced
2 15-ounce packages raisins, light
  and dark
2 11-ounce packages currants
1 cup sherry
5 cups sifted cake flour
1 teaspoon each: cinnamon,
  cloves and mace
2 teaspoons salt
2 cups butter
1 1-pound package brown sugar
12 eggs, well beaten
1 cup strawberry jam
1 cup light molasses
1 cup walnuts

Combine candied fruits, peels, dates, raisins and currants. Pour over sherry; let stand overnight. Sift flour with spices and salt 3 times. Cream butter, gradually add sugar, beating until light and fluffy. Add eggs slowly, beating well. Add sherried fruit, jam, molasses, and nuts mixing well. Gradually work in flour mixture. Pour into 5 paper-lined (9x5x3-inch) loaf pans. Bake at 250 degrees for 3½ to 4 hours. Test for doneness with wire tester or straw. Remove from pans, cool on wire rack. Wrapped cold cakes in cheese cloth dipped in sherry, brandy or rum and store at least 2 weeks remoistening cheese cloth once a week. Can keep at least 6 weeks if cloth is kept moist and stored in cool place.

Jacki Falkenroth, University of Nevada-Reno
Chicago Northwest Suburban, Illinois

WHITE FRUIT CAKE

1 pound butter (no substitute)
1 pound light brown sugar
4 cups flour, all purpose
1 teaspoon baking powder
½ teaspoon salt
7 eggs, separated
1 ounce lemon extract
1 pound pecans (¾ pound is ok)
¾ pound candied cherries, cut in half
¾ pound candied pineapple, cut

Sift flour, baking powder and salt together, using one cup flour to coat cut fruit and nuts. Cream butter and sugar well, add the egg *yolks*, beating until a light creamy mixture and add the lemon extract then the remaining flour mixture. Fold in well beaten egg whites. Fold this into the fruit and nuts. This requires a large container. Bake in a well-greased Bundt pan. (I flour it.) Put cake batter in the pan as smoothly as you can, cover with wax paper and refrigerate overnight. Before removing wax paper mash down as firmly as you can. Bake at 250 degrees for 3 hours, but check it at 2½ hours. Place pan of boiling water of bottom rack while baking. LET PAN COOL BEFORE REMOVING.

Ruby Dudley Collins, Southern Methodist University
Fort Worth, Texas

FUDGE DELIGHT CAKE

Cake:
1 stick margarine
½ cup oil
1 cup water
4 tablespoons cocoa
2 cups flour
2 cups sugar
2 unbeaten eggs
½ cup sour cream
1 teaspoon baking soda
1 teaspoon vanilla
Frosting:
1 stick margarine, melted
6 tablespoons milk
2 tablespoons cocoa
1 box powdered sugar
1 teaspoon vanilla
½ cup nuts (chopped)

In medium-size saucepan, place margarine, oil, water and cocoa. Cook to a rapid boil, then turn off heat. Add flour and sugar. Stir and then add the eggs, sour cream, soda, and vanilla. Stir until well mixed but do not beat. Bake in 18x12x1 inch greased and floured sheet pan at 375 degrees for 20 minutes. If you use a slightly smaller pan, bake about 30 minutes.

Frosting: Fix frosting about 5 minutes before cake is done and pour frosting over cake as soon as you take it out of the oven. Heat the margarine, milk, and cocoa until dissolved. Turn off heat and add sifted powdered sugar, vanilla, and nuts. Pour over hot cake. Let cool and cut.

Gwen Nichols Durrenberger, University of Texas
Evansville, Indiana

LOUISE'S GRAHAM CRACKER CAKE

½ cup shortening
1 cup sugar
3 egg yolks
2 cups graham cracker crumbs
2 tablespoons flour
¼ teaspoon salt
2 teaspoons baking powder
1 cup milk
3 stiffly beaten egg whites
1 cup chopped nuts
Large package Cool Whip

Cream shortening and sugar. Add egg yolks and beat until fluffy. Mix flour, salt, baking powder, crumbs and add alternately with milk. Fold in egg whites and nuts. Bake in 2 greased cake pans at 350 degrees for 30 minutes. Frost generously with Cool Whip.

Cookbook Committee

ITALIAN CREAM CAKE

Cake:
5 egg whites
2 cups sugar
1 stick butter
½ cup vegetable shortening
1 tablespoon vanilla
5 egg yolks
1 cup buttermilk
2 cups flour
1 tablespoon soda
½ teaspoon salt
2 cups coconut
1 cup pecans, chopped
Icing:
8 ounce cream cheese
1 teaspoon vanilla
¼ stick butter, melted
Box powdered sugar

Beat egg whites until stiff; set aside. Cream together: sugar, butter, and shortening. Add vanilla and egg yolks. Add buttermilk alternately with flour, soda, and salt sifted together. Stir in coconut and pecans. Fold in egg whites and pour into three 9 inch cake pans. Bake at 350 degrees for about 30 minutes or until done.
For icing, blend together cream cheese and butter. Add vanilla and sugar. Ice when cooled.

Margaret McGill Kunkel, Texas Tech University
Dallas, Texas

SOUTHERN JAM CAKE

2 cups sugar
¾ cup butter or margarine
4 eggs
1 teaspoon soda
1 cup buttermilk — put soda in buttermilk
1 cup raisins (optional)
3½ cups sifted flour
2 cups jam (seeded blackberry or raspberry jam or preserves)
1 cup chopped nuts (pecans or mixture of pecans and English walnuts)
2 teaspoons each of cloves, nutmeg and cinnamon

Mix and cream butter and sugar. Add eggs one at a time, beating well after each addition. Combine spices and flour, add alternately with buttermilk and soda. Add jam, raisins and nuts. Bake in a 350 degree oven in a 10½ inch round angel food pan, which has been greased and floured. Cooking time is about 1½ hours.
Frosting: Caramel, using your favorite recipe or butter cream, in which I substitute 2 tablespoons of the same kind of jam used in cake, for 2 tablespoons of milk in the frosting.

Catherine Gardner Bowling, Vanderbilt University
Creve Coeur, Missouri

JELLY ROLL

3 eggs
1 cup sugar
3 tablespoons milk
1 cup flour
2 teaspoons baking powder
½ cup currant or plum jelly for filling, beat with fork

Beat egg whites until stiff. Set aside. Beat yolks, add sugar and beat together. Add milk. Fold in beaten whites. Fold in flour and baking powder. Spread evenly on large buttered tin 12x16 inches. Bake at 350 degrees until light brown. Cut off edges (¼ inch) with a sharp knife. Spread cake while hot with jelly. Loosen cake with spatula and gently roll.

Gertrude Bolton Rash, Iowa State University
Dallas, Texas

Cake:
½ cup milk
1 tablespoon butter or margarine
2 eggs
1 cup sugar
1 teaspoon vanilla
1 cup flour
1 teaspoon baking powder
¼ teaspoon salt
Topping:
3 tablespoons butter or
  margarine
5 tablespoons brown sugar
2 tablespoons milk or cream
½ cup coconut or nuts

LAZY-DAISY CAKE

For cake, heat milk and butter (or margarine) together in small pan. Beat eggs, sugar and vanilla in medium sized bowl. Add flour, baking powder and salt to egg mixture, beating a little. Stir in hot milk and butter mixture. Pour into a greased and floured 8x8 inch square or 7x11 inch rectangular pan. Bake at 350 degrees for 30-35 minutes, or until cake springs back at light touch. Remove from oven.

For topping, heat all ingredients together until well mixed. Spread hot topping over warm cake and broil until golden brown.

Best served slightly warm.

Mary M. Callander, University of Maryland
Alexandria, Virginia

4 eggs, separated, room
  temperature
1 cup sugar
¼ teaspoon cream of tartar
½ cup sugar
3 tablespoons lemon juice
1 cup whipping cream, whipped

LEMON TORTE

Beat egg whites with a little salt until frothy. Add ¼ teaspoon of cream of tartar; continue beating until whites form points. Gradually beat in 1 cup sugar. Spread meringue in greased 9-inch pie pan and bake for a total of 1¼ hours. For the first 20 minutes, bake at 275 degrees and the balance of the time at 300 degrees. Cool. Beat egg yolks until lemon colored. Add ½ cup sugar, beat until thick. Add 3 tablespoons lemon juice and cook in double boiler until thick. Cool. Whip cream. Spread half on cooled meringue; then lemon custard. Top with rest of cream. Chill 24 hours to blend flavors.

Georgiana Post McClenaghan, Oregon State University
Nashville, Tennessee

Cake:
2 sticks butter
½ cup cocoa
4 eggs
2 cups sugar
1½ cup self-rising flour
1½ cup nuts
1 teaspoon vanilla
1 cup miniature marshmallows
Frosting:
1 pound confectioners sugar
¼ cup milk
⅓ cup cocoa
½ stick butter, melted

MISSISSIPPI MUD

For cake, melt butter. Remove from heat. Add cocoa, then eggs, then sugar and vanilla. Mix well. Blend in flour, then nuts. Pour in greased and floured 9x13 inch pan. Bake at 350 degrees for 30-40 minutes. Sprinkle on marshmallows. Return to oven until marshmallows are melted. Combine all ingredients for the frosting and frost the cake.

Pam Rutherford, Vanderbilt University
Nashville, Tennessee

Connie Brandon, Vanderbilt University
Nashville, Tennessee

OATMEAL CAKE

Cake:
1 cup raw oatmeal
1¼ cups boiling water
¼ pound butter
1 cup brown sugar
1 cup white sugar
2 beaten eggs
1½ cups flour
1 teaspoon soda
1 teaspoon cinnamon
½ teaspoon nutmeg
¼ teaspoon salt
Icing:
6 tablespoons butter
½ cup brown sugar
½ cup white sugar
¼ cup evaporated milk
1 3-ounce can flaked coconut
1 cup chopped pecans (optional)

For cake, pour boiling water over oatmeal and butter, set aside to cool for about 20 minutes. Add brown sugar, white sugar and beaten eggs. Sift together flour, soda, cinnamon, nutmeg and salt; add to oatmeal mixture. Pour into a buttered and floured pan (13x9 inch). Bake at 350 degrees for about 35 minutes.

For icing, mix butter, brown sugar, white sugar, evaporated milk and coconut. Spread on cake while hot. Broil until bubbly.

Allys Field Boyle, University of Denver
Dallas, Texas

Corinne Lawton Mayborn, Texas Tech University
Dallas, Texas

ORANGE CAKE I

1¼ cups sugar
1 orange
½ cup shortening
1 cup raisins
2 beaten eggs
1 cup buttermilk
2 cups flour
½ teaspoon salt
1 teaspoon baking powder
1 teaspoon baking soda

Combine ¼ cup sugar and the juice of the orange, stirring until sugar is dissolved. Cream 1 cup sugar with shortening. Add eggs. Sift flour with salt, baking powder and baking soda. Add alternately with the buttermilk. Add raisins which have been ground with orange peel. Mix until well blended. Bake in oiled loaf pan at 350 degrees for about 45 minutes. Pour sugar and juice over cake while still in pan and warm. This cake can also be baked in a 9x13 inch pan and covered with the sugar and juice mixture while warm.

Ann Martin, Vanderbilt University
Dallas, Texas

ORANGE CAKE II

1 cup butter, room temperature
1½ cups sugar
3 eggs, separated
2 cups flour
1 teaspoon baking powder
1 teaspoon baking soda
1 cup sour cream
Grated rind of one orange
½ cup chopped walnuts or pecans
¼ cup orange juice
⅓ cup Grand Marnier
2 tablespoons slivered, blanched almonds

Heat oven to 350 degrees. Cream butter and *1 cup sugar.* Beat in egg yolks. Sift together dry ingredients and add alternately with sour cream. Stir in orange rind and nuts. Beat egg whites and fold in. Grease 9 inch tube pan and pour in batter. Bake 50 minutes. Combine ½ cup sugar, orange juice and liqueur. Spoon over hot cake. Let cake cool before removing from pan. Decorate top with almonds.

Note: I use a bundt pan for this cake as it looks attractive. However, I use a rather heavy one that is not teflon lined. When I have used the lightweight teflon lined bundt pans popular now for the bundt cake mixes, the cake gets too brown and the baking time needs to be decreased. I don't feel the cake rises as well in this teflon bundt pan either.

Susan K. Sismondo, University of Michigan
Westchester County, New York

Cake:
2 cups sifted flour
2 teaspoons baking powder
½ teaspoon salt
1⅓ cup sugar
⅔ cup shortening
1½ teaspoon vanilla
3 eggs
¾ cup milk
Glazes
Decorative frosting

6 ounce package semi-sweet
  chocolate pieces
2 tablespoons shortening
¼ cup light corn syrup
2 teaspoons vanilla
3 tablespoons water

1¾ cups sifted confectioners
  sugar
4 teaspoons cold water
¼ teaspoons vanilla

2 cups granulated sugar
⅛ teaspoon cream of tartar
1 cup hot water
3⅓ cups sifted confectioners
  sugar
2 teaspoons vanilla
Red or green food coloring*

PETITS-FOURS

Cake: Sift flour with baking powder and salt. Blend sugar with shortening and vanilla. Beat in eggs, one at a time. Add flour mixture, alternately with milk. Beat batter ½ minute. Turn into a well greased and lightly floured 12x15x1-inch jelly roll pan. Bake in a pre-heated 350° oven for 30 minutes or until toothpick inserted in center comes out clean. Turn onto a wire rack to cool. Wrap entire cake in foil and keep until the next day. When ready to ice, place cake on a pastry board and cut into 90 (2"x1") pieces. Brush off crumbs and arrange cakes in rows on a wire rack. Place rack in a large shallow pan. Quickly pour glaze over the cakes. Don't be afraid to pour, moving steadily from left to right covering tops and sides of cakes. Scoop up all the icing that has dripped through the rack, reheat with 1 teaspoon of water over hot water until of good pouring consistency. Pour over another batch of cakes. Continue until all cakes have one coating of glaze. Each time a frosting is re-heated, add 1 teaspoon water. Put a second coat of glaze by repeating above process with a new batch of glaze. When icing on cakes is set, decorate with decorative icing or glazed fruits.

CHOCOLATE GLAZE FOR PETITS-FOURS

Place chocolate pieces, shortening, corn syrup and water in top of a double boiler. Place over hot (not boiling) water and cook until chocolate has melted. Stir in vanilla. Covers 30 petits-fours.

DECORATIVE FROSTING FOR PETITS-FOURS

Combine all ingredients. Place in decorating tube and decorate tops of glazed petits-fours.
Variation: Can be tinted to accent color of petits-fours.

VANILLA GLAZE FOR PETITS-FOURS

In saucepan, combine granulated sugar, cream of tartar and hot water. Cook over low heat stirring constantly until sugar is dissolved. Cook gently without stirring to 226° or to a thin syrup. Cool until lukewarm (110°) or until pan may be held in hand. Add confectioners sugar (more or less if necessary) to make a pouring consistency. Stir in vanilla and add a few drops of food coloring. Glazes about 30-35 petits-fours.
Variation: Omit vanilla, add mint flavoring and tint green.

*optional

Jacqueline LeDuc, Rutgers University
Short Hills, New Jersey

PISTACHIO CAKE

Cake:
1 box white cake mix
1 package pistachio pudding mix
1 cup corn oil
1 cup club soda
3 beaten eggs
½ cup chopped nuts (almonds)
Icing:
1 cup milk
1 package pistachio pudding mix
1 large carton Cool Whip

Mix all ingredients for cake together and beat for 4 minutes. Put in a greased and floured bundt pan. Bake at 350 degrees for 35-50 minutes, until toothpick comes out clean. Mix all ingredients for the icing together. When cake is cool, cover with icing and refrigerate. Delicious!

Audrey Shafer, Past Grand President,
University of Missouri-Columbia
Greater Kansas City

RED PLUM CAKE

Cake:
2 cups sugar
1 cup oil
3 eggs
2 cups flour
1 teaspoon cinnamon
1 teaspoon cloves
½ teaspoon soda (baking)
¼ teaspoon salt
2 jars (4 ounces) red plum baby food
1½ teaspoon red food coloring
¾ cup pecans (optional)
Topping:
1 cup powdered sugar
2 tablespoons lemon juice
Barely boil and pour over cake while hot.

Cream sugar, oil, and eggs. Sift together flour, spices, soda, and salt. Add to creamed mixture, mixing well. Add red plum baby food, food coloring, and pecans. Pour in greased and floured bundt pan. Bake at 350 degrees for one hour.

Connie Shirey, Midwestern State University
Wichita Falls, Texas

Carol Edgington Thornburgh, Florida State University
DeRidder, Louisiana

Ann Sokol Heath, Iowa State University
Dallas, Texas

POLKA DOT CAKE

1¼ cups chopped dates
1 cup hot water
¾ cup shortening
1 cup sugar
2 eggs
2 cups sifted flour
1 teaspoon baking soda
½ teaspoon salt
1 teaspoon vanilla
1 6-ounce package chocolate chips
½ cup chopped nuts

Combine dates with water; set aside to cool. Cream together shortening and sugar. Add eggs, mix well. Sift together dry ingredients. Then add flour mixture alternately with date mixture, mixing well after each addition. Stir in vanilla and ½ cup chocolate chips. Pour into greased 13x9x2 inch pan. Sprinkle nuts and ½ cup chocolate chips on cake batter before baking. Bake at 350 degrees for 30-35 minutes.
Needs no additional icing — perfect for picnics.

Marianne Smith, University of Kentucky
Dixon, Kentucky

POPPY SEED CAKE I

½ pound butter
1½ cups sugar
4 beaten egg yolks
¼ cup poppy seed
1 teaspoon baking soda
1 cup sour cream
2 cups cake flour (1¾ cup regular)
2 teaspoon vanilla
4 egg whites, beaten stiff

Cream butter and sugar (5 to 8 minutes). Add poppy seed to 4 well beaten egg yolks; add to butter and sugar mixture. Add soda and sour cream. Add flour and vanilla. Fold in beaten egg whites. Bake for 1 hour in 10 inch ungreased tube pan at 350 degrees. Invert for one hour until cool.

Jacquelyn Cooper Pirkle, Arizona State University
Balboa Island, California

POPPY SEED CAKE II

1 package yellow cake mix
1 package vanilla instant pudding
1 cup sour cream
⅓ cup sherry
½ cup cooking oil
¼ cup poppy seed
4 eggs
Glaze:
1 cup powdered sugar
2 tablespoons sherry or lemon juice or water

Blend all together at medium speed for 2 minutes. Put into greased and floured bundt pan; bake at 350 degrees for 40 to 50 minutes. Cool 25 minutes with top side up. Invert and pour glaze over.

Irene Braden Loosley, Oklahoma University
Dallas, Texas

Jeri Lynn Franey, University of Northern Iowa
Prospect, Kentucky

POUND CAKE

2 sticks margarine
½ cup vegetable shortening
3 cups granulated sugar
5 beaten eggs
3 cups flour
1 cup milk
2 teaspoons lemon extract

Beat eggs until fluffy. Set aside. Combine margarine and shortening and mix well. Add sugar and mix until mixture is very well creamed. Add eggs, mix thoroughly. Combine milk and lemon extract and add alternately with the flour, in thirds. Pour into well-greased and floured large tube pan. Bake at 300 degrees for two hours.

Barbara H. White, University of Maryland
Washington, D.C.

BUTTERSCOTCH-CREAM CHEESE POUND CAKE

3 cups sugar
2 sticks margarine
¼ cup vegetable shortening
1 teaspoon vanilla
8-ounce cream cheese
3 cups flour
6 eggs
1 small package butterscotch chips
1 cup pecans (chopped)
Save 2 tablespoons flour to coat nuts

Cream first 5 ingredients together. Add alternately flour and eggs. Fold in pecans and butterscotch chips. Bake at 325 degrees for 1½ hours or until done, in a greased and floured bundt or tube pan.

Violet Baswell Mahaffey,
Birmingham-Southern College
Birmingham, Alabama

COCONUT POUND CAKE

2 sticks butter
1 stick margarine
3 cups sugar
6 eggs
3 cups flour
1 cup milk
1 teaspoon almond extract
1 teaspoon vanilla extract
1 large can coconut

Cream butter, margarine, and sugar. Add eggs, one at a time; beating well after each one. Add flavorings. Add flour and milk — alternating. Add coconut. Bake 1½-2 hours at 300 degrees, in a large buttered and floured, bundt pan.

Dawn Chappell, University of California
Riverside, California

5 FLAVORS POUND CAKE

½ pound butter
½ cup vegetable shortening
3 cups sugar
5 eggs, beaten
3 cups flour
½ teaspoon salt
½ teaspoon baking powder
1 cup milk
1 teaspoon rum flavor
1 teaspoon butter flavor
1 teaspoon lemon flavor
1 teaspoon coconut flavor
1 teaspoon vanilla flavor

Cream butter and shortening. Cream again with sugar. Beat eggs until lemon colored. Add to butter mixture. Mix flour, baking powder and salt. Add to mixture alternately with milk. Add flavorings. Spoon into floured and greased 10 inch tube pan. Bake for 1½ hours at 325 degrees.

Topping: Dissolve over low heat, 1 cup sugar, ⅓ cup water and 1 teaspoon of each of the 5 flavorings. Spoon over cake in pan while both are hot. Let cool in pan.

Sharon A. Kocsis, University of Maryland
Silver Spring, Maryland

AUNT SUE'S POUND CAKE

3 cups flour
2¼ cups sugar
1½ cups vegetable shortening
6 eggs
2¼ teaspoons baking powder
¾ cup milk
1 teaspoon vanilla

Place ingredients in mixing bowl. Beat with electric mixer at medium speed for 20 minutes. Mixture can be divided into two greased/floured loaf pans or into one tube pan. Bake one hour and 15 minutes at 325 degrees.

Nancy Sinclair Henry, William and Mary
Alexandria, Virginia

OLD-FASHIONED POUND CAKE

1 pound butter
2 cups sugar
4 cups cake flour sifted with
2 teaspoon baking powder
Pinch salt
10 eggs
1 teaspoon vanilla

Cream butter and sugar well. Add flour. Beat in eggs one at a time until well blended. Add salt and vanilla. Beat well. Bake in greased 10 inch tube pan one hour at 325 degrees. (Makes enough for 2 8-inch bundt pans.)

Lynne Ayers, Vanderbilt University
Nashville, Tennessee

PUMPKIN POUND CAKE

1 cup margarine or vegetable
  shortening
3 cups sugar
3 eggs
2 cups pumpkin (16 ounce can)
3 cups sifted flour
1 teaspoon baking powder
1 teaspoon soda
1 teaspoon cinnamon
1 teaspoon nutmeg
1 teaspoon ground clove
1 teaspoon allspice

Cream together shortening and sugar. Add eggs and pumpkin and mix well. Sift dry ingredients together and add slowly to the creamed mixture. This is a heavy pound cake type batter, thorough mixing is necessary. Add no additional liquid. Pour into a greased and floured angel food tube pan. Bake at 325 degrees for 1¼ hours. If not done, bake an additional 15 minutes. Cool in pan. Dust with powdered sugar or drizzle with thin glaze. Serve with whipped cream or ice cream.

Anita Stewart Vieson, Ohio Wesleyan University
Dayton, Ohio

PRUNE CAKE

Cake:
1½ cups sugar
1 cup cooking oil
3 eggs
2 cups flour
1 teaspoon nutmeg
1 teaspoon cinnamon
1 teaspoon allspice
1 teaspoon salt
1 teaspoon soda
1 cup buttermilk
1 cup nuts
1 cup cooked chopped prunes
1 teaspoon vanilla
Icing:
1 cup white sugar
½ cup buttermilk
¼ pound butter
½ teaspoon soda
1 tablespoon corn syrup
½ teaspoon vanilla

For cake, beat together first 3 ingredients. Sift together next 6 ingredients (flour and spices). While beating first 3 ingredients, add flour mixture alternately with buttermilk. Add nuts, prunes, and vanilla. Bake in greased pans at 300 degrees for 40 minutes. *For icing,* stir all ingredients until dissolved over medium heat until the mixture reaches soft ball stage. Pour at once over cake.

Lynne Ayers, Vanderbilt University
Nashville, Tennessee

PUMPKIN CAKE

Cake:
2 cups sugar
4 eggs
1½ cups pumpkin
1½ cups oil
2 cups flour
1 teaspoon salt
2 teaspoons soda
3 teaspoons cinnamon
Icing:
1 stick margarine
1 8-ounce package cream cheese
1 pound package confectioners
  sugar
1 teaspoon vanilla
1 cup nuts (optional)

Cream sugar, eggs; add oil and pumpkin. Then add flour, salt, cinnamon and soda. Mix well. Use angel food or bundt cake pan. Bake at 350 degrees for 1 hour. Let cool on rack. Spread icing on cooled cake.

Sue Ward Ragsdale, Southern Methodist University
Dallas, Texas

NANCY'S PUMPKIN CAKE

Crust:
One box yellow cake mix, minus
   one cup
½ cup melted margarine
1 egg
Filling:
One large can of pumpkin
3 eggs
2 teaspoons cinnamon
½ cup brown sugar
⅔ cup milk
Topping:
One cup cake mix
½ cup granulated sugar
¼ cup softened margarine
⅓ cup chopped nuts

Crust: Mix cake mix and margarine, add one egg and stir. Press into greased 9x13 inch pan.
Filling: Mix together ingredients and pour over crust.
Topping: Mix by hand and sprinkle over filling. Sprinkle with chopped nuts. Bake at 350 degrees for one hour or until light brown.

Nancy Ann McNary, West Virginia University
Eighty-Four, Pennsylvania

SKI CAKE

½ cup vegetable shortening
½ cup sugar
2 cups flour
3 teaspoons baking powder
1 cup milk
1 teaspoon vanilla
⅔ cup coarsely shaven unsweeten
   chocolate
2 egg whites
½ cup sugar
Topping:
½ cup butter
1½ cups sugar (powdered)
2 egg yolks
6 ounces chocolate chips

Cream shortening, add ½ cup sugar, mix well. Sift cake flour and baking powder into shortening mixture alternately with milk. Add vanilla and chocolate. Beat egg whites very stiff and add to ½ cup sugar, add to batter. Bake in two 8 inch layers at 350 degrees. Cool cake completely.
Topping: Cream butter, beat in 10X sugar to make it soft and fluffy. Beat in 2 egg yolks until very light and mix into above. Frost cooled cake, refrigerate 5 to 10 minutes. Melt chocolate chips over hot water, let it cool slightly, and pour over top of frosting. Refrigerate 5 to 10 minutes more to set.

Sarah Bristor, Michigan State University
Birmingham, Michigan

BOILED RAISIN SPICE CAKE

Cake:
1 cup raisins
2 cups water
1 egg
1 cup granulated sugar
½ cup shortening
1 teaspoon each: cinnamon,
   nutmeg, cloves (scant
   teaspoon)
2 cups all purpose flour
1 teaspoon baking soda
½ teaspoon salt
½ cup chopped nuts
(1 teaspoon vanilla)
Icing:
1 square baking chocolate
2 tablespoon margarine, or
   substitute
1 teaspoon vanilla
1 pound powdered sugar
Evaporated milk

Cake: Preheat oven to 350 degrees. Wash raisins and boil them 20 minutes in the 2 cups water. Drain water from raisins and *save*. Add cold water to make 1 cup. Cream the egg, sugar and shortening, spices and vanilla together until fluffy and light. Add 1 cup flour, then boiled raisins, then 1 cup flour, with ½ teaspoon salt and 1 teaspoon baking soda. Add 1 cup raisin water to mixture. (Add nuts with raisins if desired.) Mix all well. Spoon into cupcake papers or into square baking pan or 2 8-inch round pans (greased unless teflon). Bake at 350 degrees until tester shows it is done. Remove from oven, leave in pan. Ice while warm in pan. Use following recipe or any chocolate icing recipe.
Chocolate Icing For Boiled Raisin Spice Cake: Melt chocolate and margarine or its substitute in a mixing bowl over hot water (or in double boiler). Add vanilla and sugar and enough evaporated milk to make it spreadable on a warm cake. Beat well with an electric mixer. Spread on warm cake.

Lillian Brighton Spaid, Pennsylvania State University
Lititz, Pennsylvania

RUM CAKE

1 cup chopped pecans
1 package yellow cake mix
1 3¾-ounce package instant
    vanilla pudding
4 eggs
½ cup cold water
½ cup cooking oil
½ cup rum
Glaze:
¼ pound margarine
¼ cup water
1 cup granulated sugar
½ cup rum

Grease and flour tube or bundt cake pan. Sprinkle nuts in bottom. Mix cake ingredients together and pour batter over nuts. Bake for 1 hour at 325 degrees. Cool. Invert on serving plate. Poke holes all over top and sides, slowly drizzle glaze over, allowing cake to absorb it.

Glaze: Melt margarine in saucepan. Stir in water and sugar. Boil 5 minutes, stirring constantly. Remove from heat, stir in rum. Optional: whipped cream as a garnish.

Connie Hays Strohmyer, University of Nebraska
Lincoln, Nebraska

SODA CRACKER TORTE

Crust:
3 egg whites
¼ teaspoon cream of tartar
1 cup sugar
16 soda crackers
½ cup chopped pecans
Topping:
1 pint fresh strawberries or sliced
    peaches (sweetened)
Whipped topping

Crush soda crackers fine. Mix with sugar and pecans. Beat egg whites and cream of tartar until stiff peaks form. Fold egg white mixture into cracker mixture. Bake in buttered 8 or 9 inch pie tin for 30 minutes at 325 degrees. Cool. Cut into wedges and serve with whipped topping and fresh strawberries or sliced peaches.

Caroline Hardy Howard, Iowa State University
Centerville, South Dakota

SULTANA CAKE

¼ pound butter (or ½ cup butter
    substitute)
1 cup sugar
2 eggs, well beaten
¾ cup Sultana raisins (white)
½ cup candied cherries, and cut
    lemon and orange peel
⅓ cup milk
2 cups flour (measure before
    sifting)
1 teaspoon baking powder
¼ teaspoon salt
½ teaspoon almond flavoring
Hazel nuts and cherries

Cream butter and sugar, add well-beaten eggs, folding in gently; add fruit and peel and gradually add milk and flour with baking powder and salt with last of the flour. Add flavoring and mix well. Pour into greased and floured loaf pan. Decorate the top very liberally with shelled hazel nuts and candied cherries. Bake for at least an hour in a moderate oven (about 350 degrees). A sheet of aluminum foil over the top of the pan during the first part of the baking will prevent the top from getting too brown. This is an old Scottish recipe. It keeps well and is nice for Christmas giving and eating.

Carol Ryrie Brink, University of Idaho
La Jolla, California

BLACK WALNUT CAKE

2 sticks butter or margarine
2 cups sugar
4 eggs
2 teaspoons baking powder
1 cup milk
1 can finely cut coconut
16 ounces graham cracker
  crumbs
1 cup chopped black walnuts
Filling:
1 pound of powdered sugar
1 stick melted butter
1 small can crushed pineapple

Cream butter and sugar thoroughly. Beat in eggs one at a time. Stir in coconut. Mix the baking powder with cracker crumbs. Add alternately with milk. Stir in the nuts last. Divide batter between three large round cake pans, that have been lined with wax paper. Bake for 25 to 30 minutes in a 350 degree oven. When cool, frost between layers and on top. Combine filling ingredients. This cake is much better if made a day ahead of serving.

Zay Lynn Oliveira, University of Wyoming
Fairport, New York

WINE CAKE

1 1-pound 3-ounce package
  yellow cake mix
1 package vanilla instant pudding
  mix
4 eggs
¾ cup oil
¾ cup sherry (dry, medium, or
  cream)
1 teaspoon nutmeg

Combine all ingredients. Mix with electric beater about 5 minutes at a medium speed. Pour batter into greased angel food cake pan. Bake at 350 degrees about 50 minutes or until done. Cool in pan about 5 minutes before turning out on rack. Sprinkle with powdered sugar.

Lucy Crimmins Eichorn,
Southern Methodist University
Dallas, Texas

CHOCOLATE CUPCAKES

1 package Bordo cut, sugared
  dates or 1 package dates cut in
  pieces
1 cup boiling water
1 teaspoon baking soda
1 cup sugar
1 cup margarine
2 eggs
2 tablespoons cocoa
1¾ cups flour
½ teaspoon salt
Chocolate chips
Chopped nuts
Powdered sugar

Soak dates and soda in the boiling water for 10 minutes. Cream sugar and margarine; add eggs and cocoa. Add flour and salt alternately with the date mixture. Spoon into cupcake tins lined with paper muffin holders, either the foil ones or gay colored ones. Top each cupcake with a few chocolate bits and chopped nuts, if desired. Bake at 350 degrees for 20 minutes. When slightly cool, dust tops with powdered sugar. Makes 24 medium size cupcakes. These freeze very well, but add powdered sugar when defrosted. These are moist and tender, a favorite of our family, and easy to make as an electric beater does all the work.

Elise Bossort Bell, University of Wisconsin
Milwaukee, Wisconsin

SURPRISE CUPCAKES

8 ounces cream cheese, softened
⅓ cup sugar
1 egg
Dash salt
6 ounces chocolate bits (semi-sweet)
Chocolate or yellow cake mix

Cream softened cheese with sugar, add salt and egg. Stir in chocolate bits. Place in refrigerator. Mix cake for cupcakes. Pour into cupcake tins, filling only halfway. Drop rounded teaspoon of cheese mixture into cupcake. NOTE: If using cupcakes uniced, put ½ teaspoon of cake mix on top of cheese mixture. Bake at 375 degrees for 20 minutes. Yield: 30 cupcakes. Can be made ahead and frozen unfrosted, then frost when ready.

Barb Tate, Vanderbilt University
Cincinnati, Ohio

Cookies

ALMOND MERINQUES

1 cup sugar
½ cup water
2 egg whites
½ cup finely chopped almonds
Green coloring

Boil sugar and water to 245 degrees. Beat egg whites until stiff and pour syrup over them. Beat again. Fold in almonds. Tint green. Drop on well-greased cooky sheet in *very* small drops (size of a dime). Bake at 250 degrees for 25-30 minutes.

Gertrude Bolton Rash, Iowa State University
Dallas, Texas

BEACON HILL COOKIES

1 cup (6 ounces) semi-sweet chocolate chips
2 egg whites
½ cup sugar
½ teaspoon vanilla
½ teaspoon vinegar
Dash of salt
¾ cup chopped pecans

Melt chocolate over hot water. Beat egg whites with salt until foamy. Gradually add sugar, beating well. Then beat until stiff peaks will form. Beat in vanilla and vinegar. Fold in chocolate and nuts. Drop by teaspoonfuls on greased cookie sheet. Bake at 350 degrees for 10 minutes. Remove from cookie sheet immediately. Makes 36 cookies.

Gertrude Bolton Rash, Iowa State University
Dallas, Texas

Frances Jacobs Finks, Southern Methodist University
and Syracuse University
Dallas, Texas

Georgiana Post McClenaghan, Oregon State University
Nashville, Tennessee

BRAZIL NUT DROPS

1 cup butter (or ½ cup butter and
    ½ cup margarine)
1 cup sugar
2 eggs
2¼ cups flour
¼ teaspoon salt
½ teaspoon soda
1½ teaspoon vanilla
½ cup moist shredded coconut
2 cups Brazil nuts (each cut into
    3-4 pieces)

Cream shortening, add sugar gradually and cream thoroughly. Blend in eggs. Sift flour, salt, soda together then blend into butter mixture. Stir in vanilla, nuts, and coconut. Drop by teaspoonfuls onto lightly greased baking sheet. Bake 15 minutes in moderate oven (350 degrees).

Mrs. John L. Strong, U.C.L.A.
Monterey Bay, California

BOURBON BALLS

1 cup vanilla wafer crumbs
1 cup powdered sugar
¼ cup bourbon
1½ tablespoons white corn syrup
    mixed with bourbon
1 cup finely chopped pecans
2 tablespoons cocoa

Mix crumbs, cocoa, sugar and nuts. Add mixed syrup and bourbon. Mix and roll into 1 inch balls, then roll in powdered sugar, or cocoa or finely chopped nuts. Store in container for 2 days or more to ripen.

Latane Jordan Graham, Memphis State University
Dallas, Texas

DOUBLE RICH BROWNIES

Brownies:
2½ ounces unsweetened
    chocolate
1 cup shortening
1 cup sugar
1 cup brown sugar
4 eggs
1 teaspoon baking powder
1 teaspoon vanilla
1 cup flour
1 cup nuts
Frosting:
2½ cups sugar
3 tablespoons cocoa
1 tablespoon white corn syrup
¾ cup sweet milk
1 teaspoon vanilla
1 stick margarine

Brownies: Melt chocolate and shortening and allow to cool. Beat sugar and eggs until well blended and add chocolate mixture. Combine baking powder and flour and add to chocolate mixture. Stir in vanilla and nuts. Bake at 325 degrees for about 30 minutes in a 13x9x2 inch pan.
Frosting: Combine all ingredients except margarine and cook until soft ball forms. Remove from heat and add margarine and beat until ready to spread.

Cindy Sanders, University of Kentucky
Princeton, Kentucky

FAMILY FAVORITE BROWNIES

1 cup margarine
2 cups sugar
4 eggs
½ cup cocoa or 2 squares bitter chocolate, melted
1½ cups flour
1 teaspoon vanilla
Pinch of salt
½ cup chopped walnuts
Powdered sugar

Cream margarine and sugar together. Add eggs and beat well. Sift cocoa and flour together and stir into mixture. Add vanilla, salt and nuts. Beat well. Spread in greased 11¾x7½ inch pan. Bake at 350 degrees for about 35 minutes. Cool before cutting into squares. (Recipe can be doubled and baked in a 15½x10½ inch pan.) Sprinkle powdered sugar on brownies while in pan and still warm.

Margaret Godbold Briscoe,
Southern Methodist University
St. Louis, Missouri

Anne Yeager, Southern Methodist University
Dallas, Texas

FUDGE BROWNIES

Cake:
1 cup sugar
½ cup cocoa
½ cup flour
½ cup melted butter or margarine (1 stick)
2 well beaten eggs
½ cup nuts
Icing:
1 cup powdered sugar
2 tablespoons cocoa
2 tablespoons hot coffee
1 tablespoon melted butter

For cake, melt butter in 8x8 inch pan in 350 degree oven. Combine with all other ingredients. Bake for 20 minutes. (Will be more like fudge than a cake brownie.) Combine all ingredients for the icing and ice the brownies when cool. (Optional)

Gayle Christensen Avant,
Georgia State College for Women
Tallahassee, Florida

MARY'S BLACK RIVER BROWNIES OR BROWNIES DELUXE

Brownies:
4 eggs, beaten
1 cup vegetable oil
4 squares chocolate, melted
2 cups sugar
1½ cups sifted flour
1 teaspoon baking powder
¼ teaspoon salt
2 teaspoons vanilla
1 cup chopped nuts
Frosting:
Miniature marshmallows
2 cups powdered sugar
⅓ cup cocoa
¼ cup butter
4 tablespoons cream
¼ teaspoon salt
1 teaspoon vanilla

Combine ingredients for brownies and bake at 350 degrees for 20 minutes in a 15x10x1 inch greased pan. Sprinkle liberally with miniature marshmallows and broil . . . WATCH CAREFULLY!!! Spread frosting over melted marshmallows.

Mary Carlson Paterson, University of Illinois
Williams Bay, Wisconsin

Elise Berthon, Birmingham-Southern College
Birmingham, Alabama

BUTTERSCOTCH THINS

Graham crackers
1 cup margarine
1 cup brown sugar
1 cup nuts, chopped

Layer graham crackers on a greased cookie sheet that has sides. Don't break or crush them, but leave them whole. Boil margarine, sugar and nuts for 5 minutes. Pour evenly over graham crackers. Bake at 350 degrees for 10 to 15 minutes. When cool, cut into squares as the crackers are scored.

Cookbook Committee

CARAMEL CHOCOLATE SQUARES

60 caramels
½ cup evaporated milk
1 package German chocolate cake mix
¾ cup melted butter
½ cup evaporated milk
1 cup pecans
1 cup chocolate chips

Melt caramels and ½ cup evaporated milk in double boiler and set aside. Grease and flour a 2-quart utility dish. Mix cake mix with butter and ½ cup evaporated milk. Divide batter and put half in baking dish. Spread with chopped nuts and bake 8 minutes at 350 degrees. Remove from oven and sprinkle 1 cup chocolate chips on top. Pour caramel mixture over all. Then put other half of cake batter on top. (Do this carefully to spread it out.) Return to oven for 18 minutes. Remove and allow to cool. Put in refrigerator for about an hour for caramel to set up. Cut into small squares. May be frozen. Sinfully good!

Audrey Shafer, Past Grand President,
University of Missouri
Greater Kansas City

CHOCOLATE DROP COOKIES

½ cup shortening
1 cup brown sugar
2 eggs
1½ cups flour
½ teaspoon salt
1 teaspoon baking soda
½ cup cocoa
½ cup milk
1 cup chopped nuts
1½ teaspoons vanilla

Cream shortening and sugar together. Add eggs and beat until fluffy. Add vanilla. Sift flour, cocoa, baking soda and salt together. Add sifted dry ingredients alternately with milk. Stir in chopped nuts. Drop by teaspoonfuls onto ungreased baking sheet, spaced 2 to 3 inches apart. Bake at 375 degrees for about 10 minutes. These may be frosted with a chocolate cream frosting made of ⅓ cup cocoa, 1⅓ cups confectioners' sugar, 2 tablespoons butter, 3 tablespoons milk and ½ teaspoon vanilla.

Sara Hess McElhaney, Iowa State University
Dallas, Texas

NO-BAKE CHOCOLATE DROP COOKIES

1 stick margarine, melted
2 cups sugar
½ cup milk
¼ cup cocoa
1 teaspoon vanilla
½ cup peanut butter
3 cups quick oats
¾ cup coconut (optional)

Bring first 4 ingredients to a good boil and boil one minute in an open pot. Add vanilla and peanut butter and mix well. Add quick oats and coconut (optional). Mix and drop by teaspoonfuls on wax paper. Makes 7 dozen small cookies. Store in metal box. Keep well — freeze well. One cup of chopped nuts may be substituted for the peanut butter.

Betty Hodnett, Oklahoma State University
Stillwater, Oklahoma

Wendy A. Schneider, Ohio Wesleyan University
Dallas, Texas

CHOCOLATE BALL COOKIES

2 cups powdered sugar
1½ cups crunchy peanut butter
3 tablespoons melted margarine
1½ cups chocolate chips
1/5 bar paraffin wax

Combine sugar, peanut butter and margarine together. Mix well. Refrigerate for 1 hour. Roll into balls. Dip into melted chips and paraffin. Refrigerate to set.

Peg Walker Thiesen, University of Nebraska at Omaha
Omaha, Nebraska

CHOCOLATE MINT STICKS

2 cups sugar
4 eggs, beaten
1 cup butter or margarine
1 teaspoon vanilla
4 squares unsweetened chocolate
1 cup sifted flour
1 cup nuts, chopped, optional
Glaze:
2 squares unsweetened chocolate
2 tablespoons butter
Frosting:
2 tablespoons (heaping) Spry
¾ to 1 box powdered sugar
Green food coloring
Milk
Peppermint flavoring

In double boiler, melt butter and chocolate together. Remove from heat and add sugar, eggs and vanilla. Blend well. Add flour and nuts, blending well again. Bake in a 13x9-inch greased pan at 350 degrees about 30 minutes. (Should feel done to the touch, they should be chewy and not overdone.) Cool completely! Frost with the Spry, sugar to which milk, green food coloring and peppermint flavoring have been added to make good consistency (1 to 2 teaspoons peppermint or what tastes good to you.) Let set and harden. For the glaze, melt the chocolate and butter in double boiler. Drizzle over frosting quickly. Then tilt pan to cover frosting completely. Cool, then refrigerate. Cut into bars to serve.

Lois A. Price, Bowling Green State University
Fairfax, Virginia

CHOCOLATE NUT CLUSTERS

¼ cup butter or substitute
½ cup sugar
1 egg
1½ teaspoons vanilla
2 ounces unsweetened chocolate
½ cup flour
¼ teaspoon salt
¼ teaspoon baking powder
2 cups broken walnuts

Cream together butter and sugar. Add egg and vanilla. Mix well. Blend in chocolate that has been melted and cooled. Sift together flour, salt and baking powder; and stir into creamed mixture. Stir in the walnuts. Drop by small teaspoons on ungreased cookie sheet. Bake at 350 degrees for about 10 minutes. Makes about 3 dozen cookies.

Dorothy Kenney, Syracuse University
Syracuse, New York

CHOCOLATE PEPPERMINT COOKIES

Cookie:
2 squares unsweetened chocolate
½ cup butter
2 eggs
1 cup sugar
¼ teaspoon peppermint extract
½ cup flour
¼ teaspoon salt
Frosting:
1 cup powdered sugar
2 tablespoons butter
1 tablespoon evaporated milk
½ teaspoon peppermint extract
A drop or two of green food
   coloring
Glaze:
2 squares unsweetened chocolate
2 tablespoons butter

Cookie: Melt chocolate and butter. Add eggs which have been beaten with sugar. Stir in remaining cookie ingredients and bake in a buttered 8-9" square cake pan. 350 degrees — 30 minutes. Cool.
Frosting: Mix frosting ingredients, spread on cookies and chill.
Glaze: Melt butter and chocolate. Spread over frosting. Store in refrigerator.

Dawn Chappell, University of California
Riverside, California

CHOCOLATE SHERRY CREAM BARS

Base:
4 ounces baking chocolate
1 cup margarine
4 eggs
2 cups sugar
½ teaspoon salt
1 teaspoon vanilla
1 cup flour, sifted
Filling:
½ cup butter
4 cups powdered sugar
¼ cup cream or ½ & ½
4 tablespoons sherry
1 cup chopped walnuts or pecans
Topping:
1 6-ounce package chocolate bits
3 tablespoons water
4 tablespoons butter

Base: Preheat oven to 325 degrees. Melt chocolate and margarine over boiling water and let cook slightly. Beat eggs until light. Add sugar gradually. Then add chocolate mixture, flour sifted with salt, and vanilla. Beat one full minute. Pour into greased and floured 10x14x1 inch pan. Bake 25 minutes.
Filling: Beat butter and sugar together, adding cream and sherry gradually. When light and fluffy, add nuts and mix well. Spread over base. Chill in refrigerator or freezer.
Topping: Melt bits with water and butter over boiling water. Mix well and dribble over filling, spreading to cover (work fast). Let harden in refrigerator or freezer before cutting into bars. Makes 3 to 4 dozen. Store in refrigerator or freezer. Better in freezer and can be eaten frozen or thawed (most people don't care, they just eat them fast).

Carolyn Ray Leeming, Washington University
Phoenix, Arizona

CHOCOLATE WAFERS

1 cup butter
2 cups sugar
3 eggs
3 ounces chocolate
1⅓ cups flour
2 cups chopped nuts
1 teaspoon vanilla

Cream butter and sugar, add beaten eggs, then melted chocolate and vanilla. Stir in the nuts and flour. Drop by scant teaspoonfuls on a greased baking sheet. Place well apart — they will spread. Bake at 350 degrees for about 10 minutes.

"A favorite for three generations."

Dorothy Heryford Marshall, Iowa State University
Pittsburgh, Pennsylvania

CHRISTMAS WREATH COOKIES

¼ cup butter
3 cups miniature marshmallows
1½ teaspoons green food coloring
4 cups unsweetened corn flakes
Cherry quarters or red hots for
    berries (or other red dried fruit)

Butter 2 cookie sheets. Heat butter and marshmallows over low heat stirring constantly until marshmallows are melted. Stir in the green food coloring. Remove pan from heat and mix in the cereal with a wooden spoon until completely covered with the green marshmallow mixture. Butter hands and shape small amounts of mixture into wreath shapes on the cookie sheets. Work fast because the mixture cools rapidly and then it is hard to work with. Place red candy or fruit for berries. After cookies are set, store in single layers separated by waxed paper. Store 1 week only in an air tight container.

"Great family project. Easy for kids aged 3 and up to help."

Sheila Cornish Bell, University of Idaho
Spokane, Washington

COWBOY COOKIES

2 cups sifted flour
1 teaspoon soda
½ teaspoon baking powder
½ teaspoon cinnamon
¼ teaspoon nutmeg
½ teaspoon salt
1 cup shortening
1 cup white sugar
1 cup brown sugar
2 eggs
2 teaspoons vanilla
2 cups oatmeal
1 package chocolate chips or 1
    cup maraschino cherries
1 cup chopped nuts

Cream shortening, add white sugar, brown sugar, eggs, vanilla. Add soda, baking powder, cinnamon, nutmeg, and salt to sifted flour. Sift together into shortening/sugar/egg mixture. Stir in oatmeal, chopped cherries and chopped nuts. Drop generous teaspoonfuls of dough onto greased cookie sheet. Bake at 350 degrees for 10-12 minutes.

Note: 1 package chocolate chips may be used instead of cherries OR separate dough into two equal parts. Add ½ cup cherries to part and ½ package chocolate chips to the other part.

Cindy Drevo, University of Nebraska
Lincoln, Nebraska

DANISH COOKIES

1¼ pound (5 cups) flour (scant)
¾ pound (1½ cups) butter, oleo
   or shortening
½ pound (1 cup) sugar
½ teaspoon salt (1 teaspoon if
   shortening is used)
2 eggs
1 cube (¾ inch square or 1
   heaping teaspoon ammonia
   carbonate, baker's ammonia,
   available in pharmacy, mashed
   fine and dissolved in a bit of
   water).
Flavor as desired (2 teaspoons
   vanilla or orange or lemon
   flavoring).

Mix well, roll thin and cut with floured cookie cutter. Brush top with beaten whole egg to decorate with sugar. Bake in moderately hot oven, 350 to 375 degrees for 8 to 10 minutes.
Note: Ammonia Carbonate (Baker's Ammonia) has to be bought at a pharmacy. It comes in cubes, crystals or powdered form.

Carol Turner, Southern Methodist University
Springfield, Missouri

DATE CASSEROLE COOKIES

2 well beaten eggs
1 cup sugar
1 cup dates, cut up
1 cup coconut
1 cup nut meats
¼ teaspoon almond extract

To well beaten eggs, add sugar. Beat again and then add dates, coconut, nut meats, and almond extract. Place mixture in a 2 quart casserole. Bake at 350 degrees for 30 minutes. Remove from oven and beat with a *wooden* spoon. Scrape from edges as you beat. Work with 2 teaspoons and form into balls OR 1 teaspoon and your fingers and form into balls. Roll in granulated sugar. Keep in refrigerator.

Doris Erwin Hawkins, Iowa State University
Washington, D.C.

DATE-FILLED PINWHEEL COOKIES

1 pound dates, cut up
½ cup sugar
1 cup water
3 eggs
1 cup white sugar
1 cup brown sugar
1 cup shortening
4 cups flour
1 teaspoon soda
½ teaspoon salt
1 teaspoon vanilla

Boil first 3 ingredients and let cool. Mix remaining ingredients. Divide dough. Roll thin and spread with above mixture. Roll as cinnamon rolls. Chill in refrigerator. When chilled, slice and bake. Bake at 350 degrees for about 25 minutes.

Barbara Apple Keffer, Iowa State University
Tryon, North Carolina

ENGLISH TOFFEE COOKIES

1 cup butter
1 cup sugar
1 egg, separated
1 teaspoon vanilla
2 cups sifted flour
½ cup finely chopped pecans or almonds

Cream butter and sugar together. Add egg yolk, vanilla and sifted flour. Spread and press very thin on 2 cookie greased sheets almost to the edge. Brush with slightly beaten egg white. Sprinkle with pecans. Bake at 300 degrees for 40 minutes. Cut in shapes as soon as taken from oven.

Arthetta White Swafford, Oklahoma University
Tulsa, Oklahoma

Mary Dovell Long, University of California
Culver City, California

FRUIT COOKIES

1½ cups sugar
1 cup butter, worked to a cream
3 well beaten eggs
½ cup molasses
1 teaspoon soda in ½ cup sour milk or buttermilk
1 cup raisins
1 cup currants
1 cup chopped candied pineapple
1 cup cut candied cherries
1 cup chopped nuts
1 teaspoon baking powder
3 cups flour

Cream butter and sugar. Add beaten eggs and molasses. Stir in soda and sour milk. Add flour and baking powder. Blend in raisins, currants, candied pineapple, candied cherries and nuts. Add enough more flour to make a soft dough if necessary. Do not roll. Take out a small amount and put on a floured board to cut. Place on a greased cookie sheet and bake at 350 degrees for 12 minutes. May serve plain or when cool, ice and sprinkle with red or green sugar.

Icing: Powdered sugar, little butter and milk or cream.

Harriet Lishen Baldwin, University of Missouri
Dallas, Texas

FRUIT CAKE COOKIES

3 eggs
1-1½ cups brown sugar, firmly packed
⅔ cup butter, melted
1 teaspoon soda, dissolved in
1 teaspoon buttermilk
1 teaspoon vanilla
3 cups flour, sifted with
1 teaspoon cloves
2 teaspoons cinnamon
½ teaspoon salt
Fruits and Nuts:
½ pound almonds
½ pound pecans
½ pound glazed cherries
½ pound citron
½ pound pineapple
1 pound white raisins

Cut the fruit and nuts the night before and pour ½ cup sherry over top — cover tight and let soak overnight. Next day, toss fruit and nuts in sifted dry ingredients. Add batter made of first 6 ingredients above. Drop by teaspoonful on baking sheet and bake at 375 degrees until done. These may be made weeks in advance and stored in air tight tins until wanted. Dribble a glaze of powdered sugar and brandy over the top of the cookies before serving.

Pauline Peacock Little, Iowa State University
Greenville, North Carolina

GINGERBREAD CHORISTERS

½ cup shortening
⅓ cup molasses
1½ cup sifted flour
⅔ cup sugar
¼ teaspoon salt
½ teaspoon soda
¾ teaspoon ginger
1 tablespoon water
1 cup rolled oats

Beat together shortening and molasses until creamy. Sift together flour, sugar, salt, soda and ginger. Add to shortening mixture. Add water. Blend in oatmeal mixing until well combined. Knead dough gently for a few seconds. Sprinkle confectioners' sugar over board; roll out to ⅛ inch thickness. Cut with ginger boy and girl cutters dipped in powdered sugar. Place on greased cookie sheets. Bake in 350 degree oven for about 8 minutes. Allow to cool for a few minutes before removing. Cool and decorate with powdered sugar frosting. Rolled cookies that are especially nice to cut in shapes and decorate for Christmas — delicious anytime.

Patricia Smith Dieterich, University of Iowa
Ridgefield, Connecticut

GINGER COOKIES

¾ cup bacon fat
1 cup granulated sugar
1 cup molasses
1 teaspoon ginger
½ teaspoon cloves
½ teaspoon allspice
2 teaspoon soda in 3 tablespoons hot water
3⅔ cups sifted flour

Measure molasses and bacon fat into large bowl. Mix well. Add sugar, then soda in hot water. Add flour and spices. Mix, place in a bowl, cover with saran wrap and chill. Roll a quarter at a time, thin as possible. Cut with a floured cookie cutter, sprinkle with sugar and bake at 375 degrees for about 12 minutes.
Note: Butter or margarine may be used instead of bacon fat.

Ruth Buckman Armstrong, Syracuse University
Dallas, Texas

LEMON LOVENOTES

Crust:
1 cup flour
¼ cup powdered sugar
½ cup butter or margarine
Topping:
2 beaten eggs
1 tablespoon flour
1 cup granulated sugar
½ teaspoon baking powder
1 tablespoon lemon juice

Crust: Mix all ingredients well. Pat into an 8x8 inch pan. Bake at 350 degrees for 15 minutes or until golden brown.
Topping: Mix all ingredients well. Pour over baked crust. Bake 20 to 25 minutes more at 350 degrees. Then sprinkle with powdered sugar. Cut into squares when cool.

Terri Leinsteiner,
California State University-Long Beach
Lindsay, California

Polly Grove Haliday, Northwestern University
Evanston North Shore, Illinois

Elizabeth Maurer Wilkinson,
Southern Methodist University
Golden, Colorado

LEMON COOKIES

1 cup flour
½ cup corn starch
¼ teaspoon salt
½ teaspoon nutmeg
¼ pound plus 4 tablespoons butter
½ cup powdered sugar
2 teaspoons grated lemon rind

Cream butter, sugar and lemon together. Sift flour, corn starch, salt and nutmeg together, and add to butter mixture. Form or roll into small balls and place on ungreased baking sheet. Flatten with the bottom of a water glass dipped in powdered sugar. Bake at 325 degrees for about 10 minutes, or until light yellow around edges. These are wonderful for teas.
"They melt in your mouth."

Sara Hess McElhaney, Iowa State University
Dallas, Texas

AUNT MAE'S MUNCHERS

1 can sweetened condensed milk
1 6-ounce package chocolate chips
1 package (11 crackers) graham, crushed

Mix crushed graham crackers, condensed milk and chocolate chips. Press into a 8x8 inch slightly greased pan. Bake at 350 degrees about 15 to 20 minutes or until top is slightly browned. Cut into bars.

Peggy Larson Stromer, University of Nebraska
Milton, Wisconsin

NANAIMO'S

1 stick margarine
5 tablespoons cocoa
¼ cup sugar
1 egg
¼ teaspoon vanilla
1 package graham crackers crushed (2 cups)
1 cup coconut
½ cup nuts
1 stick butter, melted
2 cups powdered sugar
3 tablespoons milk
2 tablespoons vanilla *instant* pudding mix
4 squares semi-sweet chocolate
1 tablespoon butter

Melt margarine, cocoa and sugar together in saucepan over low heat and add the next five ingredients. *Press* very firmly into 9x12 inch pan. Refrigerate. Mix the melted butter, powdered sugar, milk and instant puddng mix together and spread on the first layer. Melt the semi-sweet chocolate and butter together and carefully spread over the top. Cut in small squares to serve. Easy and just delicious. Freezes beautifully.

Peggy Habegger, University of Washington
Seattle, Washington

OATMEAL COOKIES

1 cup bacon drippings
1 cup brown sugar
2 cups flour
2 cups rolled oats
¼ cup milk
1 cup raisins
2 beaten eggs
2 teaspoons cinnamon
½ teaspoon salt
1 teaspoon soda
1 teaspoon vanilla

Cream drippings and sugar til light and fluffy — add eggs, milk, and vanilla. Add oatmeal and raisins — mix well. Sift flour, soda, salt and cinnamon, add and mix well. Drop from a teaspoon on to greased cookie sheet. Bake about 12 minutes at 350 degrees.
Note: Butter or margarine may be used instead of bacon drippings.

Barbara Barott Lentz, University of Nevada-Reno
Greater Kansas City

Peggy Joy Habegger, University of Washington
Seattle, Washington

OATMEAL BUTTER COOKIES

2 sticks butter or margarine
½ cup sugar
1 cup flour
1½ cups quick cooking oatmeal
1 teaspoon vanilla
Powdered sugar

Cream butter or margarine with sugar until light and fluffy. Add flour and oatmeal with vanilla and blend. Allow to chill for about 30 minutes, then form into small balls. Arrange on an ungreased baking sheet and flatten with the bottom of a glass over which a damp cloth has been stretched. Bake at 350 degrees for 10 to 12 minutes, or until delicately browned. Remove from the baking sheet to a wire cake cooler and dust, while hot, with powdered sguar.

Dorothy Cooley Thompson, Iowa State University
Milwaukee, Wisconsin

MOM'S OATMEAL AND COCONUT COOKIES

2 cups flour
1 teaspoon salt
1 teaspoon soda
2 cups brown sugar
4 cups rolled oats
1 cup coconut
1 cup butter
2 eggs
Nuts (optional)

Mix well and form into balls, size of walnuts. Flatten and bake in a 375 degree oven until lightly brown. Will freeze. Crispy.

Karen Lee Kendall, Vanderbilt University
Nashville, Tennessee

PECAN CRISPS

1 cup brown sugar, packed
½ cup butter or substitute
1 egg
2 cups flour plus ¼ teaspoon salt
½ teaspoon soda
½ teaspoon cream of tartar
½ teaspoon vanilla
½ cup chopped pecans

Cream sugar and butter; add egg and vanilla. Mix well. Add flour, salt, soda, and cream of tartar. Blend in chopped pecans. Form into two rolls and wrap in wax paper. Refrigerate until firm or overnight. Slice in thin pieces and place on ungreased cookie sheet. Bake at 350 degrees for about 8 to 10 minutes.

Sara Hess McElhaney, Iowa State University
Dallas, Texas

PEANUT-BUTTERSCOTCH SQUARES

1½ cups flour
½ cup margarine
½ cup brown sugar
1½ cup sugar
Nuts (½ cup) chopped
½ cup honey
1 6-ounce package butterscotch chips
½ cup peanut butter
2 cups Rice Chex mashed up

Cream margarine and brown sugar. Stir in flour and chopped nuts. Press in ungreased 9x13 inch pan. Bake at 350 degrees for 15 minutes. In saucepan, combine sugar and honey; heat to boiling. Remove from heat. Add butterscotch pieces and peanut butter. Stir until butterscotch is melted. Stir in cereal. Spread over baked layer. Cool. Cut into squares.

Janice Impey, University of Illinois
Chicago N.W. Suburban, Illinois

POTATO CHIP COOKIES

1 cup sugar
½ pound soft margarine
1 egg yolk
1½ cup flour
¾ cup crushed potato chips
1 cup chopped nuts
1 teaspoon vanilla

Combine ingredients, saving potato chips and nuts for the last addition. Drop by spoonfuls on ungreased cookie sheet. Bake at 350 degrees for about 12 minutes.

Ruth Hendrix Stoufer, Iowa State University
Beverly Hills and Los Angeles, California

POTATO FLAKE COOKIES

1 stick margarine
1 cup sugar
1 egg
1¼ cup biscuit mix
1 teaspoon coconut flavoring
1 cup instant potato flakes

Cream margarine and sugar. Add the egg, biscuit mix, coconut flavoring and instant potato flakes. Mix all ingredients well. Bake on ungreased cookie sheet ten minutes at 325 degrees. Remove from oven and cool 3 to 5 minutes. Makes 40 to 50 drop cookies.

Grace Pitchford Killingsworth, Oklahoma University
Dallas, Texas

PRETZEL COOKIES

2 cups white sugar
1 pound margarine
1 whole egg
1 teaspoon vanilla
5 cups flour
1 teaspoon baking powder

Cream sugar and margarine until fluffy. Then add vanilla and egg. Beat well. Add flour to mixture. This mixture is stiff. Use a cookie press (I use a star design). Squeeze dough through press and make a circle design. Bake at 350 degrees until cookie is slightly brown. This recipe makes about 100 or so cookies. These are easy to make and oh! so delicious.

Ella Dodds Mistrot, University of Texas
Dallas, Texas

DICK'S PUMPKIN BARS

4 eggs
1⅔ cups sugar
1 cup cooking oil
1 16-ounce can pumpkin
2 cups flour
2 teaspoons baking powder
2 teaspoons cinnamon
1 teaspoon salt
1 teaspoon baking soda
Cream Cheese Frosting:
1 3-ounce package cream cheese, softened
½ cup butter, softened
1 teaspoon vanilla
2 cups powdered sugar

Bars: Beat together eggs, sugar, oil, and pumpkin until light and fluffy. Stir together the flour, salt, cinnamon, baking soda and baking powder. Add to pumpkin mixture and mix thoroughly. Spread on ungreased 15 by 10 by 1 inch baking pan. Bake at 350 degrees for 25 to 30 minutes. Cool. Frost with Cream Cheese Frosting. Top with chopped nuts if desired. Cut in bars.
Frosting: Cream together the cream cheese and butter. Stir in vanilla. Add powdered sugar, a little at a time, beating well, until mixture is smooth.

Victoria Friede, University of Wisconsin-Milwaukee
Lawrence, Kansas

RANGER COOKIES

1 cup margarine
1 cup brown sugar
1 cup white sugar
2 eggs
1 teaspoon vanilla
2 cups flour
½ teaspoon baking powder
½ teaspoon salt
1 teaspoon soda
2 cups crisp rice cereal
2 cups quick oatmeal
1 cup coconut
1 cup raisins, optional
1 cup nuts, optional

Cream margarine and sugars, add eggs, vanilla, flour, baking powder, salt and soda. After these are well blended, add the remaining ingredients. Drop by spoonful on cookie sheet. Bake at 350 degrees for about 10 minutes.

Ruth Hawley Sokol, Iowa State University
Iowa City, Iowa

Dorothy Cooley Thompson, Iowa State University
Milwaukee, Wisconsin

SPRINGERLE COOKIES

4 eggs
1 pound powdered sugar
1 tablespoon lemon peel, grated
3 (+) cups regular flour
1 teaspoon baking powder
1 drop anise oil (from drug store)

Beat eggs well. Stir in sugar and beat in mixer for at least 10 minutes. Add lemon, flour, baking powder and anise oil. It should get very stiff and might be necessary to mix by hand. Roll on floured and powdered sugar covered board to ½ inch thick. Imprint with springerle board. Cut apart and place on greased and floured cookie sheet. Let stand overnight. Bake at 325 degrees for 20 minutes. (Do not let get brown). Cool and store in airtight container.

Betty Boefer Keller, University of Missouri
Bartlesville, Oklahoma

SUGAR COOKIES

½ cup butter or margarine
1 cup sugar
2 eggs
1 teaspoon vanilla
½ teaspoon salt
2¾ cups flour
3 teaspoons baking powder

Cream butter and sugar thoroughly. Add eggs and beat well. Add vanilla. Sift flour, salt and baking powder into the creamed mixture. Mix well. Chill 15 minutes. Roll ⅛ inch thick on a slightly floured board. Cut with floured cutter, and sprinkle with sugar. Place on ungreased baking sheet. Bake at 400 degrees for about 10 minutes.
For holidays, sprinkle with red or green sugar.

Sara Hess McElhaney, Iowa State University
Dallas, Texas

DOWN-HOME SUGAR COOKIES

3 tablespoons water
2 cups sugar
3½ cups sifted flour
3 teaspoons baking powder
Dash salt
¾ cup bacon fat
1 teaspoon ground nutmeg
3 eggs
½ teaspoon ground cloves

Cream bacon fat and sugar, then mix in a combination of beaten eggs, 1 cup flour, and baking powder. Add spices, water and 2 cups flour. The remaining ½ cup flour is worked in until the dough is stiff enough to roll. Refrigerate for 1 to 2 hours, roll, cut and sprinkle with sugar. Bake at 400 degrees for 8-10 minutes.
"Don't let the bacon fat scare you. These cookies *don't* taste greasy."

Donna Berra Cutler, Washington University
St. Louis, Missouri

BARBARA'S 7 LAYER COOKIES

1 stick butter
1 cup graham cracker crumbs
Shredded coconut
6-ounce package of chocolate chips
6-ounce package of butterscotch chips
1 can sweetened condensed milk
1 cup chopped walnuts

Melt butter in a 9x13 inch baking pan in 350 degrees oven. Sprinkle with graham cracker crumbs. Add coconut, chips, sweetened condensed milk and top with walnuts. Bake at 350 degrees for 30 minutes. Cut into squares while still warm but not hot. Allow to cool. Yields about 50.

Cookbook Committee

SAND TARTS

½ pound margarine
½ cup sifted powdered sugar
2 cups sifted all purpose flour
1 cup chopped pecans
1 teaspoon vanilla

Add sugar to softened margarine and mix well. Add flour, nuts, vanilla. Shape into balls or crescents and bake on an ungreased cookie sheet at 325 degrees for 15-20 minutes or until light brown. Roll on powdered sugar while warm.

Gayle Howard Young, University of Texas
Dallas, Texas

Latane Jordan Graham, Memphis State University
Dallas, Texas

LITTLE WAFFLES
(A French Cookie)

4 eggs
1 cup sugar
1 cup melted margarine
2¼ cups sifted flour
1 teaspoon vanilla
Raisins and/or nuts (optional)

Mix all ingredients together and let batter stand in refrigerator overnight. Bake by teaspoonful at medium heat on waffle iron. One teaspoonful in each section of waffle iron for just a minute or two.

Mary Alice Betts, William and Mary
Winter Park, Florida

ZUCCHINI DROP COOKIES

1 cup zucchini, peeled and grated
1 teaspoon soda
1 cup sugar
½ cup shortening
1 egg beaten
1 cup raisins
2 cups flour
1 teaspoon cinnamon
½ teaspoon cloves
½ teaspoon nutmeg
½ teaspoon salt

Beat zucchini, soda, sugar, and shortening. Add egg and beat well. Sift flour and spices together and add to other mixture. Add raisins and stir in. Drop on greased cookie sheet. Bake at 375 degrees for 12-15 minutes.

Margaret Gatlin 'Meg' Smith, Florida State University
Minneapolis-St.Paul, Minnesota

Candy

CARAMEL CORN

2 cups brown sugar
½ cup white corn syrup
½ pound butter or margarine
3 poppers of popped corn

Boil caramel sauce for 5 minutes. Pour hot sauce over popped corn and bake at 250 degrees for 1 hour. Use 2 or 3 large cake pans that have been greased well. Stir occasionally while baking to redistribute the syrup.

Carolyn Hill Chaffin, North Dakota State University
Carrollton, Texas

COLORADO GORP (SNACK)

1 cup quick-cooking rolled oats
1 cup peanuts (shelled)
¼ cup wheat germ
½ cup honey
½ cup almonds, pecans or walnuts
2 tablespoons vegetable oil
1 cup M&M candies
½ cup chopped, mixed dried fruit
½ cup raisins

In a bowl combine oats, peanuts, wheat germ and nuts. Combine honey and oil and stir into oat mixture. Spread out in a 9x9x2 inch baking pan. Bake at 300 degrees for 30 to 40 minutes or until light brown, stirring every 10 minutes. Remove from oven and transfer to another lightly greased pan to cool. Break up large pieces. Stir in dried fruit, raisins and candy. Store in a tightly covered container or plastic "zip lock" bag. This is a high energy building snack, just perfect for outdoor activities! Makes 6 cups.

Winnie Unger Johnson, University of Denver
Denver, Colorado

DADDY'S FUDGE

4 cups of sugar
2 cups of milk
4 squares unsweetened chocolate
1 inch square butter
2 teaspoon vanilla

Simmer until you can form a hard ball. To form hard ball, drop a few drops from spoon into a dish of lukewarm water. Try to form a ball. If so, take off stove and place pan in sink with 1 to 2 inches of water (in sink). Add butter and vanilla, do not stir. Just let cool. When cool, then beat. Beat until it turns a different color brown. Pour onto a greased plate and let cool.

Sandy MacNeal, Purdue University
West Lafayette, Indiana

DARK AND CREAMY FUDGE

4 1-ounce squares baking
  chocolate
2 cups sugar
⅔ cup half and half
Pinch of salt
1 tablespoon butter

Bring first four ingredients to a boil over medium high heat, stirring constantly. After mixture boils, stop stirring. Continue boiling until a few drops off the end of the spoon into a cup of *cold* water forms a soft ball. Remove immediately from the stove and do not stir. Put butter in mixture and allow it to cool until you are able to dip a finger into the middle without burning. Stir mixture until it is stiff enough (but still creamy — it will become dull in sheen) to hold its shape when dropped off the end of a spoon. Drop into bite size pieces onto saran wrap. If too stiff, take up into hands and mold into balls or roll into a log and slice. If undercooked, re-cook and follow previous directions. This is a triple Gamma Phi Beta legacy recipe, as it has been handed down through the generations. Several pounds of it are sold every year at the Milwaukee Alumni Christmas boutique.

Mae Rowe Luecker, University of Wisconsin
Margaret Luecker Martin (daughter),
University of Wisconsin
Catherine Martin Brown (granddaughter),
Iowa State University
Anne Martin (granddaughter)
University of Arizona
Sent by Catherine Martin Brown
Milwaukee, Wisconsin

PSI PINK CARNATION MINTS

2½ cups powdered sugar
3 ounces cream cheese
½ teaspoon flavoring (flavoring
  and coloring as desired)
Food coloring for any color
  desired to correspond with
  molds

Mix and knead as for pie dough. Roll in balls the size of a marble. Roll in a small amount of granulated sugar. Press in a rubber mold. Unmold at once. When using the carnation mold, press the pink colored mixture in the flower part and then in the stem part, press the green mixture. These mints have become a tradition at Gamma Phi Beta activities at Oklahoma University.

Betty Mae Conner Jones, Oklahoma University
Dallas, Texas

SUPER CHOCOLATE CANDY

1 bar of German chocolate
  (baking type)
1 package of peanut butter chips
1½ cups of pecan halves

Melt chocolate and chips in microwave for about 1½ minutes on reheat. Stir halfway through. (Can be done on stovetop over water in double boiler. Stir frequently.) Add nuts and drop on wax paper in teaspoon size pieces. For variety add ½ cup of shredded coconut.

Sandra Graham Cude, Memphis State University
Dallas, Texas

BB's DIVINITY

2¾ cups sugar
Scant ¾ cup white corn syrup
Scant ½ cup boiling water
2 egg whites
Pinch of salt
1 teaspoon vanilla

Have egg whites at room temperature and in a large mixing bowl before starting. Mix sugar, syrup, salt and boiling water in heavy saucepan and cook over low heat until sugar dissolves. Cook until it forms a soft ball when tested in ice water. While this is cooking, beat egg whites stiff. When candy reaches soft ball stage, pour ⅓ of the cooked mixture over the stiffly beaten egg whites. Return other ⅔ of the mixture to the heat and cook to crack stage. When it reaches the crack stage, pour it over the first mixture. Add vanilla and beat until the candy cools and will hold its shape. Working quickly, drop candy by teaspoonfuls onto cookie sheet or waxed paper. Add nuts or maraschino cherries for decoration as desired. This recipe never fails!

Karen Rawlings, University of Missouri
Columbia, Missouri

MILLIONAIRES

1 pound caramels
3 tablespoons water
2 cups pecans
8 ounce milk chocolate bar
⅓ of a quarter pound paraffin bar

Melt together slowly the caramels and water. Stir in the pecans. Drop by teaspoon on a buttered cookie sheet. Chill until firm. Melt over low heat in a double boiler the chocolate bar and paraffin. Dip each chilled caramel in the warm chocolate and place on buttered plate until firm and cool. They are great!

Annabel Jones, Oklahoma University
Norman, Oklahoma

PEANUT BUTTER BALLS

2 cups peanut butter
1 pound margarine or butter
2 boxes powdered sugar
2 teaspoon vanilla
12 ounces chocolate chips
½ of a bar paraffin (½ of a
  quarter pound bar)

Combine the first four ingredients. Make in balls and refrigerate for 30 minutes. Melt 12 ounces of chocolate chips and ½ bar paraffin. Melt the chips and paraffin over low heat in a double boiler. Dip the chilled balls in the chocolate mixture and let harden. Use a toothpick for dipping. This makes a large amount so could be halved.

Janet Lynn Jones, Oklahoma University
Norman, Oklahoma

SUGAR AND HONEY PECANS

1½ cups sugar
¼ cup honey
½ cup water
½ teaspoon vanilla
3 cups pecan halves
¼ teaspoon salt

Combine sugar, honey, water and salt in a saucepan; cook over medium heat, stirring constantly, until sugar is dissolved. Continue cooking, without stirring, to 242 degrees Fahrenheit on the candy thermometer, or until a little in cold water forms a firm ball. Remove from heat. Add vanilla and pecans; stir gently until mixture becomes creamy. Turn onto waxed paper. With fork, separate pecans. Let dry. Makes about 1¼ pounds.

Nell Taylor Wolfe, Iowa State University
Westchester County, New York

Desserts

BAKED ALEUTIANS
(Miniature Baked Alaskas)

One sponge layer cake
Three egg whites
Six tablespoons sugar
¼ teaspoons lemon juice
Cream of tartar (¼ teaspoon)
1½ pints ice cream (strawberry, peach or peppermint)
Pastel colored paper muffin cups

Place a thin circle of sponge cake in the bottom of each paper muffin cup and set the cups into standard muffin baking tin. Top the cake with a scoop of very solidly frozen ice cream. Beat three egg whites with ¼ teaspoon lemon juice, salt or cream of tartar until they begin to stiffen. Then add, one at a time, 6 table-spoons of sugar, beating after each addition. Cover the ice cream completely with the egg whites. The secret is to really seal in the ice cream. This is sometimes difficult to accomplish with a big Alaska, much easier with the small ones. Set the whole thing into the freezer. When ready to serve, simply slide the muffin tray into a very hot oven (400 degrees) and leave for three to four minutes or until very lightly tinged with gold. Serve in their paper cups at once. Serves six.

Sheila Smith, Kent State University
New York City

ANGEL FOOD CAKE DESSERT

1 angel food cake
1 cup boiling water
1 package strawberry gelatin
½ pint whipping cream
1 package frozen strawberries

Slice angel food cake in three layers. Dissolve gelatin in boiling water and add strawberries. Chill until firm. Whip cream and add to strawberry mixture. Spread between layers of cake and chill until ready to serve. This can be made a day in advance. Serve plain or with whipped cream. Note: Cake will retain its shape better if returned to the pan while chilling. Chill for 24 hours. Or chill and serve in a beautiful dish.

Christine Lynn Aden, Colorado State University
Fort Collins, Colorado

AUDREY'S ANGEL FOOD CUSTARD DESSERT

1 large angel food cake cut into
   12 or 16 wedges and laid in
   9x13x2 inch dish
Custard:
⅔ cup sugar
5 egg yolks
1½ cups milk
Pinch of salt
2 teaspoons lemon gelatin
1 pint whipping cream
1 teaspoon vanilla

Cook egg yolks, milk, sugar and salt until it coats spoon. While hot add the gelatin which has been dissolved in a little cold water. Let cool. Then add whipped cream and vanilla. Pour custard over the cake wedges in dish and place in refrigerator for 24 hours. Cut into squares and serve.

Mary C. Lawrence Engle, Kansas University
Houston, Texas

CHERRY ANGEL FOOD CAKE DESSERT

1 angel food cake, broken into
   small pieces
1 3-ounce package cherry gelatin
1 3¾-ounce package instant
   vanilla pudding mix
1 21-ounce container cherry pie
   filling
1 cup boiling water
1 cup milk
8 ounces sour cream

Place broken pieces of angel food cake into a 9x13 inch glass dish. Mix gelatin with boiling water and allow to stand until partially cooled. Add cherry pie filling to gelatin and mix well. Pour gelatin and cherry mixture over the pieces of angel food cake. Place in the refrigerator until set. Combine instant vanilla pudding mix and milk, beating until smooth and thick. Add sour cream to the pudding and mix thoroughly. Spread sour cream and pudding mixture on top of cake and cherry mixture. Return to the refrigerator until time to serve. Serves 12.

Sheryl Stoner Myhra, Iowa State University
Dallas, Texas

APPLE CHUNKIES

½ margarine stick
¾ cup sugar
1 egg
1 teaspoon vanilla
1 cup flour
1 teaspoon baking powder
¼ teaspoon salt
1 peeled, chopped apple
½ cup chopped nuts

In 1½ quart saucepan melt margarine and sugar, mix using wooden spoon, and cool. Beat in 1 egg and vanilla. Sift together flour, baking powder, salt. Stir into margarine-sugar mixture. Stir in apple chunks and nuts. Lightly grease 8x8 inch pan. Bake at 350 degrees for 30 minutes. Cut into squares and serve while still warm.

Carol Lehrer Wilson, Colorado State University
Colorado Springs, Colorado

APPLE CRISP

1 cup sugar
¾ cup sifted flour
1 teaspoon cinnamon
½ teaspoon salt
¾ cup quick oats
1 stick cold butter or margarine
Apples, McIntosh or other
cooking variety

Mix crumb mixture together with a pastry blender. Finely cut in butter — mixture should be crumbly. Butter a baking dish. Slice washed and peeled apples into dish. (For apples which are not tart, sprinkle with a few drops of lemon juice.) Cover apples with crumb mixture. Bake at 375 degrees for 45 minutes or until apples are tender and topping is crisp. Serve warm, with vanilla ice cream, whipped cream or hard sauce.

Rosalind Nichols Bartlett,
Pennsylvania State University
Erie, Pennsylvania

MARILYN'S APPLE CRISP

8-9 cooking apples, peeled and
sliced
3 tablespoons apricot nectar
1 cup white sugar
¾ cup all purpose flour
⅓ cup butter or margarine
1 teaspoon cinnamon

Place sliced apples into an oblong baking dish. Cover with the apricot nectar. Working with a pastry blender or fingertips, mix remaining ingredients until well blended and sprinkle over the apples. Bake at 350 degrees for 1 hour.

Pat O'Connell Mullins, St. Louis University
Dallas, Texas

GOMMIE APPLES
(Six Generation Recipe)

6 to 8 medium baking apples
(Jonathan or Delicious fine)
1 cup sugar
¼ cup water (or more if apples
are not juicy)
¼ cup cornstarch
1½ cups milk
1 lump butter
¾ cup sugar
1 pinch salt
1 teaspoon vanilla
Nutmeg and cinnamon

Peel and quarter apples. Cover the bottom of a glass 8x11 inch baking pan, then add water and sprinkle sugar. Bake in 350 degree oven until done, about one hour. On top of stove, mix ¼ cup or more milk and the cornstarch, then add rest of milk, butter, sugar and salt. Cook on medium heat, stirring constantly until it gently bubbles, then a couple minutes more. Add vanilla and pour over apples in baking dish or serving dish. Serve warm or chilled. Sprinkle with cinnamon and nutmeg.

Sue Lytle Yett, Iowa State University
Mobile, Alabama

ADAH'S BREAD PUDDING

½ cup honey
4 cups bread, cubed
1 quart milk
5 eggs, slightly beaten
¼ cup sugar
¼ teaspoon salt
2 teaspoons vanilla
¾ cups raisins

Mix honey and bread cubes and cook over low heat until honey is absorbed. Blend milk, slightly beaten eggs, sugar, salt and vanilla. Add to bread mixture. Remove from heat. Add raisins to bread mixture. Pour into buttered baking dish. Sprinkle cinnamon on top. Place dish in pan of hot water. Bake at 350 degrees for one hour.

Cookbook Committee

PEACH BLANC MANGE

⅓ cup sugar
3 tablespoons cornstarch
¼ teaspoon salt
2¼ cups milk
1½ teaspoons vanilla
Fresh or frozen peaches
Lady fingers
Whipping cream

Mix sugar, cornstarch and salt in saucepan. Stir milk in gradually. Cook over medium heat, stirring constantly, until mixture boils. Boil 1 minute. Remove from heat. Blend in vanilla. Place lady fingers in bottom of pyrex pie dish. Peel and slice two or three fresh peaches, and place on top. Pour pudding mixture over top. Chill. Serve with whipped cream on top. Serves 6-8. Real "Ladyfood".

Margaret Clarke Linn (Cissy), University of Missouri
St. Louis, Missouri

BLUEBERRY BUCKLE

¾ cup sugar
¼ cup butter
2 eggs
½ cup milk
1½ cups flour
2 teaspoons baking powder
½ teaspoon salt
½ teaspoon nutmeg
½ teaspoon ground cloves
1½ cups fresh or frozen
   blueberries
Topping:
½ cup sugar
⅓ cup flour
½ teaspoon cinnamon
¼ cup butter

Mix sugar, butter, eggs and milk until well blended. Sift flour, baking powder, salt, nutmeg and cloves. Stir into sugar mixture. Fold in blueberries. Spread in greased 9 inch square pan. Combine topping ingredients until they crumble and sprinkle over batter. Bake in 375 degree oven for 45-50 minutes. Served to the campers at Sechelt Camp.

Debbie Berto, University of British Columbia
North Vancouver, B.C.

MICHELLE'S BLUEBERRY CREAM FLAN

1 package yellow cake mix (one
   layer)
1 can blueberry pie filling (or any
   flavor)
1 package vanilla instant pudding
Whipped topping for garnish

Grease and flour flan pan. Bake cake according to package directions in flan pan. Cool. Invert pan onto large serving plate. Spread center of cake with vanilla pudding prepared according to package directions. Top with pie filling. Garnish with whipped topping.

Cookbook Committee

BROWNIE PUDDING

1 cup enriched flour
2 teaspoons baking powder
½ teaspoon salt
¾ cup granulated sugar
2 tablespoons cocoa
½ cup milk
1 teaspoon vanilla
2 tablespoons shortening
 (melted) or cooking oil
¾ to 1 cup chopped nuts
¾ cup brown sugar
¼ cup cocoa
1¾ cups hot water

Sift together flour, baking powder, salt, granulated sugar and cocoa. Add vanilla, milk and shortening; mix until smooth. Add nuts. Pour into greased 8-inch square cake pan. Mix brown sugar and cocoa and sprinkle over batter. Pour hot water over entire batter. Bake in moderate oven (350°) for 40-45 minutes. (This turns out upside-down, with sauce on the bottom!)

Beth McCallon Wheeler,
Southern Methodist University
Dallas, Texas

BAKED FUDGE

4 well beaten eggs
2 cups sugar
½ cup flour
½ cup cocoa
1 cup melted butter
1 cup chopped pecans
2 teaspoons vanilla
¼ teaspoon salt

Beat eggs and dry ingredients until blended. Mix in butter. Add remaining items. Pour into an ungreased 9 by 9 inch pan. Set into a large pan with boiling water. Bake at 325 degrees for 45 minutes or until set (like custard). Do not over bake. Cool. Serve 2 inch squares with whipped cream.

Betty Boefer Keller, University of Missouri
Bartlesville, Oklahoma

FROZEN CHERRY DESSERT

1 20-ounce can crushed
 pineapple, undrained
1 can cherry pie filling
1 large carton whipped topping
1 can sweetened condensed milk
½ cup chopped walnuts

Mix all ingredients together in a large bowl. Spread in a 9x13 inch pan and freeze. Let stand at room temperature about 10 minutes before serving.

Lee Kennedy Hardacre, Wittenberg University
Dayton, Ohio

CHERRY JUBILEE

½ cup softened butter
1½ cups confectioners
 (powdered) sugar
2 eggs
½ pound vanilla wafers or graham
 crackers (finely crushed)
1 can cherry pie filling (1 pound 6
 ounce size)
½ pint whipping cream (whipped)

Cream butter and powdered sugar until light and fluffy. Add eggs, one at a time; beat thoroughly. Cover bottom of large baking dish (9x13x2 inch) with half of the crumbs. Spread butter mixture over crumbs. Cover with layer of cherry filling. Spread whipped cream over cherries. Sprinkle top with remaining crumbs. Chill in refrigerator overnight. Serves 12.

Polly Grove Haliday, Northwestern University
Evanston-North Shore, Illinois

CHERRY SURPRISE

Batter:
¼ cup butter
½ cup sugar
½ cup milk
1 egg
2 tablespoons baking powder
1 cup flour
Topping:
1 2-pound can unsweetened
  cherries
1 cup sugar
¼ teaspoon salt

Batter: Cream together butter and sugar. Stir in alternately, dry ingredients and milk. Beat until smooth. Beat in egg. Pour into greased baking dish. Cover with topping.
Topping: Mix together cherries, sugar and salt. Pour over batter. Bake in a 350 degree oven for 1 hour.
"The surprise is that the cherries end up on the bottom! Great served warm with ice cream."

Ann Mullen Bronsing, Indiana State University
St. Louis, Missouri

CHOCOLATE DELIGHT

Crust:
1 cup flour
1 stick oleo
1 cup pecans, chopped
First Layer:
1 8-ounce package cream cheese
1 cup powdered sugar
1 cup Cool Whip
Second Layer:
1 small box instant chocolate
  pudding
1 small box instant vanilla
  pudding
3 cups milk

Crust: Mix until crumbly; press into 9x13 inch pan. Bake at 350 degrees for 20 minutes. Let Cool. *First Layer:* Let Cool Whip thaw and cream cheese soften. Mix well and place on top of crust. *Second Layer:* Mix well and place on top of first layer. Let set. Top with 1½ cups of Cool Whip and sprinkle with pecans and shaved chocolate. Freeze and thaw just before serving.
"Great for bridge, church dinner and husbands even love it too!"

Patty McWilliams, Texas Tech University
Dallas, Texas

Marijo K. Kitko, Pennsylvania State University
Beccaria, Pennsylvania

CHOCOLATE DELIGHT

8 ounces German sweet chocolate
4 eggs, well beaten
1 cup whipping cream, whipped
1 teaspoon vanilla
¼ cup sugar
¾ cup chopped nuts
1 angel food cake, baked and
  cooled
¼ cup chopped nuts for topping

Melt German chocolate. Cool slightly. Pour over and mix well with beaten eggs. Whip cream, gradually adding vanilla and sugar. Add to chocolate and egg mixture. Also add ¾ cup chopped nuts. Tear angel food cake into small pieces. (Do not use crusty outsides). Line a 13x9 inch pan with half the cake pieces. Pour half the filling over cake. Put remaining cake pieces in pan and pour the rest of the filling over them. Sprinkle with the chopped nuts. Chill overnight. Serve with whipped cream and a cherry.

Cindy Drevo, University of Nebraska
Lincoln, Nebraska

CHOCOLATE DESSERT

1 cup flour
¾ cup butter
¾ cup chopped walnuts
2 medium sized cartons whipped topping
1 cup powdered sugar
8 ounces cream cheese
2 packages instant chocolate pudding
2½ cups cold milk
Chocolate mints

Mix and pat in the bottom of a 9x13 inch pan the flour, butter and walnuts. Bake at 350 degrees for 15 minutes. Mix together and put on the cooled crust the powdered sugar, cream cheese and one bowl of whipped topping. Mix together the pudding mix and milk and put on top of second layer. Then spread on more whipped toppings. Shave 3-layer type chocolate mints on top.

Donna Lammert, University of Northern Iowa
Omaha, Nebraska

CHOCOLATE IGLOO

1 envelope plain gelatin, softened in 1 tablespoon cold water
⅓ cup sugar
¼ teaspoon salt
1¾ cups milk
1 package German sweet chocolate
3 slightly beaten egg yolks
3 egg whites
1 teaspoon vanilla
⅓ cup sugar
2 cups whipped cream
Chocolate curls
Additional chocolate

Combine ⅓ cup sugar, salt and milk and sweet chocolate in saucepan. Cook until chocolate melts. Blend with beater. Add small amount to egg yolks and stir vigorously. Gradually add rest of mixture, stirring constantly. Cook about 5 minutes until slightly thickened. Stir in gelatin and chill until partly thickened. Beat egg whites until foamy. Add vanilla. Slowly add ⅓ cup sugar. Beat until stiff peaks form. Fold into chocolate mixture and chill in round mold. Unmold onto a layer of chocolate cake the same diameter as the mold. Cover with whipped cream and decorate with curls.

Mary Jane Brown Monnig, Washington University
St. Louis, Missouri

CHOCO-MINT FREEZE

1¼ cup finely crushed vanilla wafers (28)
4 tablespoons melted butter or margarine
1 quart peppermint ice cream, softened
½ cup butter
2 squares unsweetened chocolate
3 eggs
1½ cup sifted powdered sugar
1 teaspoon vanilla
½ cup chopped pecans

Toss together vanilla wafers and butter or margarine. Reserve ¼ cup crumb mixture; press remaining mixture into a 9x9x2 inch baking pan. Spread with one quart peppermint ice cream and freeze. Melt ½ cup butter and 2 squares unsweetened chocolate over low heat. Gradually stir into 3 well-beaten egg yolks with 1½ cup confectioner's sugar, ½ cup chopped pecans and 1 teaspoon vanilla. Cool thoroughly. Beat 3 egg whites until stiff peaks form. Beat chocolate mixture until smooth; fold in egg whites. Spread over ice cream, top with the reserved crumb mixture, freeze. To serve, cut into two inch squares.

Joanne Carlen, Southwest Missouri State University
Chesterfield, Missouri

CHOCOLATE MOUSSE CRUNCH

Crust:
2 cups chocolate wafers, crushed
⅓ cup butter, melted
Mousse:
1 cup milk
2 squares unsweetened chocolate
Pinch of salt
½ pound (about 32) marshmallows
1 egg yolk, slightly beaten
1 teaspoon vanilla
1 cup whipping cream, whipped

Crust: Mix and press into bottom and sides of an 8-inch square pan. Bake at 375 degrees for eight minutes — then chill. *Mousse:* Heat milk, chocolate, salt and marshmallows over low heat, stirring constantly till chocolate and marshmallows melt. Stir small amount into egg yolk, mixing constantly, then return to hot mixture. Cook and stir over low heat one minute. Add vanilla. Chill until partially set, stirring occasionally. Fold in whipped cream. Four into crust and freeze until firm. Can decorate top with little chocolate bugle bits.

Linda Allman Hahn, University of Texas
Dallas, Texas

FRESH CRANBERRY DELIGHT

1 pound raw cranberries (frozen)
½ cup sugar, extra fine
10-ounce package marshmallows, diced
1 cup grated fresh coconut or canned angel shred
1 cup pecans
1 pint whipping cream

Grind frozen cranberries, add sugar and marshmallows. Whip cream and fold into cranberries. Fold in coconut and nuts. Let stand in refrigerator at least 24 hours before serving. Can also be frozen in tight container for several weeks. To serve, fill tart shells, cream puffs or meringue rings with cranberry mixture, or serve in chilled sherbets fringed with sugar and a sprig of mint. Serves 12 to 14.

Posy Erb, Washington State University
Olympia, Washington

CREME ALEXANDER

1 envelope plain gelatin, softened in 4 tablespoons cold water
2 ounces shaved sweet chocolate
⅓ cup milk
2 tablespoons sugar
⅓ cup gin
1 ounce brandy
1 cup whipping cream
¼ cup powdered sugar
Additional whipped cream
Slivered toasted almonds

In double boiler, mix chocolate, milk, and sugar and cook until chocolate melts. Add gelatin. Stir until smooth. Remove from heat; then stir in gin and brandy. Whip cream with powdered sugar and fold into gelatin mixture. Spoon into demitasse or cocktail glasses and refrigerate until firm. Serve with whipped cream and almonds. Serves 8. "Superb!"

Mary Jane Brown Monnig, Washington University
St. Louis, Missouri

PEACH MELBA SUNDAE CREPES

10 dessert crepes
1 10-ounce package frozen raspberries
⅓ cup currant jelly
3 tablespoons butter
¼ teaspoon almond extract
1 1-pound can peach slices (drained)
10 scoops (French vanilla) ice cream (preferably homemade)
¼ cup slivered almonds

Thaw raspberries; force through a strainer. In saucepan, combine seedless raspberry puree, jelly, butter and almond extract. Bring to a boil over moderate heat. Add peaches. Cool for several minutes. With large spoon, scoop ice cream onto each crepe. Fold over. Spoon peaches and sauce over. Sprinkle with almonds. Serve immediately. Makes 10 crepes.

Cathy Rieder, University of California-Los Angeles
Rancho Palos Verdes, California

FORGOTTEN DESSERT

6 egg whites
1½ cup sugar
¼ teaspoon salt
½ teaspoon cream of tartar
1 teaspoon vanilla
6 egg yolks
¾ cup sugar
Juice and rind of 1½ lemons
Pinch of salt
1 cup whipping cream
Chopped nuts

Beat egg whites to froth. Add cream of tartar and beat stiff. Add sugar gradually, then salt and vanilla. Spread in 9x12 inch ungreased pan. Preheat oven to 425 degrees. Put pan in oven, close door and count slowly to 10. Turn off heat and leave in oven overnight. Do *not* open door until morning. Put egg yolk mixture in double boiler and cook until thick. Cool. Whip 1 cup whipping cream to which add 1 tablespoon sugar. Spread whipped cream on cooled meringue. Freeze until whipped cream is hard, then spread cooled lemon-egg yolk mixture over it. Top with chopped nuts. Cover and keep refrigerated. Can be made ahead and frozen. Serves 12.

Mary Wilcox Rietman, William and Mary
Northern Virginia

SPICY FRUIT COMPOTE

2 29-ounce cans cling peach
  halves, drained
2 3-inch long cinnamon sticks
½ teaspoon ground allspice
⅛ teaspoon ground ginger
⅛ teaspoon ground nutmeg
2 29-ounce cans pear halves,
  drained
1 17-ounce can figs, drained
½ cup brandy
3 medium bananas

One day ahead, drain syrup from peaches into 1 quart saucepan; stir in cinnamon sticks, allspice, ginger and nutmeg over medium heat. Heat to boiling. Reduce heat to low, cover and simmer 10 minutes stirring occasionally. Remove sauce from heat, cool. In large bowl, combine pears, figs, drained peaches and brandy. Pour peach syrup mixture over fruit. With rubber spatula, gently toss mixture to mix well, cover and refrigerate overnight. Slice bananas into ½ inch chunks, stir gently into fruit a few minutes before serving. Serves 12. This is wonderful to serve around the holiday season.

Kathy Garret Stephenson, Kansas University
Greater Kansas City

HOT SPICED FRUIT

½ cup raisins
1 pound can peach halves
1 pound can pineapple chunks
½ cup orange marmalade
2 tablespoons margarine
1 cinnamon stick
⅛ teaspoon nutmeg
⅛ teaspoon ground cloves

Drain fruit, reserving 1½ cups syrup. Combine marmalade, margarine, spices and reserved syrup. Bring to a boil and cook two to three minutes. Reduce heat, gently stir in fruit. Warm for 20 minutes. Makes 6-8 servings. Serve warm!

Sally Wells Bauman, University of Wisconsin-Madison
Milwaukee, Wisconsin

GAMMA PHI DELIGHT

2 small packages chocolate chips
4 eggs
½ cup sugar
1 pint whipping cream, whipped
1 angel food cake
1 teaspoon vanilla
Nuts

Melt chocolate chips in double boiler. Beat 4 egg yolks and add to chocolate. Let cool. Beat 4 egg whites until stiff — add ½ cup sugar and 1 teaspoon vanilla. Fold this into chocolate mixture. Break a large angel food cake into small pieces in bottom of 11x13 inch pan (use a fork to break). Fold whipped cream into 1st mixture and pour on broken cake. Sprinkle with nuts. Put in ice box overnight or about eight hours.

"This recipe was special to the Gamma Phi's at OSU. Our cook would only fix it for our initiation banquets."

Karen Schott Lawson, Oklahoma State University
Dallas, Texas

GARDEN PARTY DELIGHT

6 cup cakes (unfrosted)
Favorite ice cream
4 egg whites
⅛ teaspoon cream of tartar
½ cup sugar
6 3-inch clay flower pots, new
3 straws cut in half
6 fresh flowers

Place fresh cupcake in bottom of unused clay flower pot. It will fit snugly. Now fill with favorite ice cream to the top of the flower pot. Cover. Place pots in muffin tin and return to freezer for a few hours. Just before serving, prepare baked Alaska meringue. Beat until stiff 4 egg whites, ⅛ teaspoon cream of tartar, and beat ½ cup sugar in gradually. Beat until very stiff. Heap meringue on top of ice cream. Seal all edges of pot with meringue. Brown in hot oven, 450 degrees, for 5 minutes or until brown. (for easier handling, keep pots in muffin tin). If flowers are inserted after removing from oven, stick a half straw into ice cream and cupcake before freezing, then insert flower stem into straw.

This was served at the 30th anniversary of the Cedar Rapids Alumnae chapter in April, 1978. It was a real conversation piece, cute and simple. My boys, 7 and 10, put it together for me.

Nancy Boza Klopp, Bowling Green State University
Cedar Rapids, Iowa

MOTHER'S GINGERBREAD

½ cup sugar
½ cup shortening
2 eggs, beaten
½ cup molasses
1 cup boiling water
2 cups flour
1 teaspoon soda
1 teaspoon ginger

Cream sugar and shortening. Add eggs. Mix well. Add the molasses. Sift the dry ingredients. Add to above mixture, alternating with the hot water. Pour into 8 by 12 inch pan which has been greased. Bake in a 350 degree oven for about 40 minutes. Makes about 8 generous servings. Very delicious, old fashioned ginger bread. Serve with whipped cream or a custard sauce.

Verla Oare, University of Arizona
Phoenix, Arizona

HEAVENLY HOTS

1 cup sour cream
3 tablespoons flour
1½ teaspoons sugar
½ teaspoon baking soda
2 eggs, beaten

Add sour cream to beaten eggs and blend until smooth. Add rest of ingredients. Spoon onto hot griddle. Brown and turn as for pancakes. Serves 3. Serve with fruit or sauce as a crepe.

Chris Loveberg Montgomery,
California State University-San Diego
Orange County, California

ICE CREAM

2 teaspoons lemon extract
1 teaspoon vanilla
8 eggs
2 quarts skim milk
2 cups sugar
¼ teaspoon salt

Mix above ingredients in a large mixing bowl. Put in conventional freezer and follow freezer directions for making ice cream.

Sue Ann Thompson Griffin,
Southern Methodist University
Bartlesville, Oklahoma

ICE CREAM CRUNCH SQUARES

1 cup all purpose flour
¼ cup quick cooking rolled oats
¼ cup brown sugar
½ cup butter or margarine
½ cup nuts, chopped
1 quart ice cream, any flavor, depending on type of nuts chosen

Combine flour, oats and brown sugar; cut in butter or margarine until mixture is blended. Stir in nuts. Bake in a 13x9 inch pan at 375 degrees for 15 minutes. Stir while still warm. Cool. Spread half into 9x9 inch pan. Put ice cream on top, then other half of crumb topping over all the ice cream. Freeze. Cut into squares to serve.

Carol Genmer Massey,
University of Wisconsin-Madison
Glencoe, Illinois

ICE CREAMWICH

1½ cups Rice Krispies
¼ cup brown sugar (firmly packed)
¼ cup melted butter or margarine
1 cup flaked coconut
½ cup chopped pecans
1 quart brick vanilla ice cream

Lightly mix rice crispies, sugar, butter, coconut, nuts and press ½ of mix into an 8x8 inch pan (or rectangle pan of similar volume). Cut ice cream into slices, and place on top of mixture. Sprinkle top with remaining cereal and nuts. Freeze. At serving time, cut into squares and top with coffee liqueur of your choice.

Latane Jordan Graham, Memphis State University
Dallas, Texas

RICE CHEX ICE CREAM FREEZE

1 cup coconut
½ cup chopped walnuts
⅓ cup melted butter
⅔ cup packed brown sugar
2 cups finely rolled Rice Chex
½ gallon vanilla ice cream, softened
Topping:
1 6-ounce package chocolate chips
1 6-ounce can evaporated milk
1 pint jar marshmallow cream

Mix coconut, walnuts, brown sugar and Rice Chex together. Add melted butter and stir until coated. Spread ⅔ of mixture into 9x13x2-inch cake pan. Spread ½ gallon ice cream over mixture. Top with remaining ⅓ of mixture. Cover and refreeze until ice cream is cold, approximately 4 hours. To make topping, melt all ingredients in double boiler. Pour over individual pieces of ice cream and serve. Any remaining topping may be stored in refrigerator.

Linda Frantel, University of Wisconsin-Oshkosh
Milwaukee, Wisconsin

ICE CREAM DESSERT

1 cup butter or margarine
3 squares melted chocolate (or 9 tablespoons cocoa)
4 eggs, separated
¾ cup chopped nuts
Graham cracker crumbs
1 cup confectioners sugar
1 teaspoon vanilla
½ gallon vanilla ice cream

Butter a long baking dish and sprinkle with graham cracker crumbs. Cream the butter, sugar, chocolate, egg yolks, nuts and vanilla. Beat egg whites until stiff. Fold egg whites into chocolate mixture. Spread this over the graham cracker crumbs in the dish and freeze for several hours. Soften ice cream to spreading consistency and spread over the frozen chocolate layer. Top with chopped nuts or some shaved chocolate. Return to freezer.

Kiki Phillips, Washington University
State College, Pennsylvania

ICE CREAM TORTE

24 macaroons, crushed
¾ gallon chocolate ice cream
¾ gallon coffee ice cream
8 Heath bars, crushed
1 medium-sized can chocolate syrup or fudge sauce

Butter springform pan. Pat in one half of the crushed macaroons. Add softened chocolate ice cream. Dribble with chocolate syrup. Add remaining macaroons. Add softened coffee ice cream. Dribble with chocolate syrup. Top with Heath bars. Wrap in foil and freeze overnight. Serves 16.

Patty Borland, University of California-Long Beach
South Bay, California

COFFEE ICE CREAM DESSERT

2 dozen cookies (chocolate), crushed
½ cup melted butter
3 squares unsweetened baking chocolate
¼ pound butter
⅔ cup sugar
Dash salt
⅔ cup evaporated milk
½ pint whipping cream whipped
½ teaspoon vanilla
¼ cup confectioners sugar
½ gallon coffee ice cream

Combine cookie crumbs and ½ cup melted butter. Line bottom of a 9x13 inch pan with mixture. Place softened ice cream over crumbs and freeze. Melt chocolate and ¼ pound of butter. Stir in sugar and salt. Cook till small bubbles form. Stir in milk and cook, stirring constantly, till slightly thick. Pour over ice cream. Put back in freezer. Combine whipped cream, vanilla and confectioners sugar; spread over chocolate. Freeze till serving time. Let stand 2 or 3 minutes at room temperature before cutting in squares to serve. Serves 12.

Teek Schonberg, Iowa State University
Omaha, Nebraska

LEMON ANGEL SUPREME

Base:
6 egg whites
¼ teaspoon salt
¼ teaspoon cream of tartar
1½ cups sugar
1 teaspoon vanilla extract
Filling:
6 ounces cream cheese
1 cup powdered sugar
1 teaspoon salt
2 cups whipped cream or dream whip
2 cups miniature marshmallows
Lemon Sauce:
6 egg yolks
1½ cups sugar
¼ cup flour
½ teaspoon salt
½ cup lemon juice
1 cup water
½ cup butter
2 lemon rinds, grated

Base: Beat whites until frothy. Gradually add remaining ingredients, beating until stiff peaks form. Pour into a buttered 9x11 inch pan. Place in preheated 450 degree oven on the middle rack. Turn oven off. Leave overnight.
Filling: To prepare, blend cream cheese, sugar and salt. Fold in whipped cream and marshmallows. Spread over baked base. Serve with lemon sauce.
Sauce: Cook in double boiler until thick, about 20 minutes. Stir in butter and grated rind of two lemons. Serves 12.

Maxine Leverett Trager,
Southern Methodist University
Dallas, Texas

LEMON CAKE PIE

1 tablespoon butter
2 tablespoons flour
1 cup sugar
1½ cups milk
Juice and grated rind of 1 lemon
2 eggs, separated

Cream butter, sugar and flour together. Beat egg whites until stiff. Beat egg yolks and add with milk to butter mixture. Add lemon juice and rind. Fold in egg whites. Pour into buttered two quart baking dish. Place in pan of hot water and bake at 350 degrees until light brown. Serve hot or cold.

Gertrude Bolton Rash, Iowa State University
Dallas, Texas

LEMON CUSTARD DESSERT

1 cup sugar
2 tablespoons butter or margarine
1½ cups milk
3 eggs
5 tablespoons lemon juice
Grated rind of 1 lemon
4 tablespoons flour
Pinch of salt

Cream butter well and add sugar gradually. Cream well. Add salt, flour, lemon juice and rind. Mix thoroughly. Stir in beaten egg yolk mixed with milk. Fold stiffly beaten egg white. Pour in custard cups and place in pan of water. Bake in moderate oven — 350 degrees for 45 minutes. May be served with whipped cream or Cool Whip.

Dorothy Jackson Myers,
Southern Methodist University
Dallas, Texas

LIME DELIGHT

1⅓ cups hot water
1 package small lime gelatin
¼ cup creme de menthe
1 pint vanilla ice cream

Dissolve lime gelatin in hot water. Cool slightly. Add liqueur and ice cream. Freeze in parfait glasses. Remove 5 minutes prior to serving. Serve with chocolate shavings and cookie, if desired. Nice and light!

Kay Johnson Marovich, Kansas State University
South Bay, California

LAZY MAN'S MERINGUES

2 egg whites
⅔ cup granulated sugar
1 small bag chocolate chips
(optional) or ground pecans
(optional) or nothing!

Heat oven to 370 degrees. Beat until very stiff the whites of 2 eggs and ⅔ cup of granulated sugar. Stir in a small bag of chocolate chips, or a small amount of ground pecans, or nothing! Drop spoonfuls onto ungreased cookie sheet. Put in oven and turn off heat. Go to bed and don't peep! "I peeped once and it was a disaster!" (Verbal P.S. by Mary Tom)
Note: Mary Tom McCurley (1910-1974) was an active and much beloved Gamma Phi from Goucher College. This was her recipe.

Harriet McCurley Trout, Goucher College
Richmond, Virginia

MAXINE'S DILEMMA

1 stick margarine
1¼ cup flour
½ cup chopped pecans
1 8-ounce package cream cheese
2 boxes chocolate pudding (not instant)
1 cup powdered sugar
½ of 8-ounce container whipped topping
3 cups milk
1 teaspoon vanilla
½ cup chopped pecans

To make crust, blend margarine, pecans and flour until mealy. Then press into large 8x10 inch pan and bake for 20 minutes at 375 degrees. Cool. Mix cream cheese, powdered sugar and whipped topping until creamy. Spoon into crust. Let stand for one hour in refrigerator. Mix two boxes of chocolate pudding with 3 cups of milk and 1 teaspoon vanilla and cook according to directions. Cool. Pour over cream cheese mixture. Top with the remaining whipped topping and sprinkle with ½ cup chopped pecans. When set, cut into squares.
"Maxine" is Maxine Boatright, KTVY television personality, Oklahoma City

Rosemary Andrews Lurie, Oklahoma University
Oklahoma City, Oklahoma

HELEN'S PEACH COBBLER

1 cup water
One quart peaches, cut up
1½ cups sugar
1 cup flour
1 cup sugar
1 cup milk
2 teaspoons baking powder
One stick butter

Put water, 1½ cups sugar, and peaches into a saucepan and cook to a good boil. Remove from heat. Make a batter of flour, 1 cup sugar, milk, and baking powder. Melt one stick of butter in baking pan. Pour batter into a 13x9x2 inch pan, pour fruit over batter and bake slowly at about 350 degrees until brown on top.

Elise Hodges Weed, Oklahoma University
Dallas, Texas

PEPPERMINT DESSERT

1 large peppermint candy stick
(6½ ounces), crushed
2 cups miniature marshmallows
1 cup nuts, chopped
¾ pint cream, whipped, or 2 9-
ounce cartons whipped topping
1 cup graham cracker crumbs

Whip cream until stiff. Fold in candy and marshmallows, add nuts. Butter 8x13x1½ inch pan, and use ¾ cup graham cracker crumbs to line pan, sides and bottom. Spoon mixture into pan, top with ¼ cup crumbs. Chill 12-24 hours. Either cut into squares and serve on plates or spoon into dessert dishes. May top with maraschino cherries if desired. (This is a pale pink color naturally; I have tinted it green with food coloring on occasions).

Virginia Arnold Auld, University of Missouri
Greater Kansas City

PISTACHIO DELIGHT

1 small carton whipped topping
1 16-ounce can crushed
pineapple, including syrup
1 16-ounce can fruit cocktail,
including syrup
1 small package pistachio instant
pudding mix
1 cup miniature marshmallows
¼ cup finely chopped nuts, any
kind

Put all in mixing bowl and fold or mix together and chill in refrigerator for two hours. Do not add any water to pudding mix as syrup from canned fruit takes care of the liquid. Serves 12 or more.

Karlene C. Franzen, Wittenberg University
Philadelphia North Suburban, Pennsylvania

PISTACHIO FROZEN DESSERT

50 Ritz crackers, crumbled
1 cube margarine
2 packages pistachio pudding
(small size boxes)
1½ cups milk
1 quart vanilla ice cream
9-ounce Cool Whip
3 Heath candy bars, crumbled

Melt margarine. Mix with cracker crumbs. Press into 13x9 inch pan and bake 10 minutes at 350 degrees. Soften ice cream and mix with pudding and milk until blended and smooth. Pour evenly over crumb crust. Freeze. Spread Cool Whip over ice cream layer. Sprinkle Heath bars over all. Thaw about 1 hour before serving. Serves: 12 to 16.

Sharon Stahlman Ashby, East Texas State University
Diamond Bar, California

POIRE AU GRATIN

3 fresh pears, peeled and sliced in
⅜ inch slices *or*
1 can pears, halves or slices,
drained
⅓ cup apricot jam
⅓ cup Vermouth or white wine
Macaroons *or* slivered, blanched
almonds, *or* almond extract
Butter

Place pears in buttered dish. Top with apricot jam and Vermouth. Crumble macaroons and sprinkle over top. Dot top with 1 tablespoon butter. Bake at 425 degrees for 20-25 minutes. Serves 4. Serve with cream if desired. Good hot or cold. Once you've made this a few times you discover that the proportions of ingredients are not crucial . . . put in what you have. You can also take canned peaches, undrained, add some cornstarch to thicken, a drop or two of almond extract, bake and serve warm over vanilla ice cream.

Susan K. Sismonde, University of Michigan
Westchester County, New York

POT DE CREME

1 6-ounce package semi-sweet
chocolate pieces
2 tablespoons sugar
Pinch of salt
1 egg
1 teaspoon vanilla
¾ cup milk

Place first 5 ingredients in an electric blender. Heat milk just to boiling. Pour over ingredients. Cover. Blend one minute. Pour immediately into 6 serving dishes (pot de crème pots or demitasse cups). Chill 4 hours or longer. Serve with whipped cream. Serves 6. This is real "ladyfood" that men and children will love.

Sylvia Hardy Trewin, Iowa State University
Richardson, Texas

GRANDMOTHER'S ENGLISH PLUM PUDDING (from Manchester, England)

¼ pound suet (ground)
1⅛ cups brown sugar
½ cup milk
2 eggs, well beaten
1 cup seedless raisins
1½ cups currants
⅓ cup preserved orange peel
⅓ cup crystallized lemon peel, cut
fine
⅓ cup citron, cut fine
½ cup blanched almonds,
chopped
1 cup sifted flour
1 teaspoon soda
1 teaspoon salt
½ teaspoon nutmeg
1 teaspoon cinnamon
¼ teaspoon mace
1 cup stale bread crumbs

Mix together the suet, brown sugar, and milk, and add the eggs. Mix the fruits, peels and nuts with ¼ cup of the flour. Mix and sift the remaining flour with the soda, salt and spices. Add the fruit mixture, crumbs and flour to the suet mixture. Mix well and turn into greased 1½ quart mold. Cover and steam 2½ hours. Serve hot with any desired sauce. I like a foamy, hard sauce with brandy.

Polly Peacock Little, Iowa State University
Greenville, North Carolina

SCANDINAVIAN PUDDING

1 package unflavored gelatin
½ cup cold water
5 eggs, separated
¾ cup sugar
Juice of 1 lemon or 2 tablespoons
  sherry
Pinch salt
½ pint whipping cream
Maraschino cherries or almonds

Soak gelatin in water 5 minutes. Dissolve over boiling water; cool to lukewarm. Set aside. In large mixing bowl beat egg yolks well. Add sugar a little at a time, beating constantly. Add lemon juice or sherry and continue beating. Add cooled gelatin mixture and beat again. Add salt to egg whites and beat until stiff. Fold into egg mixture. Pour into 1½ quart bowl (a glass one is best as this is the serving bowl). Chill until firm. Just before serving, spread whipped cream over top and garnish with halved maraschino cherries or toasted almonds. Serves 8.

Ardis McBroom Marek, Past Grand President,
Northwestern University
LaJolla, California

WHIRL PUDDING

1½ cups flour
¾ cup chopped pecans
1½ sticks butter, melted
1 cup powdered sugar
½ of a 9-ounce container of
  whipped topping
8-ounce package cream cheese,
  room temperature
2 small packages chocolate or
  pistachio instant pudding mix
3 cups cold milk

Mix flour, pecans and melted butter together and press into a 9x13 inch pan. Bake at 350 degrees for 30 minutes. Cool on baking rack. Cream powdered sugar and cream cheese together. Stir in whipped topping and spread mixture on cooled crust. Beat milk and both packages of pudding together until mixture is thick. Pour on top of above layer. Spread remaining half of whipped topping over pudding. Garnish as desired.

Pat O'Connell Mullins, St. Louis University
Dallas, Texas

MOM'S RASPBERRY DELIGHT

1 package frozen raspberries,
  thawed
1 small can crushed pineapple
1 3-ounce package raspberry
  gelatin
1 package unflavored gelatin
6 ounces cream cheese
½ cup confectioners sugar
1 cup whipping cream

Combine juices of raspberries and pineapple. Add water, if necessary, to make 1¾ cups liquid. Heat to a boil, add raspberry gelatin, then cool slightly. Add raspberries. Refrigerate in mold until gelatin is firm enough but soft enough so next layer will gel to it. Add ¼ cup cold water to unflavored gelatin. Stir and let soften. Heat in double boiler to dissolve, then cool. Cream together cream cheese and whipping cream. Beat until stiff. Add confectioners sugar. Blend cool gelatin into crushed pineapple. Fold this into cream cheese mixture. Spoon over raspberry gelatin. Refrigerate overnight and serve.

Joan Lonnborg DeLaGarza,
University of Wisconsin-Madison
Dallas, Texas

AUNT HILDA'S RHUBARB DESSERT

4 cups sliced rhubarb
½ cup sugar or more to taste
1 small package red gelatin
  (raspberry or strawberry)
1 small box white or yellow cake
  mix (2 cups)
1 cup water
½ cup melted butter

Layer ingredients in order given above in 8x11 inch pan. Bake at 350 degrees for 40 minutes.

Jacki Falkenroth, University of Nevada-Reno
Chicago Northwest Suburban, Illinois

RUSSIAN ROLL

1 tablespoon gelatin
2 cups scalded milk
Yolk of three eggs
½ cup sugar
¼ teaspoon salt
1 teaspoon vanilla
1 cup whipping cream, whipped
  very stiff
1 angel food cake
½ cup chopped nuts (pecans or
  almonds)

Dissolve gelatin in cold water. Add boiling milk, salt and sugar. Pour the mixture on the beaten egg yolks, stirring constantly. Cook in a double boiler ten minutes. Remove from fire and cool. When it begins to set, fold in the stiff whipped cream. Allow to set or stiffen. Put between and on top of angel food cake (either loaf or round) sliced into layers. Cover with chopped pecans or slivered almonds. Garnish with maraschino cherries if desired. This may be made ahead and kept cold. Slice to serve.

Lorraine Forister Grigsby, University of Wyoming
Cheyenne, Wyoming

STRAWBERRY DESSERT

1½ cups crumpled stick pretzels
½ cup sugar
½ cup soft butter or margarine
1 8-ounce package cream cheese,
  softened
1 cup sugar
1 large carton whipped topping
2 3-ounce packages strawberry
  gelatin
2 cups hot water
2 packages frozen strawberries

Mix pretzels, sugar, butter well and spread in a 9x13 inch pan. Bake at 350 degrees for 5 to 7 minutes and cool. Mix cream cheese with sugar, cream well and fold in one large carton whipped topping. Spread on cooled pretzel mix. Mix gelatin with two cups hot water; add frozen strawberries, slightly broken up. Spread on top of both mixtures and refrigerate until set. Delicious! Serves 12-15.

Mary Rice Raber, University of Washington
Seattle, Washington

FROSTY STRAWBERRY SQUARES

Topping:
1 cup flour
¼ cup brown sugar
½ cup chopped pecans
½ cup melted butter
Squares:
3 egg whites
⅔ cup sugar
1 10-ounce package frozen
  berries
1 tablespoon lemon juice
1 quart whipped topping

Place topping ingredients in pan and bake at 350 degrees for 20 minutes, stirring twice while baking. Cool and spread ⅔ of topping into 9x13 inch pan. Beat other 4 ingredients for 10 minutes until very stiff. Fold in one quart whipped topping and spread over ⅔ of topping in pan. Sprinkle remainder of topping mixture over this. Freeze for 12 hours. Serve direct from freezer. Serves 12.

Sharyn Marie Wehrli Behnke, University of Illinois
Evansville, Indiana

STRAWBERRIES ROMANOFF

1 pint sour cream
1 cup light brown sugar
Dash nutmeg
Dash cinnamon
1 teaspoon light rum
Fresh strawberries

Mix first five ingredients together and serve over fresh strawberries, that have been stemmed and washed. Serves 10 to 12 desserts.

Gloria Swanson Nelson, Oklahoma University
Dallas, Texas

FRESH STRAWBERRY FROZEN YOGURT

1 pint basket (10 ounces)
   strawberries, rinsed and hulled
¼ cup sugar
½ cup light corn syrup
2 cups (16 ounces) plain yogurt

Turn the berries, sugar and corn syrup into a blender container. Blend at medium speed until liquified — about 30 seconds. Add yogurt. Blend at medium speed until well mixed — about 10 seconds. Pour into 9x5x3 inch metal loaf pan. Freeze until firm — about 4 hours. Whirl in a blender at medium speed until liquified about 1 minute. Return to loaf pan. Cover and freeze until firm — about 3 hours. Before serving, let stand at room temperature about 10 minutes. Makes about 1½ pints.
Note: For a luscious, soft frozen strawberry yogurt, stir occasionally during the second period of freezing and serve before firm. Count on this taking less than 3 hours.

Harriet Lishen Baldwin, University of Missouri
Dallas, Texas

TOFFEE-MOCHA FROZEN TORTE

2 packages lady fingers, split
½ gallon vanilla ice cream,
   softened
1½ tablespoons instant coffee,
   dissolved in 2 tablespoons hot
   water
5 Heath chocolate bars, crushed
1 cup whipped cream
2 tablespoons cognac

Line bottom and sides of 8 inch or 9 inch spring form pan with split lady fingers. Combine crushed candy, ice cream and dissolved coffee. Pour into spring form pan. Freeze solid. Before serving whip cream, add cognac, spread over top of torte.

Lawrie Kern Branson, University of Maryland
Olney, Maryland

M'MAMA'S BLUEBERRY TARTS

1 can sweetened condensed milk
⅔ cup lemon juice
1 can blueberries, drained
8-10 tart shells, baked

Beat milk while gradually adding lemon juice. (Food processor works well for this step). Fold in gently blueberries and spoon into prebaked tart shells. Chill. Top with whipped cream and a cherry.

Sandra Graham Cude, Memphis State University
Dallas, Texas

MINI-PECAN TARTS

Crust:
1 cup flour
½ cup margarine
3 ounce package cream cheese
2 tablespoons powdered sugar
Filling:
1 egg, beaten until fluffy
1 teaspoon melted margarine
1 cup brown sugar
1 teaspoon vanilla
1 cup chopped pecans

To make crust, blend like pastry and make into 24 balls. Lightly grease tart pans. Use thumbs to press into pans on both bottom and sides.
For filling: Mix all ingredients well and fill tarts. Sprinkle with chopped pecans. Bake at 325 degrees for 25 minutes. Remove when cool and store covered. Makes 24 tarts.

Diane Walter Prah, Miami University
Milwaukee, Wisconsin

GLORIA'S INDIVIDUAL FRUIT TARTS

2 8-ounce packages cream
cheese, softened and whipped
¾ cup sugar
2 eggs
1 tablespoon lemon juice
½ teaspoon vanilla
1 can fruit pie filling
Vanilla wafers

Put a vanilla wafer in bottom of paper cupcake cup. Mix cream cheese, sugar, eggs, lemon juice and vanilla. Pour mixture into cupcake cup. Top with fruit pie filling. Bake at 300 degrees for 15 minutes. Chill.

Cookbook Committee

MANDARIN ORANGE TARTS

1 envelope unflavored gelatin
softened in —
2 tablespoons water
1 cup boiling water
1 cup sugar
½ cup orange juice
A drop or two of red and yellow
food coloring
1 cup whipping cream, whipped
1 10-ounce can mandarin orange
sections, drained
8 tart shells

Stir boiling water into softened gelatin. Dissolve sugar in this. Stir in orange juice and food coloring, tinted to make a pale orange color. Chill until almost set. Fold whipped cream into gelatin mixture, and pour a spoonful into each tart shell. Divide orange sections among the shells, and cover with remaining gelatin mixture. Chill for several hours until set. Various berries could be substituted for oranges.

Barbara Ash Clark, University of Texas
Nashua, New Hampshire

BUTTERSCOTCH NUT TORTE

Torte:
6 egg yolks
6 egg whites
1½ cups sugar
2 cups graham cracker crumbs
1 teaspoon baking powder
1 cup chopped nuts
½ teaspoon salt
1 pint whipping cream (whipped)
1 teaspoon almond extract
Butterscotch Sauce:
1 cup brown sugar
1 tablespoon flour
¼ cup butter
¼ cup orange juice
¼ cup water
1 beaten egg
½ teaspoon vanilla

Torte: Ingredients at room temperature. Beat egg yolks at high speed until thick. Combine sugar, baking powder and salt. Add to yolks gradually. Add vanilla and almond extract. Beat egg whites until stiff. Fold in egg whites. Fold in crumbs and nuts. Bake in 2 9-inch tins greased and wax paper lined at 325 degrees for 35 minutes. Cool. Top with whipped cream and spoonfuls of butterscotch sauce. Drizzle sauce over the edge.
Butterscotch Sauce: Combine all but vanilla in saucepan. Blend and stir constantly. Cook at low heat until mixture thickens. Add vanilla and cool. Serves 10-12.
"Scrumptious looking as well as eating."

Virginia Anderson Wells, Northwestern University
Milwaukee, Wisconsin

RHUBARB TORTE

Torte:
1 cup sugar
3 tablespoons cornstarch
4 cups sliced rhubarb
½ cup water
Few drops red food coloring
1 recipe graham cracker crust
1 4-ounce carton whipped topping
   (non-dairy frozen variety)
1¾ cup miniature marshmallows
1 package instant vanilla pudding
Graham Cracker Crust:
1 cup graham crackers, crumbled
2 tablespoons sugar
4 tablespoons melted butter

Preheat oven to 350 degrees. Prepare graham cracker crust by combining the ingredients, reserving 2 tablespoons of crumbs. Pat remainder in a 9x9x2 inch pan. Bake for 10 minutes; cool. Combine sugar and cornstarch; stir in rhubarb and water. Cook, stirring, until thickened. Reduce heat; cook 2 to 3 minutes. Add food coloring. Spread on cooled graham cracker crust. Cool. Fold marshmallows into thawed whipped topping. Spoon on rhubarb mixture. Prepare pudding according to package directions; spread over all. Sprinkle with reserved crumbs. Chill. Serves 9.

Phyllis Donaldson Choat, University of Nebraska
Omaha, Nebraska

STRAWBERRY TIFFANY TORTE

3 cups vanilla wafer crumbs
½ cup melted margarine
1 8-ounce package cream cheese
2 cups milk
1 4-serving size instant vanilla
   pudding
1 quart strawberries, sliced
2 2-ounce packages dessert
   topping mix

Combine crumbs and margarine, reserve 1 cup for topping. Press remaining crumb mixture into bottom of greased 9x13x2 inch pan. Gradually add ½ cup milk to softened cream cheese, mixing well until blended, then add pudding mix and remaining milk. Beat slowly 1 minute. Pour over crust; cover with layer of strawberries. Prepare dessert topping as directed on package; spread over strawberries and top with remaining crumbs. Chill several hours or overnight. Serves 12-15.

Sue Ward Ragsdale, Southern Methodist University
Dallas, Texas

TOFFEE MERINGUE TORTE

6 egg whites, room temperature
2 teaspoons vanilla
½ teaspoon cream of tartar
Dash salt
2 cups sugar
6 ounces of Heath bars (frozen
   and crushed) or 1 package Bits
   O'Brickle
Dash salt
1 pint whipping cream

Beat egg whites, adding vanilla, cream of tartar and salt, until soft peaks form. Gradually add sugar, beating to stiff peaks. Cover 2 cookie pans with ungreased paper. Draw a 9 inch circle on each and spread meringue evenly within circles, flattening peaks. Bake at 275 degrees one hour. Turn off heat, leave in oven minimum of 4 hours. Whip cream. Fold crushed candy into it. Frost the 2 meringues like a 2 layer cake. Garnish with additional crushed candy. Chill overnight. Serves 16.

Peggy Cook Evans, University of Missouri
Greater Kansas City

PEACH SOUP

2 cups water
1 cup sugar
2 sticks cinnamon
2 teaspoons whole cloves
⅓ cup arrowroot (or cornstarch)
1 bottle dry white wine
2 pounds frozen peaches (defrost in refrigerator)
3 pounds peaches, well ripened
Garnish:
1 cup fresh blueberries
½ cup heavy cream
½ cup sour cream
2 tablespoons confectioners' sugar

Soup: Place water, sugar, spices in a saucepan and bring to boil. Cover and simmer for 30 minutes. Combine arrowroot with wine, add syrup, stirring carefully so mixtures are well blended. Bring to boil, stirring occasionally, set aside to cool. Meanwhile, place defrosted peaches with juices in the food processor or electric blender. Process to a smooth puree. Add to the syrup. Peel fresh peaches, halve and remove pits, then cut into slices. Add to the soup. Refrigerate until cold.

Garnish: Combine heavy cream and sugar, whip until mixture holds a peak. Fold into sour cream. When peach soup is cold and you are ready to serve, place in individual dessert dishes with a dollop of cream on top. Sprinkle with blueberries or other berries of your choice.

Posy Erb, Washington State University
Lafayette, Indiana

STRAWBERRY CRUNCH

1 cup flour
½ cup margarine
¼ cup brown sugar
½ cup chopped nuts
2 egg whites
1 teaspoon lemon juice
½ cup sugar
1 10-16 ounce package frozen strawberries
Large carton whipped topping

Mix flour, margarine, brown sugar and chopped nuts. Bake in 9x13 inch pan at 275 degrees, stirring every 15 minutes, ending up with crumbs. Cool. Remove ½ cup crumb mixture and reserve. Spread remainder evenly in bottom of pan. In biggest mixing bowl, beat the egg whites till foamy with lemon juice and sugar. Throw in package of thawed frozen strawberries. Beat 20 minutes at highest speed. Fold in large container of whipped topping. Pour on crust and sprinkle with reserved crumbs. Freeze covered, overnight. Serve frozen, it cuts easily. Serves 12.

Helen Peckworth, University of Maryland
Chicago Northwest Suburban, Illinois

MILDRED'S DELICIOUS TIDBITS

White bread (suggest Pepperidge Farms toasting loaf because of thick slices.
1 can sweetened condensed milk
Shredded coconut

From thick slice of bread, remove crust. Cut bread into 4 strips. Dip bread in condensed milk. Roll in shredded coconut. Place on baking sheet, and bake at 350 degrees until coconut is golden and crisp.

Harriet McCurley Trout, Goucher College
Richmond, Virginia

TORTONI SQUARES

⅓ cup chopped toasted almonds
2 tablespoons melted butter or margarine
1⅓ cups finely crushed vanilla wafers
1 teaspoon almond extract
1 12-ounce jar apricot preserves
3 pints vanilla ice cream, softened
Whipping cream (optional)

Mix vanilla wafer crumbs, almonds, almond extract and butter. Put layer of crumbs in bottom of 9 inch square pan, buttered, then layer of ice cream and layer of apricot preserves, sprinkle with crumbs. Repeat layers, ending with crumbs on top. Freeze several hours, until ice cream is firm. Cut in squares and top with whipped cream if desired. Serves 9.

Dorothy Chase Jones, Southern Methodist University
Dallas, Texas

RASPBERRY TRIFLE

1 10-ounce package frozen raspberries, thawed
2 teaspoons cornstarch
3-ounce package (12 double) ladyfingers, separated
¼ cup sherry
3 ¼-ounce package vanilla instant pudding mix
2 cups milk
½ cup sliced almonds
1 cup whipping cream

In a saucepan stir a little of the raspberry syrup into the cornstarch, keeping it smooth; stir in the remaining syrup and berries, reserving a few for garnish. Cook over moderate heat, stirring constantly until clear and slightly thickened; cool. Sprinkle the ladyfingers with sherry; arrange half of them around the bottom of a 6-cup glass bowl. Prepare the pudding mix with the milk as package directs. Whip the cream and reserve ½ cup for garnish; fold the rest into the pudding. Layer half the berries, pudding and nuts over the ladyfingers in the bowl. Arrange remaining ladyfingers around the side of the bowl. Repeat layers of berries, pudding and nuts. Chill.

Susan M. Hume, William and Mary
Northern Virginia

STRAWBERRY TRIFLE

1 package frozen strawberries or 1 quart fresh sliced berries
1 package vanilla custard
1 butter pound cake
6-8 tablespoons sugar
6-8 tablespoons sherry
½ cup chopped pecans (optional)
Whipped cream

Prepare custard and cool to set. In a large glass bowl, layer cake, custard and berries. Sprinkle sugar and sherry over each layer of berries. Refrigerate for at least 3 hours before serving to let flavors mingle. Top with whipped cream and nuts.

Cathy Boudreaux Griffin, Louisiana State University
Central New Jersey

FROZEN WINE "CAKE"

1 pound marshmallows
2 cups creme sherry
1 quart whipped heavy cream
Sliced almonds

Melt marshmallows a few at a time in creme sherry in the top of a double boiler. Chill until slightly congealed. Fold in the whipped heavy cream. Pour into mold. Freeze 24 hours. Serve in thin slices, topped with sliced almonds. Serves 12-16.

Carolyn Coe Cole, University of Texas
Dallas, Texas

"YOU'LL LIKE IT" OR "YUMMY"

1 3-ounce package orange or
   orange-pineapple gelatin
1 3-ounce package apricot gelatin
2 cups boiling water
1 20-ounce can crushed
   pineapple, juice drained and
   saved
1 20-ounce can mandarin orange
   segments, juice drained and
   saved
1 pint soft orange sherbet

Dissolve the boxes of gelatin in cups boiling water. Add strained pineapple and mandarin orange segments. Add 2 cups juice reserved from fruit (or juice and water to make 2 cups). Stir above ingredients together well. Add 1 pint soft orange sherbet and mix well. Chill in refrigerator (not freezer) for overnight or 12 hours. This may be molded, set only in a large bowl and spooned into serving dishes, or poured into individual dessert molds.

Lillian Brighton Spaid, Pennsylvania State University
Lititz, Pennsylvania

MILDRED'S YUMMY MORSELS

Fig Newtons
Powdered sugar

Cut each Fig Newton in three strips. Roll each strip in powdered sugar.

Harriet McCurley Trout, Goucher College
Richmond, Virginia

Pies

PIE CRUST

⅔ cup shortening
1½ cups flour
½ teaspoon salt
¼ teaspoon baking powder
1 teaspoon sugar
¼ cup milk

Combine shortening, flour, salt, baking powder and sugar. Mix until shortening is cut into fine pieces. Add milk until proper consistency to roll out. This makes 2 large or 3 small single crust pies, or one double crust pie.

Barbara B. Derrick, Iowa State University
Ft. Worth, Texas

AUNTIE'S PIE CRUST

3 cups flour
1½ cups shortening
1½ teaspoon salt
2 tablespoons sugar
1 egg
1 tablespoon vinegar
2 tablespoons water

Sift dry ingredients together. Cut shortening into flour mixture very well. Add egg, vinegar and water; mix well. Makes 4 9-inch pie crusts. This crust can be handled as much as you like. Can be refrigerated or frozen, if wrapped tightly.

Mary Jo Ringhofer, Memphis State University
Germantown, Tennessee

NEVER FAIL PIE CRUST

3 cups flour plus extra for rolling
1¼ cup shortening *or* 1 cup lard
1 egg
5½ tablespoons water
1 teaspoon vinegar

Mix flour, shortening and salt. Beat egg, water and vinegar. Mix in well in center of flour. This makes 2 two crust pies.

Peggy Larson Stromer, University of Nebraska
Milton, Wisconsin

GRAHAM CRACKER PIE CRUST

1 cup graham cracker crumbs
2 tablespoons sugar
4 tablespoons melted butter

Preheat oven to 350 degrees. Combine ingredients and press into and along sides of a 9-inch pie pan. Bake for about 10 minutes. Cool before filling.

Cookbook Committee

EASY APPLE PIE

3 cans (16 ounces) apple pie
  filling
½ cup raisins
1 8-ounce can Pillsbury Quick
  Crescent Dinner Rolls
2 tablespoons granulated sugar
Cinnamon

Spoon apple pie filling into a 12x8-inch baking dish. Sprinkle with cinnamon and raisins. Unroll both halves of dough into flat, rectangular sheets. Fit dough to cover the baking dish. Combine sugar and about ¼ teaspoon cinnamon; sprinkle evenly over dough. Bake at 375 degrees for 25 minutes. Serve warm with ice cream or cheese. Serves 8 to 10.

Pat O'Connell Mullins, St. Louis University
Dallas, Texas

MOM'S APPLE PIE

5 medium Winesap or McIntosh
  apples, pared and thinly sliced
1 cup sugar
½ teaspoon nutmeg
½ teaspoon cinnamon
1 tablespoon flour
Butter
1 recipe for double crust pastry

Roll out pastry. Place in pie pan. Mix all other ingredients. Place in pastry and dot with butter. Place top of pastry on pie and seal. Bake at 350 degrees for 40-45 minutes. For pie crust pastry see Never Fail Pie Crust.

Lynne Ayres, Vanderbilt University
Nashville, Tennessee

RED ROCKER APPLE PIE

Crust:
2½ cups flour
½ pound shortening
1 teaspoon sugar
½ teaspoon salt
½ teaspoon cinnamon
5 tablespoons ice water
Filling:
5 cups apples, peeled, cored and
  sliced
1 cup sugar
1 teaspoon cinnamon
½ teaspoon flour
2 tablespoons margarine, melted
½ teaspoon salt

For the crust, blend all the dry ingredients and cut in cold shortening. Moisten with ice water. Chill before rolling.

To make the filling, mix sugar, spices, flour, salt and melted margarine together. Stir apples into mixture. If apples are dry, add some water and lemon juice. Roll pastry, add filling, put on slashed top crust. Bake at 450 degrees for 10 minutes, then reduce heat to 400 degrees and cook until pie has bubbled about 10 or 15 minutes and apples are tender. Total baking time about one hour.

This pie, in its 94th year, is served warm at Greater Kansas City Alums' annual antique and art show.

Mrs. Elspeth Rankins Byers, Vanderbilt University
Greater Kansas City

APRICOT PIE

6 ounces raspberry jelly
Juice of ½ lemon
1 large can apricot halves
1 baked 9 inch pie shell
Whipping cream, if desired

Put jelly into pan and cook slowly on low flame, stirring constantly. When jelly begins to boil, add lemon juice. Cool. Drain apricot halves and place them in circles in pie crust. Pour cooled jelly over apricots. Refrigerate 2 hours or more. Serve as is or with whipped cream.

Doris Erwin Hawkins, Iowa State University
Silver Springs, Maryland

BLACK BOTTOM PIE I

1¾ cup milk
4 egg yolks
½ cup sugar
⅛ teaspoon salt
1 tablespoon cornstarch
1 envelope gelatin
¼ cup water
2 squares chocolate, melted
2 tablespoons sugar
1 teaspoon vanilla
4 egg whites
⅛ teaspoon cream of tartar
½ cup sugar
1 tablespoon rum
½ pint whipping cream
Baked pie crust

Combine sugar, salt and cornstarch. Add milk slowly, then beaten egg yolks. Cook over slow heat until thick, but do not allow to boil, as it will curdle. Remove from heat and add gelatin softened in ¼ cup water. Stir until gelatin is dissolved. Divide this custard in half, adding one half to chocolate, 2 tablespoons sugar and vanilla. Pour this into large baked pie crust and let cool until firm. Keep the other half warm so it will not congeal. Beat egg whites with cream of tartar until foamy. Add ½ cup sugar and beat until very stiff. Fold in reserved custard and rum and spread over chocolate layer. Chill until firm. Before serving pile ½ pint sweetened whipped cream, to which vanilla has been added, on top. Sprinkle with grated chocolate. This pie is better if it sets at least 12 hours or overnight. Serves 8.

Barbara Derrick, Iowa State University
Fort Worth, Texas

BLACK BOTTOM PIE II

1¼ cups ginger snap crumbs
¼ cup melted butter
2 cups milk, scalded
4 egg yolks, well beaten
½ cup sugar
1½ tablespoons cornstarch
1½ squares melted chocolate
1 teaspoon vanilla
1 tablespoon gelatin
2 tablespoons water
4 egg whites, room temperature
½ cup sugar
¼ teaspoon cream of tartar
2 or more tablespoons whiskey or
   rum
Whipping cream

Blend ginger snaps and melted butter together, pat into 9 inch pie pan. Bake at 400 degrees for ten minutes. Cool. Add egg yolks to scalded milk very slowly. Combine sugar and cornstarch and stir into egg-milk mixture. Cook over hot water, stirring occasionally, until it coats a spoon. Remove from heat and take out one cup. Add the melted chocolate to the cup of custard and beat well as it cools. Add vanilla. Pour into crust. Chill. Dissolve the gelatin in cold water. Add to remaining custard and cool. Beat the egg whites, add sugar and continue beating; add cream of tartar and continue beating; add whiskey or rum. Fold this into the plain custard and pile on chocolate mixture. Chill. Cover top of pie with whipped cream and decorate with shavings of bitter chocolate. Serves 6-8.

Georgiana Post McClenaghan, Oregon State University
Nashville, Tennessee

CHEESE PIE

Crust:
22 Lorna Doone cookies
½ stick butter
Filling:
½ pound cream cheese
1 egg
¼ cup sugar
1 teaspoon vanilla
Top:
3 tablespoons sugar
1 teaspoon vanilla
½ pint sour cream

Mix cookies with melted butter or margarine. Press into 9 inch pie pan. Mix other ingredients with softened cream cheese. Pour into pie shell, bake at 325 degrees for 15 minutes. Mix topping ingredients well, pour over baked, cooled filling. Bake 10 minutes at 325 degrees. Pie is better if chilled overnight.

Gretchen Youse Rein, Kansas University
Greater Kansas City

EASY CHEESE PIE

1¼ cups fine graham cracker crumbs
¼ cup sugar
6 tablespoons butter or margarine, melted
4 packages (3 ounces each) cream cheese, softened
2 cups cold milk
2 tablespoons sugar
½ teaspoon vanilla
1 package (3¾ ounces) Jello Lemon or Vanilla Instant Pudding and Pie Filling

Combine crumbs, ¼ cup sugar and butter, press firmly on bottom and sides of an 8 inch square or 9 inch pie pan. Chill while preparing filling. Beat cream cheese until very soft. Blend in ½ cup milk. Add remaining milk, sugar, the vanilla and pie filling. Mix and beat as package directs. Pour into crust. Chill until firm, at least 2 hours. *Note:* for crumb garnish, reserve 2 tablespoons of crumb mixture.

Ginny Scott Slagle, University of Iowa
Gretna, Louisiana

CHESS PIE

1 cup unsalted butter
2 cups sugar
½ cup flour
⅛ teaspoon salt
6 egg yolks
1 cup evaporated milk
2 teaspoons vanilla
⅓ teaspoon lime juice
1 teaspoon honey
2 9-inch unbaked pie shells

Cream butter and sugar. Add egg yolks, then flour, milk and remainder of the ingredients. Fill two 9 inch unbaked pie shells. Bake 45 minutes at 350 degrees.

Eleanore Evenson Ericson, University of Minnesota
Sarasota, Florida

CHOCOLATE CHESS PIE

1½ cup sugar
3½ tablespoons cocoa
½ stick melted butter
2 eggs, beaten
⅔ cup evaporated milk
1 teaspoon vanilla
1 unbaked pie shell

Mix sugar and cocoa, then add melted butter, eggs, milk and vanilla. Pour into unbaked pie shell. Bake 40-45 minutes at 350 degrees.

Sunshine Hollar Davis, Southern Methodist University
Nashville, Tennessee

CHOCOLATE CHIP PIE

1 stick melted margarine
4 eggs, beaten
1 cup sugar
1 cup white corn syrup
1 cup broken pecans
1 small (6-ounce) package
    chocolate chips
2 unbaked pie shells

Divide the nuts and chips in bottom of 2 unbaked pie shells. Pour mixture of butter, sugar, eggs and syrup over nuts and chips. Bake at 350 degrees between 30 and 40 minutes. Makes two pies.

Connie Lynne Brandon, Vanderbilt University
Nashville, Tennessee

FRENCH CHOCOLATE PIE

½ cup butter
¾ cup sugar
2 squares unseetened chocolate,
    melted
2 eggs
½ pint whipping cream (whipped)
Graham cracker crust.

Cream butter with sugar. Stir in chocolate. Add eggs, one at a time, beating 5 minutes after each addition, at high speed. Fold in whipped cream. Pour into crust. Chill until firm. This may be made the day before serving. One teaspoon of vanilla may be added to the mixture for more flavor.

Edith Cameron McMillan, Memphis State University
Starkville, Mississippi

Peggy Larson Stromer, University of Nebraska
Milton, Wisconsin

FRENCH SILK PIE

1½ sticks butter
¾ cup sugar
1½ ounces (1 or 1½ squares)
    unsweetened chocolate, melted
    and cooled, (not solid)
1 teaspoon vanilla
2 eggs
1 pie shell, baked
Whipped cream

Bake pie shell. Cream butter, add sugar gradually. Beat well. Blend in cooled chocolate and vanilla. Beat well. Add 1 egg and beat 5 minutes until fluffy. Add other egg and beat 5 minutes. Filling should be stiff not runny or grainy. If not stiff enough put in freezer for short time. Should keep peaks easily. Put in shell. Refrigerate until serving. Top with whipped cream sweetened with sugar and vanilla.

Vicki Freund Campbell, Soutern Methodist University
Dallas, Texas

GERMAN CHOCOLATE PIE

½ bar German chocolate
½ cup margarine
1 teaspoon vanilla
3 eggs
1 cup sugar
3 tablespoons flour
1 cup chopped nuts
Whipped cream or ice cream

Melt margarine and chocolate over low heat. Cool. Add vanilla. Combine eggs, sugar and flour and beat on high speed for about 3 minutes. Fold chocolate mixture into egg mixture and add nuts. Pour into greased 9 inch glass pie pan and bake at 325 degrees for 35 minutes. Let set in refrigerator 4-6 hours or overnight. Serve with whipped cream or ice cream. Serves 6-8. This pie has no crust — it will form its own.

Floreine Dietrich Allen, Oklahoma University
Bartlesville, Oklahoma

CHOCOLATE SUNDAE PIE

First Layer:
1 cup flour
1 cup pecans, chopped fine
1 stick butter, melted
Second Layer:
1 cup powdered sugar
1 8-ounce package cream cheese
1 cup whipped topping
Third Layer:
1 package chocolate pudding and
  pie filling
1½ cups milk
Fourth Layer:
1 package vanilla pudding and pie
  filling
1½ cups milk
Fifth Layer:
½ cup pecans (chopped)

First Layer: Melt butter, add flour and pecans and press into 9x15 inch dish. Bake 15-20 minutes at 375 degrees. Cool before adding second layer.
Second Layer: Cream together sugar, cream cheese and whipped topping until fluffy. Spread on top of cooled first layer.
Third Layer: Cook according to directions. Cool completely before spreading onto second layer.
Fourth Layer: Cook according to directions. Cool completely before spreading onto third layer. Instant puddings, with the same amount of milk, may be substituted if desired.
Fifth Layer: Spread remainder of large container of whipped topping onto fourth layer. Sprinkle with ½ cup chopped pecans.

Marilyn Cooke Sullivan, University of Iowa
Dallas, Texas

CHERRY-CHEESE PIE

1 9-inch crumb crust or baked pie
  shell
1 8-ounce package cream cheese
1⅓ cups (15 ounces) sweetened
  condensed milk
⅓ cup lemon juice
1 teaspoon vanilla
1 can (1 pound, 6 ounces) cherry
  pie filling or cherry glaze

Soften cream cheese to room temperature, then whip until fluffy. Gradually add sweetened condensed milk while continuing to beat until well blended. Add lemon juice and vanilla, blend well. Pour into crust and chill 2 to 3 hours before spreading with cherry glaze. To make glaze, blend ½ cup cherry juice, 2 teaspoons sugar and 2 teaspoons cornstarch. Cook until thick, add a drop of food coloring, add 1 cup drained pitted sour cherries.

Elaine Campbell Simpson, University of Iowa
Washington, D.C.

CRANBERRY PIE

1½ cups cranberries
1 cup raisins
1 cup boiling water
1 cup sugar
2 tablespoons flour
1 tablespoon butter
1 teaspoon vanilla
9 inch pie shell

Boil cranberries and raisins in water for five minutes. Mix sugar and flour and add to cranberry mixture. Remove from heat and add butter and vanilla. Cool. Pour into baked 9 inch pie shell. At serving time, top with whipped cream.

Sara Hess McElhaney, Iowa State University
Dallas, Texas

FRUIT WHIP PIE

1 tablespoon granulated gelatin
3 tablespoons cold water
3 egg yolks
1 cup sugar
¼ teaspoon salt
½ cup orange juice
½ cup pineapple juice
2 tablespoons lemon juice
½ cup whipped cream
3 egg whites
1 baked crust
Strawberries (fresh, frozen or canned)

Soak gelatin in cold water for five minutes. Beat egg yolks. Add half of sugar, salt and juices. Cook in double boiler until slightly thick and creamy. Stir frequently. Add gelatin and stir until dissolved. Cool and fold in cream. Beat whites until stiff, add rest of sugar and beat until creamy. Add to gelatin mixture and pour into crust. Top with berries and chill until firm. Serves 6 to 8 with a flourish.

Geraldine Epp Smith, University of Missouri
St. Louis, Missouri

NO-CRUST FUDGE PIE

2 eggs, well beaten
1 cup sugar
½ cup butter or margarine, melted
½ cup flour
5 tablespoons cocoa
¼ teaspoon salt
1 tablespoon vanilla
1½ cups broken pecans

Mix all ingredients well. Pour into 8 inch pie pan. Bake at 350 degrees for 20 to 25 minutes. Serves 6.

Margaret Gatlin "Meg" Smith, Florida State University
Minneapolis, Minnesota

FUDGE PIE

½ cup melted butter
2 cups sugar
1 cup flour
4 eggs
2 squares melted chocolate
2 teaspoons vanilla

Beat butter and sugar together. Add eggs. Mix well. Add flour and mix. Add melted chocolate and vanilla. Pour into pie pan. Need no crust. Bake at 325 degrees for 25 minutes. Serve plain or with whipped cream.

Active Chapter, Southern Methodist University
Dallas, Texas

GRASSHOPPER PIE

Crust:
15 oreo cookies
4 teaspoons melted butter
Filling:
30 large marshmallows
¾ cup cream
2 jiggers cream de menthe
½ pint whipping cream

To make crust, crush cookies add melted butter, pack into 9 inch pie pan and chill.
For the filling, melt marshmallows in ¾ cup cream. Cool. Add creme de menthe. Fold in whipped cream. Pour filling into crust. Refrigerate.
May be topped with grated chocolate.

Dawn Chappell, University of California-Riverside
Riverside, California

ICE CREAM PIE

18 oreo cookies
1/3 cup margarine
1/2 gallon vanilla ice cream
1 tablespoon boiling water
1 tablespoon instant coffee
3 squares semi-sweet chocolate
2 tablespoons margarine
1/2 cup sugar
Small can evaporated milk
Topping:
Small container whipped topping
1/2 to 1 cup nuts

Crush cookies and mix with margarine. Press into bottom and sides of 9x13 inch pan. Mix softened ice cream with coffee and water mixture. Spread over cookies. Put in freezer to harden for 1/2 day, or overnight. Melt chocolate and add other ingredients. Cook until thick, about 10 minutes. Let cool completely and pour on top of ice cream. Return to freezer and let harden. Mix whipped topping and nuts, spread over frozen chocolate sauce.

Elizabeth Quick, Indiana University
Mt. Pleasant, Michigan

KEY LIME PIE

Baked 9 inch pie crust or crumb
crust
2 teaspoons grated lime peel
1/2 cup fresh lime juice
3 egg yolks
1 14-or 15-ounce can of
sweetened, condensed milk
1 egg white
Whipped cream topping

Stir the lime juice, one teaspoon of the grated peel and the egg yolks into the milk until the mixture is thick and evenly colored. Beat the egg white until stiff but not dry, and fold into the milk mixture. Chill pie well and serve with the topping lightly sprinkled with the remaining lime peel.

Sylvia Hardy Trewin, Iowa State University
Richardson, Texas

KOKOMOKO PIE

1/4 cup melted butter or margarine
1 quart coffee ice cream
1 ounce Kahlua (coffee liqueur)
Sliced almonds
2 cups flaked coconut
3 ounces chocolate sauce (ice
cream topping kind)
Whipped dessert topping or
whipped cream

Mix together butter and coconut and press into a 9 inch pan or pie plate. Bake at 300 degrees for 20 to 30 minutes or until golden. Cool, then fill with 1 quart coffee ice cream. Freeze until ready to serve. (No minimum time.) Mix chocolate sauce and Kahlua together. Cut pie into serving pieces. Pour sauce over each, top with whipped topping and sliced almonds.

Diane Dross Nichols, Indiana University
South Bend, Indiana

HONEY'S LEMON CHIFFON PIE

1 tablespoon cornstarch
1 tablespoon water
4 large eggs, separated (room temperature)
1 cup sugar
½ teaspoon salt
5 tablespoons lemon juice
2½ teaspoons grated lemon rind
1 prebaked pie shell

Dissolve cornstarch in water. Beat egg yolks in top of double boiler and gradually add sugar and dissolved cornstarch. Add salt and mix well. Add lemon juice slowly so it does not curdle. Add lemon rind. Cook in double boiler until mixture thickens, about 10 minutes. Set mixture aside to cool. Beat egg whites to peaks. Fold cooled mixture into egg whites gently but thoroughly. Put in baked pie shell and bake at 375 degrees for 15 minutes or until pie puffs up and is golden brown. (This recipe may be made with lime or orange instead of lemon. A drop of green or orange food coloring makes them especially pretty. The lemon needs no color.)

Linda Crothers, University of Washington
Seattle, Washington

LEMON MERINGUE PIE A LA MODE

⅓ cup butter
2 teaspoons grated lemon rind
⅓ cup lemon juice
¼ teaspoon salt
1 cup sugar
2 eggs
3 egg yolks
1 quart vanilla ice cream
1 baked 9 inch pie shell, cooled (should have high, fluted rim)
3 egg whites
½ cup sugar

Melt butter in top of double boiler. Add lemon rind and juice, salt, and 1 cup sugar. Beat whole eggs and yolks; stir into butter mixture. Cook over boiling water until thick and smooth, stirring constantly. Remove from heat; *cool thoroughly.* Soften ice cream slightly. Press half the ice cream into bottom of pie shell. Carefully spread half the lemon filling over the ice cream. Freeze pie until layers are firm. Keep remainder of ice cream frozen until ready to use. Repeat layers, using rest of ice cream and lemon filling. Freeze pie until firm. Beat egg whites until foamy. Beat in ½ cup sugar gradually; continue beating until meringue is stiff but not dry. Quickly spread meringue on pie, sealing to the pastry edge. Place pie on a board. Bake at 475 degrees for 4 to 5 minutes or until lightly browned. Return pie to freezer until serving time.

Carribelle Conway, Goucher College
Washington, D.C.

OLD FASHIONED LEMON PIE

1¼ cups sugar
1 tablespoon cornstarch
1 tablespoon flour
3 eggs
¼ cup melted butter
¼ cup lemon juice
2 tablespoons grated lemon rind
¼ cup milk
1 8-inch pie crust, unbaked

Mix dry ingredients in a bowl. Add beaten eggs, lemon juice, rind and milk. Beat until smooth. Pour into 8 inch unbaked pie crust and bake at 375 degrees for 30 to 40 minutes.

Ann Culley Dye, West Virginia University
Morgantown, West Virginia

MAGIC MACAROON PIE

12 saltine crackers, finely crushed
12 pitted dates, chopped or cut up
½ cup pecans or English walnuts (chopped fine)
¾ cup sugar
3 egg whites
½ teaspoon baking powder
½ teaspoon almond flavoring

Crush saltines. Add nuts and dates. Beat egg whites until foamy and then add baking powder, sugar and almond flavoring. Beat until very stiff, then add saltines, nuts and date mixture and fold into well-buttered pie pan. Bake 25 minutes at 325 degrees. Serve with or without whipped cream.

Frances Kirk Cranfill, University of Tulsa,
Washington University
Dallas, Texas

MERLIN'S MILE-HIGH PIE

Crust:
Whites of 4 eggs
½ teaspoon cream of tartar
Pinch of salt
1 cup sugar
Filling:
2 quarts each of chocolate, peppermint-stick, and vanilla ice cream
Topping:
Whites of 8 eggs
1½ cups sifted sugar
Sauce:
1½ cup minted chocolate sauce

Crust: Beat 4 egg whites frothy; add tartar, salt, beat stiff; beat in sugar gradually, stiff peaks. Form high-sided shell in well-greased 9 inch pie pan. Bake for 40 minutes at 300 degrees. Freeze.

Filling: Beat 1 quart chocolate ice cream soft; pour into crust; refreeze. Beat second quart chocolate, level on first layer, refreeze. Similarly add 2 layers peppermint-stick, 2 layers vanilla, refreezing each. When hard-frozen, invert on cold metal; remove pan; substitute 12 inch paper doily topped by 12 inch wooden disc; reinvert; freeze.

Topping: Beat 8 egg whites to peaks; beat sugar in gradually, stiff peaks, chill.

Serving: Preheat oven to 500 degrees, 15 minutes before serving, remove from freezer; cover ice cream thickly with topping sealing to crust, piling excess on top; sift sugar on meringue. Bake to delicate brown. Remove to serving tray. Slice in wedges. Add prewarmed sauce. Serves 12-14.

A smashing success at any party!

Ralphine Ronald Staring, Idaho University
Bowie, Maryland

MILLIONAIRE PIE

3 egg whites
1 cup sugar
1⅓ cup pecans *or* walnuts
1 teaspoon vanilla
21 Ritz crackers
1 8-ounce package softened cream cheese
¾ cup powdered sugar
8 ounce can drained crushed pineapple
½ pint heavy cream, whipped

For the crust, crunch crackers, cut nuts fine. Beat egg whites while adding sugar slowly and beat until stiff. Add vanilla. Fold in crackers and nuts. Pour into a greased 10 inch pie pan. Bake at 350 degrees for 30 minutes. Cool. Combine the cream cheese and confectioners sugar and spread on top of the cooled crust. For the icing, combine the pineapple and heavy cream (fold pineapple into cream). Spread on top of the filling. Make a ring of nuts on top with pineapple and cherries on top. Chill overnight.

Carolyn Vestal Kelly, Southern Methodist University
Dallas, Texas

MINCE MEAT FOR PIE OR TARTS

3 pounds cooked beef, ground
1 pound chopped suet
6 pounds apples, chopped
3 pounds raisins (one white)
2 pounds currants
1 pound chopped citron
½ cup rind of lemon and orange
2 tablespoons cinnamon
1 teaspoon nutmeg
3 pounds brown sugar
1 32-ounce can apple juice
1 cup apple jelly
Orange juice (about 1 cup)
Salt to taste

Simmer all together for two hours, stirring occasionally. Seal in glass jars/or freeze in amount for a pie. One tablespoon brandy may be added to each jar.
A delicious rich pie! The filling is ready to be baked, just make a 2 crust pie. Fill with the filling. Bake at 425 degrees for about 30 minutes. Serve warm with a hard sauce or ice cream.

Suzanne Schwantes Coil, Kansas University
Lawrence, Kansas

OPEN-FACE PEACH PIE

3 cups sliced fresh peaches
¾ cup sugar
¼ cup flour
2 tablespoons butter
2 tablespoons milk or light cream
1 unbaked 9 inch pie crust

Combine sugar, butter and flour to make crumbs. Sprinkle half of this mixture over the bottom of the unbaked crust. Arrange sliced peaches over crumbs. Cover peaches with remaining crumb mixture. Pour milk or cream over all. Bake at 425 degrees for 10 minutes, then reduce heat to 325 degrees and bake for 30 more minutes.

Sara Hess McElhaney, Iowa State University
Dallas, Texas

PEANUT BUTTER PIE

1 graham cracker crust (9 inch)
1 3-ounce package cream cheese
1 cup powdered sugar
½ cup milk
¾ cup crunchy peanut butter
1 9-ounce container whipped topping

Cream cheese and sugar, add milk and "work in" the peanut butter. Fold in whipped topping. Pour into graham cracker crust. Refrigerate at least 2 or 3 hours before serving. The pie freezes very well.

Doris Erwin Hawkins, Iowa State University
Washington, D.C.

LOG CABIN PECAN PIE

2 cups Log Cabin syrup
⅓ cup coarsely chopped pecans
¾ cup pecan halves
3 tablespoons butter
¼ cup sugar
2 tablespoons flour
¼ teaspoon salt
4 well-beaten eggs
½ teaspoon vanilla
1 8-inch unbaked pie shell

Bring syrup to boil in 1½ quart saucepan; boil gently uncovered for 8 minutes. Cool about 15 minutes. Sprinkle coarsely chopped nuts in pie shell. Arrange pecan halves on top. Cream butter; blend in sugar, flour and salt. Stir in eggs, vanilla and syrup and pour into pie shell. Bake at 375 degrees for 55-60 minutes, or until puffed and browned. Cool before serving.

Kay Johnson Marovich, Kansas State University
South Bay, California

PECAN PIE

3 eggs, beaten
1 cup white corn syrup
⅛ teaspoon salt
1 teaspoon vanilla
1 cup brown sugar or white sugar
2 tablespoons flour
3 tablespoons melted butter
1 cup whole pecans
1 unbaked 9 inch pastry shell

Mix all ingredients except sugar and flour which are then mixed and added to first mixture. (If you prefer, put pecans on uncooked pastry shell and pour mixture on top.) Bake at 400 degrees for 15 minutes, until it begins to set, then to 350 degrees for 35 minutes.

Billie Loomis Smith, University of Washington
Seattle, Washington

Lynne Ayers, Vanderbilt University
Nashville, Tennessee

Latane Jordan Graham, Memphis State University
Dallas, Texas

Frances Ballard, Southern Methodist University
Dallas, Texas

QUICK PINEAPPLE PIE

Prepare 2 graham cracker crusts
Filling:
1 can sweetened condensed milk
⅓ cup lemon juice
1 large can crushed pineapple
1 7-ounce can coconut (2 cups)
1 cup chopped nuts
1 large Cool Whip

Combine all filling ingredients. Pour in pie crust and chill. Can be frozen and taken out to thaw about 1 hour before serving. Two pies.

Harriet Lishen Baldwin, University of Missouri
Dallas, Texas

PINK CARNATION PIE

2 cups premium shredded
  coconut
2 tablespoons butter, melted
5 tablespoons Creme de Noyaux
1½ quarts vanilla ice cream

Coat the coconut with butter and pat firmly into a 9 inch pie pan. Bake at 350 degrees until toasted. Cool. Blend the Creme de Noyaux and the slightly softened ice cream. Pour into pie shell and freeze. Garnish with pink carnations.

Georgiana Post McClenaghan, Oregon State University
Nashville, Tennessee

Catherine Gardner Bowling, Vanderbilt University
Creve Coeur, Missouri

Karen Diehl Greening, Washington University
St. Louis, Missouri

Pam Rutherford, Vanderbilt University
Nashville, Tennessee

PUMPKIN PIE I

1½ cups pumpkin
1 cup sugar
¼ teaspoon salt
3 egg yolks
½ teaspoon vanilla
¾ cup evaporated milk or half and half
¼ teaspoon ginger
¼ teaspoon cloves
½ teaspoon nutmeg
1½ teaspoons cinnamon
3 egg whites
1 unbaked 10 inch pie shell

Beat egg whites until stiff and set aside. Beat egg yolks until light yellow; add sugar, salt, vanilla and spices. Beat until thick. Add pumpkin and milk and mix thoroughly. Fold in egg whites. Pour into pie shell. Bake at 425 degrees for 10 minutes and 325 degrees for 50 minutes longer or until a knife inserted in the center comes out clean.

Glenda Gay Beach Condon and Susan Beach Spiller,
Colorado State University
Windsor, Colorado

PUMPKIN PIE II

2 cups stewed and strained pumpkin or canned pumpkin
2 cups rich milk or thin cream
½ cup brown sugar
½ cup granulated sugar
2 eggs
¼ teaspoon ginger
½ teaspoon salt
1 teaspoon cinnamon
1 teaspoon vanilla

Mix pumpkin with milk, sugar, beaten eggs, ginger, salt, cinnamon and vanilla. Beat 2 minutes, pour into a 9 inch pie tin, which has been lined with pastry. Place in oven at 425 degrees for 15 minutes, reduce heat to 350 degrees and bake 45 minutes, cool. Serve with whipped cream.

Ann Culley Dye, West Virginia University
Morgantown, West Virginia

PUMPKIN CHIFFON PIE I

1 can pumpkin
1¼ cup milk
1¼ cup sugar
½ cup flour
2 tablespoons sorghum
3 eggs, separated
½ teaspoon salt
1 tablespoon butter
1 teaspoon ginger
1 teaspoon cinnamon
½ teaspoon cloves
¼ teaspoon nutmeg
Dash vanilla
Baked pie shell

Beat egg yolks, sift flour with spices. Add pumpkin and sugar to egg yolks. Mix, then add sorghum, salt, flour mixture and milk. Cook over low heat until thickened, add butter and dash of vanilla, just before removing from heat. Beat egg whites stiff adding 1 tablespoon sugar. When pumpkin mixture is cool, fold egg whites in gently. Pour into baked pie shell and refrigerate. Serve topped with whipped cream. Filling can be made ahead and refrigerated, but do not put into pie shell until ready to serve.

Sue Ann Wiltse Fagerberg, Kansas State University
Overland Park, Kansas

PUMPKIN CHIFFON PIE II

3 eggs, separated
¾ cup brown sugar
1½ cups pumpkin
½ cup milk
½ teaspoon salt
1 tablespoon cinnamon
1 envelope gelatin
¼ cup cold water
¼ cup sugar
½ teaspoon nutmeg
9 inch baked pie shell
Whipping cream

Combine 3 beaten egg yolks with brown sugar, pumpkin, milk and spices. Cook in double boiler until thickened, stirring constantly. Soak one envelope gelatin in cold water and stir into hot mixture. Chill until partly set, about one hour. Beat 3 egg whites, add ¼ cup sugar and beat stiff. Fold into gelatin mixture. Pour into 9 inch pie shell and chill until set. Garnish with whipped cream sprinkled with nut meats.

Kay Conrad, University of Idaho
Corvallis, Oregon

PARADISE PUMPKIN CREAM PIE

1 package plain gelatin
1 small box butterscotch pudding-pie filling
2 teaspoons pumpkin pie spice
1½ cups pumpkin
1 cup milk
⅓ cup dark brown sugar (packed)
2 eggs (separated)
½ pint whipping cream (whipped)
1 baked pie crust

Mix gelatin, pudding powder, pumpkin, spice, egg yolks and milk in saucepan. Cook, stirring, over medium heat until mixture boils, then remove from stove and set in pan of cold water. Stir frequently until cool to the touch. Make stiff meringue of egg white and add brown sugar. Fold into pumpkin mixture. Fold in whipped cream and pour in a baked pie crust. Refrigerate overnight or 8 to 10 hours before serving.

Mary Jo Ringhofer, Memphis State University
Germantown, Tennessee

PUMPKIN ICE CREAM PIE

¼ cup honey or ½ cup sugar
¾ cup canned pumpkin
¼ teaspoon ginger
¼ teaspoon cinnamon
Dash nutmeg and cloves
⅓ cup broken pecans
¼ teaspoon salt
1 quart vanilla ice cream
1 baked 10 inch pie shell
Topping:
Whipped cream
Pecan halves

Combine honey, pumpkin, spices and salt. Bring just to a boil, stirring constantly. Cool, then fold into softened vanilla ice cream and pecans. Spread in baked pastry shell. Freeze until firm. Remove from freezer about 1 hour before serving. Trim with whipped cream and pecan halves.

Karlene C. Franzen, Wittenberg University
Fort Washington, Pennsylvania

Barbara Missert Sassaman, Syracuse University
Manilius, New York

RASPBERRY FLUFF PIE

Crust:
1¼ cups oatmeal
½ cup flaked coconut
½ cup brown sugar
½ cup butter or margarine, melted
Filling:
1 3-ounce package raspberry gelatin
1 cup hot water
1 10-ounce frozen package raspberries, thawed
1 pint vanilla ice cream

Combine oatmeal and coconut in shallow pan. Bake at 350 degrees for 10 minutes. Stir in brown sugar and melted butter. Press mixture onto bottom and sides of a 9 inch pie pan. Chill. Dissolve gelatin in 1 cup hot water and stir in raspberries and juice. Blend in softened ice cream. Chill until partially set. Pour into chilled crust. Can be frozen and made ahead.

Sally Wells Bauman, University of Wisconsin-Madison
Whitefish Bay, Wisconsin

MARY PEOPLE'S RUM PIE

No definite measurements
About 1 quart vanilla ice cream
About ½ pound bakery (not boxed) macaroons
About ¼ cup rum
Some nuts

Cover bottom of a 9-inch pie pan with macaroons. Cover macaroons with rum. When rum has sunk in, add as much ice cream as you wish. Put macaroons around the edge. Top with crumbled macaroons, put in freezer. Same day or later, take out of freezer and put a few nuts on top, blanched almonds or such. Serve immediately.

Harriet McCurley Trout, Goucher College
Richmond, Virginia

RUM CREAM PIE

9 egg yolks
1½ cups sugar
1½ tablespoons gelatin
¾ cup water
1½ pint heavy cream, whipped stiff
¾ cup clear rum
2 graham cracker crusts
Bitter-sweet chocolates

Combine egg yolks and sugar and beat until light. Dissolve gelatin in water and bring to a boil over medium heat. Stir into egg mixture, beating briskly. Let cool slightly. Fold whipped cream into egg mixture and add rum slowly. Pour into pie crusts and refrigerate to set. When ready to serve, grate bittersweet chocolate on top. Makes two large pies.

Patricia Smith Dieterich, University of Iowa
Ridgefield, Connecticut

FRESH STRAWBERRY PIE

1 quart strawberries
¾ cup sugar
2 tablespoons cornstarch
⅓ cup water
Red food coloring
Juice of half a lemon

Bake a 9 inch pie shell at 400 degrees until crisp and golden brown about 10 minutes. Combine sugar, cornstarch and water. Cook until it begins to thicken, then add ½ quart berries cut in half. Cook until thick and clear. Add red food coloring and lemon juice. Pour over other half of berries placed in pie shell. Cool and serve with whipped cream or ice cream.

Barbara B. Derrick, Iowa State University
Ft. Worth, Texas

FROZEN STRAWBERRY PIE

1 1-pound package frozen strawberries, do not thaw
1 cup sugar
⅛ teaspoon salt
2 egg whites
1 teaspoon lemon juice
½ pint whipping cream
1 teaspoon vanilla
1 graham cracker crust

Make graham cracker crust first and refrigerate. Whip cream, add vanilla and refrigerate. Place strawberries, broken apart with a fork, egg whites, lemon juice, sugar and salt in large mixing bowl and beat at medium speed for 10 to 15 minutes, until mixture is stiff and holds shape. Fold in whipped cream. Pile lightly in graham cracker crust and freeze. Serves 12-16.

Beatrice Brown Freeman, Iowa State University
Aiken, South Carolina

STRAWBERRY PIE

1 9-inch pie shell, baked
1¼ cups water
1 cup sugar
3 tablespoons cornstarch
3 tablespoons water
Fresh strawberries, one quart
Red food coloring
Dash of salt

Wash and slice strawberries. Mash about ⅓ of them. Bring water and sugar to a rolling boil in a saucepan. Gradually add cornstarch dissolved in 3 tablespoons of water. Stir constantly. Add mashed berries. Add a few drops of red coloring to make the sauce a bright color. Remove from stove; add salt and stir well. Add rest of the berries. Cool slightly and pour into baked pie shell. Refrigerate. Serve with whipped cream or topping.

Virginia Gray Douglas, University of Washington
Seattle, Washington

"TU TU" PIE

1 cup sugar
¼ cup cornstarch
¼ pound butter or margarine
2 eggs
1 tablespoon bourbon
1 cup chopped pecans
1 small package chocolate chips
1 deep pie shell

Melt butter. Put sugar, cornstarch, melted butter or margarine and eggs into blender and mix for a few seconds then add the bourbon and mix again. Remove ingredients from blender and put into a large bowl and add by hand the pecans and chocolate chips. Pour into unbaked pie shell. Bake at 350 degrees about 50 minutes or until done.

Note: This is quite rich and will serve 6 to 8 depending on the size of the pieces.

Doris Erwin Hawkins, Iowa State University
Silver Spring, Maryland

YOGURT PIE

1 graham cracker pie shell
1 small carton lime or lemon
  yogurt
1 small carton fruit flavored
  yogurt
1 carton whipped topping
  (9-ounce)

Mix last three ingredients. Put in pie shell and refrigerate. May top with shaved chocolate or coconut or chopped nuts.

Elaine Campbell Simpson, University of Iowa
Washington, D.C.

Joanie Johnson Maines, California State University
Fresno, California

INDEX

A

A CHICKEN DISH BY MOTHER, 87
ADAH'S APPLE CAKE, 194
ADAH'S BREAD PUDDING, 239
ADAH'S SWEET FRENCH DRESSING, 153
ALMOND MERINGUES, 218
ALMOST RAVIOLI, 70
ANGEL FOOD CAKE DESSERT, 236
ANGOSTURA DIP, 8
ANN'S PINEAPPLE-CARROT CAKE, 197
ANN'S SWISS ENCHILADAS, 95
APPETIZER CREAM PUFFS, 14
APPLE CAKE, 194
APPLE CHUNKIES, 237
APPLE CRISP, 238
APPLE PUDDING CAKE, 195
APPLE SAUCE CAKE, 195
APRICOT MUFFINS, 45
APRICOT PIE, 261
ARTICHOKE BITES, 8
ARTICHOKE HEARTS AND SPINACH AU
   GRATIN, 172
ARTICHOKE PATE, 8
ASPARAGUS CANAPES, 8
ASPARAGUS PARMESAN CHEESE
   CASSEROLE, 172
ASPARAGUS SALAD, 122
AUDREY'S ANGELFOOD CUSTARD
   DESSERT, 237
AUDREY'S STICKY CINNAMON BUNS, 40
AUNT HILDA'S RHUBARB DESSERT, 253
AUNTIE'S PIE CRUST, 259
AUNT MAE'S MUNCHERS, 228
AUNT SUE'S COLE SLAW DRESSING, 152
AUNT SUE'S POUND CAKE, 213
AVOCADO COCKTAIL, 9
AVOCADO-CRANBERRY SALAD, 123
AVOCADO IN ASPIC, 122
AVOCADO MOUSSE, 123
AVOGOLEMONO SOUP, 156

B

BB'S DIVINITY, 235
BACON STUFFED MUSHROOMS, 19
BAGHDAD BISQUE, 157
BAKED ALEUTIANS, 236
BAKED AVOCADOS WITH CRAB
   MEAT, 101
BAKED CHEESE FONDUE, 73
BAKED CHICKEN BREASTS, 80
BAKED CHICKEN BREASTS WITH
   ALMONDS, 80
BAKED CHICKEN SANDWICHES, 99
BAKED FUDGE, 240
BAKED OMELET, 79
BAKED PINEAPPLE DRESSING FOR
   HAM, 167
BAKED PORK CHOPS, 115
BAKED STUFFED SHRIMP, 108
BAKED SLICED TOMATOES, 189
BAKED VEGETABLE MEDLEY, 190
BAMBI'S CRAB CASSEROLE, 105

BANANA NUT BREAD, 38
BANANA BREAD, 38
BANANA CAKE & TOPPING, 195
BARBARA'S 7 LAYER COOKIES, 232
BARBECUED RIBS, 118
BARBECUED SPARERIBS, 118
BARBECUE SALAD, 124
BARBECUE SAUCE, 168
BARBEQUE CHICKEN WINGS, 15
BARBECUED-BROILED ROAST, 58
BAR-B-Q BEEF, 58
BAR-B-QUED BRISKET, 59
BARLEY CASSEROLE, 173
BASIC MAYONNAISE AND SOUR CREAM
   BLUE CHEESE VARIATION, 155
BEACON HILL COOKIES, 218
BEAN SOUP, 157
BEEF AND BACON ROLLS HERBED
   RICE, 58
BEEF AND RICE CASSEROLE, 63
BEEF CARBONNADE, 60
BEEF QUICHE, 70
BEEF ROLL-UPS, 9
BEEF STROGANOFF, 63
BEEF-ZUCCHINI-CASSEROLE, 63
BEER BATTER FOR FISH, 105
BEER BREAD, 38
BEER CHEESE, 10
BEST BROCCOLI CASSEROLE, 176
BEST EVER SALAD, 124
BETTY'S FRESH MUSHROOM SALAD, 138
BEV'S CHICKEN CREAM
   ENCHILADAS, 96
BEV'S GOLDEN GLAZED CHICKEN, 86
BLACK BOTTOM PIE I, 261
BLACK BOTTOM PIE II, 261
BLACK WALNUT CAKE, 217
BLUEBERRY CHEESECAKE, 199
BLUEBERRY BUCKLE, 199
BLUEBERRY AND PINEAPPLE
   SALAD, 124
BOB'S GASPACHO, 160
BOEUF BOURGUIGNONNE, 59
BOILED RAISIN SPICE CAKE, 215
BOLOGNA STACKS, 9
BOURBON BALLS, 219
BRAUNSCHWEIGER DIP, 9
BRAZIL NUT DROPS, 219
BRENDA'S ORANGE COOLER, 34
BRENNAN'S PRALINE PARFAIT
   SAUCE, 165
BRISKET OF BEEF, 59
BROCCOLI CASSEROLE I, 175
BROCCOLI CASSEROLE II, 176
BROCCOLI CASSEROLE III, 176
BROCCOLI, CAULIFLOWER, BRUSSEL
   SPROUT, CHEESE CASSEROLE, 181
BROCCOLI-RICE CASSEROLE, 176
BROCCOLI SUPREME, 177
BROCCOLI ZITI, 177
BROILED ZUCCHINI, 190
BROWN STONE FRONT CAKE, 196

BROWNIE PUDDING, 240
BRUNCH EGGS, 77
BRUNCH EGGS AND POTATOES, 78
BRUNCH EGG CASSEROLE, 77
BUTTER PECAN BUNDT CAKE, 197
BUTTERMILK BISCUITS, 39
BUTTERMILK CAKE, 197
BUTTERSCOTCH-CREAM CHEESE POUND
  CAKE, 212
BUTTERSCOTCH NUT TORTE, 255
BUTTERSCOTCH THINS, 221

C

CABBAGE SALAD, 126
CAESAR SALAD, 125
CALICO BEANS, 174
CALIFORNIA BUFFET EGGS, 78
CALIFORNIA CRAB SPREAD, 15
CALIFORNIA GREEN CHILI
  ENCHILADAS, 96
CALIFORNIA SALAD, 125
CANDIED BRANDIED CRANBERRIES, 165
CARAMEL CHOCOLATE SQUARES, 221
CARAMEL ROLLS, 52
CARAMEL CORN, 233
CARLA'S CHEESE BALL, 10
CARROT CASSEROLE, 178
CASSIE'S CRAB SOUFFLE, 104
CELERY SEED DRESSING, 152
CHALUPAS, 64
CHAMPAGNE PUNCH, 32
CHAMPAGNE PUNCH, 32
CHARLIE'S COQUILLE ST. JACQUES, 100
CHARLIE'S CORNBREAD, 43
CHEDDAR CHEESE SOUP, 157
CHEESE BALL, 10
CHEESE BALL, 10
CHEESE BONBONS, 11
CHEESE CAKE, 198
CHEESE CAKE, 199
CHEESE CHILE CUBES, 73
CHEESE CORN CASSEROLE, 180
CHEESE GRITS, 182
CHEESE PIE, 262
CHEESE PUFFS, 12
CHEESE SHORTBREAD, 53
CHEESE SOUFFLE, 74
CHEESE SPREAD, 12
CHEESY APRICOT SALAD, 122
CHEESY CHICKEN CASSEROLE, 82
CHERRY AND COKE MOLD, 127
CHERRY ANGELFOOD CAKE
  DESSERT, 237
CHERRY-CHEESE PIE, 264
CHERRY FRUIT SALAD, 127
CHERRY JUBILEE, 240
CHERRY SALAD, 127
CHERRY SURPRISE, 241
CHESS CAKE, 198
CHESS PIE, 262
CHICKEN ALMOND SALAD, 129

CHICKEN AND DRESSING BAKE, 85
CHICKEN AND RICE CASSEROLE, 92
CHICKEN AND SPINACH SOUP, 160
CHICKEN BALL, 79
CHICKEN BREAST DIVINE, 80
CHICKEN CASSEROLE I, 81
CHICKEN CASSEROLE II, 81
CHICKEN CHILI, 84
CHICKEN-CRAB VALENTIN, 82
CHICKEN CREPES EXCELSIOR, 83
CHICKEN CRISP CASSEROLE, 84
CHICKEN DINNER FROM BALI, 85
CHICKEN DIVAN, 87
CHICKEN ENCHILADAS, 97
CHICKEN FILLING FOR
  ENCHILADAS, 96
CHICKEN KIEV, 88
CHICKEN MAXIMILLIAN, 89
CHICKEN MONTE CARLO, 89
CHICKEN MOUSSE, 128
CHICKEN NOEL, 89
CHICKEN ON THE VINE, 95
CHICKEN PARMESAN, 91
CHICKEN PARMESAN AND RICE, 91
CHICKEN PATE, 13
CHICKEN PILLOWS, 90
CHICKEN-RICE CASSEROLE I, 91
CHICKEN-RICE CASSEROLE II, 91
CHICKEN SALAD, 128
CHICKEN SOPPA, 93
CHICKEN SQUARES, 93
CHICKEN STRATA, 94
CHICKEN STUFFED AVOCADO, 123
CHICKEN TETRAZZINI, 94
CHICKEN VERONIQUE, 94
CHICKEN WITH GARLIC BUTTER, 86
CHICKEN WITH SESAME RICE, 92
CHILI I, 72
CHILI II, 72
CHILI-CHEESE DIP, 15
CHILI RELLENOS I, 74
CHILI RELLENOS II, 75
CHILI RELLENOS CASSEROLE, 75
CHILLED CUCUMBER SOUP, 159
CHINESE COLESLAW, 126
CHINESE SPARERIBS, 118
CHOCOLATE BALL COOKIES, 222
CHOCOLATE BUNDT CAKE, 202
CHOCOLATE CAKE I, 201
CHOCOLATE CAKE II, 201
CHOCOLATE CHEESECAKE I, 200
CHOCOLATE CHEESECAKE II, 200
CHOCOLATE CHERRY CAKE, 202
CHOCOLATE CHESS PIE, 262
CHOCOLATE CHIP CAKE, 203
CHOCOLATE CHIP PIE, 263
CHOCOLATE CUPCAKES, 217
CHOCOLATE DELIGHT I, 241
CHOCOLATE DELIGHT II, 241
CHOCOLATE DESSERT, 242

CHOCOLATE DROP COOKIES, 221
CHOCOLATE GLAZE FOR
   PETITS-FOUR, 210
CHOCOLATE IGLOO, 242
CHOCOLATE MINT STICKS, 222
CHOCOLATE-MOUSSE CRUNCH, 243
CHOCOLATE NUT CLUSTERS, 223
CHOCOLATE PEPPERMINT
   COOKIES, 223
CHOCOLATE SAUCE, 164
CHOCOLATE SHERRY CREAM BARS, 223
CHOCOLATE SUNDAE PIE, 264
CHOCOLATE TOPPING FOR ICE
   CREAM, 164
CHOCOLATE WAFERS, 224
CHOCO-MINT FREEZE, 242
CHRISTMAS CAKE, 203
CHRISTMAS CHERRY CAKES, 204
CHRISTMAS WASSAIL, 35
CHRISTMAS WREATH COOKIES, 224
CINNAMON BREAD, 40
CINNAMON COFFEE CAKE, 41
CINNAMON CRUMB CAKE, 41
CLAM CHOWDER-NEW ENGLAND STYLE, 158
CLAMS CASINO, 100
COCKTAIL HOT DOGS, 17
COCOA COLA CAKE, 204
COCONUT POUND CAKE, 213
COFFEE ICE CREAM DESSERT, 247
COFFEE PUNCH, 32
COLD AVOCADO SOUP, 156
COLD CARROT SALAD, 126
COLD CUCUMBER SOUP, 159
COLD OVEN POPOVERS, 50
COLD POACHED SALMON WITH LEMON
   SAUCE, 107
COLD SPAGHETTI SALAD, 143
COLESLAW, 126
COLORADO GORP (SNACK), 233
CONVENTION CHEESETTES, 11
COOKIE'S CRABBY CANAPE, 15
COQUILLE ST. JACQUES, 101
CORN AND BROCCOLI CASSEROLE, 181
CORN PUDDING, 180
COTTAGE CHEESE-CUCUMBER
   MOLD, 131
COTTOI'S TUNA SALAD, 149
COUNTRY CRUST BREAD, 39
COWBOY COOKIES, 224
CRAB AND CHEESE BAKE, 101
CRAB DIP, 13
CRAB IMPERIAL MOUSSE, 13
CRAB MEAT AU GRATIN I, 103
CRAB MEAT AU GRATIN II, 103
CRAB SELDOVIA, 102
CRABMEAT SHERRY CASSEROLE, 104
CRAB-SHRIMP CASSEROLE, 104
CRANBERRY BREAD, 42
CRANBERRY CAKE WITH BUTTER
   SAUCE, 204

CRANBERRY CHICKEN FOR TWO, 83
CRANBERRY FRUIT NUT BREAD, 43
CRANBERRY NUT SALAD, 131
CRANBERRY ORANGE SALAD, 131
CRANBERRY PIE, 264
CRANBERRY-RASPBERRY MOLD, 131
CRANBERRY SALAD, 130
CRANBERRY SOUR CREAM SALAD, 131
CREAMY CASHEW CHICKEN, 81
CREAMY CUCUMBER ASPIC, 132
CREAMY FROZEN FRUIT SALAD, 134
CREME ALEXANDER, 243
CREOLE CRAB-RICE CASSEROLE, 105
CRESCENT CINNAMON TWISTS, 41
CRUMB CAKE, 205
CRUNCHY GAZPACHO, 135
CURRIED CHICKEN DIP, 12
CURRIED CHICKEN SALAD, 128
CURRIED TUNA, 149
CURRIED VEGETABLE SALAD, 151
CURRY IN A HURRY, 111

D
DADDY'S FUDGE, 233
DANISH COOKIES, 225
DARK & CREAMY FUDGE, 234
DATE AND NUT CAKE, 205
DATE BREAD, 43
DATE CASSEROLE COOKIES, 225
DATE-FILLED PINWHEEL COOKIES, 225
DAVID EYRE'S PANCAKE, 49
DECORATIVE FROSTING FOR
   PETITS-FOURS, 210
D-LISH VELVET HOT FUDGE, 164
DEL MAR TUNA SALAD, 148
DEVILED CRAB, 102
DILL DIP, 16
DILLED GREEN BEANS, 174
DIANE'S RUSSIAN TEA, 35
DICK'S PUMPKIN BARS, 230
DIP FOR RAW VEGETABLES, 28
DIP FOR SHRIMP, 24
DIRTY RICE, 99
DIVINE CRAB PATE, 14
DOTTIE'S CHOCOLATE BUTTERMILK
   CAKE, 202
DOTTIE'S SHRIMP BALL, 24
DOTTIE'S SWEDISH MEATBALLS, 18
DOUBLE RICH BROWNIES, 219
DOWN-HOME SUGAR COOKIES, 232
DYNAMITE DILLY CHEESE BREAD, 44

E
EASIEST-EVER CHICKEN, 85
EAST INDIA CURRIED LAMB, 112
EASY APPLE PIE, 260
EASY AU GRATIN POTATOES, 183
EASY BRUNCH CASSEROLE, 75
EASY CHEESE PIE, 262
EASY CHICKEN AND RICE
   CASSEROLE, 90

EASY COLESLAW, 126
EASY CREAM OF CORN SOUP, 158
EASY CREAMED CHICKEN, 83
EASY ELEGANT CHICKEN, 87
EASY FROZEN FRUIT SALAD, 135
EASY FRUIT SALAD, 133
EASY HOT CHOCOLATE MIX, 30
EAT MORE, 64
EASY POP-UP BREAD, 50
EASY TOMATO ASPIC, 147
EGG-CHEESE CASSEROLE, 77
EGGPLANT BEEF CASSEROLE, 61
EGG TORTILLA CASSEROLE, 78
EGGS GOLDENROD, 78
ELEGANT WISCONSIN HOT POTATO
    SALAD, 140
ENDIVE AND HEARTS OF PALM, 132
ENGLISH PEA SALAD, 132
ENGLISH TOFFEE COOKIES, 226
ESCALOPES DE TERNERA, 71
ETHEL DRAKE'S GERMAN BERRY
    CAKE, 196
EVA'S CAULIFLOWER, 179

F
FABULOUS FISH FILLETS, 106
FABULOUS ROLLS, 51
FALL FRUIT SALAD, 134
FAMILY FAVORITE BROWNIES, 220
FANNIE BELLE'S CHICKEN
    CASSEROLE, 82
FANTASTIC FLANK STEAK, 62
FIVE CUP SALAD I, 132
FIVE CUP SALAD II, 133
5 FLAVORS POUND CAKE, 213
FLUFFY FRENCH DRESSING, 153
FORGOTTEN DESSERT, 244
FRANCES' AMBER PUNCH, 32
FRANCES' FRUIT PUNCH, 32
FREEZER STRAWBERRY JAM, 165
FRENCH CHOCOLATE PIE, 263
FRENCH DRESSING, 153
FRENCH MUFFINS, 45
FRENCH ONION SOUP, 162
FRENCH SALAD, DRESSING, 153
FRENCH SILK PIE, 263
FRESH APPLE BREAD, 38
FRESH CRANBERRY DELIGHT, 243
FRESH STRAWBERRY FROZEN
    YOGURT, 254
FRESH STRAWBERRY PIE, 273
FRITO SALAD, 133
FROSTED SALAD, 133
FROSTY STRAWBERRY SQUARES, 253
FROZEN CHERRY DESSERT, 240
FROZEN FRUIT DAIQUIRIS, 31
FROZEN FRUIT SALAD, 135
FROZEN STRAWBERRY PIE, 273
FROZEN WINE "CAKE", 258
FRUIT CAKE, 205

FRUIT CAKE COOKIES, 226
FRUIT CHEESECAKE, 199
FRUIT COOKIES, 226
FRUIT DRESSING, 154
FRUIT SAUCE FOR HAM, 167
FRUIT WHIP PIE, 265
FUDGE BROWNIES, 220
FUDGE DELIGHT CAKE, 206
FUDGE PIE, 265

G
GALA PECAN SPREAD, 21
GAMMA PHI DELIGHT, 245
GARDEN PARTY DELIGHT, 245
GARLIC COCKTAIL PICKLES, 22
GERMAN CHOCOLATE PIE, 263
GINGERBREAD CHORISTERS, 227
GINGER COOKIES, 227
GLAZED CARROTS, 179
GLORIA'S INDIVIDUAL FRUIT
    TARTS, 255
GLORIA'S MUSHROOMS AU GRATIN, 182
GLORIOUS MEDLEY, 69
GOMMIE APPLES, 238
GRAHAM CRACKER PIE CRUST, 260
GRANDMA KAY'S HAWAIIAN MEATBALLS, 68
GRANDMA SULLIVAN'S IRISH SODA
    BREAD, 46
GRANDMA'S EGG SOUFFLE, 76
GRANDMOTHER'S COFFEE CAKE, 41
GRANDMOTHER'S ENGLISH PLUM
    PUDDING, 251
GRAPEFRUIT COOLER, 31
GRAPEFRUIT SALAD MOLD, 135
GRAPENUT BREAD, 44
GRASSHOPPER PIE, 265
GREEN BEANS WITH HERBED
    BUTTER, 175
GREEN CHILI BITES, 13
GREEN CHILI SOUFFLE, 74
GREEN RICE, 184
GREEN RICE CASSEROLE, 185
GREEN VEGETABLE CASSEROLE, 190

H
HAM DELIGHTS, 16
HAM FILLING FOR CREPES, 114
HAM LOAF, 114
HAM LOAF SUPREME, 114
HAMBURGER CASSEROLE, 64
HAMBURGER-CHEESE DIP, 17
HAMBURGER PARMESAN, 65
HAMBURGER PIZZA DIP, 17
HAMBURGER STROGANOFF, 65
HARTWELL FARM CORN PUDDING, 180
HEAVENLY HOTS, 246
HELEN'S PEACH COBBLER, 249
HERBED AND CHEESEY FRENCH BREAD, 44
HOLIDAY PUNCH, 33
HOMEMADE STEAK SAUCE, 168
HOMEMADE TOMATO SOUP, 163

HOMEMADE YOGURT, 156
HONEY ORANGE BREAD, 48
HONEY'S LEMON CHIFFON PIE, 267
HONOLULU SHRIMP, 25
HOOVER CASSEROLE, 64
HORSERADISH CARROTS, 178
HOSPITALITY PUNCH, 34
HOT ARTICHOKE-CHEESE BARS, 172
HOT BUTTERED RUM, 35
HOT CELERY SALAD, 127
HOT CHEESE DIP FOR FONDUE, 15
HOT CHICKEN SALAD I, 129
HOT CHICKEN SALAD II, 129
HOT CHICKEN SALAD III, 129
HOT CRAB SPREAD, 14
HOT CRANBERRY PUNCH, 33
HOT CURRIED FRUIT, 128
HUT CURRIED FRUIT, 134
HOT FRUIT SALAD, 134
HOT GERMAN POTATO SALAD, 140
HOT PUNCH, 34
HOT PUNCH, 34
HOT SPICED FRUIT, 244
HOT SPICED PECANS, 21
HOT TUNA DELIGHTS, 111

I
ICE CREAM, 246
ICE CREAMWICH, 246
ICE CREAM CRUNCH SQUARES, 246
ICE CREAM DESSERT, 247
ICE CREAM PIE, 266
ICE CREAM TORTE, 247
ICED GAZPACHO, 160
IMPOSSIBLE QUICHE, 119
IOLA'S SHRIMP DIP, 23
ITALIAN CREAM CAKE, 207
ITALIAN EGGPLANT APPETIZER, 16
ITALIAN ZUCCHINI CASSEROLE, 192

J
JALAPENO RICE, 185
JANE NOLAN'S SHRIMP DIP, 24
JANE'S BROCCOLI-RICE CASSEROLE, 177
JANE'S CRAZY STEW, 62
JAN'S SAUSAGE AND LENTILS, 117
JELLY ROLL, 207
JENNIEBELLE'S FIVE BEAN
    CASSEROLE, 174
JOANIE'S CARROTS, 125
JUICY MEAT LOAF, 68
JULIE'S BAKED BEANS, 173

K
KASHA, 182
KATHARINE'S SHRIMP AND CHEESE
    CASSEROLE, 109
KATHRYN'S UNUSUAL SPINACH SALAD, 144
KEY LIME PIE, 266
KOKOMOKO PIE, 266
KOLACHY, 46

KUWAIT CHICKEN, 88

L
LAKE SHORE CASSEROLE, 115
LAMB SHANKS, 113
LAMB STEW WITH ARTICHOKES, 113
LASAGNA CASSEROLE, 66
LASAGNA, 66
LAZY-DAISY CAKE, 208
LAZY MAN'S MERINGUES, 249
LEG OF LAMB WITH COFFEE
    GRAVY, 112
LEMON ANGEL SUPREME, 248
LEMON BAKED CHICKEN, 88
LEMON BREAD, 46
LEMON CAKE PIE, 248
LEMON COOKIES, 228
LEMON CUSTARD DESSERT, 248
LEMON LORENOTES, 227
LEMON MERINGUE PIE A LA MODE, 267
LEMON TORTE, 208
LIME DELIGHT, 248
LINCOLN LOGS, 17
LINDA'S BUBBLING PINEAPPLE
    PUNCH, 33
LINDA'S COLD CUCUMBER SOUP, 159
LINDA'S GAZPACHO, 161
LINDA'S PINEAPPLE PARTY PUNCH, 33
LITTLE WAFFLES, 232
LOG CABIN PECAN PIE, 269
LOLLY'S BEEF BURGUNDY, 62
LOUISE GRAHAM'S CRACKER CAKE, 206
LOUISE'S BAKED CORN IN SOUR
    CREAM, 180
LOUISE'S EGGPLANT CASSEROLE, 181
LOUISE'S GROUND BEEF CASSEROLE, 61
LOUISE'S SCALLOPED ASPARAGUS, 173
LOUISE'S STUFFED TOMATO, 189
LUSCIOUS CARROTS, 178

M
MACARONI-CHICKEN CASSEROLE, 89
MACARONI SAUTE, 65
MADRAS CHICKEN CURRY, 84
MAGIC MACAROON PIE, 268
MANDARIN ORANGE SALAD, 136
MANDARIN ORANGE TARTS, 255
MAPLE NUT LOAF, 47
MARGARET'S CHRISTMAS CAKE, 203
MARGARET'S TAMALE BALLS, 27
MARILYN'S APPLE CRISP, 238
MARINATED MUSHROOMS I, 19
MARINATED MUSHROOMS II, 19
MARINATED SALAD, 136
MARY PEOPLE'S RUM PIE, 272
MARYLAND LADY CRAB CAKES, 102
MARYLAND SEASHORE CRAB, 103
MARY'S BLACK RIVER BROWNIES OR
    BROWNIES DELUXE, 220
MARY'S "DELICIOUS" QUICHE, 75
MAXINE'S DILEMMA, 249

MEAT AND CHEESE LOAF, 67
MEAT BALLS IN SAUCE, 20
MEATLESS TACO SALAD, 146
MELON GINGER COCKTAIL, 18
MERLIN'S MILE-HIGH PIE, 268
MEXICAN BEEF SANDWICH, 71
MEXICAN CHEF SALAD, 137
MICHELLE BLUEBERRY CREAM
  FLAN, 239
MICHELLE'S ITALIAN TOMATO
  SALAD, 147
MICHIGAN STATE CRAB AND AVOCADO
  DIP, 14
MIGUEL'S SALADA, 137
MILDRED'S DELICIOUS TIDBITS, 257
MILDRED'S YUMMY MORSELS, 259
MILK PUNCH, 34
MILLIONAIRE PIE, 268
MILLIONAIRES, 235
MINCE MEAT FOR PIE OR TARTS, 269
MINI-PECAN TARTS, 255
MISSISSIPPI MUD, 208
MIXED VEGETABLE RELISH, 166
M'MAMA'S BLUEBERRY TARTS, 254
MOLDED CHICKEN SALAD, 130
MOLDED CRANBERRY SALAD, 130
MOLDED STRAWBERRY SALAD, 144
MOLDED TOMATO SALAD, 147
MOLLY'S SCALLOPED CELERY, 179
MOM'S APPLE PIE, 260
MOM'S HOT FUDGE SAUCE, 164
MOM'S NEW ENGLAND
  SUCCOTASH, 188
MOM'S OATMEAL & COCONUT
  COOKIES, 229
MOM'S POTATO SALAD, 139
MOM'S RASPBERRY DELIGHT, 252
MOM'S RICE, 185
MONKEY BREAD, 47
MOSTLY MUSHROOM SALAD, 137
MOTHER'S DATE-NUT BREAD, 44
MOTHER'S GINGERBREAD, 245
MOTHER'S PETITE CHERRY
  CHEESECAKES, 201
MOTHER'S RED CABBAGE, 178
MOTHER'S WATERGATE SALAD, 152
MUSHROOM APPETIZERS, 18
MUSHROOM SOUP, 162
MUSTARD SAUCE, 167

N
NANAIMO'S, 228
NANCY'S PUMPKIN CAKE, 215
NEVER FAIL PIE CRUST, 259
NEVER-FAIL QUICK SPAGHETTI
  SAUCE, 168
NEW ENGLAND CLAM CHOWDER, 158
NINE DAY SLAW, 142
NO-BAKE CHOCOLATE DROP
  COOKIES, 222
NO-CRUST FUDGE PIE, 265

NOLA'S WEST TEXAS OKRA, 182
O
OATMEAL BREAD, 47
OATMEAL BUTTER COOKIES, 229
OATMEAL CAKE, 209
OATMEAL COOKIES, 228
OATMEAL REFRIGERATOR ROLLS, 48
OLD FASHIONED EGG NOG, 31
OLD FASHIONED LEMON PIE, 267
OLD-FASHIONED POUND CAKE, 213
OLIVE CHEESE PUFFS, 20
OMAR'S DRESSING, 154
OMEGA'S FRENCH CHOCOLATE, 30
ONE MEAL HEALTH MUFFINS, 45
ONION CASSEROLE, 183
ONION SOUP, 162
OPEN FACE HAMBURGERS, 72
OPEN-FACE PEACH PIE, 269
ORANGE CAKE I, 209
ORANGE CAKE II, 209
ORIENTAL SPINACH SALAD, 143
OVEN BEEF STEW OR STROGANOFF, 63

P
PAL'S COCOA APPLE CAKE, 194
PARADISE PUMPKIN CREAM PIE, 272
PARKERHOUSE ROLLS, 49
PARMESAN CHEESE BREAD, 49
PARMESAN CHEESE SANDWICH, 20
PARMESAN GARLIC CHEESE SPREAD, 12
PARMESAN POPOVERS, 50
PARTY POPS, 22
PARTY POTATO CASSEROLE, 184
PARTY SANDWICHES, 72
PARTY SOUP, 162
PEACH BLANC MANGE, 239
PEACH MELBA SUNDAE CREPES, 243
PEACH SOUP, 257
PEANUT BUTTER BALLS, 235
PEANUT BUTTER PIE, 269
PEANUT-BUTTERSCOTCH
  SQUARES, 229
PEANUT STICKS, 21
PECAN CHEESE BALL, 11
PECAN CRISPS, 229
PECAN PIE, 270
PEERLESS PIERCE'S PERFECT MEAT
  LOAF, 68
PEPPER BEAN CASSEROLE, 175
PEPPERMINT DESSERT, 250
PETITS-FOURS 210
PICKLED ARTICHOKES, 8
PICKLED PEACHES, 165
PICKLED VEGETABLES, 152
PIE CRUST, 259
PINEAPPLE CREAM CHEESE
  BLOCKS, 138
PINEAPPLE MINT FREEZE SALAD, 138
PINK CARNATION PIE, 270
PINK SALAD, 139

PIQUANT COCKTAIL MEATBALLS, 18
PISTACHIO CAKE, 211
PISTACHIO DELIGHT, 250
PISTACHIO FROZEN DESSERT, 250
PISTACHIO SALAD, 139
PIZZA BY THE YARD, 69
POIRE AU GRATIN, 251
POLKA DOT CAKE, 211
POLLO BARCELONA, 90
"POOR MAN'S LOBSTER", 93
POPPY SEED BREAD I, 50
POPPY SEED BREAD II, 51
POPPY SEED CAKE I, 212
POPPY SEED CAKE II, 212
POPPY SEED DRESSING I, 154
POPPY SEED DRESSING II, 155
PORK CHOP CASSEROLE, 115
PORK CHOPS NEW ORLEANS, 116
PORK CHOPS WITH RICE, 116
POTATO CHIP COOKIES, 230
POTATO FLAKE COOKIES, 230
POTATO ROLLS, 52
POTATO SALAD FOR A CROWD, 139
POTATOES ROMANOFF, 183
POT DE CREME, 251
POUND CAKE, 212
PRETZEL COOKIES, 230
PRUNE CAKE, 214
PSI PINK CARNATION MINTS, 234
PUMPKIN BREAD, 52
PUMPKIN CAKE, 214
PUMPKIN CHEESE CAKE, 200
PUMPKIN CHIFFON PIE I, 271
PUMPKIN CHIFFON PIE II, 271
PUMPKIN ICE CREAM PIE, 272
PUMPKIN PIE I, 271
PUMPKIN PIE II, 271
PUMPKIN POUND CAKE, 214
PUNCH, 33

Q

QUICHE OVER EASY, 76
QUICHE SUPREME, 76
QUICK AND EASY LASAGNE, 67
QUICK PINEAPPLE PIE, 270

R

RANGER COOKIES, 231
RASPBERRY FLUFF PIE, 272
RASPBERRY TRIFLE, 258
RATATOUILLE, 184
RAW VEGETABLE DIP, 28
RED PLUM CAKE, 211
RED ROCKER APPLE PIE, 260
RED, WHITE AND BLUE SALAD, 140
RHUBARB COFFEE CAKE, 42
RHUBARB TORTE, 256
RICE CHEX ICE CREAM FREEZE, 247
ROAST PORK WITH SOUR CREAM
   GRAVY, 116
ROULADEN, 66

RUM CAKE, 216
RUM CREAM PIE, 273
RUSSIAN ROLL, 253
RUSTIC ALMOND COFFEE, 30
RYE LOAF DIP, 22
RYE ROUNDS, 22

S

SACK POSSET, 166
SAILOR MOKU SOUP, 161
SALAD KEY ROYALE, 136
SALAMI, 23
SALINAS SALAD BOWL, 141
SALMON BALL, 23
SALMON CROQUETTES I, 106
SALMON CROQUETTES II, 106
SALMON LOAF WITH SHRIMP
   SAUCE, 107
SALMON SOUFFLE, 107
SAND TARTS, 232
SANDRA'S SALTED PECANS, 21
SAUCE FOR VEGETABLES, 169
SAUERKRAUT SALAD, 141
SAUSAGE COOKIES, 23
SAUSAGE RING, 117
SAVORY STUFFED FILET OF BEEF, 62
SAVORY SUMMER BISQUE (COLD GREEN
   BEAN SOUP) 158
SCANDINAVIAN PUDDING, 252
SEA FOOD CASSEROLE, 108
SESAME SEED CHICKEN, 92
SEVEN LAYER SALAD, 150
SHERRIED BEEF, 61
SHRIMP AND AVOCADO SALAD, 141
SHRIMP ASPIC, 141
SHRIMP BUTTER, 24
SHRIMP CASSEROLE A LA
   STOCKTON, 108
SHRIMP CHOWDER, 163
SHRIMP/CRAB CASSEROLE, 108
SHRIMP CURRY, 109
SHRIMP MARSEILLAISE, 110
SHRIMP MOLD, 142
SHRIMP MOUSSE, 25
SHRIMP ROLL-UPS OR PINWHEELS, 25
SHRIMP SPREAD, 25
SHRIMP VIENNESE, 110
SHRIMP WITH DILL AND LEMON SAUCE, 109
SIMPLE YET SUPREMELY DELICIOUS LEEK
   SOUP, 161
SISSY'S FRUIT SAUCE, 164
SKI CAKE, 215
SKILLET MACARONI DINNER, 65
SKILLET SALAD, 142
SMOKE-FLAVORED BEEF BRISKET, 60
SODA CRACKER TORTE, 216
SOMBRERO DIP, 26
SOUR CREAM CHEESE
   ENCHILADAS, 97
SOUR CREAM CHICKEN
   ENCHILADAS, 97

SOUR CREAM COFFEE CAKE, 42
SOUR CREAM CORN BREAD, 43
SOUR CREAM SHRIMP CURRY, 109
SOURDOUGH BREAD, 54
SOURDOUGH ZUCCHINI BREAD, 56
SOUTHERN JAM CAKE, 207
SPAGHETTI WITH WHITE CLAM SAUCE, 100
SPICED PEACH SALAD, 138
SPICE APPLE PANCAKES WITH CIDER SAUCE, 48
SPICY BARLEY CASSEROLE, 173
SPICY FRUIT COMPOTE, 244
SPINACH BALLS, 26
SPINACH CASSEROLE I, 185
SPINACH CASSEROLE II, 186
SPINACH CASSEROLE III, 186
SPINACH-CHEESE APPETIZER SQUARES, 27
SPINACH-CHEESE SNACK, 27
SPINACH-DILL SALAD BOWL, 144
SPINACH DIP, 26
SPINACH DIP OR LIZA'S MYSTERY DIP, 26
SPINACH MILANESE, 186
SPINACH QUICHE, 76
SPINACH RICE CASSEROLE, 186
SPINACH RISLEY, 187
SPINACH SALAD FLAMBE, 143
SPINACH SPREAD, 27
SPRINGERLE COOKIES, 231
SQUASH CASSEROLE, 187
SQUASH SOUFFLE, 187
SQUASH OR GREEN BEAN CASSEROLE, 187
SQUASH-TOMATO-CHEESE CASSEROLE, 188
STEAK DIANE, 62
STRAWBERRIES ROMANOFF, 254
STRAWBERRY BREAD, 53
STRAWBERRY BREAD WITH SPREAD, 53
STRAWBERRY CRUNCH, 257
STRAWBERRY DESSERT, 253
STRAWBERRY PIE, 274
STRAWBERRY SALAD SUPREME, 145
STRAWBERRY TIFFANY TORTE, 256
STRAWBERRY TRIFLE, 258
STUFFED CHERRY TOMATOES, 28
STUFFED FLOUNDER, 106
STUFFED SQUASH, 188
STUFFED ZUCCHINI, 192
SUGAR AND HONEY PECANS, 236
SUGAR COOKIES, 231
SUGAR LUMP CINNAMON BREAD, 40
SULTANA CAKE, 216
SUMMER CHICKEN SALAD, 129
SUMMER SQUASH CASSEROLE, 188
SUNSHINE PUNCH, 35
SUNSHINE SALAD, 145
SUPER BISCUITS, 39
SUPER CHICKEN MOLD, 130
SUPER CHICKEN SALAD, 130
SUPER CHOCOLATE CANDY, 234

SUPER EASY TUNA CURRY, 110
SUPREME SOUR CREAM COFFEE CAKE, 42
SUPRISE CUPCAKES, 218
SUSIE'S CARROT CAKE, 198
SWEDISH GLOGG, 31
SWEDISH VEGETABLE SALAD, 145
SWEET AND SOUR BEANS, 175
SWEET AND SOUR DRESSING, 155
SWEET'N SOUR MEATBALLS, 69
SWEET AND SPICY MUSTARD, 167
SWEET POTATO CASSEROLE, 184
SWISS ENCHILADA, 98

T
TABOULI, 146
TACO SALAD, 146
TALLAHASSEE RICE, 185
TAMALE CORN, 181
TART B-B-Q SAUCE, 169
TARTAR SAUCE, 166
TEA GARDEN SALAD, 146
TERIYAKI MARINADE, 169
TERIYAKI TENDERLOIN, 70
THREE BEAN SALAD, 124
3-DAY PEA SOUP, 163
TOFFEE MERINGUE TORTE, 256
TOFFEE-MOCHA FROZEN TORTE, 254
TOMATO-RASPBERRY MOLD, 148
TOMATO SALAD RING FOR FRUIT, 147
TONGUE, 73
TORTONI SQUARES, 258
TOWERING PIZZA, 70
TRIPLE ORANGE MOLDED SALAD, 136
TUNA CASSEROLE, 110
TUNA FISH SALAD, 148
TUNA-MACARONI SALAD, 149
TUNA SALAD, 148
TUNA SALAD SUPREME, 149
TURKEY A LA ENDI, 98
TURKEY FRUIT SALAD, 150
TURKEY HOT BROWN, 98
TURKEY TETRAZZINI, 99
"TUTU" PIE, 274
TWENTY-FOUR HOUR SALAD, 150

U
UNTOSSED SALAD, 151

V
VANILLA GLAZE FOR PETITS-FOURS, 210
VEGETABLE CASSEROLE, 190
VEGETABLE DIP, 28
VEGETABLE MEDLEY, 189
VEGETABLE SALAD, 151
VIRGINIA'S TWENTY-FOUR HOUR SALAD, 151
VIVA LA CHICKEN, 95

W
WALNUT BROCCOLI CASSEROLE, 177

WALNUT CHICKEN APPETIZERS, 13
WALNUT OIL FRENCH DRESSING, 154
WALNUT RICE, 82
WANDA'S PEA THING, 183
WHIRL PUDDING, 252
WHISPERIN' SMITH, 35
WHITE BREAD, 54
WHITE FRUIT CAKE, 206
WHOLE WHEAT BREAD, 55
WILD RICE AND SAUSAGE, 118
WILD RICE CASSEROLE, 117
WINE CAKE, 217
WINTER CARROT CASSEROLE, 179
WOODCOCK, 79

Y

YAPRAK SARMA, 113
YOGURT PIE, 274
"YOU'LL LIKE IT" OR "YUMMY", 259

Z

ZUCCHINI BREAD, 55
ZUCCHINI CASSEROLE I, 191
ZUCCHINI CASSEROLE II, 191
ZUCCHINI CHEESE PUFF, 191
ZUCCHINI DROP COOKIES, 232
ZUCCHINI LASAGNE, 67
ZUCCHINI MICHELE, 192
ZUCCHINI NUT BREAD, 55

LADYFOOD
GAMMA PHI BETA DALLAS ALUMNAE
1104 Yale Circle, Plano, TX 75075

Please send me _____ copies of "Ladyfood, A Collection of Recipes Enjoyed by Ladies and Gentlemen", at $8.95 per copy, plus $1.05 to cover postage and handling. (Texas residents add 45 cents sales tax.)

Enclosed is my check for $_____

Name_____

Street Address_____

City_____State_____Zip_____

LADYFOOD
GAMMA PHI BETA DALLAS ALUMNAE
1104 Yale Circle, Plano, TX 75075

Please send me _____ copies of "Ladyfood, A Collection of Recipes Enjoyed by Ladies and Gentlemen", at $8.95 per copy, plus $1.05 to cover postage and handling. (Texas residents add 45 cents sales tax.)

Enclosed is my check for $_____

Name_____

Street Address_____

City_____State_____Zip_____

LADYFOOD
GAMMA PHI BETA DALLAS ALUMNAE
1104 Yale Circle, Plano, TX 75075

Please send me _____ copies of "Ladyfood, A Collection of Recipes Enjoyed by Ladies and Gentlemen", at $8.95 per copy, plus $1.05 to cover postage and handling. (Texas residents add 45 cents sales tax.)

Enclosed is my check for $_____

Name_____

Street Address_____

City_____State_____Zip_____

LADYFOOD
GAMMA PHI BETA DALLAS ALUMNAE
1104 Yale Circle, Plano, TX 75075

Please send me _____ copies of ''Ladyfood, A Collection of Recipes Enjoyed by Ladies and Gentlemen'', at $8.95 per copy, plus $1.05 to cover postage and handling. (Texas residents add 45 cents sales tax.)

Enclosed is my check for $_____

Name_____

Street Address_____

City_____State_____Zip_____

LADYFOOD
GAMMA PHI BETA DALLAS ALUMNAE
1104 Yale Circle, Plano, TX 75075

Please send me _____ copies of ''Ladyfood, A Collection of Recipes Enjoyed by Ladies and Gentlemen'', at $8.95 per copy, plus $1.05 to cover postage and handling. (Texas residents add 45 cents sales tax.)

Enclosed is my check for $_____

Name_____

Street Address_____

City_____State_____Zip_____

LADYFOOD
GAMMA PHI BETA DALLAS ALUMNAE
1104 Yale Circle, Plano, TX 75075

Please send me _____ copies of ''Ladyfood, A Collection of Recipes Enjoyed by Ladies and Gentlemen'', at $8.95 per copy, plus $1.05 to cover postage and handling. (Texas residents add 45 cents sales tax.)

Enclosed is my check for $_____

Name_____

Street Address_____

City_____State_____Zip_____

LADYFOOD
GAMMA PHI BETA DALLAS ALUMNAE
1104 Yale Circle, Plano, TX 75075

Please send me _____ copies of "Ladyfood, A Collection of Recipes Enjoyed by Ladies and Gentlemen", at $8.95 per copy, plus $1.05 to cover postage and handling. (Texas residents add 45 cents sales tax.)

Enclosed is my check for $_____

Name_____

Street Address_____

City_____State _____Zip_____

LADYFOOD
GAMMA PHI BETA DALLAS ALUMNAE
1104 Yale Circle, Plano, TX 75075

Please send me _____ copies of "Ladyfood, A Collection of Recipes Enjoyed by Ladies and Gentlemen", at $8.95 per copy, plus $1.05 to cover postage and handling. (Texas residents add 45 cents sales tax.)

Enclosed is my check for $_____

Name_____

Street Address_____

City_____State _____Zip_____

LADYFOOD
GAMMA PHI BETA DALLAS ALUMNAE
1104 Yale Circle, Plano, TX 75075

Please send me _____ copies of "Ladyfood, A Collection of Recipes Enjoyed by Ladies and Gentlemen", at $8.95 per copy, plus $1.05 to cover postage and handling. (Texas residents add 45 cents sales tax.)

Enclosed is my check for $_____

Name_____

Street Address_____

City_____State _____Zip_____